since 1901

The Victorians since 1901

Histories, representations and revisions

edited by
Miles Taylor
Michael Wolff

Manchester University Press
Manchester and New York
distributed exclusively in the USA by Palgrave

Published by Manchester University Press
Oxford Road, Manchester M13 9NR, UK
and Room 400, 175 Fifth Avenue, New York, NY 10010, USA
www.manchesteruniversitypress.co.uk

Distributed exclusively in the USA by
Palgrave, 175 Fifth Avenue, New York,
NY 10010, USA

Distributed exclusively in Canada by
UBC Press, University of British Columbia, 2029 West Mall,
Vancouver, BC, Canada V6T 1Z2

British Library Cataloguing-in-Publication Data
A catalogue record for this book is available from the British Library

Library of Congress Cataloging-in-Publication Data applied for

ISBN 0 7190 6724 3   *hardback*
       0 7190 6725 1   *paperback*

First published 2004

12 11 10 09 08 07 06 05 04   10 9 8 7 6 5 4 3 2 1

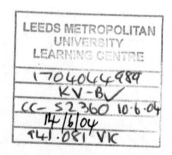
Typeset in 10 on 12 pt Sabon
by SNP Best-set Typesetter Ltd., Hong Kong
Printed in Great Britain
by CPI, Bath

Contents

Contributors

Michael Bentley is professor of modern history, University of St Andrews. He was the editor of *Companion to Historiography* (Routledge, 1997); his most recent publication is *Lord Salisbury's World: Conservative Environments in Late Victorian Britain* (Cambridge, 2001).

Timothy Boon is head of collections at the Science Museum, London, having been deputy project director of the museum's 'Making the Modern World', a major gallery showing technology and its post-1750 impact. His PhD thesis 'Films and the contestation of public health in inter-war Britain' was completed in 1999. He has published on the history of health and on museology.

Anthony Burton is former head of the research department at the Victoria and Albert Museum, London. His books include a history of the museum, *Vision and Accident: The Story of the Victoria and Albert Museum* (Victoria and Albert Museum, 1999).

Becky Conekin is a research fellow and lecturer at the London Institute's College of Fashion. She is the author of *The Autobiography of a Nation: The 1951 Festival of Britain* (Manchester University Press, 2003) and co-editor of *The Englishness of English Dress* (Berg, 2002) and of *Moments of Modernity: Reconstructing Britain 1945–1964* (Rivers Oram, 1999). She is writing a book on the notion of taste in nineteenth- and twentieth-century Britain and America.

Eric Evans is professor of social history, University of Lancaster. His many publications include *The Contentious Tithe: The Tithe Problem and English Agriculture, 1750–1850* (Routledge, 1976), *The Forging of the Modern State: Early Industrial Britain, 1783–1870* (Longman, 1983) and *Parliamentary Reform in Britain, 1770–1918* (Longman, 2000). He is Edexcel's chairman of examiners.

Miles Fairburn is professor of history and head of the history department, University of Canterbury, Christchurch, New Zealand. His latest book is

Social History: Problems, Strategies and Methods (Macmillan, 1999); he is currently researching the social foundations of working-class political conservatism in New Zealand during the first half of the twentieth century.

John Gardiner studied history at the universities of Cambridge and Kent, and has taught at Queen Mary, University of London. He is the author of *The Victorians: An Age in Retrospect* (Hambledon, 2002).

Michelle Hawley is assistant professor of English, California State University at Los Angeles. She completed her PhD, on aesthetics and citizenship in mid-Victorian poetry, at the University of Chicago in 1999.

Martin Hewitt is professor of Victorian Studies and director of the Leeds Centre for Victorian Studies at Trinity and All Saints College, Leeds. He is the editor of *An Age of Equipoise? Reassessing Mid-Victorian Britain* (Ashgate, 2000) and co-editor of *The Diaries of Samuel Bamford* (Sutton, 2000). He was a founding editor in 1996 of the *Journal of Victorian Culture*.

Christopher Kent teaches history at the University of Saskatchewan, Canada. He is the editor of the *Canadian Journal of History/Annales canadiennes d'histoire* and president of the Research Society for Victorian Periodicals. He is currently writing *Gentility and Gender: Clubland in Victorian London*.

William Lubenow is professor of history at Stockton College, New Jersey. His publications include *Parliamentary Politics and the Home Rule Crisis: The British House of Commons in 1886* (Oxford University Press, 1988) and *The Cambridge Apostles, 1820–1914: Liberalism, Imagination and Friendship in British Intellectual Life and Professional Life* (Cambridge University Press, 1998).

Helen Rogers lectures on cultural history at Liverpool John Moores University. She is the author of *Women and the People: Authority, Authorship and the Radical Tradition in Nineteenth-Century England* (Ashgate, 2000).

Miles Taylor is professor of modern British history, University of Southampton. His most recent book is *Ernest Jones, Chartism and the Romance of Politics, 1819–69* (Oxford University Press, 2003); he is currently completing a history of parliamentary representation and reform in modern Britain.

James Thompson is lecturer in modern history, University of Bristol. He is completing a book on the idea of public opinion in late Victorian and Edwardian Britain.

Stewart Weaver is professor of history, University of Rochester, New York, and the author of *The Hammonds: A Marriage in History* (Stanford University Press, 1997).

Michael Wolff is emeritus professor of English, University of Massachusetts. He co-edited *The Victorian City: Images and Reality* (Routledge, 1973) and *The Victorian Periodical Press: Samplings and Soundings* (Leicester University Press, 1982). From its inception in 1957 until 1969 he was an editor of *Victorian Studies*, and in 1968 he founded the Research Society for Victorian Periodicals.

Preface

Michael Wolff

In July, 2001 a four-day conference was held in South Kensington to commemorate the 150th anniversary of the Great Exhibition of 1851 and, more
particularly, the centenary of the death of Queen Victoria in 1901. 'Locating the Victorians' had plenary sessions, exhibits and visits to interesting
Victorian sites, but its main programme consisted of twenty-one sections
with some 300 speakers under such headings as 'Liberty and Authority',
'Pain and Pleasure', 'The Shock of the City', and so on. One such section
was 'The Victorians since 1901', organised by the editors of this volume.
Its role was to examine some of the ways in which the twentieth century
responded to the nineteenth. Most of the papers presented that day, together
with six fresh commissions, are included in this book.

It seems appropriate in this Preface for me to take a personal look at Victorian studies during the second half on the twentieth century, because my
academic career began with the founding of *Victorian Studies*, for many
years the principal journal in the field, and it may well end with 'Locating
the Victorians' and its aftermath. I also want to focus on the interdisciplinary nature of Victorian studies.

Fifty years ago, interdisciplinary study of historical periods was a relative novelty, and the crossing and blurring of standard academic disciplines
had yet to establish itself as legitimate, let alone, as it is now, commonplace.
So the timing of the first issue of *Victorian Studies*, in 1957, could not have
been better. And my own background had prepared me to be a founding
editor.

The accidents of my schooling had equipped me for an interdisciplinary
career. At my secondary school in England I was in the classical sixth. When
I went up to Cambridge in 1945 it was with a scholarship in history. I took
the first part of my degree in moral sciences (philosophy) and the second part
in English. So, before I emigrated from England in 1951 I had acquired, in
large part by chance, some training in most of the humanities. (That I had
spent my first twenty-four years in England may well have helped *Victorian
Studies* become the thoroughly transatlantic enterprise that it was from its

beginning.) In 1952, when I began graduate work in English at Princeton, I still had a hankering for history and philosophy, and I chose a dissertation topic that allowed me to make use of my reading in those subjects. I wrote on George Eliot's frame of mind during her last years when, as Marian Evans, she was working as an extraordinarily wide-ranging editor and intellectual journalist. This required me, if I wanted to understand and comment on her essays and reviews, to try to reflect that range as best I could. So I found myself getting initiated in many unfamiliar aspects of Victorian life and thought in the 1850s. The unfamiliarity lay not so much in the reviews themselves as in their being beyond the ordinary preoccupations of the discipline of English literary history. There was, then, an interdisciplinary cast to my work while I was still a graduate student.

In 1955 I joined the English department at Indiana University. Among the new people hired that year two others were Victorianists: Philip Appleman and William Madden. We wondered how we might take advantage of such an unusual clustering. Within weeks we had the idea of starting a journal. Each of us, it turned out, had experienced difficulties while writing our dissertations in getting a handle on material outside of the usual boundaries of English departments, so our first impulse was to start a journal for English literature people that would confine itself to articles and reviews outside of literature. That idea quickly evolved into a more general one, and a couple of years later *Victorian Studies* was launched as a journal of the 'humanities, arts and sciences'.

It was clear to the three editors (and, to judge from the reviews of the first issue, to many people in the field) that we were trying to do something new. Just after the launching of Sputnik in October 1957, only a month after our first issue, the *Times Literary Supplement* printed a lead article under the title 'Lend-lease' (the author was impressed by the transatlantic nature of *Victorian Studies*) which ended with this flourish:

> This interpenetration of two cultures, this intimate and solicitous refertilization of the past by the present, is a transaction of quite exceptional value; and those concerned have every right to see themselves as engaged in an enterprise at least as novel as that which has set a man-made moon revolving about the face of the earth.[1]

Victorian Studies was indeed timely. Its launch in 1957 coincided with the beginnings of Walter Houghton's work on what was to become the *Wellesley Index of Victorian Periodicals* (an outcome of his research for *The Victorian Frame of Mind*), and the founding, in London, of the Victorian Society. Also around this time ground-breaking books that spilled over departmental boundaries were being published. Richard Altick's *The English Common Reader* (1957), Asa Briggs's *Victorian People* (1954), John Holloway's *The Victorian Sage* (1953), and Raymond Williams's *Culture and Society* (1958) all appeared shortly before or just after the debut of *Victorian Studies*.

Already people in neighbouring university departments (for example, at Cambridge, Leicester, Rutgers, Sussex) had wanted, as a pioneering project, to look at the Victorians as a whole. We summed up our own intentions (and probably those of others who were already at work) in the earnest, if naïve, 'Prefatory note' to our first issue:

> Although the division of history into periods is an artificial procedure, certain times may have their own complex and individual characters; the Victorian period has such a character, and its importance can be seen more clearly now that the inevitable antipathies are passing. *Victorian Studies* hopes to capture something of the life of that era, to discuss its events and personalities, and to interpret and appraise its achievement.
>
> This hope is more likely to be realised through the coordination of academic disciplines than in departmental isolation. It is the tradition for journals to devote themselves to particular disciplines, but *Victorian Studies* will publish work addressed to all students of the Victorian age.
>
> It is by its broad approach, then, as well as by the importance of its subject, that *Victorian Studies* takes its place among scholarly journals.

The journal's early success allowed us to add Donald Gray and George Levine to our staff, making a total of five faculty all in English. That there was no one in history led to a joint appointment for me so that I could teach the undergraduate British history survey and, at the graduate level, the modern British history courses (1688 to the present). I could now claim personally to be interdisciplinary, with the title of professor of Victorian studies.

I was surely an exception. In the 1950s and 1960s most academic work on the Victorians was still the bailiwick of members of English and history and occasionally other departments – economics and art, for example. But by 2000, even though English and history still predominate, there has been such a blurring of disciplinary lines that departmental affiliations have become almost irrelevant.

As for *Victorian Studies*, in its early days we had regularly to massage the pieces we accepted into at least the appearance of being interdisciplinary. Now most pieces appearing in its pages, and in those of the other, newer, journals that concentrate on the nineteenth century, are unsurprisingly interdisciplinary. In these days it is difficult to write an ambitious piece about the Victorians from the perspective of any single discipline. In any event, it was clear to all three editors, and to many early subscribers and contributors, that we were trying to do something different from what almost all other scholarly journals were doing.

We did not know of course how interdisciplinary the submissions would be. We had arranged for our masthead a distinguished interdisciplinary advisory board. So far so good. Our first issue, however, had three articles by equally distinguished scholars: one on architecture; one on Victorian literary criticism; and one on *Punch* and the American Civil War, but only the last was even remotely interdisciplinary. For many years we found ourselves putting together issues that combined various disciplines, multi-disciplinarity rather than interdisciplinarity. From the start, however, the review section pointed the way, with coverage of recent books in politics, economics, literature, philosophy, art, science, theatre and religion.

We continued to aspire to interdisciplinarity. In 1963 we printed an editorial entitled 'Notes toward the definition of "interdisciplinary"', and in 1964, in 'Victorian studies: an interdisciplinary essay', I wrote about the pitfalls and benefits of working across disciplines.[2] Meanwhile genuinely interdisciplinary articles were hard to come by. We faced a sort of crisis when we were offered a very impressive article on *Great Expectations*. We recognised its importance at once, but it had not an ounce of the interdisciplinary about it, and so we felt obliged to reject it. It was published shortly after in another journal and went on to become a minor classic.[3] We realised then that it was idle to insist on authors tinkering with their pieces to make them meet our interdisciplinary hopes. That had been from the beginning a rather artificial procedure, and without fuss, but with reluctance, we acknowledged that *Victorian Studies* was mostly multidisciplinary rather than interdisciplinary. This seems to me to be no longer the case in 2001. Most *Victorian Studies'* articles today may well derive from a given discipline, but almost all of them bring, without strain and as though it were routine, evidence or methodology that cannot be categorised as belonging to any single discipline. Various other 'studies', particularly women's studies and urban studies, have contributed to an interdisciplinarity that is no longer self-conscious, particularly because the subjects' younger scholars are attracted by the requirement that they cast a broad net. So, even though fifty years ago we thought we could initiate an actual rather than a virtual Victorian studies, it took several academic generations before Victorian studies was thoroughly naturalised.

The generalisation that *Victorian Studies* was a pioneer holds – we were ahead of the field in our hopes if not in our pages. The journal took only one or two years to establish itself. We had a distinguished advisory board and a strong subscription list. The journal had settled in comfortably, with a steady flow of submissions. Now we were looking for ways of expanding our activities and trying something new. Our idea was to commission a book on the annus mirabilis of 1859. The result was *1859: Entering an Age of Crisis*,[4] published to the day on the centennial of Charles Darwin's *On The Origin of Species*, and dedicated to G. M. Young, the author of *Victorian England: Portrait of An Age* (1936), and featuring an impressive group of contributors on the contents page. We took it for granted that a book on a particular year would have to be interdisciplinary, and so it was, even if not all of the chapters were. Our next step was to plan a gathering at Indiana of twenty or so scholars from different fields. We had the promise of some funding, and in 1962 we decided to invite people, mostly younger scholars, to Indiana for an interdisciplinary symposium. We could think of no better title for it than the vague 'Victorian Affairs' which had the virtue

of giving us unlimited scope. This gathering turned out to be the forerun-
ner of a current – and almost defining – feature of Victorian studies, the
steady flow of conferences.

Its success led to a second conference in 1965 – 'The Victorian City', a
subject that again required contributions from many disciplines. Papers
from the first conference filled two issues of the journal, and out of the
second grew *The Victorian City: Images and Realities*[5] a collaboration
between the first professor of urban studies (H. J. Dyos at Leicester) and
the first professor of Victorian studies. Similarly, a later collected volume,
The Victorian Periodical Press: Samplings and Soundings, edited by myself
and Joanne Shattock,[6] a member of the University of Leicester Victorian
Studies Centre, could not help but be interdisciplinary. The latter book was
itself an offshoot of the work of the Research Society of Victorian Periodicals that I had started in 1968 and which had been interdisciplinary from
the outset. Indeed, one of the major differences between Victorian studies
in the 1950s and now is the current widespread use of periodicals and newspapers of all sorts, a hitherto almost hidden resource, and again one that
almost invariably requires an interdisciplinary reading. It was in 1968 also
that I visited the Centre for Contemporary Studies in Culture at Birmingham University and talked with Richard Hoggart and Stuart Hall about
applying their innovations to the nineteenth century. The word 'culture' was
not then used as pervasively as it now is, though I had often spoken of what
we were doing in Victorian studies as 'cultural history'.

Victorian studies has changed in other ways over the half-century. It has
gone from being insular to being global. What most of us meant by 'Victorian' (the concept itself being now consistently in question) was England
and things English. At the time we did not find anything incongruous in
considering 'Studies in Victorian England' as the title of the new journal.
Now the subject matter is clearly Britain and British connections with the
empire and beyond.

To finish the story of my years with *Victorian Studies*. By 1970 all the
original editors except me had left Indiana. I had asked Martha Vicinus to
be an associate editor, and when I left the next year she became editor. She
brought the journal more in line with new work and an early result was an
issue on Victorian women. She expanded this issue into a pioneering book,
Suffer and Be Still: Women in the Victorian Age.[7] The transition signalled
two other shifts: first, the increasing interdisciplinarity of the contents of
Victorian Studies, that is, from being nominally interdisciplinary to being
genuinely so; second, a maturing of Victorian studies, acknowledging new
emphases in scholarship which reflected societal changes since the 1960s.

Since 1970 I have been particularly aware of other changes, perhaps insti-
gated by the remarkable growth of the field. Work that was traditionally
often done in isolation is now more broadly collegial and collaborative. Victorian studies now has a growing network of programmes in universities
and regional societies. Perhaps the scale of the surviving evidence (all those

increases in population, literacy, legislation, and so on) and their relative novelty as historical subjects have encouraged interdisciplinarity as well as collaboration.

I hope this book recommends itself not only as telling some of the story of how the twentieth century read and responded to the nineteenth, but as another instance, through the variety of contributions and contributors, of the range and growing reach of Victorian studies.

Notes

1 'Lend-lease', *Times Literary Supplement*, 18 October 1957, p. 625.
2 Editorial, 'Notes towards the definition of "interdisciplinary"', *Victorian Studies*, 6 (1963), pp. 203–6; Michael Wolff, 'Victorian studies: an interdisciplinary essay', *Victorian Studies*, 8 (1964), pp. 59–70.
3 Julian Moynihan, 'The hero's guilt: the case of *Great Expectations*', *Essays in Criticism*, 10 (1960), pp. 60–79.
4 P. Appleman, William A. Madden and Michael Wolff (eds), *1859: Entering an Age of Crisis* (Bloomington: Indiana University Press, 1959).
5 H. J. Dyos and Michael Wolff (eds), *The Victorian City: Images and Realities*, 2 vols (London: Routledge & Kegan Paul, 1973).
6 Joanne Shattock and Michael Wolff (eds), *The Victorian Periodical Press: Samplings and Soundings* (Leicester: Leicester University Press, 1982).
7 Martha Vicinus (ed.), *Suffer and Be Still: Women in the Victorian Age* (Bloomington: Indiana University Press, 1972).

Introduction

Miles Taylor

When Queen Victoria died in 1901 much of the Victorian age died with her. Of her nine children three predeceased her. Her eldest daughter, Victoria, passed away within months of her mother's death, and her eldest son and heir, Edward, having waited a lifetime to accede to the throne, died nine years later – after one of the shortest reigns since the Restoration. And although her remaining children proved remarkably long-lived their lives were mostly played out in homage to their mother: Arthur as roving imperial statesman; Beatrice as devoted editor of her mother's diaries; and Helena as patron of nursing homes for the military. Only Louise – sculptress, salon hostess and supporter of women's higher education – carved out a career which signalled the arrival of the twentieth century rather than a replay of the nineteenth.[1] As in her own family, so too at her court: by the time Victoria died her favourite artists (Heinrich Angeli, Edwin Landseer and Franz Winterhalter), writers (Lewis Carroll, Pauline Craven and Charlotte Yonge) and the composer Felix Mendelssohn were either dead or no longer fashionable.[2] Even the enthusiasm for memorialising Victoria petered out after a decade.[3] Beyond the court at Westminster, few of Victoria's prime ministers survived their formidable sovereign. The final and longest serving of her prime ministers, Lord Salisbury, died in 1903, and only Lord Rosebery, her briefest, lived on, eventually dying in 1929. Many of the distinctive features of the Victorian constitution barely survived their head of state. Within four years of Victoria's death the first Scottish commoner – Campbell-Bannerman – became prime minister, followed eleven years later by the first Welshman – Lloyd George. In 1907 the line separating male and female spheres began to dissolve as the largest city in the world – London – confirmed the right of women to vote in local government elections. In 1909 the grip of the aristocracy on the public purse was loosened, as the People's Budget made landed incomes for the first time subject to taxation. And in 1911 the peerage relinquished its hold over the Commons, as the House of Lords' veto was scaled down from a power to refuse to a power to delay. In the same year the sway held by the plutocracy came to an end when salaries were introduced for MPs, a trend continued by the 1913 Trades Union Act which permitted unions to fund the Labour Party.[4] Above all, many of the achievements of the Victorian age were starting to lose their lustre by 1901. As Victoria lay dying, her vast dominion overseas was facing its severest challenge to date, in the shape of the war in South Africa, and her informal empire of trade was being 'invaded' by the low-cost manufacturing economies of the USA and Germany.[5] In these ways Victoria's death marked the end not only of a reign and an era but of the present. For a civilisation that had prided itself for so long on being the epitome of modernity, Victorian Britain found itself being consigned to the past with remarkable speed.

What the Edwardian years began the devastation wrought by the First World War completed. By 1918 the door was not simply closed on the Victorian age, but sealed shut. With hasty patriotism the House of Saxe-Coburg-Gotha became the House of Windsor, royal palaces were turned over to convalescent soldiers, and George V and his family remodelled themselves as a 'welfare monarchy', staving off republican and socialist sentiment with highly visible philanthropy.[6] The final generation of Victorian men became the lost generation of the war. If the Victorian era remained in the public memory at all in the years immediately following 1918 it was as the subject of satire, irony and indictment.[7] In other words, within two decades of the death of Victoria a chasm had opened up between Victorian and post-Victorian sensibilities, which went well beyond the death of one monarch and the accession of her son. Eighty or so years later we still live with the consequences of this remarkable transformation. What we know and understand as the Victorian age is not an exhibit left in a glass case in 1901. On the contrary, the Victorians have been made and remade throughout the twentieth century, as successive generations have used the Victorian past in order to locate themselves in the present. This story of adaptations and survivals has begun to be told in a handful of important recent works in historiography, cultural studies and biography.[8] *The Victorians since 1901* is an addition to this literature, its novelty being that it seeks to illustrate the process whereby the twentieth century has reinterpreted the nineteenth through a wide-ranging series of inter-disciplinary case studies across the whole of the last 100 years. The volume looks at the principal chroniclers and historians of the Victorian age, at the various media and cultural institutions through which the wider public has encountered images of the Victorians, and, finally, at the changing fashions in academic interpretation of the period. In order to set the scene this short Introduction charts the major turning points in the chronology of changing popular and scholarly attitudes towards the Victorians since 1901, and draws together some of the themes of the different chapters. It might usefully be read in conjunction with the 'Timeline of Victorian studies' at the end of the book.

I

The Victorians invented many things – including themselves. But in the very act of creation lay the seed of destruction. The appearance of the term 'Victorian' has been dated back to as early as 1851, and certainly by the Jubilee years of 1887 and 1897 it was being used to describe a distinct historical era, with its own poetry, literature and song, military heroes, drama, graphic art, dress and fashion. At least two exhibitions commemorating the 'Victorian age' were held in the 1890s, some years before the death of the queen.[9] 'Victorian' denoted the arrival of modernity, even the end of history. One writer suggested a new history of the world, beginning in 1322 BC and ending in AD 1896, to be subtitled 'The Victorian Canon', while another 'discovered' a new prehistoric era, and proposed labelling it 'the Victorian era'.[10] Such colonising of the past was not confined to the eccentric. The late nineteenth century saw the commencement of a range of encyclopaedic and antiquarian projects such as the *Dictionary of National Biography* (1885–) and the *Victoria County History* (1899–), which, together with earlier developments such as the founding of the Royal Historical Society in 1868, helped situate the late Victorians as guardians of the national past.[11] But, of course, history did not stand still, and by allowing the *DNB* and the *VCH* to reach into the contemporary epoch – casting people, places and events into stone whether ancient or modern – these monumental dictionaries of national life helped to entomb the Victorians as much as it did their predecessors.

A similar effect was achieved by the National Portrait Gallery (NPG), which moved into its present St Martin's Lane location in 1896. The NPG observed a ten-year rule whereby only a decade had to lapse after the death of some illustrious person before a portrait could be exhibited. Inevitably, nineteenth-century portraits began to fill the NPG, and by 1949 they accounted for around one-third of all the gallery's holdings.[12] In these ways the 1890s became, ironically, a kind of historical caesura. What had begun at the time of the Jubilee, in 1887, as an attempt to celebrate the distinctly contemporary character of Victoria's reign had turned into a retrospect in which the Victorians historicised everything – including their own era. As Herbert Asquith observed in 1918, unlike Queen Anne and Elizabeth I, Victoria outlived her own times. The Victorian age, he suggested – an age of '[m]aterialism, and the pursuit of wealth and comfort' – had ended at least a decade before 1901.[13]

Literary taste as well as historical scholarship detached the late nineteenth century from the rest of the Victorian era. The reaction of the Bloomsbury generation to the Victorians, exemplified by Lytton Strachey's iconoclastic *Eminent Victorians* (1918) – about which William Lubenow writes in the opening chapter of this book – and perpetuated in different ways through the inter-war years by E. M. Forster, T. S. Eliot, W. H. Auden, the Leavises and the Sitwells, is of course well known.[14] What is often overlooked, however, is just how quickly the modernist critique of the Victorian era down to the 1880s had set in prior to 1918. In their onslaught against what they saw as the excessive moralism of George Eliot, the journalistic style of Charles Dickens, the insincerity of William Thackeray and the melancholia of Alfred Tennyson, Bloomsbury followed where late nineteenth-century critics such as Henry James and Arnold Bennett had already led.[15] Despite the best efforts of writers such as G. K. Chesterton, Arthur Quiller-Couch (the subject of chapter 4, by Michelle Hawley) and George Saintsbury, the reputations of early and mid-Victorian men and women of letters were already at rock-bottom in the decade prior to the First World War.[16] For example, writing in 1908, Joseph Carr confessed that he was 'an impenitent Victorian' who disavowed the modern creed, lamenting the fact that no one over the age of 14 read Dickens.[17] Even before Strachey began his incisive muck-raking, biographers and *belles-lettristes* alike had begun to separate out the post-1880 generation. The tortured private mid-Victorian lives of Thomas and Jane Carlyle, Robert Browning and Elizabeth Barrett Browning, and the Brontë sisters, all became exposed to public view in a series of works during the first two decades of the twentieth century.[18] At the same time, later Victorian writers such as William Morris, Walter Pater, George Gissing, Thomas Hardy and even Aubrey Beardsley came to be co-opted into the modernist canon, praised for the complexity of their philosophy and aesthetics, and the authentic social realism of their prose.

Biography and autobiography contributed to the distancing of the Victorians in the opening decades of the twentieth century. The first Victorian centenary, in 1919, saw Strachey turn his attention to Queen Victoria, revealing the dead monarch to be just as emotional, melancholic and sentimental as were her subjects.[19] Prime ministers' lives, by contrast, remained public chronicles with political lessons for the present day. As Michael Bentley demonstrates in chapter 3, on the commemoration of the great statesmen, reverence for Gladstone considerably outlasted the demise of the Liberal Party. By contrast, Disraeli came to enjoy prominence as a biographical subject, not because he was a Conservative deity, but because he was a cosmopolitan romantic, who seemed free of the prejudice and hypocrisy associated with his age. Post-Victorian autobiography also manufactured distance by emphasising the gap of generations between parents and children – for example, the well-known works of Edmund Gosse, George Wyndham, Dora Montefiore and E. F. Benson.[20]

In the inter-war years, 'anti-Victorianism' was not restricted to the prose and poetry that had been produced in the middle decades of the nineteenth century. Victorian taste and design were held up for scrutiny by champions of modernism, and were found wanting. John Betjeman and Nikolaus Pevsner singled out as the dark ages of English architecture the period between the Industrial Revolution and the arts and crafts movement.[21] If the outside was bad, the domestic interior was even worse. Clive Bell condemned Victorian taste as middle-class and imitative,[22] and, as Anthony Burton shows (chapter 8), the Victoria and Albert Museum steered clear of Victoriana until the early 1950s. Victorian painting, by which was usually meant Millais, Frith and Sargent (the pre-Raphaelites by contrast were accelerated into the moderns), was blamed for never living up to the promise of Romanticism.[23] And despite its native opera and cathedral composition, Victorian Britain was written-off by music scholars as 'das Land ohne Musik' until the advent of Edward Elgar's patriotic work at the turn of the century.[24] Even that quintessential Victorian musical institution – the opera of Gilbert and Sullivan – fared badly after 1930. When Sir Henry Lytton, the leading light of the D'Oyly Carte Company died in 1934, critics opined that the Gilbert and Sullivan show was dead. The Sullivan centenary went unmarked in 1942, and in the 1940s and early 1950s the company almost disappeared from view in London, confining itself to provincial and overseas tours, until its return to Sadler's Wells in 1969.[25]

The 1930s introduced another dimension to 'anti-Victorianism': the economic depression. Unemployment opened up a further gulf between Victorian materialism on the one hand and breadline Britain on the other. As Stewart Weaver and Timothy Boon show (chapters 2 and 7), pioneers of social history, such as the Hammonds and the early practitioners of documentary realism, combined to demonise the Victorian age as one of private wealth and public squalor. Such work coincided with Hollywood's discovery of the Victorian novel. Adaptations of the Brontës and of Dickens – filmed using sets constructed in the sunny climes of California – inevitably exaggerated the contrast between the comfortable splendour of the well-to-do and the hard lot of the very poor, both past and present.[26]

'Anti-Victorianism' thus began as an assault on the public lives and letters of the famous figures of the first fifty years of Victoria's reign. It started as an understandable reaction to the over-zealous imperial triumphalism of the 1880s and 1890s – of the sort that, as Eric Evans shows (chapter 12) in considering the Victorians and the school curriculum, was perpetuated well into the twentieth century. 'Anti-Victorianism' developed in the years following 1918 as a means of emphasising the distinct quality of 'modernist' literature, although as William Lubenow shows in his discussion of Strachey (chapter 1), and likewise Michelle Hawley on Quiller-Couch (chapter 4), this break between Victorians and moderns was more subtle and contested than it might first appear. By the 1930s, the Bloomsbury assault on the nineteenth century had been extended into the arts and the social and economic history of the Victorian age.

II

When did 'anti-Victorianism' end? Chapter 5 by Miles Taylor (on G. M. Young) and chapter 6 by Martin Hewitt (on Victorian studies in the 1950s) indicate that a quiet revival had been underway even in the inter-war years.

By the late 1920s and early 1930s a number of writers were suggesting that the early and mid-Victorian literary and intellectual *mentalité* was more subtle and complicated than breezy modernists assumed. For example, Alan Bott regretted how his generation had been the first to 'build barriers against the Victorians', while E. H. Dance noted perceptively that 'Victorianism is not so much the attitude adopted by the Victorians towards their world, as the attitude adopted by posterity towards the Victorians'.[27] The wheel had turned once more, and a younger generation was turning on its modernist parents: 'The young are beginning to see merits in Tennyson, Anthony Trollope, and William Morris just because they heard their parents disparage them', suggested William Inge, the dean of St Paul's Cathedral, in 1933.[28] There was also some nostalgia involved. The political harmony of the Victorian years seemed to have been in marked contrast to the turbulence of poor industrial relations at home in the 1920s and the spread of fascism and communism abroad in the 1930s.[29] Against this backdrop book-length re-evaluations of early and mid-Victorian culture began to appear – most notably, David Cecil's *Early Victorian Novelists* (1934) and G. M. Young's *Portrait of an Age* (1936). The centenary of Victoria's accession was marked by a hugely successful film starring Anna Neagle. But, as Miles Taylor shows, G. M. Young's work sold slowly, and remained relatively neglected until the wave of Anglo-American Victorian studies' scholarship of the 1950s which, Martin Hewitt emphasises, bestowed canonical status on Young's work. In other words, up until the 1940s, the negative verdict of the Bloomsbury generation on the Victorians remained powerful. 'The giants of the age', conceded Edith Batho and Bonamy Dobrée, 'were undoubtedly giants, but they seem to us to be malformed . . . it was not an age of scepticism so much as an age of muddle'. F. R. Leavis concurred, finding room (just about) for George Eliot in his *Great Tradition* (1948), but excluding many other prominent Victorian writers.[30]

There was more interest in, if not enthusiasm for, the Victorians after the Second World War. As Becky Conekin (chapter 9, on the 1951 Festival) and James Thompson (chapter 10, on the BBC) show in their contributions to this volume, the years around the centenary of the 1851 Great Exhibition presented an occasion for the national media to reflect on the Victorian achievement, although for the most part monochromatic comparisons between nineteenth-century materialism and mid-twentieth-century social equality continued to be drawn. Anthony Burton (chapter 8) argues that it was also in 1951 that the Victoria and Albert Museum finally matched its name to its vocation, and made the decorative arts of the Victorian period the subject of a major exhibition. Indeed, by the 1950s the re-evaluation of Victorian taste was well underway, led by writers such as John Steegman, formerly of the NPG, architect Hugh Casson and Henry-Russell Hitchcock, the American architectural historian.[31] Nikolaus Pevsner now began to curb some of his earlier hostility to Victorian design, and was subsequently joined by John Betjeman.[32] Some critics remained cautious. For example, John Gloag wrote compendious accounts of Victorian taste and fashion, but remained convinced that the period had confused ornament and design. However, by the end of the decade, commentators were beginning to observe that a 'neo-Victorian age' in matters artistic had set in.[33]

The Victorian revival of the 1950s was not simply a matter of aesthetic judgement. In the first place, as John Gardiner shows (chapter 11), Victoriana began to collected, bought and sold not just by eccentric Oxonians such as Betjeman and Harold Acton but by antique-dealers and indeed a new generation of home-buyers. The 'Victorian Collector' series (1961–68), edited by Hugh Wakefield, was one sign of this new-found enthusiasm for nineteenth-century knick-knacks.[34] Secondly, as Britain emerged from post-war austerity and turned its attention to urban renewal and reconstruction, the built environment of Victorian Britain came under threat. In 1956, the Society for the Protection of Ancient Buildings joined the campaign to oppose the destruction of the Imperial Institute (built in 1893) in South Kensington – 'a memorial of one of our greatest periods'.[35] Two years later, the SPAB, which already boasted a Georgian Group, created another sub-division to cover the Victorian period. Betjeman was taken on as advisor, and the Victorian Society was formed, going on to enjoy mixed success in the 1960s. The Society helped save some landmarks of Victorian London (notably, the St Pancras Hotel, and the streets to the south of the British Museum), while others were lost (most famously, the Euston Hotel and the Coal Exchange on Lower Thames Street). Of equal importance was the network of regional branches inspired by the Victorian Society, and through its conferences, exhibitions and publications a permanent lay community of enthusiasts and experts was created.[36]

Significantly, some of the 1950s' revival of interest in Victorian taste came from America. After all, American history had its own 'Victorian' period – lasting from 1865 to 1914 – and the distinctive artistic and architectural culture of America in those decades produced less of a twentieth-century backlash than did its equivalent in Britain. As early as 1939, R. B. Mowat had included American intellectual life in his survey of the Victorian age, and in 1957 John Maass produced a sympathetic picture of pre-modernist American architecture of the 'Victorian' period.[37] Ironically, the milieu which had produced the first anti-Victorian – Henry James – was now reclaiming its own Victorian past. North American academic scholarship in the 1950s also began to subject Victorian culture to serious critical attention. The launch of a new journal in 1957, *Victorian Studies* – described by Michael Wolff, one of its founding editors, in the Preface to this volume – was a manifestation of this critical focus, but there were many others. Synthetic surveys produced by Jerome Buckley and Walter Houghton, major bibliographic projects such as the *Wellesley Index to Victorian Periodicals* (directed by Houghton), definitive editions of the lives and letters of figures such as Matthew Arnold (Michigan), John Stuart Mill (Toronto), and Robert Browning (Ohio) all helped to produce a renaissance of Victorian scholarship across the Atlantic. Writers whose reputations had been battered by Bloomsbury, such as Tennyson, Thackeray and George Eliot, now began to receive appreciative coverage, while Matthew Arnold's pronouncements on mid-Victorian culture came to enjoy privileged status among conservative and radical critics alike.

Where North American academics in the late 1950s spearheaded the revival of interest in the public intellectual face of Victorian Britain, their British counterparts delved into the private and parochial life of the nineteenth century. The social history boom of the 1960s and 1970s transformed what was known about the Victorians – from suburbs to slums, religion to riots, drink and drugs, and class and sex in all their varieties. Enterprising publishers such as Gregg (the 'Victorian Social Conscience'), Frank Cass ('Library of Victorian Times'), and Leicester University Press ('The Victorian Library') established reprint series devoted to the Victorian period. A Victorian Studies Centre was established at Leicester, and in 1965 some of the best of the new social history was featured in the 'Victorian City' conference.[38] There were many reasons why the Victorian era became the fixed object of the gaze of the new social historians. The Victorian period was the first information age, and a hallmark of the new social (and economic) history was its quantitative imperative. Where better to look for statistical correlation of historical trends than a civilisation which had collected so many facts and figures. The trail left by the Victorians – their newspapers and periodicals, parliamentary blue books and records of associational life – was a researcher's treasure-trove, and not surprisingly between 1965 and 1975 Ph.Ds in British universities on the nineteenth century accounted for over half of all Ph.Ds in British history after 1485.[39] Moreover, as social history took off in the older civic universities and in the new out-of-town campuses, the landscape of Victorian Britain was still highly visible from the doorsteps of many academics. As Asa Briggs, the pre-eminent scholar of the British revival in Victorian studies, observed of Leeds: 'The past was a visible element in the present. The very pace of recent change – social and topographical – even greater perhaps in Leeds than in most Victorian cities – is giving greater urgency to the work of the nineteenth-century historian.'[40]

Most importantly, however, the Victorian era offered to the 1960s' generation confirmation of its own modernity. The relaxation in the Wilson years of the laws relating to divorce, homosexuality, age of majority and censorship, together with the sea-change in attitudes towards sexual and racial discrimination brought on by the women's movement worldwide and the civil rights campaign in America, made the Victorians seem very old, very different and, above all, very unenlightened. Not surprisingly, when Mrs Thatcher swung back the political pendulum in the early 1980s and began preaching the virtues of 'Victorian values' – self-help, *laissez-faire* and an aggressive promotion of national interests – Britain's leading social historians had ammunition at the ready for their counter-attack on the prejudices of Victorian culture.[41] As Eric Evans shows in his contribution, this debate went to the very heart of what British school-children should be taught about the national past. Sixty-five years after Strachey's *Eminent Victorians*, interpretations of the nineteenth century remained as politically charged as ever.

III

In the twenty years since such partisan skirmishes over 'Victorian values' peace has broken out in Victorian studies. The Victorians are more ubiquitous than ever. Patrick Leary describes in his chapter the considerable variety of Victorian resources now available on the internet. James Thompson provides an overview of recent television costume dramas and documentaries which take the Victorians as their subject. And John Gardiner shows how the Victorian period has been exploited by the tourist and heritage industry. There are now probably as many views about the Victorians as there are journals and societies devoted to the period. Several contributors to *The Victorians since 1901* show how, despite today's global and anglophone information community, Victorian historiography still conforms to national stereotype. Christopher Kent (chapter 14) describes the discipline in North America, where the commitment to documenting and recording Victorian intellectual and literary life remains paramount, despite the ebb and flow of different methodologies and theoretical approaches. Miles Fairburn (chapter 15) considers the particular preoccupations of Victorian studies in Australia and New Zealand, where social and intellectual historians have made less impact on the subject. There, as in Ireland, 'Victorian' can connote colonial assumptions of metropolitan and English superiority which sit uncomfortably in the post-imperial age. And Helen Rogers (chapter 16) describes how Victorian studies in Britain itself has now retreated from the micro-history so favoured by social historians in the 1960s, and has returned to larger issues of periodisation and national identity. Beyond the English-speaking world, the subject flourishes with specialist academic societies in France (Société française d'études victoriennes et edouardiennes) and Germany (Prince Albert Society).

Victorian studies is thus in a state of flux – but flux of the healthy variety. The 2001 centenary of Victoria's death was marked by a series of conferences and volumes which were remarkably free of the exaggerated reverence or scorn which characterised the previous anniversaries of 1919, 1937 and 1951. We are now encouraged to look back at the Victorians and admire their modernity and energy, sympathise with their moral dilemmas, and appreciate the complexity of their attitudes towards race, sex and class.[42] One hundred years on it seems as though we are at last learning to live with the Victorians.

Notes

1 On Victoria's death, see Jerrold M. Packard, *Farewell in Splendour: The Death of Queen Victoria and Her Age* (New York: Dutton, 1995); Tony Rennell, *Last Days of Glory: The Death of Queen Victoria* (London: Viking, 2000). On the subsequent lives of her children, see John van der Kiste, *Queen Victoria's Children* (Gloucester: Sutton, 1986), ch. 5.

2 For Victoria's taste in art, see Oliver Miller, *The Victorian Pictures in the Collection of Her Majesty the Queen*, 2 vols (Cambridge: Cambridge University Press, 1992), vol. 1, pp. xiii–lxi.

3 John Plunkett, 'Remembering Victoria: the national memorial to the great queen outside Buckingham Palace', *The Victorian*, 1 (1999), pp. 4–9; Tori Smith, ' "A grand work of noble conception": the Victoria memorial and imperial London' in Felix Driver and David Gilbert (eds), *Imperial Cities: Landscape, Display and Identity* (Manchester: Manchester University Press, 1999), pp. 21–39.

4 Peter Clarke, 'The Edwardians and the constitution' in Donald Read (ed.), *Edwardian England* (London: Croom Helm, 1982), pp. 40–55.

5 Andrew S. Thompson, *Imperial Britain: The Empire in British Politics, c. 1880–1932* (Harlow: Pearson Education, 2000), chs 4–5; Paul Kennedy, *The Rise of the Anglo-German Antagonism, 1860–1914* (London: Allen & Unwin, 1980), chs 17–18.

6 Frank Prochaska, *The Republic of Britain, 1760 to 2000* (London: Allen Lane, 2000), pp. 156–77.

7 For different views of the relationship between the First World War and public memory, see: Paul Fussell, *The Great War and Modern Memory* (Oxford: Oxford University Press, 1975); Robert Wohl, *The Generation of 1914* (Cambridge, MA: Harvard University Press, 1979); Jay Winter, *Sites of Memory, Sites of Mourning: The Great War in European Cultural History* (Cambridge: Cambridge University Press, 1995).

8 Peter Mandler and Susan Pedersen (eds), *After the Victorians: Private Conscience and Public Duty in Modern Britain: Essays in Memory of John Clive* (London: Routledge, 1994); Gary Day (ed.), *Varieties of Victorianism: The Uses of a Past* (London: Macmillan, 1998); Martin Hewitt (ed.), *An Age of Equipoise? Reassessing Mid-Victorian Britain* (Aldershot: Ashgate, 2000); Matthew Sweet, *Inventing the Victorians* (London: Faber, 2001); Christine Krueger (ed.), *Functions of Victorian Culture at the Present Time* (Athens: Ohio University Press, 2002); John Gardiner, *The Victorians: An Age in Retrospect* (London: Hambledon & London, 2002).

9 G. M. Young, *Portrait of An Age* (London: Phoenix Press, 2002 [1936]), p. 89. A selection of 'Victorian' retrospectives from the 1880s and 1890s might include: C. R. Low, *Soldiers of the Victorian Age* (London: Chapman & Hall, 1880); E. C. Stedman, *Victorian Poets* (New York: Houghton & Co., 1887); Margaret Oliphant, *The Victorian Age of English Literature*, 2 vols (London: Percival and Co., 1892); Hugh Walker, *The Greater Victorian Poets* (London: Swan Sonnenschein & Co., 1895); Frederic Harrison, *Studies in Early Victorian Literature* (London: Edward Arnold, 1895); John Southward, *Progress in Printing and the Graphic Arts during the Victorian Era* (London: Simpkin & Marshall, 1897); Augustin Filon, *The English Stage: Being an Account of the Victorian Drama* (London: J. Milne, 1897); *Victorian Costumes: A Record of Ladies' Attire,*

1837–97 (London: S. Miller, 1897); John Taylor, *Victorian and Patriotic Songs* (London: G. Philip & Son, 1900). The two exhibitions were: 'The Victorian Exhibition' at the New Gallery, London, 1887; and 'Victorian Art' at the Guildhall, City of London, 1897.

10 C. A. L. Totten, *The Canon of History, Secular in Particular. Or, the Victorian Canon: An Astro-Chronologico-Historical Digest of the Times of the Gentiles, etc* (New Haven, CT: Our Race Publishing Co., 1896); F. F. Arbuthnot, *The Mysteries of Chronology, with a Proposal for a New English Era to be Called the Victorian* (London: Heinemann, 1900).

11 Colin Matthew, *Leslie Stephen and the New Dictionary of National Biography* (Cambridge: Cambridge University Press, 1997); R. B. Pugh, 'The *Victoria County History*', *British Studies Monitor*, 2 (1971), pp. 15–23.

12 Calculated from the *Catalogue of the National Portrait Gallery, 1856–1947* (London: National Portrait Gallery, 1949).

13 H. H. Asquith, *Some Aspects of the Victorian Age*, Romanes Lecture (Oxford: Clarendon Press, 1918), pp. 3–5.

14 S. P. Rosenbaum, *Victorian Bloomsbury: The Early Literary History of the Bloomsbury Group* (London: Macmillan, 1987), ch. 3; Jonathan Rose, *The Edwardian Temperament, 1895–1919* (Athens: Ohio University Press, 1986), pp. 38–9, 163–5.

15 E. W. F. Tomlin, 'Dickens' reputation: a reassessment' in Tomlin (ed.), *Charles Dickens, 1812–70: A Centenary Volume* (London: Weidenfeld & Nicolson, 1969), pp. 238–63; Elton E. Smith, 'Tennyson criticism, 1923–1966: from fragmentation to tension in polarity', *Victorian Newsletter*, 31 (1967), pp. 1–4; Gordon Haight, *A Century of George Eliot Criticism* (London: Methuen, 1966), pp. xii–iv; J. C. Olmsted, *Thackeray and His Twentieth Century Critics: An Annotated Bibliography, 1900–75* (London: Garland, 1977), pp. xiv–vi. For the role of Bennett and James, see: Arnold Bennett, 'My literary heresies' (1904) in *The Author's Craft and Other Critical Writings of Arnold Bennett*, ed. Samuel Hynes (Lincoln: University of Nebraska Press, 1968), pp. 231–41; R. W. B. Lewis, 'Henry James: the Victorian scene' in W. R. Louis (ed.), *More Adventures with Britannia: Personalities, Politics and Culture in Britain* (London: I. B. Tauris, 1998), pp. 83–98.

16 John Coates, *Chesterton and the Edwardian Cultural Crisis* (Hull: Hull University Press, 1984); Gertrude White, 'Chesterton as literary critic', *Chesterton Review*, 10 (1984), pp. 424–34; Harold Orel, *Victorian Literary Critics* (London: Macmillan, 1984), ch. 6; Dorothy Richardson Jones, *'King of the Critics': George Saintsbury, 1845–1933, Critic, Journalist, Historian, Professor* (Ann Arbor: University of Michigan Press, 1993).

17 Joseph Carr, *Some Eminent Victorians: Personal Recollections in the World of Art and Letters* (London: Duckworth, 1908), p. vi.

18 Sandra Donaldson, *Elizabeth Barrett Browning: An Annotated Bibliography of the Commentary and Criticism, 1826–1990* (New York: G. K. Hall, 1993), p. 2; N. Young, *Carlyle: His Rise and Fall* (London: Duckworth, 1927), chs 28–9; Jean-Pierre Petit (ed.), *Emily Brontë: A Critical Anthology* (Harmondsworth: Penguin, 1973), pp. 54–9.

19 Strachey's *Queen Victoria* was not published in book form until 1921, but it was serialised in the *New Republic* during 1919. Jay Dickson, 'Surviving Victoria' in Maria DiBattista and Lucy McDiarmid (eds), *High and Low Moderns:*

Literature and Culture, 1889–1939 (Oxford: Oxford University Press, 1996), pp. 23–46.

20 Philip Dodd, 'The nature of Edmund Gosse's *Father and Son*', *English Literature in Transition*, 22 (1979), pp. 270–80; Nancy W. Ellenberger, 'Constructing George Wyndham: narratives of aristocratic masculinity in fin-de-siècle England', *Journal of British Studies*, 39 (2000), pp. 487–517; cf. Dora Montefiore, *From a Victorian to a Modern* (London: E. Archer, 1927); E. F. Benson, *As We Were: A Victorian Peep-Show* (London: Longmans, 1930).

21 John Betjeman, *Ghastly Good Taste, or a Depressing Story of the Rise and Fall of English Architecture* (London: Chapman and Hall, 1933), chs 7–8; Nikolaus Pevsner, *Pioneers of the Modern Movement: From William Morris to Walter Gropius* (London: Faber, 1936); Tim Mowl, *Stylistic Cold Wars: Betjeman versus Pevsner* (London: John Murray, 2000), pp. 46–8, 146.

22 Clive Bell, 'Victorian taste', *Listener*, 23 June 1936, p. 1235; cf. John Betjeman, '1830–1930 – Still going strong: a guide to the recent history of interior decoration', *Architectural Review*, 67 (1930), pp. 231–40.

23 John Piper, 'Victorian painting', *Listener*, 20 November 1941, p. 698.

24 Nicholas Temperley, 'Xenophilia in British musical history', *Nineteenth Century British Music Studies*, 1 (1999), pp. 3–19.

25 *The D'Oyly Carte Opera Company in Gilbert and Sullivan Operas: A Record of Productions, 1875–1961*, comp. Cyril Rollins and R. John Witts (London: Michael Joseph, 1962); *D'Oyly Carte Centenary: 100 Years of Gilbert and Sullivan* (London : D'Oyly Carte Opera Trust, 1975); David Cannadine, 'Gilbert and Sullivan: the making and unmaking of a British "tradition"' in Roy Porter and Paul Thompson (eds), *Myths of the English* (Cambridge: Polity, 1992), pp. 12–32; Tony Joseph, *The D'Oyly Carte Opera Company, 1875–1982: An Unofficial History* (Bristol: Bunthorne Books, 1994), chs 10–11.

26 H. Mark Glancy, *When Hollywood Loved Britain: The Hollywood 'British' Film, 1939–45* (Manchester: Manchester University Press, 1999), pp. 74–8; Jeffery Richards, *The Age of the Dream Palace: Cinema and Society in Britain, 1930–39* (London: Routledge & Kegan Paul, 1984), pp. 254–5.

27 Alan Bott, *Our Fathers, 1870–1900: Manners and Customs of the Ancient Victorians: A Survey in Pictures and Text* (London: Heinemann, 1931), p. 2; E. H. Dance, *The Victorian Illusion* (London: Heinemann, 1928), p. 2.

28 W. R. Inge, 'Introduction' to *The Post Victorians* (London: Nicholson and Watson, 1933), p. vii.

29 Arthur Baumann, *The Last Victorians* (London: Ernest Benn, 1927), pp. 16–17; Peter Quennell, *Victorian Panorama: A Survey of Life and Fashion from Contemporary Photographs* (London: B. T. Batsford, 1937), p. vi.

30 E. C. Batho and B. Dobrée, *The Victorians and After* (London: Cresset Press, 1938), pp. 37, 40. F. R. Leavis, *The Great Tradition: George Eliot, Henry James, Joseph Conrad* (London: Chatto & Windus, 1948).

31 John Steegman, *Consort of Taste, 1830–1870* (London: Sidgwick & Jackson, 1950); Hugh Casson, *An Introduction to Victorian Architecture* (London: Art & Technics, 1948); H. R. Hitchcock, 'Victorian Monuments of Commerce', *Architectural Review*, 105 (February 1949), pp. 61–74, and *Early Victorian Architecture in Britain*, 2 vols (New Haven, CT: Yale University Press, 1954).

32 Nikolaus Pevsner, 'Victorian thought on architecture', *Listener*, 26 July 1951, pp. 137–9; 'Victorian churches and buildings', *ibid.*, 2 August 1951, pp. 177–9;

'The late Victorians and William Morris', *ibid.*, 9 August 1951, pp. 217–19; Peter Ferriday (ed.), *Victorian Architecture* (London: Jonathan Cape, 1963).

33 John Gloag, *Victorian Taste: Some Social Aspects of Architecture and Industrial Design, from 1830–1900* (London: Adam & Charles Black, 1962), p. xv; Joanna Richardson in the *Listener*, 11 June 1959, p. 1031.

34 The series, published by Herbert Jenkins, featured titles on Victorian embroidery, costume, silver and silver-plate, pottery, lace and porcelain.

35 Society for the Protection of Ancient Buildings, *Report of the Committee for the 74th to 80th years (1952–57)* (London: SPAB, 1957), p. 28.

36 Paul Thompson, 'The Victorian Society', *Victorian Studies*, 7 (1964), pp. 387–92; Alan Crawford, 'Victorian heritage: twenty-five years of the Victorian Society', *History Today*, 33 (1983), pp. 45–8.

37 R. B. Mowat, *The Victorian Age: The Age of Comfort and Culture* (London: George G. Harrap, 1939); John Maass, *The Gingerbread Age: A View of Victorian America* (New York: Rinehart, 1957); D. W. Howe (ed.), *Victorian America* (Philadelphia: University of Pennsylvania Press, 1976).

38 Later published as H. J. Dyos and Michael Wolff (eds), *The Victorian City: Images and Realities*, 2 vols (London: Routledge & Kegan Paul, 1973).

39 By comparison, in 1960 PhDs on the nineteenth century accounted for 39 per cent of all British universities' PhDs in post-1485 studies, and by 1990 it had fallen back to the same proportion: calculated from *Theses in History* (London: Institute of Historical Research, 1958–90).

40 Asa Briggs, *Victorian Cities* (London: Odhams Press, 1963), p. 10.

41 Raphael Samuel, 'Mrs Thatcher and Victorian values' in Samuel, *Island Stories: Unravelling Britain. Theatres of Memory* (London: Verso, 1998), vol. 2, pp. 330–48; James Walvin, *Victorian Values* (London: Andre Deutsch, 1987); Gordon Marsden (ed.), *Victorian Values: Personalities and Perspectives in Nineteenth Century Society* (Harlow: Longman, 1990); T. C. Smout (ed.), *Victorian Values: A Joint Symposium of the Royal Society of Edinburgh and the British Academy* (Oxford: Oxford University Press, 1992).

42 'Roundtable: locating the Victorians, 2001', *Journal of Victorian Culture*, 7 (2002), pp. 111–33; Sweet, *Inventing the Victorians*; Martin Hewitt, 'Prologue: reassessing the age of equipoise' in Hewitt (ed.), *Age of Equipoise*, pp. 1–38; A. N. Wilson, *The Victorians* (London: Hutchinson, 2002).

Part I
Histories

1

Lytton Strachey's *Eminent Victorians*: the rise and fall of the intellectual aristocracy

William C. Lubenow

God's calls are many, and they are strange. (Lytton Strachey)[1]

Introduction

When Lytton Strachey published *Eminent Victorians* in 1918 he sent copies to his mother and to his kinsman Walter Raleigh, the professor of English at Oxford University. He wrote to his mother: 'Its appearance is rather good, I think, don't you?' Strachey received a letter in which Raleigh expressed his approval of Strachey's book.[2] That Strachey should have wanted his mother's and his kinsman's approval has real point because dynastic families like theirs were both the subject of his book and the target of his mockery. Strachey's friends admired his book, though not uncritically. Dennis Robertson, the Apostle and economist, wrote to J. R. M. Butler, the son of the master of Trinity College:

> I wonder if you have read Strachey's Eminent Victorians, & what you thought of it. I confess it amused me greatly. I think it is unfair certainly to Cromer, and probably to Arnold and others, and that it has sacrificed too much to his sense of the dramatic and the ludicrous to produce a really true work. And I imagine some people find the whole method offensive, though I think the greatest personalities like Florence & Gordon (and Hartington) emerge from it greater rather than less.[3]

It gave Lowes Dickinson 'some consoling and profitable hours' during the horror of the war.[4] Bertrand Russell's warder had to remind him that prison was no amusing matter when Russell burst out laughing while reading it.[5]

Eminent Victorians was tremendously influential. It sold 35,000 hardbound copies in Britain and the United States. It was translated into Polish, Romanian, Spanish, Italian and Japanese in Strachey's lifetime.[6] From the beginning, *Eminent Victorians* had its critics. F. A. Simpson famously accused Strachey of being morally flawed: 'In the last resort he did not care enough for truth.' Strachey's portraits 'are not merely false but falsified'.[7]

And even recently these criticisms are muttered in the Senate House discussions in Cambridge. In the discussion of the Fourth Report of the Board of Scrutiny on 24 October 2000 the president of Wolfson College described Strachey's methods as 'ugly and vulgar', and carried out with 'considered and calculated cunning'.[8] As Noel Annan remarked: 'Historians never mention Strachey's name without a curse.'[9]

On the other hand, Strachey's book was a revolution in biographical writing. Michael Holroyd said that Strachey liberated twentieth-century biography from respectability;[10] and Richard Holmes called attention to the ways in which Strachey reshaped biographical literature. Strachey was 'less of a story–teller, than a destroyer of illusions and a liberator of forms'. Strachey 'released a generation of brilliant experiments in biographical narrative, who at last began to ask *how* can lives be genuinely reconstructed: what is memory, what is time, what is character, what is "evidence" in the human story?'[11] Reviewers of biographies continue to cite Strachey and his methods with approval.[12] Strachey's work unleashed a century of British biography. It was a literary movement which, as Holroyd has argued, 'used biography as an instrument against the sterility of postmodernism'. This biographical tradition helped 'to establish identity in an age of fading authority'.[13]

The importance of *Eminent Victorians* might be accounted for by referring to Strachey's slashing style, to the verve and vim with which he conducted a revolution in the writing of biography. It might be accorded to Strachey's iconoclastic manner and the way he revealed the flaws and defects of his famous subjects. As Strachey expressed his aim in the Preface: 'Je n'impose rien; je ne propose rien: j'expose' (10). Such an approach may not appeal to all tastes, but it is refreshing in its narrative power. This chapter, however, offers another argument for the importance of *Eminent Victorians*. It was a tract for the times. It was a polemic which charted the rise and fall of families like his own, families which belonged to what Noel Annan famously called the 'intellectual aristocracy'.[14] As such it is about modernism and at the same time is an exercise in modernism. *Eminent Victorians* describes the fragmented world of the late nineteenth century and reveals the discontinuous, cross-cutting multidimensionalism which characterised it.

The rise of the intellectual aristocracy

Let us note those selected by Strachey as subjects. His eminent Victorians were neither great landed magnates nor powerful plutocrats. They were people from families like his own; people who were attached to the universities, the schools, the professions and the world of public service. They were the children of families soaked in evangelicalism who had their roots in country rectories and in the professions of the 'Old Corruption'. As the fiscal–military–confessional state of the old regime collapsed, they were left behind, faced with the task of forging a place for themselves in the world of the new professions. Their task was to define a new kind of authority and status. Some of them came out of Clapham. Some of them ended in Bloomsbury. They were families of empire – and if not to the actual empire, like Arnold, they belonged to the empire of the mind which produced recruits for empire, or, like Manning, they belonged to the empire of the spirit with ultramontane connections on the continent and in Rome.

Manning's father had been a West Indian merchant; Arnold's father, a collector of customs. Gordon's father had been a lieutenant-general in the Royal Artillery and his mother's family were merchants. Nightingale's father was the son of a banker, a cultivated country gentleman who loved travel; her mother was the daughter of William Smith, who worked aggressively for the abolition of slavery.

The task of such families was to find a new kind of authority and identity for themselves. Strachey, in describing his own family, called attention to their indeterminate social circumstances:

> What happened was that a great tradition – the aristocratic tradition of the eighteenth century – had reached a very advanced state of decomposition. My father and mother belonged by birth and breeding to the old English world of country-house gentlefolk – a world of wealth and breeding, a world in which such things as footmen, silver, and wine were necessary appurtenances of civilized life. But their own world was different: it was the middle class professional world of the Victorians, in which the old forms still lingered but debased and enfeebled.[15]

Older forms of authority had been signified by the law, birth and wealth, as well as by confessional creed.[16] De Tocqueville and Marx thought that aristocratic notions of honour and authority had been displaced in the nineteenth century by conceptions of interest; but, as one modern author has observed, honour and authority had been democratised and made invisible.[17]

Social value was desacralised and defetishised (though perhaps *re*sacralised and *re*fetishised would be more accurate) by attaching it to the experiences of professional life. The author of Miss Nightingale's *DNB* entry put the point aptly: she 'taught nurses to be ladies' and she 'brought ladies out of the bondage of idleness to be nurses'.[18] At the end of her life Nightingale was named to the Order of Merit, an award formed in 1902 to give honour and authority to imagination. Strength, courage and morality were no longer derived from fantasies of martial valour, or from birth, property or law. Now they were conceived of as properties established by talent, ability and service in the public sphere. They were the values of the 'competition wallahs', measured by success in competitive examinations rather than on the field of battle. This transformation of honour and authority was part of a much larger historical process, what one scholar has called 'a shift from a court-based culture to a club-based culture'.[19] The repeal of

the Test and Corporation Acts (1828) and the emancipation of Catholics
(1829) required new ideas of loyalty. Politics was liberated from confessional creeds. As new forms of dignity, meaning, and value were created,
identity replaced status. Instead of the bright, clear borders that the law,
family lineage and wealth gave to social worth, the identities of eminent
Victorians were contested on murky frontiers the limits of which were
indefinite and uncertain.

The old indicators of social worth were no longer of much value. Burke's
Landed Gentry doubled in size; licenses for armorial bearing increased; and
the knightage was enlarged. But the doubling of Burke was a result of
enhanced displays of pedigree rather than the inclusion of new families.
Most new licenses for armorial bearings were granted for humble display
on writing paper or on family cutlery – the small things which make up the
seriousness of life – rather than for the grand purposes of the College of
Arms. Knighthoods went to the new orders – the Star of India (1861), the
Order of the British Empire, the Royal Victorian Order (1869) – precisely
those orders which recognised achievement in the world of public service
rather than circumstances of birth and wealth.[20] Burke, armorial bearings,
even knighthoods, were old social wine-skins that stretched and cracked as
new and different wine was poured into them.

The old system of honours had become devalued. When Arthur Balfour
was named to the Order of Merit in 1916, Sir G. O. Trevelyan wrote to
him: 'The public is evidently very jealous of the maintenance of the standard of the Order; and no wonder when all other honours are so cheap.'[21]
Lytton Strachey's father, Richard Strachey, was offered a barony for his services to India. After an intense family discussion, he refused it. As his grand-
son put it:

> But in his circle – earnest, agnostic, and liberal-minded – it simply was not
> done to receive a reward for work which, in itself, was reward enough, and –
> more to the snobbish point, perhaps – honours which were so abundantly dis-
> tributed to the unworthy.[22]

Richard Strachey, 'to avoid trouble and after many misgivings', accepted a
knighthood. His wife resented even that. Hitherto, she had been *the* Mrs
Richard Strachey; henceforth she would be only another Lady Strachey
(there were already several others).

The new regime of social worth to which the eminent Victorians belonged
required new social containers. Those containers were the directories of the
professions, such as *Crockford's Clerical Directory* (1869–), Foster's *Men
at the Bar* (1885), the matriculation lists for the public schools and for
Oxford and Cambridge colleges, and especially the *Dictionary of National
Biography* (1885–). The *DNB* measured social authority by imagination
and education. For the nineteenth century there are 955 entries for soldiers,
1,585 for clergymen, and 1,674 for writers.[23] Its editors were not the 'last
grand men of letters'; they were in 'the vanguard of those who gave liter-

ary studies professional standards'[24] and thereby confirmed the cultural and social capital of the country.

The method and the authority of the eminent Victorians were literary. These are precisely the aspects and attributes of their careers to which Strachey drew attention. Manning belonged to a class of ecclesiastics 'who have been distinguished less for saintliness and learning than for practical ability'. He 'seemed almost to relive in his own person that long line of administrative clerics' (13). It was, above all, Manning's careerism which Strachey found striking. For Manning 'the most subtle and terrible temptation of all was the temptation of worldly success' (44).

Strachey describes Miss Nightingale's correspondence as having been 'the most formidable of all her duties'. She lay all before her in her 'sarcasm', with her 'terrible' nicknames, and with the 'virulence of its volubility'. 'Her soul pent up all day in the restraint and reserve of a vast responsibility, now at last poured itself out in the letters with all its natural vehemence, like a swollen torrent through an open sluice. Here, at least, she did not mince matters' (127). Her report *Notes Affecting the Health, Efficiency, and Hospital Administration of the British Army*, written after her return from the Crimea, was an 'extraordinary composition'. It filled 'more than eight hundred closely printed pages, laying down vast principles of far-reaching reform, discussing the minutest details of a multitude of controversial subjects, containing an enormous mass of information of the most varied kinds – military, statistical, sanitary, architectural' (142–3).

Arnold's 'piety and industry' gave him 'a conspicuous place among his fellow students' at Winchester and Oxford (163). While the boys' 'main study remained the dead languages of Greece and Rome' at Rugby, Dr Arnold 'introduced modern history, modern languages, and mathematics' (170–1). He 'became known, not merely as a headmaster, but as a public man. He held decided opinions upon a large number of topics; and he enunciated them' (174). He never completed his commentary on the New Testament or his work on Church and state because 'Dr. Arnold's active mind was diverted from political and theological speculations to the study of philology and historical composition' (179). His letters and journals, recording his reflections and impressions in France or Italy, show us that Dr Arnold preserved 'in spite of the distractions of foreign scenes and foreign manners his accustomed habits of mind' (180–1). He entered into the study of Sanskrit and Slavonic, brought out an edition of Thucydides and engaged, the while, 'in a voluminous correspondence upon a multitude of topics with a large circle of men of learning' (179). General Gordon was an engineer who was claimed by adventure and, 'plunged into the whirl of high affairs . . . his fate was mingled with the frenzies of Empire and the doom of peoples' (189). At the end of the Crimean War he went to Bessarabia to 'assist in determining the frontier between Russia and Turkey' (191). With a faith that was 'mystical and fatalistic' as well as 'highly unconventional', he 'opened his Bible, read and noted down his reflections on scraps of paper, which, periodically pinned together, he dispatched to one or other of his religious friends and, particularly, his sister Augusta. The published extracts from these voluminous outpourings lay bare the inner history of Gordon's spirit, and reveal the pious visionary of Gravesend in the restless hero of three continents' (198, 200–1). After his adventures in China Gordon became private secretary to Lord Ripon when Ripon was Indian Viceroy but resigned three days after arriving in Bombay because he could not fulfil the more mechanical features of the job.

These were the attributes of ambitious people using literary wit to secure places for themselves in the public world. They spoke the language of power. Strachey described the force and form of this language in another place:

> Nothing is more interesting than to watch the magic of style springing out unexpectedly from the utterances of great men of action bringing an alien sweetness into the hard world of fact, wonderfully lending to expressions of business or of duty the glamour of passion and romance. The sentences of these natural stylists, thrown off amid the hazards of administration or of arms, possess often enough a distinctive quality of their own – a racy flavour of actual life which is rarely caught save by the greatest or least literary man of letters.

The 'mere writer' could only 'like a silkworm spin out his precious materials from inside him' and 'could hardly hope to rival the man of genius whose imagination has been quickened and whose tongue has been loosened by what Burke calls the "overmastering necessities" of events'.[25]

It goes beyond the scope of what can be done in this chapter to detail the intellectual content of the culture that the eminent Victorians expressed in the language of power. It was critical. It was liberal. It dealt with the question of the professions. It was non-technical. It was non-materialistic. It was non-confessional. However, since so much of their effort was given over to religious questions, it is perhaps worthwhile to say something about this issue.

The religion of the eminent Victorians, liberated from the coldness of political, constitutional and legal restraints, became polymorphous, intense and exaggerated. Prepared to correct the mistakes of the Church, as she was prepared to correct so much else, Miss Nightingale 'unravels, in the course of three portly volumes, the difficulties – hitherto, curiously enough, unsolved – connected with such matters of Belief in God, the Plan of Creation, the Origin of Evil, the Future Life, Necessity and Free Will, Law, and the Nature of Morality' (153). Then there was Dr Arnold's schoolmasterly piety. 'He would treat the boys at Rugby as Jehovah had treated the Chosen People; he would found a theocracy; and there should be Judges in Israel' (168). Then there was General Gordon's mystical, fatalistic and highly unconventional faith. He wrote to his sister: 'I died long ago, and it will not make any difference to me; I am prepared to follow the unrolling of the scroll' (198, 207). Then there was Cardinal Manning's cosmopolitan ultramontanism: he 'flung himself into the fray with the unyielding intensity of fervour, that passion for the extreme and the absolute, which is the very lifeblood of the Church of Rome' (61).

It was above all a religion released on the public world, for earthly duty rather than for heavenly delights. The eminent Victorians were people of driving ambition who sought to reconstruct the world in their own image. As Strachey puts it about Manning: 'meetings, missions, lectures, sermons, articles, interviews, letters – such things came upon him in redoubled multitudes, and were dispatched with an unrelenting zeal' (104). And about Miss Nightingale Strachey said: 'She tasted the joys of power, like those whose aristocratic rule was based upon invisibility, with the mingled satisfactions of obscurity and fame. And she found the machinery of illness hardly less effective as a barrier against the eyes of men than the ceremonial of the palace' (152). The eminent Victorians translated to the public world the earnest values of those non-confessional institutions. Maynard Keynes, who, like Strachey, emerged from such a family, described, in a witty, informal lecture to the Civil Service Association, how this worked. Keynes's utterances, like so many statements that came out of Bloomsbury, cannot be taken absolutely literally. Nevertheless, they have the ring of truth to them. The Treasury, which he characterized as 'very clever' and 'very dry', was recruited from the universities. Citing 'aesthetic methods' in such instruments as the Treasury Draft, which enabled only certain things to be done and 'made a great many things impossible', Keynes likened Treasury control to conventional morality. 'This frigid body', he said, regulated against enthusiasm and 'overwhelming wickedness'. The Treasury, therefore, 'came to possess attributes of institutions like a college or a City company, or the Church of England'.[26] Strachey singled out for attention the members of families, like his own, whose claim to authority came from professional and literary talent rather than birth or wealth.

The fall of the intellectual aristocracy

The method of the eminent Victorians was disturbing and disorienting. As a consequence, in their rise, alas, was also their fall. The nineteenth-century families of the intellectual aristocracy hedged their reputations in the respectability and piety of their two-volume biographies[27] – a literary form on which Strachey heaped contempt. But those families also created, assembled and preserved assiduously the materials that would destroy them. Their letters, their family memoirs, published and unpublished, were mirrors of consciousness and devices of self-doubt that could be used for self-evaluation and criticism.[28] From such materials could be drawn the ideas which reveal feet of clay and the inner weaknesses of those families. Fitzjames Stephen's 'Autobiographical recollections', which he himself called 'a strange performance', was, in his own view, essential, 'if anyone should ever care to know what sort of man I was then'.[29] Edmund

Sheridan Purcell's biography of Manning,[30] which one scholar has called 'one of the most extraordinary scandals in literary history',[31] is surely an example of the way in which biographical materials once preserved in a kind of pious innocence could be selected and quoted against their subject. Of course, Strachey mined Purcell heavily in his account of Manning.

In recreating their conceptions of identity, and authority, free from birth, wealth, and confessional loyalties, the eminent Victorians established indeterminate social positions for themselves. To achieve authority in the various forms they assumed they had to mimic the various intellectual, moral and political characteristics of the respectable professional bourgeoisie. They cut across the faultlines of religion, society, and politics in the nineteenth century. It is this cutting across, this highly multidimensional feature of the problem, which is so interesting. But they were, in fact, creating the various features of bourgeois society that they were seeking to mimic. To mimic and recast, therefore, was no simple adaptive mechanism.[32] In fact, mimicry and recasting suggests a kind of inauthenticity that undermined the authority they sought to achieve and which they had to protect themselves from and defend themselves against.

Because they were not authentic, the eminent Victorians had to be sincere. They were not what they seemed to be. Sincerity was a carapace that was difficult for them to get out of, or to get into. They constructed and invented. But they were also sceptical and self-critical. Strachey turned their criticism and scepticism against the eminent Victorians. Through the intimacy of biography, Strachey created a space in which he could evaluate his own kind. As Strachey put it in a famous letter to Maynard Keynes, the generations of the eminent Victorians lived in a 'glass case age'. Their refusal 'to face any fundamental question fairly – either about people or about God – looks at first sight like cowardice; but I believe it was simply the result of an incapacity for penetration – for either getting out of themselves or into anything or anybody else'.[33] *Eminent Victorians*, as a consequence, is a criticism of the Whig interpretation of history. It is not Protestant history. It is not triumphalist history. It is not history as progress.

Because their authority was literary, the social identity of the eminent Victorians was unstable. Letters, being what they are, it could hardly be otherwise. The regime of letters was based on the power of *Wissenschaft*. The prestige of a philological revolution had stripped letters of their representational claims, but conferred the far greater authority (and emotional risk) of linguistic autonomy.[34] Manning, Nightingale, Arnold and Gordon did not discover or detect their identities; they chose them.[35] Possibility creates choice. Possibility undermines some conceptions of identity while, at the same time, it allows for others to be formed and chosen. The eminent Victorians, and others whose social worth is expressed by their listing in the *DNB*, were people of letters and learning who created an intellectual tradition with its own internal cleavages. It was a tradition which, at the

same time, sustained loyalty to a regime, the very qualities of which qualified them for the *DNB*, and, at the same time, subverted it. There is point
to the fact that the *DNB* was one of the monuments to British national
identity.[36] There is also point to the fact that so many of the subjects in the
DNB were writers who gave expression to a fragile literary life. A fragile
literary life was, therefore, an expression of a fragile national identity.

Strachey was a modernist writing about modernism. Because he was one
of them, he detected the twitchy, internal perturbations and contradictions
of the careers of the eminent Victorians. That is the significance of his
wit and the irony of his treatment. As Strachey said himself, he would
attack his subjects in 'unexpected places', in their 'obscure recesses' (p. 9).
Manning, therefore, was 'supple and yielding' (13). It was necessary to be
careful, 'and Manning was careful indeed' (30). Manning's 'secret imagination was haunted by a dreadful vision' (44). Manning spun round Odo
Russell 'his spider's web of delicate and clinging diplomacy' (88). Miss
Nightingale might seem the 'perfect lady' to the casual observer, but 'the
keener eye' perceived 'the serenity of high deliberation in the scope of the
capacious brow, the sign of power in the dominating curve of the thin nose,
and the traces of a harsh and dangerous temper – something peevish, something mocking and yet something precise – in the small and delicate mouth'
(126). Back from the Crimea, she set herself to the reform of the whole of
Army medicine: 'A demoniac frenzy had seized upon her. As she lay upon
her sofa, gasping, she devoured blue-books, dictated letters, and in the inter-
vals of her palpitations, cracked her febrile jokes' (134). She could 'dissect
the concrete and distasteful fruits of actual life', but she could not 'construct a coherent system of abstract philosophy' and 'was never at home
with a generalization'. 'Like most great men of action – perhaps like all –
she was simply an empiricist' (155).

Everything about Dr Arnold 'denoted energy, earnestness, and the best
intentions', but 'his legs, perhaps, were shorter than they should have been'
(165). His reforms proved to be empty. He was an earnest enthusiast who
attempted to make his pupils Christian gentlemen according to Old Testament principles, but he founded a system that worshipped merely athletics
and good form (187). General Gordon 'was by nature *farouche*' (197). He
had never been confirmed though he took the sacrament every day (191).
'The Holy Bible was not his only solace.' Under the strong African sun 'he
would drink nothing but pure water; and then . . . water that was not so
pure' (203). He told Lord William Beresford that 'the world was not big
enough for him, that there was "no king or country big enough"; and then
he added, hitting him on the shoulder, "Yes, that is flesh, that is what I hate,
and what makes me wish to die"' (205–6). Therefore, 'it was not in peace
or rest, but in ruin and horror, that he reached his end' (189). The social
authority of Arnold, Nightingale, Manning, and Gordon, therefore, was
entwined with their moral weaknesses, and Strachey called attention to
both.

Conclusion

By stressing the ironies and the background of *Eminent Victorians*, this chapter may seem to strip out some of its vehemence and to undermine Strachey somewhat, making him more like the eminent Victorians than he would have liked. However, by calling attention to their inner anxieties and contradictions, it has actually reconceived the eminent Victorians, making them more like Strachey than they would have liked. And thus this chapter comes to its upshot. The rise and the fall of the intellectual aristocracy are perhaps inadequate or incorrect metaphors with which to explore the themes of *Eminent Victorians*. There are not two stories here; it is a single story. Their fall was in their rise. Their very virtues were their vices. The British literary forcefield, in which both the eminent Victorians and Strachey himself were located, was multi-polar: it was both centripetal and centrifugal. When he wrote *Elizabeth and Essex* (1928), Strachey quoted the lines from Virgil that Freud had used as the motto for the *Interpretation of Dreams*: 'If I cannot bend the beings in Heaven, I will stir the shades below.'[37] Through an interest in the dynamics of the inner life, Strachey could criticise and change the very regime of which he was a part. The eminent Victorians and Strachey lived on the edge of their own social world. Their social identities were multiple; their lives of letters were indeterminate. They were able, as one prominent historian has said about a very different social group, to overcome 'inertia and unthinking traditionalism' and to form a new system of social authority and a new regime of social worth because 'they were inquiring people with deep roots outside the political system for which they were working but one which they were in no way dependent'.[38] They created a literary world that could sustain innovation because it was an unsystematic system and a non-traditional tradition. It consisted in an ambiguous and unstable repertoire whose internally contradictory elements could be drawn out and thrown up with different emphases under different circumstances. Unsurprisingly, the more successfully they deployed those repertoires the more vulnerable they were to accusations of inauthenticity. By making words flesh the eminent Victorians and Strachey made words mortal: corruptible, fleeting, dying. They sought both authority and meaning, objectives that could be reconciled with only the greatest difficulty or not at all. As they came to realise, there might be two (or more) truths; those truths might be inconsistent with each other, yet they might all be true. Therefore, when Strachey said that 'God's calls are many, and they are very strange', he located the Victorians in literary families who devised the procedures of their liberal world.

Notes

1 Lytton Strachey, *Eminent Victorians* (London: Penguin, 1986), p. 112. From here on, citations of and extracts from *Eminent Victorians* refer to this edition's pagination.

2 Lytton Strachey to Jane Strachey, 11 May 1918, Oriental and India Office Library, London, Strachey Papers, Mss EUR F/127/341.

3 Dennis Robertson to J. R. M. Butler, 17 August 1918, Trinity College, Cambridge, J.R.M. Butler Mss A1/114.

4 Goldsworthy Lowes Dickinson to Lytton Strachey, 24 May [1918], British Library, London, Strachey Papers, Add. Ms 60664, fol. 146.

5 On Bertrand Russell's time in jail see Russell to Robin Mayor, 7 March 1918, Mayor Papers (Mayor's Papers were in the possession of the late Lady Rothschild until her death).

6 Michael Holroyd, *Lytton Strachey: The New Biography* (New York: Farrar, Straus & Giroux, 1994), p. 427.

7 F. A. Simpson, 'Max Beerbohm on Lytton Strachey', *Cambridge Review*, 4 December 1943, p. 70. I am grateful to Dr Gordon Johnson for this reference.

8 'Report of the discussion, 24 October 2000', *Cambridge University Reporter*, 1 November 2000, p. 149.

9 Noel Annan, *Our Age: Portrait of a Generation* (London: Weidenfeld & Nicolson, 1990), p. 83.

10 Holroyd, *Lytton Strachey*, pp. 428–9.

11 Richard Holmes, *Sidetracks: Explorations of a Romantic Biographer* (New York: Farrar, Straus & Giroux, 2000), p. 373.

12 Michiko Kakutani, 'In the course of human events, Lady Luck had a role', *New York Times*, 14 November 2000, p. E7; Benson Bobrik, 'The brethren', *New York Times Book Review*, 10 December 2000, p. 39.

13 Michael Holroyd, 'Our friends are dead', *Guardian*, 1 June 2002, p. 40.

14 N. G. Annan, 'The intellectual aristocracy' in J. H. Plumb (ed.), *Studies in Social History: A Tribute to G. M. Trevelyan* (London: Longmans, Green & Co., 1955), pp. 241–87.

15 Lytton Strachey, 'Lancaster Gate (1922)' in *The Shorter Strachey*, ed. Michael Holroyd and Paul Levy (Oxford: Oxford University Press, 1980), p. 9.

16 Robert Nye, 'Codes of honour in France: a historical anthropology', *Ethnologia Europea*, 21 (1991), p. 6.

17 William Reddy, *The Invisible Code: Honor and Sentiment in Postrevolution France, 1815–1848* (Berkeley: University of California Press, 1997), p. 19.

18 Stephen Paget, 'Florence Nightingale', *Dictionary of National Biography, 1901–1911*, Supplement 2 (London: Smith, Elder & Co., 1912), vol. 3, p. 19.

19 Paul Langford, 'Politics and manners from Sir Robert Walpole to Sir Robert Peel', *Proceedings of the British Academy*, 94 (1997), pp. 118, 125.

20 F. M. L. Thompson, 'Britain' in David Spring (ed.), *European Landed Elites in the Nineteenth Century* (Baltimore, MD: Johns Hopkins University Press, 1977), pp. 30–1, 38–41.

21 Sir G. O. Trevelyan to Arthur Balfour, 9 June 1916, Balfour Papers, BL, Add. Ms 49, 792, fol. 3.

22 Typescript of Richard Strachey's 'Unfinished Autobiography', BL, Add. Ms 61, 729, fols 18–19. This Richard Strachey (1902–1976) was the son of Ralph Strachey.

23 H. C. G. Matthew, *Leslie Stephen and the* New Dictionary of National Biography (Cambridge: Cambridge University Press, 1997), p. 15. See also Lynn Trev Broughton, *Men of Letters, Writing Lives: Masculinity and Literary Auto/Biography in the Late Victorian Period* (London: Routledge, 1999), pp. 29–36.

24 Noel Annan, *Leslie Stephen: The Godless Victorian* (Chicago and London: University of Chicago Press, 1984), pp. 84ff., 342–3.

25 Lytton Strachey, 'The prose style of men of action', *Spectator*, 25 January 1908, p. 142.

26 J. M. Keynes, 'The civil service and financial control', *The Collected Works of John Maynard Keynes*, vol. 16: *Activities, 1914–1919, The Treasury and Versailles* (Cambridge: Cambridge University Press for the Royal Economic Society, 1971), p. 299.

27 Holmes, *Sidetracks*, p. 373.

28 Christopher Tolley, *Domestic Biography: The Legacy of Evangelicalism in Four Nineteenth-Century Families* (Oxford: Clarendon Press, 1997), pp. 56–101.

29 'Autobiographical recollections', Cambridge University Library, James Fitzjames Stephen's Papers, Add. Ms 7349/19.

30 E. S. Purcell, *Life of Cardinal Manning, Archbishop of Westminster*, 2 vols (London: Macmillan & Co., 1896).

31 See David Newsome, *The Convert Cardinals: John Henry Newman and Henry Edward Manning* (London: John Murray, 1993), pp. 7–11.

32 For an interesting discussion of mimicry in the literary and scientific life of Vladimir Nabokov, see Mark Ridley, 'Humbert's humming-birds: butterfly mind – Nabokov, Linnaeus, Lepidoptera, and *Lolita*', *Times Literary Supplement*, 4 August 2000, pp. 3–4.

33 Lytton Strachey to John Maynard Keynes, 11 March 1906, King's College, Cambridge, Keynes Papers.

34 Linda Dowling, 'Victorian Oxford and the science of language', *Proceedings of the Modern Language Association*, 97 (1982), pp. 160–78. See also Stefan Collini, 'Genealogies of Englishness: literary history and cultural criticism in modern Britain', in Ciaran Brady (ed.), *Ideology and the Historians* (Dublin: Lilliput Press, 1991), pp. 131–2, 136, 140.

35 For identity choice, as distinct from identity discovery or detection, see Amartya Sen, 'East and West: the reach of reason', *New York Review of Books*, 20 July 2000, p. 37, and his *Reason Before Identity*, Romanes Lecture (Oxford: Oxford University Press, 1999).

36 Julia Stapleton, 'Political thought and national identity in Britain, 1850–1950' in Stefan Collini, Richard Whatmore, Brian Young (eds), *History, Religion, and Culture: British Intellectual History, 1750–1950* (Cambridge: Cambridge University Press, 2000), pp. 245–6.

37 Murray H. Sherman, 'Lytton and James Strachey: biography and psychoanalysis', in Norman Kiell (ed.), *Blood Brothers: Siblings as Writers* (New York: International Universities Press, 1983), pp. 350–2.

38 The phrases are Sir Michael Howard's and he used them to describe the old Whig tradition in British politics; see his 'Per ardua', *New Statesman and Nation*, 26 January 1957, pp. 106–7. I owe this reference to Peter Stansky.

2

The bleak age: J. H. Clapham, the Hammonds and the standard of living in Victorian Britain

Stewart Weaver

No survey of retrospective, twentieth-century assessments of the Victorian age would be complete without some discussion of what used to be called the standard of living debate. For fifty years, roughly from the mid-1920s to the mid-1970s, the question, variously defined, of the material effect of the Industrial Revolution on the industrial working class sustained more scholarly controversy than any other within the confines of modern British history. And though interest in the question has since slackened (along with interest in labour history generally), it continues tacitly to inform every representation of the Victorian age. Everyone, that is to say, who reflects on Victorian social life is at heart an 'optimist' or a 'pessimist', perceives either material (and moral) improvement or material (and moral) degradation. In the main, of course, this gross dichotomy simply recapitulates Victorian prejudices: what is the standard of living debate if not a variation, in a new scholarly key, of what Carlyle called 'the condition of England question'? Yet in this case the variation is of considerable interest in its own right, especially for the way in which it first emerged in the 1920s and 1930s. The climax of the standard of living debate in the 1960s, its great culmination in E. P. Thompson's *The Making of the English Working Class* (1963), is more familiar, much reviewed, much discussed.[1] My limited purpose here, then, is to revisit the debate at its creative origin. Too often disposed of in a preliminary paragraph, the original confrontation between J. H. Clapham, on the one hand, and J. L. and Barbara Hammond, on the other, was in fact the definitive one that set the enduring terms of this debate. At the same time, however, it was a richer, subtler, more wide-ranging affair than, say, the later confrontation between R. M. Hartwell and Eric Hobsbawm over the level of real incomes. In reconstructing in some depth and contextual detail this opening act in the standard of living debate, I hope to recapture its original spirit and to recover a critical moment in the making of 'the Victorians since 1901'.

I

The standard of living debate may be said to have begun on 13 September 1926, when in the Preface to the first volume of his *Economic History of Modern Britain* (1926) J. H. Clapham derided 'the legend that everything was getting worse for the working man, down to some unspecified date between the drafting of the People's Charter and the Great Exhibition'.[2] Statisticians had long known better, had long known, that is, that after the price fall of 1820–21 the purchasing power of wages in general was definitely greater than it had been prior to the revolutionary and Napoleonic wars. But social historians, Clapham suggested, had consistently ignored the statistical evidence, preferring instead to follow 'a familiar literary tradition'. Who, specifically, Clapham had in mind here among social historians, he did not say. Nor need he have done: his readers, in 1926, would immediately have recognised the slighting allusion to J. L. and Barbara Hammond.

For the Hammonds were, in 1926, at the height of their literary celebrity. Between 1911 and 1919, they had collaborated on a popular trilogy of books – *The Village Labourer* (1911), *The Town Labourer* (1917) and *The Skilled Labourer* (1919) – the cumulative effect of which was to install the Industrial Revolution at the centre of Britain's historical consciousness. They had followed their trilogy, in 1923, with a sprightly life of *Lord Shaftesbury*, the great Victorian humanitarian, and then a textbook, *The Rise of Modern Industry* (1925), which, as late as 1960, was described by no less eminent an authority than R. H. Tawney as 'the most original introduction to the social and economic aspects of history available in English'.[3] By 1960, however, already indeed by the time of Lawrence Hammond's death in 1949, the Hammonds had fallen into relative obscurity – relative, certainly, to the oddly comparable (and roughly contemporary) couple of Sidney and Beatrice Webb. The Hammonds's books have never been out of print, but few read them nowadays, and mention of their names seldom rouses more than a dim flicker of recognition. The argument the Hammonds started, in other words, has long outlived them, and in coming to terms with it we do well to remind ourselves briefly of who they were.[4]

Lawrence Hammond was born in 1872 in Drighlington, Yorkshire. His father, a keen home-ruler, made Gladstone into 'a sort of fourth person of the Trinity', and Hammond himself, throughout his life, felt a little unsure of the distinction between God and the Grand Old Man.[5] After five years at Bradford Grammar School, where he earned a reputation as a fiery radical, Hammond went up to St John's College, Oxford, in 1891, to read Greats with Sidney Ball, the Fabian disciple of T. H. Green. There he met Lucy Barbara Bradby, who, from a childhood spent at Toynbee Hall, Samuel Barnett's mission settlement in Whitechapel, had come up to Lady Margaret Hall in 1892 to read Greats with L. T. Hobhouse, and made herself conspicuous (initially) by becoming the first woman to ride about

town on a bicycle. Neither she nor her husband ever studied history in any
formal academic way. 'Armed with a little Latin and Greek, and with the
habits of mind formed by a study of a complete and significant civilisation,
we stepped into a world where men breathed the air of strictest science',
they once wrote in accounting for the tragic tone of *The Town Labourer*.[6]
While over at Cambridge, J. H. Clapham, their precise contemporary, was
studying economic history with Alfred Marshall and William Cunningham
– the very founders of the new academic discipline – the Hammonds were
reading Arnold Toynbee, whose posthumous *Lectures on the Industrial
Revolution* (1884) were really a traditional moral indictment of what
Toynbee called 'a period as disastrous and as terrible as any through which
a nation ever passed'.[7]

Lawrence Hammond's first historical work was an admiring, not to say
worshipful study of Charles James Fox (1903), in whom he somehow contrived to find the father of modern Liberalism. From Fox he had meant to
go on to a life of William Cobbett, the renegade anti-Jacobin turned 'poor
man's friend'; but early in his research, while 'dipping in a desultory way'
into Cobbett's *Political Register*, he was (he and his wife later recalled)
'startled to come upon a series of events quite new to him: the rising in the
southern counties in 1830'.[8] As it happened, the Home Office records on
which an investigation of the Swing rising would rest had just been opened
to public scrutiny. Here was an irresistible opportunity, and, leaving
Cobbett to their young friend G. D. H. Cole, Lawrence and Barbara
together turned to the far broader study of social conditions in the industrial age. They never contemplated a trilogy. It was only when their book
was in production, and the printers had made 'the horrifying discovery' that
it ran to 560 pages, that Barbara Hammond 'by a Herculean effort' devised
a scheme for breaking the book into first two and then, when even that
proved unwieldy, three volumes: one on rural conditions, another on urban,
and a third on the history of the skilled trades.[9] The first of the three, *The
Village Labourer*, appeared against the backdrop of the constitutional
upheaval of 1911.

Originally subtitled 'A Study of the Government of England before the
Reform Bill', *The Village Labourer*, despite its canonical (if controversial)
status as a work of rural history, was really, as Tawney noted, more of an
essay on 'the social philosophy of the English ruling classes'.[10] The 'mind
of the enclosing class' interested the Hammonds as much as enclosure itself,
though they did devote two highly original chapters to the 'actual method
of Parliamentary enclosure' – the precise manner and means by which it
was carried out. They never questioned its agricultural logic; they never
denied (though people think they did) that enclosure 'made the soil of
England immediately more productive' and capable of sustaining more
people than it had previously. But they did emphasise the high price
paid in the extinction of the old village life. No reader of Fielding or
Richardson could make the mistake of idealising this life, they noted. But,

for as long as it survived, the common-field system with its attendant right of access to common pasture had 'formed a world in which the villagers lived their own lives and cultivated the soil on a basis of independence'. Enclosure killed that world. Agriculture was revolutionised. Rents leapt up. 'England seemed to be triumphing over the difficulties of a war with half the world', the Hammonds said; but, in place of the old peasant with his customary rights and status, and his 'share in the fortunes and government of his village', now stood the village labourer 'with no corporate rights to defend, no corporate power to invoke, no property to cherish, no ambition to pursue, bent beneath the fear of his masters, and the weight of a future without hope'.[11]

Needless to say, this cataclysmic view of the social effect of enclosure is highly controversial and has never received much academic assent. Among the first to dispute it at the time was J. H. Clapham, the author of a book on the Abbé Sieyès and the politics of the French Revolution – a final, belated, expression of his undergraduate attachment to Lord Acton – but then the rising authority on English economic history. *The Village Labourer*, Clapham said in his review in the *Economic Journal*, was a 'brilliantly written social tragedy', but it was bad social history. Enclosure, left to stand alone, appeared 'both more important and less inevitable than it actually was'. The book throughout gave Clapham the utterly unscientific impression that 'but for greed things could have gone on very well as they were'. Nowhere did the Hammonds suggest how common-field agriculture was to meet the needs of a rapidly expanding population. Nowhere did they undertake any serious study of the effect of enclosure on prices, wages or rents. Instead, Clapham complained, a few notorious instances of abuse had been made to stand as somehow typical of the age and landowning class. The concluding account of the labourers' rising of 1830 – the Hammonds' main contribution to historical study – was 'so wretched, so infinitely discreditable to the governors of England', that one could well understand 'how its shadow got thrown back over every preceding page'. But, on the whole, Clapham concluded, the picture was altogether 'out of drawing'. The Hammonds complained somewhere of the 'simplifying philosophy of the eighteenth century', while themselves grossly simplifying its economic history.[12]

In their Preface to a new edition of *The Village Labourer*, issued in September 1913, the Hammonds responded briefly to these and other criticisms, reminding readers that more than half of their book was concerned with causes of the rural labourer's degradation *other* than enclosure: 'The book is a study in government', they insisted, 'a discussion of the lines on which Parliament regulated the lives and fortunes of a class that had no voice in its own destinies.'[13] It was, in short, a political as much as a social history, as was, to their minds, its famous sequel *The Town Labourer*, which appeared against the backdrop of war and reconstruction in 1917. There the subject was explicitly the Industrial Revolution, but it was not their purpose, the Hammonds said, to 'trace the long struggles of inventors, or the rapid triumphs of the leaders of enterprise, nor even to examine the result of all this energy in terms of national power and national wealth'. They were here concerned, rather, with 'the fortunes of the mass of the people engaged in the industries that produced this wealth', and these, they were certain, had declined. 'The revolution that had raised the standard of comfort for the rich had depressed the standard of life for the poor', they wrote – a sentence in which, unknowingly, they named the debate to come. But the Hammonds never understood 'the standard of life' in purely material terms. The Industrial Revolution was 'a social revolution', creating, as their subtitle said, 'a new civilisation' with problems and a character of its own. Industry was 'the new power' abroad in the land; and regardless of their wage levels – the Hammonds did not even enter into these – urban workers

> felt of this new power that it was inhuman, that it disregarded all their instincts and sensibilities, that it brought into their lives an inexorable force, destroying and scattering their customs, their traditions, their freedom, their ties of family and home, their dignity and character as men and women.[14]

A generation of historians weaned on E. P. Thompson's *The Making of the English Working Class* will at once recognise this sort of language. Indeed, the most striking thing about *The Town Labourer* eighty-five years on is the extent to which it anticipates much, since Thompson, of what has passed for 'the new labour history'. Discipline, power, surveillance, supervision, control, coercion, punishment: these are the positively Foucauldian themes the book pursues in making the case for urban degradation. Scarcely any evil associated with the factory system, the Hammonds conceded, was a new evil in kind. Hours had always been long, pay had always been poor, children had always worked, homes had always been uncomfortable. What the Industrial Revolution did was to turn the traditional discomforts of life into a 'rigid system'. It introduced 'an alien power' into workers' lives, and added a suffocating discipline to all the evils which they had suffered. If machinery had lightened the drudgery of labour, it nevertheless introduced a 'wearing tension', a sense of an inexorable and inhuman power overshadowing all. Even the masters felt it, and not a few of them worked with the men to assuage it. But 'the industrial system itself was so contrived', the Hammonds argued, 'as to make the public spirit, or the human sympathy, or the generous common-sense of the best employers dependent on the selfishness or indifference or the blind greed of the worst'. Thus the fateful hardening of class conflict, the permanent souring of relations between rich and poor: that, far more than declining wages, was the social tragedy to which *The Town Labourer* was really addressed. The Industrial Revolution may have delivered society from its primitive dependence on the forces of nature; but, in return, the Hammonds insisted, it had taken society prisoner.[15]

From their 'picture of the social conditions created by the great changes of the Industrial Revolution', the Hammonds turned in *The Skilled Labourer*, the third and concluding volume of their trilogy, to 'the detailed history of particular bodies of skilled workers during those changes'.[16] From the general character of the age to a few specific experiences of it: that was the stated idea. But it left *The Skilled Labourer*, in a peculiar sense, a supplement to the second volume: as one reviewer put it – 'more, indeed, a series of detailed and voluminous footnotes ... than a separate entity in itself'.[17] The concluding chapters on the Luddite movement and the adventures of Oliver the Spy are among the most memorable of the entire trilogy. But the book as a whole is too much the product of *The Town Labourer*'s leavings; and *The Skilled Labourer* – despite being the first of the Hammonds' books to earn a short notice in the *English Historical Review* – made a relatively slight impression on their contemporaries. Still, it was a potent culmination to a masterful trilogy, the combined import of which, D. C. Coleman has written, 'was massively to confirm and disseminate the catastrophic version of the Industrial Revolution'. With passion, vigour and evident sincerity, the Hammonds had 'carried the catastrophic version beyond merely the readership of those absorbing the Industrial Revolution as part of the study of economic history' and made it something of a common national possession.[18]

Having seen their trilogy through, the Hammonds (more by accident of publisher's interest than deliberate design) now extended their interpretation of the Industrial Revolution into the early Victorian period by way of a short life of Lord Shaftesbury that had been commissioned by Constable for its 'Makers of the Nineteenth Century' series. As it happened, Lawrence Hammond's great-grandfather had been a tenant farmer (and occasional poacher) on Shaftesbury's Dorset estates, so he felt entitled to approach the great humanitarian with a certain degree of informed scepticism. *Lord Shaftesbury* is a witty and playful book, somewhat in spirit of Lytton Strachey's *Eminent Victorians* (1918). Yet it is also an admiring book that fully credits Shaftesbury for that gradual softening of the industrial system which, for the Hammonds, was the most notable feature of the early Victorian age. True, Shaftesbury never supported John Fielden's campaign for a minimum wage for the handloom weavers. Arguments for working-class enfranchisement fell foul of his aristocratic prejudice, just as arguments for national education fell foul of his religious prejudice. Still, on balance, the Hammonds felt, Shaftesbury 'did more than any single man, or any single Government in English history, to check the raw power of the new industrial system'. The Factory and Mine Acts that he sponsored were, in their view, 'events of the Victorian age not less decisive than the measures that removed the burden of the Corn Laws and swept from the government of England some of the worst of its ancient abuses'.[19]

From 'Shafter' (as they fondly called him), the Hammonds turned, in the early 1920s, to an economic history textbook that deepened their engagement with the Victorian age. Originally commissioned by Methuen & Co. as the third volume of a proposed four-volume economic and social history of England to be edited by G. D. H. Cole, *The Rise of Modern Industry* was 'an attempt to put the Industrial Revolution in its place in history', the Hammonds said, to display it against the background of earlier, and better, economic civilisations.[20] For in their general pessimism about the industrial age the Hammonds were as yet unrelenting: inexcusable poverty amid scandalous plenitude; a grave disproportion of political power; a general disposition to regard the working class as idle and profligate; the shameful extension of child labour; the corruption and deterioration of town life. In short, 'the curse of Midas' had fallen on Great Britain in the eighteenth century in the form of modern industry. By the middle decades of the nineteenth century, however, the forces of Christian compassion, working-class Jacobinism and liberal humanism had combined to inspire the factory laws, the civil service, sanitary reform and municipal incorporation, and all those other 'contributions that England was to make to the task of creating a society out of this new chaos'. The curse of Midas had not been dispelled, but it was tamed and controlled, even weakened, by Victorian public spiritedness. And now, writing on the eve of the General Strike and amid industrial decline, the Hammonds hoped to recall that Victorian spirit and bring it to bear on the economic crisis of their time.

II

Despite the misgivings of those in whom its very eloquence aroused doubts as to its academic authority, *The Rise of Modern Industry* enjoyed great success as a textbook. Together with new or recent editions of each part of the labourer trilogy, it confirmed the Hammonds's arrival as the leading social historians of their time. They were now at the height of their public influence and thus ripe for critical scrutiny, the first serious product of which came in 1925 with the appearance of M. Dorothy George's *London Life in the 18th Century*. According to 'the more modern school of social historians', began this classic study, the late eighteenth century saw 'the beginning of a dark age, in which there was a progressive degradation of the standards of life, under the blight of a growing industrialism'. But the social history of London obstinately and emphatically refused to conform to this image. Improvement, not degradation, could be traced in all aspects of London life from about 1750, George said, and it became marked, she insisted, between 1780 and 1820 – the very heart of the Hammonds's dark age. Of course London was in a sense exceptional. It underwent a revolutionary transformation in the course of the eighteenth century, 'but the direct results of what is called the industrial revolution were not conspicuous there', George conceded, and Lawrence Hammond, in his *New Statesman* review, happily enlarged on this point. London was a commercial town, he said; it had confronted its dark age in the seventeenth century

when the spoils of India and the new Atlantic trade had visited on it something of the same destructive force that the steam engine was to visit on
Manchester. But the Industrial Revolution had spared it. 'It was like a storm
that passed over London and broke elsewhere', Hammond wrote, satisfied
that this accounted for the evidence of its improvement.[21]

Needless to say, modern scholarship resists this tidy separating out of
London from the industrial scene.[22] But at the time it seemed to satisfy and
pre-empt any general challenge to the Hammonds' view of things. G. T.
Griffith's *Population Problems in the Age of Malthus* (1926) was harder to
finesse. In common with all catastrophists, the Hammonds had always
assumed that the new industrial system, with its reckless extension of the
money wage to women and children, had given a general stimulus to
population. Population growth, that is to say, was in their minds a dependent variable: the Industrial Revolution was creating its own labour force
and then degrading it, for 'it is well known', they had written, in one of
those unsubstantiated assertions that so irked Clapham, 'that population
increased with a decline in the standard of life'.[23] But had it? Griffith's far
more scientific assertion was that a falling death rate associated with
improvements in public health accounted for the eighteenth century rise in
England's population. Population growth, in his mind, was an *independent*
variable, and the obvious implication was that far from degrading a surplus
population it had called into being, the Industrial Revolution had come
along just in time to avert subsistence famine: not curse, but blessing.[24]

Compared to that of Mrs George, here was a fundamental challenge, a
revisionist assertion that went to the heart of the Hammonds's sombre argument. They handled it in two ways. First, they gracefully conceded the
point, withdrawing the more demographically suspect passages from subsequent editions of *The Town Labourer* and revising their Preface to allow
for the possibility of a falling death rate.[25] But then, in their defence,
Barbara Hammond (without, she said, wandering out of regions where the
simple arithmetic of schoolroom days would serve as her guide) undertook
a critical examination of the census statistics on which Griffith's conclusions were based. Her essential discovery was that the parish registers on
which he had relied seriously under-reported mortality rates, ignoring as
they did most extra-parochial burials.[26] In the context of the Nonconformist
north, this was a telling point that for the moment eroded confidence in
statistical proofs of improved urban conditions in the early nineteenth
century.

Such confidence was soon to revive, however, with the appearance in
December 1926 of the first volume of J. H. Clapham's magisterial *Economic
History of Modern Britain*. Here, behind a ponderous 600-page profusion
of facts and figures lay three essential claims: that the Industrial Revolution
was both more gradual and local, and less significant nationally than the
Hammonds had allowed; that, far from declining, the wages of every group
of urban or industrial workers for which information was available, with

the one grave exception of cotton (hand-loom) weavers, had risen markedly between 1780 and 1850; and that, far from being blind or indifferent to the evils arising from unrestrained growth, British governments in the early nineteenth century had been as caring and responsive as the circumstances of the time allowed. In aspects of each of these assertions, Clapham had been anticipated in a tentative way by other, less ambitious, scholars. But his was the first complete, sustained and explicit act of interpretive revision. With Clapham, a Macaulayan optimism once more came of age.[27]

Hammond's first response to it was measured and, as his friend G. M. Trevelyan said, 'very gentlemanlike'.[28] Clapham's work, he said in his *Guardian* review, was 'one of the chief achievements of our time in the writing of modern economic history'. One laid it down 'with the greatest respect for its learning, its gravity, its amazing grasp and handling of detail, and its wide and dispassionate outlook'. Still, when it came to the fortunes of the working class, Clapham spoke too much as the economist who valued life on its statistics. Surely he would admit, Hammond hoped, that in judging the relative happiness of an age one had to take other things into account.[29] Privately, Clapham did. 'Your suggestion of neglected imponderabilia is perfectly fair', he wrote to Hammond. In print, though, he would, he said, 'let [his] dogmata stand', and so the issue was joined between two perspectives on the industrial past, between, on the one side, the old moral catastrophism that had culminated in the Hammonds and, on the other, what Lawrence Hammond privately derided as 'the new school which argues that if only one paid attention to statistics it would become clear that everything went well at the Industrial Revolution'.[30]

Later participants in 'the standard of living debate' have often characterised the Hammonds' response to Clapham as feeble; and it is true that they were too quickly inclined to yield the statistical ground.[31] 'Statisticians smite and we offer the other cheek', Barbara once quipped to Lawrence.[32] But we have seen how, over the question of death rates, she had smitten Griffith in return, and now Lawrence did some smiting of his own over working-class wages. In a June 1927 *Contemporary Review* essay he took Clapham to task for investing unwarranted confidence in A. L. Bowley's expressly tentative nineteenth-century wage indices; and, in a more formal reply of January 1930, 'The Industrial Revolution and discontent', he caught him out in the elementary statistical fallacy of concocting an 'average wage' out of an average of county averages that ignored the number of workers in each respective county and thus concealed the fact, as Hammond calculated it, that 60 per cent of England's labourers fell below it. *Touché*, Clapham noted in the Preface to his second edition. But as Hammond had gone on, in spite of this quibble, to concede that 'so far as statistics can measure material improvement there was improvement', Clapham saw no need, he said, 'to maintain an arithmetical wrangle'. With Hammond's contention that 'on what men enjoy and what they suffer through their imagination, statistics do not throw a great deal of light', he professed himself in most profound agreement. And there, for the moment, the matter rested, with England's leading 'optimist' and leading 'pessimist' respectfully agreeing not so much to differ as 'each to keep to his own end of the field'.[33]

III

'This sudden effort to rehabilitate the Industrial Revolution is extremely interesting – part of the general reaction I suppose', wrote L. T. Hobhouse to J. L. Hammond in May 1927. Clapham's book had not impressed him. 'It is the kind of history that leaves you with the impression that nothing has ever happened', he assured Barbara Hammond, who herself had likened Clapham's work to 'a badly cooked cake'.[34] Badly cooked or not, Clapham's cake had clearly left the Hammonds unsure of themselves, and they were increasingly inclined to shift their arguments away from the whole vexed business of 'standards of living'. The new phrase in their lexicon was 'discontent'. 'We have tried', they wrote in reply to a spirited attack on *The Town Labourer* by a fanatical anti-socialist named Anna Ramsay, 'to describe happiness and unhappiness that statistics can neither create or comprehend; to interpret the discontent and the despair that haunted a world entering, as we are now told, with such firm and buoyant steps upon a Golden Age'.[35] The sarcasm is clear, and in private the Hammonds continued to deride what they called 'the Clapham Complex' – the tendency to look with unmoved complacency on the terrors of the Industrial Revolution. Publicly they yielded to it, however, and turned their attention from poverty to discontent. Why was it, Lawrence Hammond asked in 'The Industrial Revolution and discontent', that the ordinary workman, who was presumably richer in the first half of the nineteenth century than he had ever been, was also unprecedentedly rebellious? Was it simply, as many argued, that discontent became articulate when things, having been at their worst, then improve – when 'the first experience of progress makes people expect and desire more progress'? Not quite, Hammond said: 'For discontent depends on imagination, and in judging an age you have to consider how its imagination is satisfied and not merely how its material needs are met.'[36] Here, in preview, was the qualitative and culturalist genealogy of misery that had always been implicit in the Hammonds's work but which Clapham had forced into the open. Its full and classic assertion came in late 1930 with the appearance of what is really the fourth and crucially qualifying volume of the labourer trilogy: *The Age of the Chartists, 1832–1854*.

Ruthlessly abridged and reissued four years later as *The Bleak Age* – no concession there to the Clapham Complex – *The Age of the Chartists* in its original form was misleadingly titled, for as the Hammonds said it was not, in any sense, a history of the Chartist movement. It was, rather, as their subtitle said, 'A Study of Discontent', and it began with a famous and frequently quoted (and, as it turned out, premature) concession.

Statisticians tell us that when they have put in order such data as they can find, they are satisfied that earnings increased and that most men and women were less poor when this discontent was loud and active than they were when the eighteenth century was beginning to grow old in a silence like that of autumn. The evidence of course is scanty, and its interpretation not too simple, but this general view is probably more or less correct.

Again, how then are we to account for the discontent of which the Chartist agitation in its several forms in the 1830s and 1840s was only the most obvious expression? How to account for 'the resentment of men convinced that there is something false and degrading in the arrangement and the justice of the world'? Clearly, there were non-statistical elements involved, and to learn what they were it was necessary, the Hammonds said, to look more closely into the character of this new society, 'the general colour of its life'. Never mind wages. What was it, the Hammonds ask in perfect anticipation of E. P. Thompson, in the conditions and the setting of English social life in the first half of the nineteenth century that aroused in the working class a furious sense of wrong?

To the more classically than statistically educated Hammonds, ancient history suggested the answer. Class struggle in ancient Greece had been as bitter and incessant as at any time in history. But it had also been 'veiled or softened by the moral influence of common possession'. In Athens, as in Rome, 'the practice of social fellowship was stimulated by the spectacle of beautiful buildings, and the common enjoyment of the arts and culture of the time'. Early nineteenth-century Manchester, on the other hand, gave no quarter to public amenity, to playgrounds, theatres or libraries. Individual opportunity was the new world's only remedy for the threat of social disturbance. Private acquisition took the place in Manchester that common enjoyment had occupied in Rome, and the result was 'a low and grovelling mode of living' that went far, the Hammonds thought, towards explaining popular discontent. They gave two full chapters to 'the loss of playgrounds', to the enclosure and development of what little was left of urban commons and common fields, for to their minds it was this more than anything that signified the disregard of the public interest that characterised the age and effectively annulled any incremental rise seen in the material standard of living. A higher wage, to put it crudely, was no substitute for fresh air in affirming the value of the workman, whose life (whatever his income) had been reduced to a dreary and miserable round of eating, drinking, working and sleeping.[37]

About Chartism itself the Hammonds had surprisingly little to say. It was 'imagination in action', a moral revolt against a conception of society that rewarded the employer with riches and leisure-time while reducing the workman to a drudge. The famous six-point Charter from which the movement took its name was, in this view, significant only as a symbolic rallying point, for 'Chartism was not a precise logical demand for a particular reform', the Hammonds said, with characteristic (if always sympathetic) liberal condescension: 'it was a protest as incoherent as the life that had provoked it'. And, long after its official collapse amid the relief and ridicule of London, the same imaginative force that had sustained it went hopefully and more usefully into the causes of public health, public education, temperance and trade unionism. Chartism, in other words, was a civilising influence. For all its revolutionary rhetoric, it was – along with factory reform and trade unionism – an essentially constructive working-class contribution to the taming of English industry in favour of culture and amenity. And in the Hammonds's minds it thus accounted for the advent of the Victorian 'age of equipoise'. Challenged to account for the great transition from the turbulence of the 1830s and 1840s to the tranquility of mid-century, the Hammonds insisted, quite originally for their time, not on the accident of rising incomes, but on working-class agency, on the degree to which workers had persisted in 'a steady and responsible quarrel with the conditions of their lives'.[38]

IV

'I have not heard that Clapham has resigned yet', Tawney teased Lawrence Hammond in early 1930.[39] Far from resigning, indeed, Clapham proceeded to carry his remorselessly empirical project deep into the Victorian period, essentially unmoved and unprovoked by the Hammonds's latest work. The Hammonds had not bowed to criticism, but they had disarmed it, as T. H. Marshall noted, and moved to a plane of argument where Clapham would never follow.[40] Privately, Trevelyan put the same point in a more approving way: 'You have used the criticisms directed against your earlier work by Clapham, Mrs. George and others to lead you not back but *on* to the discovery of another layer of truth', he wrote to Lawrence Hammond, 'viz. that it was loss of amenities, in the widest sense, even more than material conditions in their purely economic aspect, which caused the trouble.'[41] Rural preservationist that he was, Trevelyan was thinking here especially of the loss of open spaces, and for the Hammonds too this sad historical fact loomed ever larger as they watched the assault of motor car and suburb on the countryside they loved. From *The Age of the Chartists*, Barbara Hammond moved on independently to a history of commons and open space preservation that would come to occupy the whole of her remaining scholarly life. With her husband, meanwhile, she also undertook a commissioned life of Sir James Stansfeld (1820–98), a reasonably prominent Victorian radical and a leader, along with Josephine Butler, in the campaign to repeal the Contagious Diseases Acts. Regrettably, Stansfeld had left behind little biographical material. Such papers as existed threw very little light on his career as a cabinet minister, still less on his tastes, his habits or the range of his mind. The book that ultimately emerged in 1932, then, was less a biography than a study or, as Tawney described it, a tribute 'to one whose sacrifice of personal ambitions to a crusade of mercy in an unpopular, and to some repellent, field, public life has not too many parallels to show'.[42]

Excepting *The Bleak Age* (their Penguin Books abridgement of *The Age of the Chartists*), *James Stansfeld: A Victorian Champion of Sex Equality* was the Hammonds's final collaborative effort. Barbara now worked exclusively on her never-to-be-completed study of commons preservation, while Lawrence turned, first, to a short and unrevealing life of the legendary C. P. Scott, and then, finally, to his magnum opus on *Gladstone and the Irish Nation*. A very long book – the magisterial product not just of ten years of research but of a lifetime's reflection on the Grand Old Man – *Gladstone* had the misfortune to appear at the moment of the Munich Agreement, and it has never received anything like the attention or acclaim it deserves. For if not 'the most formidable and incisive piece of original research yet published on the history of England or Ireland in the second half of the nineteenth century', as M. R. D. Foot once claimed it to be, *Gladstone and the Irish Nation* does stand 'unsurpassed as the basis for a historical understanding of [Gladstone's] career'.[43] Of course, in subject and purpose it bears little relation to the more famous labourer trilogy: his final book emerged out of the second side of Hammond's political nature, the old liberal, anti-imperial, little England side. Yet, in a broad sense *Gladstone* was J. L. Hammond's final riposte to the 'Clapham complex' – the tendency to measure the standard of living in purely material terms. Gladstone had taken little interest in social problems; Carlyle's condition-of-England question left him unmoved. But he had, Hammond said, 'a unique feeling for the life of a society as the expression of its spirit and character'.[44] Almost alone among Victorian statesmen, he had an innate faith in the wisdom and judgement of ordinary people, and by acting on that faith, by appealing not to individual self interest but to national self respect, Gladstone repaired the ravages of the industrial age and restored the English working class to a wholly immeasurable sense of cultural possession.

Notes

1 For a still useful anthology of important contributions to the debate from the 1930s to the 1970s, see A. J. Taylor (ed.), *The Standard of Living in Britain in the Industrial Revolution* (London: Methuen & Co., 1975).

2 J. H. Clapham, *An Economic History of Modern Britain: The Early Railway Age, 1820–1850* (Cambridge: Cambridge University Press, 1926), p. vii.

3 R. H. Tawney, 'J. L. Hammond, 1872–1949', *Proceedings of the British Academy*, 46 (1960), p. 279.

4 For a complete biography of the Hammonds, see: S. A. Weaver, *The Hammonds: A Marriage in History* (Stanford, CA: Stanford University Press, 1997).

5 J. L. Hammond to Gilbert Murray, 12 Dec. 1928, Bodleian Library, Oxford, Murray Papers, vol. 141, fol. 41.

6 J. L. Hammond and B. Hammond, ' "A socialist fantasy": a reply', *Quarterly Review*, 252 (April 1929), p. 292.

7 A. Toynbee, *Lectures on the Industrial Revolution* (London: Longmans, Green, 1928), p. 11.

8 Hammond, ' "A socialist fantasy" ', p. 290.

9 J. L. Hammond to Gilbert Murray, 16 June, 1911 Murray Papers, vol. 40, fols 89–90.

10 Tawney, 'J. L. Hammond', p. 274.

11 J. L. and B. Hammond, *The Village Labourer, 1760–1832: A Study in the Government of England Before the Reform Bill* (London: Longmans, Green & Co., 1911), pp. 33–5, 82–4, 105.

12 J. H. Clapham, 'The village labourer', *Economic Journal*, 22 (June 1912), pp. 248–52.

13 Hammond and Hammond, *The Village Labourer*, 2nd edn (London: Longmans, Green & Co., 1913), p. xii.

14 J. L. Hammond and B. Hammond, *The Town Labourer, 1760–1832: The New Civilisation* (London: Longmans, Green & Co., 1917), pp. 2, 4, 18, 36.

15 Hammond and Hammond, *The Town Labourer*, pp. 18–19, 31.

16 J. L. Hammond and B. Hammond, *The Skilled Labourer, 1760–1832* (London: Longmans, Green & Co., 1919), p. vii.

17 Walter P. Hall in *American Historical Review*, 26 (1921), p. 324.

18 D. C. Coleman, *Myth, History, and the Industrial Revolution* (London: Hambledon Press, 1992), pp. 24–5.

19 J. L. Hammond and B. Hammond, *Lord Shaftesbury* (London: Constable, 1923), pp. 9, 153.

20 J. L. Hammond and B. Hammond, *The Rise of Modern Industry* (London: Methuen & Co., 1925), pp. vii, 255.

21 M. Dorothy George, *London Life in the 18th Century* (London: Kegan Paul, Trench, Trübner & Co., Ltd, 1925), p. 1; J. L. Hammond, 'Eighteenth century London', *New Statesman*, 21 March 1925, pp. 693–4.

22 See L. D. Schwarz, *London in the Age of Industrialisation* (Cambridge: Cambridge University Press, 1992).

23 Hammond and Hammond, *The Town Labourer*, p. 14.

24 G. Talbot Griffith, *Population Problems in the Age of Malthus* (Cambridge: Cambridge University Press, 1926).

25 See the prefatory note to the revised impression of March 1928, as reprinted in the 1967 edition of *The Town Labourer*, p. xlvii.

26 Barbara Hammond, 'Urban death-rates in the early nineteenth century', *Economic History*, 1 (1926–29), pp. 419–28.

27 J. H. Clapham, *An Economic History of Modern Britain: The Early Railway Age, 1820–1850* (Cambridge: Cambridge University Press, 1926), pp. 41, 66, 315–16, 561; G. N. Clark, 'J. H. Clapham', *Proceedings of the British Academy*, 32 (1946), pp. 347–8; David Cannadine, 'The present and the past in the English industrial revolution', *Past and Present*, 103 (1984), pp. 139–41; Alon Kadish, *Historians, Economists and Economic History* (London: Routledge, 1989), pp. 239–41.

28 G. M. Trevelyan to J. L. Hammond, 1 Feb. 1927, Bodleian Library, Oxford, Hammond Papers, vol. 21, fol. 4.

29 J. L. Hammond, 'The early railway age', *Manchester Guardian*, 29 January 1927, p. 12.

30 J. H. Clapham to J. L. Hammond, 22 Oct. 1927, Hammond Papers, vol. 21, fol. 59; J. L. Hammond to Arthur Ponsonby, 2 Jan. 1928, Bodleian Library, Oxford, Ponsonby Papers, Ms Eng. Hist., c. 670, fol. 90.

31 'Clapham has had a surprisingly easy passage', noted Eric Hobsbawm in 1957, 'thanks largely to the extreme feebleness of the reply of his chief opponent, J. L. Hammond, who virtually accepted Clapham's statistics and shifted the argument entirely onto moral and other non-material territories' (quoted in Taylor (ed.), *The Standard of Living*, p. 63).

32 L. B. Hammond to J. L. Hammond, 8 Aug. 1929, Hammond Papers, vol. 14, fol. 162–3.

33 J. L. Hammond, 'New light on the industrial revolution', *Contemporary Review*, 131 (1927), pp. 741–6; J. L. Hammond, 'The industrial revolution and discontent', *Economic History Review*, 2 (1929–30), pp. 215–28; Clapham, *The Early Railway Age*, pp. ix–x; Taylor (ed.), *The Standard of Living*, p. xii; Peter Clarke, *Liberals and Social Democrats* (Cambridge: Cambridge University Press, 1978), pp. 245–7.

34 L. T. Hobhouse to J. L. Hammond, 25 May 1927, Hammond Papers, vol. 21, fol. 25; L. T. Hobhouse to L. B. Hammond, 7 Aug. 1927, *ibid.*, vol. 5, fol. 21.

35 Hammond, ' "A socialist fantasy" ', p. 292.

36 Hammond, 'The industrial revolution and discontent', p. 227.

37 J. L. Hammond and B. Hammond, *The Age of the Chartists, 1832–1854: A Study of Discontent* (London: Longmans, Green & Co., 1930), pp. 8, 30, 79; J. L. Hammond and B. Hammond, *The Bleak Age* (London: Longmans, Green & Co., 1934), p. 119.

38 Hammond, *The Age of the Chartists*, p. 2.

39 R. H. Tawney to J. L. Hammond, 27 Feb. 1930, Hammond Papers, vol. 23, fol. 33.

40 *English Historical Review*, 46 (October 1931), p. 657.

41 G. M. Trevelyan to J. L. Hammond, 2 Nov. 1930, Hammond Papers, vol. 23, fol. 134.

42 Tawney, 'J. L. Hammond', p. 288.

43 M. R. D. Foot, 'Introduction' to J. L. Hammond, *Gladstone and the Irish Nation* (London: Frank Cass, 1964), p. xxi.

44 J. L. Hammond, *Gladstone and the Irish Nation* (London: Longmans, Green & Co., 1938), p. 710.

3

Victorian prime ministers: changing patterns of commemoration

Michael Bentley

I

Old prime ministers never die; they only lose their creativity, their ability to change the image that they have built of themselves. But they gain, too, in an unsought and sometimes embarrassing transformation at the hands of posterity. Their public portrait alters as biographers and historians take a turn with the brush (or the airbrush) and bring memories or texts into line with their own preconceptions about a former age, its general culture, its political parties and the place of individuals within wider processes of development. Solely in totalitarian countries does this constant re-adjustment have its dark side. No Victorian prime minister suffered the posthumous fate of Trotsky; the most assiduous Gladstonian or Disraelian does not feel it necessary to sanctify the past or present through the deliberate falsification of historical evidence. All the same, political 'memory' plays strange tricks. Peel had become by 1901 a very different politician from the one known to those who attended his funeral. 'Gladstone' had barely been born in 1901, a twinkle in John Morley's eye. Some years would pass before Lady Gwendolen Cecil began to resuscitate her father, Lord Salisbury, and question some of the Gladstonian legends. Two world wars, an inter-war economic catastrophe and the onset of totalitarian certainties undermined the presuppositions informing both Victorian optimism and the historical method that had helped confirm it. Papers once private became public; diaries once impossible in their bulk and allusiveness received the attention of editors and annotators; cherished recollections died a natural death as the dead buried their dead; contemporary witnesses underwent posthumous torture in the Manuscripts Room of the British Museum and the repositories of 100 record offices. Mix in a wind of change, the Suez nightmare and Mr John Profumo, and you have revisionism ready-made. The conjecture of this chapter[1] is that these things are intrinsically interesting and historiographically suggestive.

At the time of the Boer War there was little to suggest the direction of the revaluations that would follow in the estimation of political personalities. Gladstone had died within recent memory and had struck contemporaries as almost too colossal to portray, except within that section of the Tory Party that had deemed him clinically mad in his later years. Salisbury was old and infirm but still massively powerful: the diminution of *his* stature over the next twenty years might have seemed odd to those whom he had led for the previous twenty. Disraeli had yet to reach coherent biography. Rather, it was the earlier years of the century that had come into historical perspective and had placed Grey and Peel within a framework that would not be shifted significantly until Carless Davis's Ford Lectures in 1926.[2] Perhaps a mild breeze blew none the less in revised editions of the sources on which high-political historians so often depend – particularly the diaries of witnesses. As it happened, one of these, the Creevey diaries, came under an editor's blue pencil during the Boer War when a Wigtownshire laird, Sir Herbert Maxwell, turned his considerable editorial energies to Creevey in a mood of apparent *insouciance*. Picture him at a dinner party in Carlton House Terrace in 1902 or 1903:

> A discussion having started on historical literature, I remarked how much it was to the detriment of the Conservative party that almost all those who, during the nineteenth century, had written British history, were Liberals or Radicals ... I thought it greatly to be desired that some competent writer should present the case for the other side ... At the time, being immersed in the preparation of *The Creevey Papers*, I gave no further thought to the subject.[3]

But, of course, thoughts have a way of entering by the back door, and the recasting of crucial texts such as *The Creevey Papers* and more especially *The Greville Memoirs* (the latter disturbing to the court when they first appeared a generation earlier but not unexpurgated until the famous Strachey and Fulford edition of 1938[4]) both played their own, largely unanalysed, part in presenting a story different from the mid-Victorian one. If that canonical version had presented a certain view of Grey, moreover, it had handed Peel to the post-Victorians already bound and gagged.

Peel crossed the line into the Edwardian age not only dead but transfigured. The process should not be a preoccupation of this discussion, the concern of which is the formative nature of post-Victorian retrospect; I have in any case considered it elsewhere.[5] It remains important, however, to understand the direction of that transfiguration which consistently pulled Peel away from Toryism and led him in the direction of a nascent Liberalism, as though trying to make out that he had been some sort of Liberal all along and that he had made his way along the road to 1846 out of a yet-unrecognised commitment to liberal values. And, of course, nothing makes a man so ripe for reconfiguration as early and unexpected death. By the 1870s Peel had turned into the instrument necessary for the politics practised in the generation of Gladstone; not the politics of the 1840s, in which he had been undoubtedly instrumental, but those of the period after the Second Reform Act when Liberalism radicalised itself and proclaimed its new morality. How fitting that Peel's son, Arthur, should have asked his friend and Oxford contemporary Charles Stuart Parker to edit the correspondence of his father and assure himself of a volume that would make Peel the harbinger of Parker's other hero, William Ewart Gladstone.[6] The bagging of Peel for the Liberal Party by the 1890s and the flushing out of Canning for the same bag by Temperley in 1905[7] completed a transformation that only the opening of the Peel Papers after the First World War, and the immersion in them of George Kitson Clark, would disturb – and then only partially. Peel would spend the first three-quarters of the twentieth century professing Liberalism to his bone-headed party and then preferring to put the country's interests before theirs or his own. It was a perspective that unified his life in a satisfying way, and one that helped to unify also Gladstone's – much the more significant achievement historiographically.

Through the first quarter of the twentieth century Gladstone dominated political memories, often because his younger contemporaries could walk ahead with his flag, take the high ground and prevent others from threatening it. Morley's three-volume *Life* of 1903 achieved this in the political sphere, at least among radicals who could look back on the events of the 1880s with equanimity. 'As time goes on', wrote Augustine Birrell in an awe-struck review, 'we see the mind of this remarkable man gaining a momentum, gathering a force – ominous of much – until at last it culminates in the prodigious effort of 1886, when that seeming revolution is complete'.[8] An anonymous contributor to the *Edinburgh Review*, published in a city and country where Liberal imperialism still meant something, ran against the tide in celebrating 'the masculine instinct that prevented [the electorate's] being swept away by personal admiration' when Gladstone went wrong over home rule,[9] a prescient observation that historians would not come to share for many decades. Edwardian Liberalism turned a tide into a flood in 1906 and the line joining that crested wave to Gladstone seemed much firmer then than now, especially when behind him, it seemed, stood Peel and Grey and Canning, presenting an unbroken tradition of enlightenment from the period before the First Reform Bill. Once Temperley had asserted Canning's place in this queue, J. R. M. Butler, on the eve of the First World War, had little difficulty in placing Grey of the First Reform Act ahead of him and behind Peel.[10] They formed the tail of an enduring conga, each holding the next one's waist, with Asquith leading the snake forward in the remote distance. Not even the appearance of the first volumes by Monypenny and Buckle on Disraeli[11] could interfere with the rhythm. The intellectual current of the time had a liberal impulse and it helped press the past into a form in which it legitimised what now seemed so obvious. Sir Charles Oman, on whom one could normally rely for remarks about democracy of a Tory sturdiness, discovered himself coining adjectives for the pre-reform political structure (*disgraceful, ridiculous, antiquated, anomalous, intolerable, ludicrous*) that he ought, granted his politics, to have directed at its subverters.[12] Hugh Cecil did his best by leaving Peel out of his 1911 study of Conservatism altogether,[13] perhaps hoping to show that one could make a history of Toryism with the liberal dimension omitted; but he struggled, even amid the death throes of the House of Lords, to make a plausible present out of such a past.

The First World War should (again) have made a dent in this liberal certitude about the past. It inaugurated a mood of national cohesiveness and purpose, a sense of peril in face of the Other, a revival of values dear to Tories: discipline, compulsion, service. It created the conditions in which the last Liberal Government to hold office in Britain came to grief. It brought down the Tsar and threw up Lenin's Bolsheviks. It does not appear unreasonable to expect a post-war historiography that would return to a Tory disposition and exhume great national figures of the past from Pitt to Salisbury. Why it did not do so remains perplexing, until we recall two things: the nature of the British intelligentsia rather than the wider population; and the kind of Toryism – the very constricted kind – that the post-war world could tolerate.

II

For British intellectuals the critical date in their political development had been not 1914 but 1886, and when they moved, almost to a man, away from Gladstone as he lurched towards Ireland they did so not out of a wish to espouse a Conservative tradition but out of a clarity of mind about Gladstone's abandoning of the Liberal one. They thought of themselves as custodians of a progressive conception of politics and placed themselves in the shadow of Grey and the liberal version of Peel rather than of Disraeli and Salisbury. After 1914 some found that they could cope with Lloyd George in small doses, but only a very few became converted to a Tory agenda. When Russia collapsed into revolution in 1917 the warning seemed to concern the dangers of extremes rather than a conservative call to arms. The radical Fourth Reform Act of 1918, moreover, placed the present in a line of development directly linked to 1832 and recalled the importance of not making the same mistakes as Liverpool's Tory governments had made at the end of *their* great war in resorting to repression of popular agitation rather than making the wise compromises now envisaged in Grey's handling of the reform crisis.

Butler's study of that crisis, written prior to the war, undoubtedly helped form the predisposition among historians; but the war itself naturally played a far weightier role. Perhaps it can be seen at its clearest in a volume that appeared in 1919, not the spectacular destruction of Victorian values and myths by Lytton Strachey, to which I shall return, but rather G. M. Trevelyan's life of the second Earl Grey which appeared in the autumn of that year. I choose it because its tone and argument together shriek the importance of authorial context and the degree to which Trevelyan's book

can be read as a tract for his times. He began the book with an appeal to
this new environment.

> A very different book is wanted now from that which would have been wel-
> comed at a time when Russell, Palmerston, and other leading actors in the con-
> flict of the great Reform Bill were still in public life . . . the trend and change
> of middle and working class opinion during the forty years of the movement
> for Parliamentary Reform over which Grey presided, are of deeper interest than
> ever in the historical perspective of our own day . . . In an age when the law
> of perpetual and rapid change is accepted as inevitable, and the difficulty is to
> obtain progress without violence, there may be profit in the story of a states-
> man who after a period of long stagnation and all too rigid conservatism, ini-
> tiated in our country a yet larger period of orderly democratic progress, and
> at the critical moment of the transition averted civil war and saved the State
> from entering on the vicious circle of revolution and reaction.[14]

The crux of the story came, for Trevelyan, in 1831, as Grey faced his
apparent revolution and had to decide whether or not to embark on reaction. Looking sideways uneasily at Lloyd George, one suspects, Trevelyan
saw in Grey a man who 'knew that the danger lay below, and therefore
made no false step on the heights above'. He inherited a country 'on the
verge of anarchy' but pulled it through with enlightenment and goodwill.
'The battle was won. The country instantly sank to rest', said Trevelyan
with Macaulayesque knowingness, 'with a sigh of profound relief.'[15]
   These intimations congealed a few years later in the year of the General
Strike when H. W. C. Davis delivered his Ford Lectures on the age of Grey
and Peel (revised and put through the press by Trevelyan in 1929, following Davis's early death), for they brought so much of the historiography of
the previous thirty years into synthesis. The tone reflected a modernist sense
of science and analysis rather than Trevelyan's romance, but the conclusions did not differ. For Whiggery itself, Davis felt little nostalgia: it offered
'a form of political optimism', but nothing more.[16] Yet Grey on the one side
and Peel on the other joined hands in courage to face the new order of
society – Grey because 'in a crisis he was bold and wary, as soon as the
moment came for action', Peel because he renounced *le parti conservateur*
and became so much more than his former leader. 'He was a loyal Tory',
Davis conceded, 'but if he had been no more than this, he would not stand
higher in the roll of British statesmen than Lord Liverpool, and indeed
would probably be rated lower than the Duke of Wellington' – which, in
face of the problems with the miners in 1926, must be low indeed.[17] Grey,
Peel and Russell were then aimed at Gladstone, that coming storm, so that
the latter became their summation, their unconscious forecast.[18]
   Extending Gladstone backwards in this way made it harder to excise him
as a Victorian paragon, though his longevity as a political hero depended
on other forms of support. The family proved aggressively protective in the
inter-war years, not merely over the famous Wright trial which demon-

strated what would happen to anyone who doubted the genuineness of Gladstone's moral claims, but over its unwillingness to divulge the diary, just as Morley had been refused access to it.[19] But the cultural barriers rose far higher than that. No one loathed Victorian morality so vividly as Lytton Strachey, and Gladstone could have been one of his victims. That even Strachey did not dare take him on[20] suggests the depth of reverence in the recollection of Gladstone, much of it, in the 1920s, still fresh and personal. The marquess of Crewe could still act in this personal role as late as 1932:

> [I]t was my good fortune to know him from my early days, through his inti-
> macy with both sides of my family. And I had the honour of filling a modest
> place in his administrations of 1886 and 1892. Better still, it was my privilege
> more than once to be his and Mrs. Gladstone's guest here at Hawarden . . .
> Almost all who adorned that happy circle have crossed the dark river . . . were
> he here, nothing could for an instant shake Mr. Gladstone's serene optimism.[21]

Optimistic in 1932? Pure moonshine, of course. Gladstone's own economic crisis in 1873–74 brought no optimism at all: it brought despair and resignation. Yet through the mists of memory, as Sir Llewellyn Woodward later complained, the Victorians appeared in roseate light with 'not a little make-believe' in the composition of their portrait.[22] The most famous and long-lasting of the 1930s' portraits, G. M. Young's *Portrait of an Age*, continued the happy story at least to the extent of retaining a Whig phraseology: 'the next advance', 'one step further', 'the tide was running fast'.[23]

The tide continued to run toward Gladstone even when no one remembered any more. Hitler played his part in it. Philip Magnus reminded readers in 1954 that Gladstone never knew about the concentration camps and the 'full shame' of the twentieth century, but he saw enough of Bismarck's era to make him fight 'to the last against the tendency to replace the worship of God by that of Caesar'; and it is clear in Magnus's case that the Caesar in mind was Hitler, whose devious evil threw into silhouette Gladstone's innocent goodness.[24] In the one case power had corrupted; in the other it had found its natural home and been used for the good of the people. No enabling acts, no Nuremberg laws, no *Kristallnacht*, but rather justice for Ireland, liberty for the citizen, the people's William. As the Nazi leadership played its game of brag over the future of Czechoslovakia, J. L. Hammond countered with *Gladstone and the Irish Nation*, a lesson from teacher to wayward prefect.[25] The war brought heroism in the fight against political evil, and some of those with the best wars became scholars in the Gladstonian tradition – Philip Magnus and M. R. D. Foot among them.[26] For older liberal intellectuals, such as Gilbert Murray, the Second World War and its grisly disclosures confirmed the wisdom, at least publicly, of the Gladstonian past, if only because 'one of the keys to Mr. Gladstone's greatness', as Murray remarked in an article entitled 'Gladstone, 1898–1948', was 'an extraordinary and, I would almost say, unworldly simplicity'.[27] The German contrast could even be achieved by leaving out Hitler altogether and contenting oneself with Bismarck, as Erich Eyck did in 1946.[28] Either way, a vision of old or new Germany gave sustenance to a culture that held Gladstone close in a form that the world of the 1960s and 1970s could not. Of course, the final appearance of the diary, beginning in 1968,[29] was crucial; but other elements need some acknowledgement.

Let me return first, however, to the second facet of explanation in considering Conservative feebleness as an historiographical persuasion between the wars – the kind of Toryism that inter-war Britain could stomach and its relationship to what had gone before. In repudiating Lloyd George and his works, the Conservative Party made a promising start in developing a hard-headed new Toryism. In substituting Baldwin, however, it discovered Lloyd George's opposite, as it were, without finding a clear identity for itself. This was a strength, electorally, as Baldwin showed over the next fifteen years. The past that this fudge required, on the other hand, showed little strength. It turned out to be a weak Disraelian affair of 'one nation' in which Baldwin could affect to believe; or it was a Peelite world of conviction politics sustained by that Liberal Peel whom the late Victorians had made. Tory historiography looked for the clarity and brilliance of a Namier. It found Kitson Clark. Looking back on *Peel and the Conservative Party*[30] leaves one conscious of the enormous distance between 1929 and today when a Tory historiography has not only come to thrive but has thriven rather better than the politics it partly celebrates. Comparing it to Davis's Ford Lectures is no less salutary, for what is striking is how much they say the same thing, not in their content but in their message. Both imply a diminuendo in sheer statesmanship after the golden generation of 1830–50. Both reflect an implicit contempt for slipperiness (Disraeli in his bad moments) and cynicism (Salisbury in all of them). Both endorse the genius of balance and judgement, and both ultimately commend a liberal universe in which the General Strike could have been handled. Could you not trust Grey or Peel to ensure a square deal? Salisbury would have called out the troops. Or think about the 1930s with its encomia on common sense, planning and the 'middle way'. Macmillan could find an appropriate past for himself by rooting around in Disraeli's more high-minded speeches. Churchill could find half a one by excavating his father's Tory democracy. What could one do with Salisbury?

Indeed, Salisbury's fate in the post-Victorian period best illustrates the spirit of the age by sketching in its darkest recesses of forgetfulness. The man who held the premiership for longer than anyone, including Gladstone, since Lord Liverpool was dead by 1903, unmanned by 1914 and all but forgotten by 1939. His daughter did what she could and Lady Gwendolen Cecil's wonderful four volumes[31] ran as a cross-current within the larger tide of inter-war historiography, reminding readers that the Gladstonian version of late Victorian politics had a tendentious element, that her father was often patently right when Gladstone went wrong, that he created a view of foreign policy which Gladstone showed himself incapable of understanding, that he built the Conservative Party into a formidable formation that dominated the post-1886 period. For the most part, however, it was as though she had never written. For sniffy Fabians like Ensor, Salisbury could not possess the *differentia* of greatness, merely the prevailing characteristics of his class.[32] Not only had Salisbury lived the life of a wealthy aristocrat but he had failed to atone for his offence by announcing progressive opinions. He had opposed democracy when all right-thinking people were supposed to be in favour of it; he had been too imperialist for any decent man; above all, he had introduced into political life the twin poisons of pessimism and class aggression. Baldwin and his colleagues needed the National Government to be something else: a vision to inspire and comfort rather than a bankers' ramp. Their history books called on the nineteenth century as a period of emerging social conscience and one-nation-ness. It called on its own depiction of Peel and a newly charged image of Disraeli to legitimise what had to be done at home; and it re-discovered Gladstone as the avatar of the peace-maker abroad.

These were bad years to be the shade of Salisbury or Palmerston, and the return to war in 1939 did not make them any better. Confronting the Nazis felt more like facing the evil Turks of the 1870s than the balance-of-power considerations that would have motivated Salisbury. One had to kick them bag and baggage out of Europe quite as emphatically as Gladstonians had hoped to kick the murdering hordes who had perpetrated the Bulgarian horrors. The generation of historians brought up in this environment and which had enjoyed a good war as its consummation ran its course after 1945 in many volumes that encapsulated the unspeakable experiences familiar to it in the mood of contrast suggested by nineteenth-century stability and sense. Each became a modulated Anthony Trollope or Mrs Gaskell, rediscovering the finer traditions of Victorian life and its greater spirits – a world in which Gladstone (or Mr Gladstone as he persisted in this generation) retained his moral pre-eminence. Those two ingredients – tradition and morality – explain in part the stranglehold of a particular way of examining the Victorians; and their presence also explains why the 1960s became a turning-point in Victorian studies and in the adjustment of Anglo-American understanding of nineteenth-century politics, forming the platform for much that has happened since in refining that understanding.

III

That such hinges happen in historiography is well-attested. A moment comes at which a discernible swing takes place – one of those Kuhnian paradigm shifts about which so much is said nowadays – and suddenly the past does not look the same any more. Political historiography inevitably attaches itself to current politics, if only at the level of intimations brought and questions asked; and in British politics the premiership of Macmillan (1957–63) spanned a period of decisive shift in the treatment of British political history. Part of the story was generational, as always. Historians brought up on inter-war perceptions of power and morality – wounded by the war with its dangers and suffering and the retrospective nightmare surrounding the Holocaust – began by the 1960s to give ground to younger people who had little recollection of Chamberlain or Baldwin and for whom the 1930s had to be treated as an historical construction rather than a facet of memory.

But part of the story was concerned also with a changing context. From the second half of the 1950s Britain experienced significant new cultural forces in the wake of substantial immigration and the coming of a youth movement with its rock music and acidic lyrics. (Whatever Bob Dylan was, he was no Gladstonian.) Universities saw an explosion of student radicalism and an ill-tempered, often vulgar, rejection of the democratic process itself. The notion of history as a preserve of 'gentlemen' had passed away in reality many years before, but it felt the need to continue now in a rather magnificent last stand against tawdriness and, of course, gentlewomen. As a self-conscious Disraelian, Harold Macmillan epitomised a passing genre – not because he was interested in Disraeli but because he wanted to manifest a version of Disraeli that clashed with the new culture, even the new Conservative culture.

It was symptomatic of this lack of interest in Disraeli for himself that the rising star of Tory letters in these years, Robert, later Lord Blake, wrote a biography of Bonar Law,[33] before turning to Disraeli himself. He produced in 1966 one of the great biographies of the century but a version of the hero dominated by crystalline intelligence, rather than sentimental notions of acting as an educator or deep thinker, and whose author located the wonder and attraction in Disraeli's humanity rather than some supposed vision. In the same year George Dangerfield's *The Strange Death of Liberal England* received its first serious challenge for thirty years in a new narrative of Liberal decline,[34] which not only threw Asquith and Lloyd George into confusion but questioned by implication the style of politics to which Dangerfield had considered them heir.

Yet of course the *historiography* of the early 1960s was not a narrative of the Right or the Centre: those years belonged to the New Left. A force of some power in historical writing since the war, especially in the Communist Party Historians' Group, Marxist analysis and the discordant ideologies that surrounded it preoccupied British intellectuals and made a significant difference to how political history as an exercise became conceived. This was no mere matter of changing the content. At stake in public argument in the 1960s was the legitimacy of political history as a form. Edward Thompson's *The Making of the English Working Class* (1963) and Eric Hobsbawm's *Labouring Men* (1964) sought to locate political explanation in a frame of mass culture and political economy that made prime ministers not quite the point at issue. It pointed to a style of political history read from the bottom up instead of from the top down. Indeed, it heralded the end of political history conceived as a constitutional study or dissection

of elites in favour of a new *histoire totale* in which the actions of politicians and cabinet ministers would have their place but only as part of a
much wider fabric carrying the impress of social elements traditionally
excluded, or so it was alleged. By bringing in the people it was possible to
bring in revolution as a serious prospect in 1831, 1848, 1867 or 1919. It
opened opportunities to see leaders such as Grey, Disraeli or Lloyd George
resembling marionettes rather than masters of their moment. For all Harold
Wilson's avowed indebtedness to Peel, the prevalent historical studies of his
period of power spoke of popular politics, trades unionism, socialism and
the rise of Labour.

Already, however, a reaction of formidable violence had begun on the
part of those sickened by what they took to be a delusion born of innocence. The roots of this disposition ran in a variety of directions. A rediscovery of Collingwood and his preferencing of intention in historical
accounts formed one of them.[35] If one wanted to understand actions in the
past then one should study those who performed them and ask what they
thought they were doing. A second ran in the direction of the archives available for study. The 1960s saw a vast interest – owing something to the
secret titillations surrounding Profumo, something to mysteries swirling
around Macmillan's succession in the Tory leadership, something to the
availability of fresh sources – in the darker operations of government and
fostered a mood of urgency about building insights from this new material
into conventional accounts of leaders written by authors who had often
depended, *faute de mieux*, on printed evidence. A third wandered towards
the Conservative Party and a group of intelligent Tory sceptics who
found Heath a poor guide to eternity and wanted to see blood flow into
Conservative thinking, or, failing that, at least to see blood flow. The upshot
is well-known among political historians of the nineteenth century. A so-
called 'Cambridge School' or (for those worried about the vastness of that
descriptor) a 'Peterhouse School' of historians – in the late 1960s, Maurice
Cowling, Edward Norman and J. R. Vincent – was held to have hatched a
conspiracy to turn back the clock, reassert the history of elites and produce
densely textured narratives in a 'mannered' style, as it was described in
Oxford. This recipe for political history did not produce biographies:
indeed, it seemed important at the time that it should not, for that way lay
sentiment and partiality in both senses. It generated instead monographs –
big books about how politics worked in the nineteenth century, with a clear
understanding that, whatever politicians said they were doing, they were
probably making it up in order to solidify their relationship with one
another and/or the external groups which they wished to inspire or appease.
Maurice Cowling's *1867: Disraeli, Gladstone and Revolution* (1967) spent
the centenary of the Second Reform Bill rubbishing revolution as any kind
of threat in mid-Victorian Britain and redefining the genius of Disraeli along
the way. Similarly, the account of Gladstone's Home Rule crisis offered by
John Vincent and Alistair Cooke in 1974 left little of Gladstone's supposed
commitments intact and introduced new ones harder to celebrate.[36] These

two texts may be seen in retrospect as signal events in a continuum of
writing in the two decades after 1965 among historians striving for a form
of cynical authenticity resting on the private records of politicians.[37]
Unmoved by the cries for history from below, they persisted in their view
that prime ministers and their cabinets made their politics from above.

Above or below, power came from the same place in both these ways
of patterning the past. It inhabited the structure itself. An implication of
both views was that the structure legislated for what its participating individuals could do; and by the structure historians of the Victorian period
meant something far firmer than Namier had intended when he wrote about
the 1760s.[38] Here one had a stylised system of relationships between
government and governed, between the governors and their supporters,
between 'the State' and its agents, between the factions of Parliament,
between Crown, Church and civil service: a world that left to its managers
as little freedom of manoeuvre as it did to its victims. Just as labour historians wanted to see governing individuals as ultimately caught in a net of
class relationships and perceptions, so the view from the cabinet room
lamented how 'broken-backed' was political activity in face of its myriad
confinements, how impossible it was for the individual to 'commit politics'.
Prime ministers went into recession. Grey became an eighteenth-century
figure rather than a saviour of the realm pregnant with nineteenth-century
ideas about democracy and revolution.[39] Peel went backwards too: away
from the alabaster 'greatest statesman of the nineteenth century', moulded
by Kitson Clark and Norman Gash, and towards an eighteenth-century
figure born too late and governing out of time.[40] Palmerston lost his isolation and found himself stitched into a developing Liberalism as tutor to
Gladstone.[41] Gladstone and Disraeli entered various cages and rattled their
bars. Salisbury acquired a 'political biography' but no one – absolutely
no one – wanted to call him a 'Victorian Titan',[42] with overtones of individual mastery and splendid, isolated genius.

Mastery, splendour and isolation we owe to Lady Thatcher. Exactly what
effect her reign will ultimately have on the development of political history
is impossible to say at present: the time-lines are too blurred and crowded.
But it is clear that those years after 1979 brought a re-affirmation of
political biography and a fresh interest in Victorian politics, if only as a
harbinger of this seemingly new phenomenon.[43] In particular, the mood
affected Salisbury who, for the first time in the twentieth century, became
a major subject of inquiry and speculation.[44] Nor was it only the supporters of Thatcherism who found their own views changing or becoming
more pressing. When Professor Peter Clarke assembled his studies of prime
ministers and other politicians under the title A Question of Leadership,
published in the year after Mrs. Thatcher's fall from power, he dedicated
the volume to two teenagers born under her cloud and hoped 'to explain
what happened before Mrs. Thatcher's premiership'.[45] The second edition
makes Mr Blair look rather like Mr Gladstone, as though a painful memory

has been expunged and the world put to rights.[46] A second element in the situation recalls the Macmillan premiership, in that Mrs Thatcher presided over a period of intense cultural and intellectual change, the consequences of which were far from Conservative. There are several words for what emerged within the intelligentsia, but 'post-structuralism' is the most accurate and helpful because it gives an immediate sense of what the change entailed. In moving away from models of political analysis that drew on a faith in identifying structures in the manner of the 1960s, an important section of academic opinion did not retreat to individualism but rather sought different sorts of collective agency to explain how British politics worked. Their thinking gave rise to a concern with language and its capacity to form a worldview, to puzzlement over what it means to 'represent' both politically and in an historical text, and to the notion of a 'cultural politics' and the place of individuals and social forces within such an idea.[47] Popular politics received some refreshment from these views in so far as they transcended a wooden commitment to 'class' as a defining condition of explanation. High politics also changed, as a younger generation of authors began to see lines of contact between various parts of the political environment about which the more austere authors of the 1970s might have been sceptical. Two recent biographical studies of British prime ministers place great stress on, for example, the quality and effectiveness of the private and public language deployed by their subjects.[48]

Considerations of space do not allow either an exposition of the theoretical challenges which these lines of thought provoke or a situation of the author's own relation to these interpretations which a reader has every right to demand. The fundamental point lies in an insistence on historiography bearing the marks of 'theory' quite as much as the substantive history that it discusses; and on its doing so quite independently of what historians consciously do and the various forms of 'influence' they acknowledge at any one time. Historians are, of course, always the first to disavow all knowledge of any '–ism' and to claim that their books have been written in an isolation ward of scholarship. You do not have to know about a contagion in order to catch it, all the same, and little patience need be wasted on a view of the subject that would render pointless all study of the context of historical writing. Scientific discoveries, evolutionary trends, long-lost male heroes, newly acquired female heroes, falling and rising gentries, rising and falling prime ministers: they all carry the imprint of their creation in a particular present and act out the purposes associated with summoning a particular past.

Notes

1 The paper on which this chapter rests comprised mainly the first half of this text which has been extended to allow for some reflection on more recent moods. One pre-emptive qualification should perhaps be registered at the outset, and that is that the argument here rests mostly on the reconstructions of *British* com-

mentators. In no sense is this exclusion meant to diminish the value and relevance of American, Australian and European contributions to historical scholarship. It may be evident from the text why a study of their responses would raise different issues from those considered here.

2 H. W. C. Davis, *The Age of Grey and Peel, Being the Ford Lectures for 1926* (Oxford: Clarendon Press, 1929).

3 Herbert Maxwell, *Evening Memories* (London: A. Maclehose & Co., 1932), p. 267; *The Creevey Papers: A Selection from the Correspondence and Diaries of the Late Thomas Creevey, MP*, ed. Herbert Maxwell, 2 vols (London: John Murray).

4 *The Greville Memoirs. A Journal of the Reign of King George IV and King William IV*, ed. Henry Reeve, 3 vols (London: Longmans, Green & Co., 1874); *The Greville Memoirs. A Journal of the Reign of Queen Victoria from 1837 to 1852*, ed. Henry Reeve, 3 vols (London: Longmans, Green & Co., 1885). *The Greville Memoirs, 1814–60*, ed. Lytton Strachey and Roger Fulford, 8 vols (London: Macmillan & Co., 1938).

5 Michael Bentley, *Lord Salisbury's World: Conservative Environments in Late-Victorian Britain* (Cambridge: Cambridge University Press, 2001), pp. 305–13.

6 C. S. Parker, *Sir Robert Peel: From His Private Papers* (London: John Murray, 1891).

7 H. W. V. Temperley, *Life of Canning* (London: James Finch & Co., 1905); cf. Dorothy Marshall, *The Life of George Canning; with an Introduction by H. Temperley* (London: Longmans, Green & Co., 1938). For the wider context of Temperley's thought, see H. W. V. Temperley and A. J. Grant, *Europe in the Nineteenth and Twentieth Centuries, 1789–1950*, rev. and ed. L. M. Penson (London: Longmans, Green & Co., 1952); and the recent assessment by John D. Fair, *Harold Temperley: A Scholar and Romantic in the Public Realm* (Newark: University of Delaware Press, 1992).

8 Augustine Birrell, 'Mr. Morley's "Life of Gladstone" ', *Contemporary Review*, 84 (1903), pp. 609–19, at 613.

9 Anon., 'Mr. Morley's Life of Gladstone', *Edinburgh Review*, 199 (1904), pp. 1–34, at 34.

10 J. R. M. Butler, *The Passing of the Great Reform Bill* (London: Longmans, Green & Co., 1914).

11 W. F. M. Monypenny and G .E. Buckle, *The Life of Benjamin Disraeli, Earl of Beaconsfield*, 6 vols (London: John Murray, 1910–20).

12 Sir Charles Oman, *England in the Nineteenth Century* (London: Edward Arnold, 1909), pp. 74–5.

13 Hon. Hugh Cecil, *Conservatism* (London; Williams & Norgate, 1912).

14 G. M. Trevelyan, *Lord Grey of the Reform Bill: Being the Life of Charles, Second Earl Grey* (London: Longmans, Green & Co., 1920), pp. vii–viii; cf. Trevelyan, *Grey of Falloden: Being the Life of Sir Edward Grey, afterwards Viscount Grey of Falloden* (London: Longmans, Green & Co., 1937).

15 *Ibid.*, pp. 312, 348.

16 Davis, *Age of Grey and Peel*, p. 272.

17 *Ibid.*, pp. 229, 287.

18 E.g. over the Encumbered Estates Act of 1848: 'It was left for Mr. Gladstone to accomplish in 1870 what both Peel and Russell had vainly tried to accomplish', *ibid.*, p. 264.

19 Captain Peter Wright made aspersions in print about Gladstone's moral propriety. The resulting trial and vindication are described in H. J. Gladstone, *After Thirty Years* (London: Macmillan & Co., 1928), Appendix 5, pp. 435–6, and Ivor Thomas, *Gladstone of Hawarden: A Memoir of Henry Neville, Lord Gladstone of Hawarden* (London: John Murray, 1936), pp. 241–3.

20 There are a few side-swipes at Gladstone in Strachey's essay on 'The end of General Gordon' about 'the darkness' at the centre of 'the sinuous creature'; but his account of Gladstone contents itself mainly with allegations of complexity: Lytton Strachey, *Eminent Victorians: Cardinal Manning, Florence Nightingale, Dr. Arnold, General Gordon* (London: Chatto & Windus, 1918), pp. 262, 282.

21 'Mr. Gladstone', *Contemporary Review*, 259 (1932), pp. 193–203, at 193–4. Even as late as 1964, G. N. Clark excused one of his own crotchets by reminding a correspondent that he 'was brought up as a Liberal while Gladstone was still alive': Clark to Denys Hay (copy), 14 July 1964, Bodleian Library, Oxford, Clark Mss 159.

22 E. L. Woodward, *The Age of Reform 1815–1870* (Oxford: Clarendon Press, 1938), p. 613.

23 G. M. Young, 'Portrait of an age', in Young (ed.), *Early Victorian England, 1830–1865*, 2 vols (London: Oxford University Press, 1934), pp. 447, 456.

24 Philip Magnus, *Gladstone: A Biography* (London: John Murray, 1954), pp. 444–5.

25 J. L. Hammond, *Gladstone and the Irish Nation* (London: Longmans, Green & Co., 1938).

26 Sir Philip Magnus-Allcroft, CBE (1906–1988). See: *Gladstone: A Biography*; *Kitchener: Portrait of An Imperialist* (London: John Murray, 1958); *King Edward the Seventh* (London: John Murray, 1964). M. R. D. Foot, CBE (1919–), with J. L. Hammond, *Gladstone and Liberalism* (London: English Universities Press, 1952); *The Gladstone Diaries*, vols 1 and 2 ed. M. R. D. Foot (Oxford: Clarendon Press, 1968); vols 3 and 4 ed. M. R. D. Foot and Colin Matthew (Oxford: Clarendon Press, 1974).

27 Gilbert Murray, 'Gladstone, 1898–1948', *Contemporary Review*, 174 (1948), pp. 134–8, at 136. A certain irony surrounds this affirmation if Peter Clarke is right that Murray voted Tory in 1951: see Clarke, *Liberals and Social Democrats* (Cambridge: Cambridge University Press, 1981), p. 286.

28 'Bismarck and Gladstone', *Quarterly Review*, 170 (1946), pp. 343–8.

29 *The Gladstone Diaries*, ed. M. R. D. Foot and Colin Matthew, 14 vols (Oxford: Clarendon Press, 1968–94).

30 G. Kitson Clark, *Peel and the Conservative Party* (London: Bell, 1929).

31 Lady Gwendolen Cecil, *Life of Robert, Marquis of Salisbury*, 4 vols (London: Hodder & Stoughton, 1921–32).

32 R. C. K. Ensor, *England, 1870–1914* (Oxford: Clarendon Press, 1936), pp. 353–4.

33 Robert Blake, *The Unknown Prime Minister: The Life and Times of Andrew Bonar Law* (London: Eyre & Spottiswoode, 1955).

34 Trevor Wilson, *The Downfall of the Liberal Party 1914–1935* (London: William Collins Sons & Co., Ltd, 1966).

35 Cf. Quentin Skinner, 'Meaning and understanding in the history of ideas', *History and Theory*, 8 (1969), pp. 3–53.

36 J. R. Vincent and A. B. Cooke, *The Governing Passion: Cabinet Government and Party Politics in Britain 1885–6* (Brighton: Harvester Press, 1974).

37 Maurice Cowling, *1867: Disraeli, Gladstone and Revolution* (Cambridge: Cambridge University Press, 1967), and *The Impact of Labour 1920–1924: The Beginning of Modern British Politics* (Cambridge: Cambridge University Press, 1971); Andrew Jones, *The Politics of Reform, 1884* (Cambridge: Cambridge University Press, 1972); Michael Bentley, *The Liberal Mind 1914–1929* (Cambridge: Cambridge University Press, 1977).

38 Lewis Namier, *The Structure of Politics at the Accession of George III*, 2 vols (London: Macmillan & Co., 1929).

39 E. A. Smith, *Lord Grey 1764–1835* (Stroud: Sutton, 1996).

40 Robert Stewart, *The Politics of Protection: Lord Derby and the Protectionist Party 1841–1852* (Cambridge: Cambridge University Press, 1971).

41 E. D. Steele, *Palmerston and Liberalism, 1855–1865* (Cambridge: Cambridge University Press, 1991), and Jonathan Parry, *The Rise and Fall of Liberal Government in Victorian Britain* (London: Yale University Press, 1993).

42 Robert Taylor, *Lord Salisbury* (London: Allen Lane, 1995); cf. Andrew Roberts's recent biography, *Salisbury: Victorian Titan* (London: Weidenfeld & Nicolson, 1999).

43 See, e.g., Michael Bentley, 'Liberal Toryism in the twentieth century', *Transactions of the Royal Historical Society*, 6th series, 4 (1994), pp. 177–201.

44 Beside Andrew Roberts's biography, see Lord Blake and Hugh Cecil (eds), *Lord Salisbury: The Man and His Policies* (Basingstoke: Macmillan & Co., 1987); David Steele, *Lord Salisbury: A Political Biography* (London: UCL Press, 2001); Bentley, *Lord Salisbury's World*.

45 Peter Clarke, *A Question of Leadership: From Gladstone to Blair*, 2nd edn (London: Hamish Hamilton, 1999 [1991]).

46 *Ibid.*, pp. 325–48.

47 Studies that come to mind are: Jon Lawrence, *Speaking for the People: Party, Language and Popular Politics in England* (Cambridge: Cambridge University Press, 1998); James Vernon, *Politics and the People: A Study in English Popular Culture c.1815–1867* (Cambridge, Cambridge University Press, 1993) and Vernon (ed.), *Re-Reading the Constitution: New Narratives in the Political History of England's Long Nineteenth Century* (Cambridge: Cambridge University Press, 1996). I reflected on these and other statements in 'Victorian politics and the linguistic turn', *Historical Journal*, 42 (1999), pp. 883–902.

48 Bentley, *Lord Salisbury's World*, pp. 295–305; Philip Williamson, *Stanley Baldwin: Conservative Leadership and National Values* (Cambridge: Cambridge University Press, 1999), pp. 13–18.

4

Quiller-Couch, the function of \
literature and modernism, 1890–

Michelle Hawley

Introduction

The emergence of Victorian studies is, by now, a familiar story. In the 1950s, a generation of scholars was ready to take a serious look at a period the values and aesthetics of which had been left behind in the wake of modernism. The recovery of the Victorians was a Janus-faced endeavour, reflecting the post-war generation's conflicted feelings about modernity. For some it provided a kind of refuge in an age that had not witnessed the mass destruction of the twentieth century. Conservative critics like Jerome Buckley and Gertrude Himmelfarb have found in the Victorian period a home for the scholarly manufacture of so-called Victorian values and virtues that seemed to be disintegrating amid American mass culture.[1] Alternatively, the Victorians appealed to other scholars because they provided a looking-glass image of twentieth-century modernity. Michael Wolff, for example, described his representative experience as an editor at *Victorian Studies*, remarking that the Victorian period 'regularly offered unexpected and troubling opportunities for understanding how the intersection of that time and place was a metaphor for the modernizing world'.[2] Despite their differences, both conservative and radical recoveries of Victorian literature share a similar point of departure: they both apparently emerged, phoenix-like, from the flame of modernism and have conspired to return literature to its historical and cultural context, bringing a host of new Victorian texts into print and into the curriculum.

Perhaps the most significant moment in the restoration of Victorian literature to the cultural landscape was the publication of Raymond Williams's *Culture and Society*. Williams's achievement was to recognise the centrality of a 'critical' concept of 'culture' that was part of a larger 'structure of feeling' connecting nineteenth- and twentieth-century British literature. A student of F. R. Leavis, Williams shared with him his commitment to the redemptive qualities of literature that spoke to and often against the fragmentation of culture in modern society. However, in returning *literary*

, to the emerging culture in which they were formed, Williams helped ..ree Victorian literature from the institutional yoking of modernism and the New Criticism, an alliance that aesthetically devalued many Victorian writings and subjected them to the disciplinary mechanism of genre.[3] As Stefan Collini has emphasised, Victorian prose did not fare well in the 1920s and 1930s; the 'almost religious significance' of the 'Holy Trinity' of poetry, drama, and the novel made it difficult to deal with Victorian moralists, who were 'consigned to the dustbin category of "non-fiction prose"'.[4]

Recently, critics have begun to suspect that our recovery of *culture*, both Victorian and categorical, has been less than complete and bears the traces of its modernist Oedipal father. Although the cultural studies tradition established by Williams broke new ground, it carried within itself some of the limits of Leavisite criticism in its oppositional stance towards society. Bruce Robbins has shown how Williams illustrates the 'limits as well as the force of opposition in culture's name . . . Because the concept of culture was critical in relation to the "society", anything that fell into the category of culture was protected . . . from all but relatively superficial criticism'. For Robbins, the predicament of Williams is significant because it exemplifies '*the* predicament of intellectuals at the present time'; that is, intellectuals inhabit the 'profound paradox of culture as, at the same time, both oppositional cutting edge and professional ground'.[5] Collini suggests that a similar predicament has come to haunt Victorian cultural studies. Structured as it is around the 'distorting' opposition between 'culture and society', Victorian cultural studies 'squeezes' its object of criticism 'out of shape' by insisting that Victorian works be classed as 'upholders of mainstream attitudes' or as 'inherently oppositional'.[6]

Ironically, both Robbins and Collini, whose intentions are to criticise the predicament of culture and recognise the self-legitimising tactics of the Jeremiad for what it is, remythologise the profession's modernist origins and self-defeating tactics. It would appear that we are stuck in a bind, in a hall of mirrors where the outside world is a projection of a professional imaginary. This chapter suggests that our familiar accounts of the rise of Victorian studies have eclipsed other stories we might tell about Victorian literature in its relationships with modernism, cultural studies and the profession. Sir Arthur Quiller-Couch, who had been Leavis's teacher at Cambridge, and Sir Walter Raleigh – the two key figures in my case study – played important roles in the history of the institutionalisation of English at Cambridge and Oxford. Although they remain peripheral players in all accounts of the history of literary criticism and in most accounts of the discipline of English literature, often described as residual 'Victorians' lingering on into the next century, their readings of Victorian literature were very much products of the twentieth century, and they cut against the grain of modernism in interesting ways. More particularly, their criticism reminds us both that the Victorians were not snuffed out of existence, and that there was, in the early twentieth century, a professional model of criticism centred not upon an opposition between the literary elite and society, but around the assumption that literature plays a vital role in the production of a liberal and democratic citizenship. Quiller-Couch and Raleigh defined literature more broadly than did those who would restrict it to the 'aesthetic', constrict it within the realm of high culture, or align it with a critical concept of 'culture' that had since Matthew Arnold, as Williams demonstrates, been detached from its 'reality in experience' and 'process'.[7] Rather, Quiller-Couch and Raleigh recognised that literature and culture were bound up with the social and political, and that they participated in the process of social transformation. Criticising those who saw nothing but 'change and decay all around them' in an age where the 'wireless', 'loud speakers', 'talkies' and 'schoolmasters' conspired to create a nostalgia for the past, Quiller-Couch reminded his readers, in an essay on the Victorian poet William Barnes, that even modernity's effects are 'conditions of organic growth'.[8]

Modernism, professionalism and Victorian literature

Before going on to develop an account of this alternative conception of English literature grounded in a radical–liberal political tradition that saw literature as intimately, if ambivalently, involved in rather than separated from 'society', this chapter briefly sketches out how the modernist myth has come to dominate our narrative about the rise of the profession and so displace the Victorian period.[9] Bruce Robbins describes the relationship between modernism and professionalism in this way:

> Modernism is said to found its cataclysmic divide between present and past on a further break with nineteenth-century literature's submission to realism (the standard of ordinary empirical observation) and authorial responsibility (the author's accountability for her or his moral standards to the public . . . Each of these commonplaces collates with those of professionalism. A minimal description, stressing the claim to esoteric, specialized knowledge as justification for a privileged local sovereignty, immediately offers several points of contact: autonomy, exclusiveness, anti-empiricism, obscurity to the layman.[10]

Robbins then carefully shows how the intertwined narratives of modernism and the professionalisation of literature are based, problematically, on temporal fictions about the 'fall' of an oppositional public and the rise of the professionalised specialist. The profession establishes itself on the basis of a story that takes a 'single path' to 'autonomy' by way of 'scientific rigour'. The 'organic society' that is so highly valued in these accounts thus reveals itself to be a founding fiction and is relegated to the status of 'an ironic backdrop' as it is sealed off from playing any role in the process of the formation of the cultural critic. The effect of these narratives is a legitimising one, for they recount the achievement of a 'specialized autonomy' that does not require social legitimation. The effectiveness of such legitimising claims

arent in the ease with which the field of literary criticism has been
to assimilate and thrive on the reservations of its staunchest opponents
n both right and left.

A re-examination of these professional critical narratives gives us a more
nuanced sense of what Victorianism stood for within the modernist and
New Critical discourse. First, it is significant that both traditional literary
critics and Marxist critics recount similar stories about the origins of
English and about how the faltering discipline was snatched from the hands
of genteel amateurs by I. A. Richards, William Empson and F. R. Leavis.
In 'The rise of English', Terry Eagleton described the birth of New Criticism in the 1920s and 1930s as a victory in the quasi-heroic battle between
the old, represented by Arthur Quiller-Couch, and the New Criticism. In
Eagleton's account, F. R. Leavis and 'the architects of the new subject' –
New Criticism – arose 'from a new social class', and were

> able to identify and challenge the social assumptions which informed its liter-
> ary judgments in a way that the devotees of Sir Arthur Quiller-Couch were
> not. None of them had suffered the crippling disadvantages of a purely liter-
> ary education of the Quiller-Couch kind . . . What the Leavises saw was that
> if the Sir Arthur Quiller-Couches were allowed to win out, literary criticism
> would be shunted into an historical siding of no more inherent significance
> than the question of whether one preferred potatoes to tomatoes'.[11]

Similarly, René Wellek's *A History of Modern Criticism* places Quiller-Couch
and his counterpart at Oxford Sir Walter Raleigh in the pre-critical dark ages,
describing them as examples of what Max Weber called the 'ideal type'.

> He is deeply afraid of an accusation of pedantry, hides his learning in under-
> statement or whimsical pleasantries, and is nevertheless proud of being a gen-
> tleman, a select being, a knight both by title and in imagination. All his writings
> are about well-established figures of the past; when he has to face the chal-
> lenge of the new, he tries to ward it off by sneers and jokes.[12]

Eagleton's and Wellek's accounts of Quiller-Couch and Sir Walter Raleigh
share several assumptions with New Criticism and modernism. Indeed, the
notion that 'literary judgement' might be reducible to mere 'taste' appears
as alarming to Eagleton and Wellek as it did to W. K. Wimsatt and Cleanth
Brooks in their *Short History* of literary criticism, who grouped Quiller-
Couch and Raleigh together with George Saintsbury and Heathcote Garrod,
arguing that they 'weakened literary history by their lack of theoretical
concern and their emphasis on critical appreciation'.[13] Second, their descriptions rehearse familiar modernist narratives about what was wrong with
Victorian literature. The Victorians had bad taste; they were overly concerned with social ranking; they were pedantic and old-fashioned; they were
emotional and subjective. Moreover, in this interesting example, Wellek's
gendering of Sir Walter Raleigh is particularly suggestive: With the contempt for criticism goes Raleigh's helplessness and sentimentality when he

praises, for example, Christina Rossetti: 'The only thing that Christina makes me want to do is cry, not lecture.'[14] Wellek not only makes a spectacle of the 'helpless' and emotional Raleigh, effeminate and rendered speechless before Christina Rossetti, but metonymically figures Raleigh as the Victorian 'Poetess', who epitomised the sentimentality and emotionalism against which T. S. Eliot, Ezra Pound and I. A. Richards crusaded.

Such evaluations of the state of criticism prior to New Criticism reveal a great deal about the formation and maintenance of the modernist and New Critical canon. John Guillory has argued convincingly that the canon is a form of cultural capital and that it 'participates centrally in the establishment of consensus as the embodiment of a collective valuation'. However, in order to establish such a consensus, the new elite needs to 'erase the conflictual prehistory of canon formation'.[15] In a discussion of New Criticism he explains how, by

> understanding that 'real' or 'true' literature is intrinsically difficult, and that it therefore must be interpreted, we can also understand why it must be studied at the university, and why those who are able to master this difficult material become sufficiently credentialed to be admired into an elite, highly educated upper class culture.[16]

In the case of the American canon, which is the primary focus of his book, Guillory goes on to show how the discussion of 'literature' came to be separated from and valued above questions concerning 'literacy', and how 'difficult' modernist poets came to be valued while poets who had been popular were devalued. In the case of the English canon we can recognise similar processes at work here.

Rather than reading Quiller-Couch and Walter Raleigh as men who were vestiges of a gentlemanly nineteenth-century humanism, insulated from the social and political changes that brought about modernism, we might also understand them as representing a sensibility Isobel Armstrong has described as Victorian *modernity*. For Armstrong,

> Victorian modernism sees itself as new, but it does not . . . conceive itself in terms of a radical break with a past. [It] . . . describes itself as belonging to a condition of crisis which has emerged directly from economic and social change . . . [It is] post-revolutionary, existing with the constant possibility of mass upheaval and fundamental change in the structure of society.[17]

The next section of this chapter suggests that Quiller-Couch's and Raleigh's conception of English needs to be recognised as a modern and democratic (which is not to say politically unproblematic) response to the expansion of the mass public sphere and a reaction against a definition of literature that is increasingly associated with high culture and professionalism. The section following, which describes the way in which the First World War shaped their understanding of the function of English, argues that their critical appreciation of Victorian literature represents less a glance backwards than a prescient critique of the modernist myths promulgated by T. S. Eliot, Ezra Pound and Lytton Strachey. The final section briefly sketches out the Victorian canon according to Arthur Quiller-Couch, suggesting that although his criticism represents a path not taken, it may yet be the path to which we are returning.

The new curriculum: writing against literature

Sir Arthur Quiller-Couch (1863–1944) and Sir Walter Raleigh (1861–1922) straddled the Victorian and modernist periods. It has been easy to forget that when they arrived at Cambridge and Oxford both men were disciplinary innovators. Shortly after being appointed the second King Edward VII chair of English in 1912, Quiller-Couch created much contention in the Cambridge senate as he sought to establish the English Tripos. The English syllabus was defined against what was perceived as the dominant ideology of the old curriculum, namely a dry-as-dust teaching of 'dead languages'. He made a passionate case for what many of his detractors saw as the pointlessness of teaching 'Hellenic to the Hellenes' and argued for the importance of allowing students to be able to study modern literature, literary criticism and comparative literature. As compared to the New Criticism, Quiller-Couch's conception of the English Tripos has a few things in common with contemporary cultural and Victorian studies. To begin with, the newly proposed Tripos was in *English*, not in English *language* or *literature*. For Quiller-Couch, studying English involved the consideration of multiple aspects of English culture, of 'what Englishmen have thought from time to time'.[18]

In its early years, Cambridge English was derisively referred to as the 'novel-reading Tripos', a designation which links the new curriculum not only with the Victorian genre of the novel, but also by extension with mass and popular readers.[19] In this incarnation, Cambridge English moved in a direction radically at odds with the process of cultural formation in the late nineteenth and early twentieth centuries, seemingly blurring what were increasingly distinct boundaries within which literary culture was sequestered. As Andreas Huyssen has lucidly delineated, modern and high art acquired a 'powerful masculine mystique' and were defined in opposition to mass and low culture, which were gendered as 'feminine and inferior'.[20] Huyssen's account helps to explain both the ideological zeal and the gendered discourse with which Leavis and the New Critical histories dismissed Quiller-Couch, for he moved towards the audience that Leavis and the New Criticism would expunge as they shifted the basis of English from the novel to modernist poetry.

Quiller-Couch had acquired his reputation as an adventure novelist writing for a popular audience. A. L. Rowse, Quiller-Couch's student and biographer, emphasises the extent to which the latter raised eyebrows: 'the national English Association opposed the ideas of a man known most notably as a Stevensonian best-seller'.[21] In his *Memoirs*, Quiller-Couch recounts with great pride the publication of his first novel, *Dead Man's Rock* (1887), which had been picked up by the same firm that broke new ground with *Treasure Island* and *King Solomon Mines*. Taking great pleasure in the fact that his book 'sold like hot cakes', Quiller-Couch did not fret much about the commodification and consumption of literature.[22] Nor did he have much time for making and maintaining distinctions between high, middle and low-brow culture. The title of his collection of critical essays written in the 1890s, *Adventures in Criticism* (1896), illustrates that, for its author, there was little contradiction or tension between his orientation as an adventure novelist and his sense of himself as a literary critic. He clearly did not see the critic's role to be the reforming of public tastes. One of the essays in this volume – 'Poor little penny dreadfuls' – took issue with those who argued that the penny dreadfuls 'demoralize the lower classes and cause violence'. Pointing out the hypocrisy behind the 'bland exhibition of bourgeois logic', that of the middle and upper classes who argued that selling 'good literature' at a 'cheap rate' would flush the penny dreadfuls from the market, he tells his reader to mark the reading materials of passengers travelling first-class from London to Paris: 'I think a fond belief in *Ivanhoe* within the reach of all would not long survive that experiment.'[23] In another essay in *Adventures in Criticism*, 'The public and letters', Quiller-Couch mocks those whose lofty cultural ideals led them to idealise a reading public which liked to read poetry and was an excellent judge of literary merit. This literary history is interesting because it does not promulgate a myth about the 'decline' of the public intellectual or his debasement amid mass culture. The matter-of-factness with which he relates anecdotes that reveal that most nineteenth-century gentlemen had not heard of Robert Browning stands in marked contrast to so many later essays by men like Lionel Trilling who would look back to the Victorian period as a golden age of literacy and of the public intellectual.

A different kind of 'public intellectual', Quiller-Couch and Raleigh were quite comfortable with the tastes of the public – the literary marketplace – and with the notion that the public did not have an intellectual and literary centre. As Franklin Court has recently surmised in his study of the institutionalisation of literature, Raleigh has been omitted from critical histories in part because of his radical cultural views. In one of his lectures, Raleigh flaunted his anti-institutionalism: 'I can't read Shakespeare anymore ... Not that I think him a bad author, particularly, but I can't bear literature. This distaste must be watched or they'll turn me out.'[24] Moreover, in 'On letters and letter writers' Raleigh makes explicit his criticism of the narrowing definition of literature that accompanied the rise in literacy:

> The simplest form of literature is the letter ... a large, though diminishing, number of educated men and women end their lives without having written a novel or a sonnet. But all practise letter-writing, and if this be really a form of literature we should all have our place in a dictionary of English authors.[25]

The 69-page chapter that follows from this Introduction offers a fascinat-ing, if idiosyncratic, critical history of letters in literature, arguing, among other things, that Byron and Keats are better known for and through their letters than through their poetry. Thus shifting the basis of literature away from the aestheticism that had dominated critical histories from Walter Pater through Saintsbury, Raleigh attacked the institution of *authorship*, and rejected the increasingly rigid distinctions between *literary* production and communication and between reader and writer. In a certain respect, Raleigh's notion of the letter-writer has an affinity with Roland Barthes's concept of 'the text'. Both express a desire to breach the distance that had come to separate reading from writing with the advent of democracy and to keep literature open as a participatory social space.[26]

Quiller-Couch also expressed a vehement dislike of the professionalising of literature, which, he believed, came to be reduced to a 'subject', divorced from life: 'I say to you that Literature is not, and should not be, the pre-serve of any priesthood ... English literature is not a mystery, not a professor's kitchen.'[27] English was a way of transmitting culture; but that culture was not defined as the best to have been thought and known. Rather, it encompassed all kinds of national cultural production. Most importantly, it was living rather than dead, and its survival depended not on its preser-vation by scholars but on the changing tastes of the young:

> But the very hope of this Chair ... relies on the courage of the young. As Lit-erature is an Art and therefore not to be pondered only, but practiced, so ours is a living language and therefore to be kept alive, supple, active in all hon-ourable use ... The novelist – well, even the novelist has his uses; and I would warn you against despising any form of art which is alive and pliant in the hands of men. For my part, I believe, bearing in mind Mr. Barrie's *Peter Pan* and the old bottles he renovated to hold that joyous wine, that even Musical Comedy, in the hands of a master, might become a thing of beauty.[28]

Such a capacious view of English literature did not limit its object of study to the realm of high culture, and encouraged criticism of a wide range of cultural productions, including musical comedy.

Quiller-Couch both wrote for popular audiences and addressed them in lectures. In fact, both he and Raleigh were better known for their lectures than for the books they had written. The *Old Cambridge*, an undergradu-ate journal, describes an audience's anticipation of Quiller-Couch's lecture on Shelley: 'the crowd made a combined attack on the deserted pavements of the courtyard. In the frenzied rush women screamed and the younger children howled.' The review continues to parody a journalistic account of a scene of mass hysteria as it recounts the crowd's response after the offi-cial announcement that Quiller-Couch had postponed his lecture: 'The women gripped their handlebars; the men, at a sharp word of command, ordered railings; and as from one voice the cry went up from the belfry: "We want Q!" '[29] Although the description is a caricature, it none the less speaks to the fact that Quiller-Couch's lectures, described by some as 'fetishes' among undergraduates, were hardly sites of 'disinterested criticism' that facilitated a privatised reflective mode of engagement with literature. Rather, they were sites of arousal, as suggested by the markedly gendered and hystericised crowd. It is often remarked on that Quiller-Couch would address his audience as 'Gentlemen', although it was frequently composed primarily of women.[30] While there are several explanations for his decision to use a masculine form in addressing a predominantly female audience – ranging from his conformity to the conventions of formal lectures to his joking protest against women's formal exclusion from Cambridge – they all draw attention to the visibility of the women. This visibility highlights another point of anxiety against which twentieth-century masculinist modernist criticism sought to defend and define itself, namely the increasing numbers of women attending Cambridge and, in particular, those studying English.

Patriotism, nationalism and anti-imperialism during the First World War

If Quiller-Couch and Raleigh were products of the Victorian period, they were hardly insulated from the events that shaped twentieth-century cultural history. D. J. Palmer emphasises that Raleigh, who never 'divorced literature from life', became increasingly uninterested in purely academic criticism with the advent of the First World War. He turned his energies away from primarily literary subjects and towards contemporary politics and the war. Commissioned to write the official history of the 'War in the Air', he travelled to the Middle East to do research that would never see light of day, for he contracted typhoid fever and died in May 1922.[31] Quiller-Couch served in the Royal Artillery as a reserve officer, took a leading part in the formation of the Territorials in Cornwall, where he recruited and organised meetings, and took university leave in 1915 to raise and train a pioneer battalion of the duke of Cornwall's Light Infantry. He lost his brother Cyril to the war and was constantly worried about his son, who fought in the Battle of the Somme in the summer of 1916.[32] His experience of the First World War shaped his understanding of the function of literature and underwrote his most significant and popular lectures in the years 1918–25. A journal entry describing one of Quiller-Couch's typical days indicates the extent to which his military and scholarly activities merged together:

> My days for a week have been 7:30 am–1:00 am. The Colonel [ie: Quiller-Couch] gets to bed at midnight, and then I consider the History of English Literature 1780–1830 . . . I have been drilling and grilling for two hours in the eye of the sun: if this letter is apparently blotted with a tear it has nothing to do with the Recording Angel . . . [It is] perspiration. I will post the General History and Shakespeare Paper tonight.[33]

It is probably no accident that the English Tripos was founded in 1917. For during the First World War, the study of English acquired a new rele-

vance, having discovered a moral purpose in keeping alive the national character while real men were dying in battle. For Quiller-Couch, the war was
taking place not only in the trenches but in academic struggles over the
study of language and literature. German philology and literary history had
invaded Cambridge and were destroying the 'living language' that beat at
the heart of British patriotism:

> [Germans] treated English literature as a thing of the past or imposed that illu
> sion upon our school, with design to prove that this particular glory of our
> birth and state is a dead possession of a decadent race ... they impose that
> hallucination upon the schools of English in our universities.[34]

As a defence against the German scholarship, which Quiller-Couch criticised for misappropriating Shakespeare, among other English writers, and
misreading into his writings a Germanicised ideal of Anglo-Saxon liberties
that glorified Germany's national crusade, both Quiller-Couch and Sir
Walter Raleigh turned to British literature, and particularly to the novel, to
re-imagine British patriotism. Unlike the imperialist nations that would

> extend their patriotism over spaces superficially; ours (or so much of as, in
> Meredith's phrase, is 'accepted of song') ever cuts down through the strata for
> its well springs, intensifies itself upon that which, untranslatable to the for
> eigner, is comprised for us in a single easy word – Home.[35]

He distinguishes 'true' British patriotism from the superficial and 'false'
rhetoric of 'Rule Britannia!', a jingoistic phrase that typifies the state-
centred nationalism and imperialism that he saw as having characterised
Germany since 1870. For Quiller-Couch, 'true' patriotism was associated
with 'shyness often translating itself into irony when it comes to talking of
that sacred emotion, love of one's country'. Irony and implicit passion were
the characteristics of national character and patriotism. 'We who seek in
English literature for the passion of patriotism, have to pride ourselves on
its being everywhere implicit.'[36] While it is a critical commonplace that the
New Criticism, with its preference for complexity, irony and ambiguity,
arose partially in response to the First World War as 'patriotism [succumbed] to internationalism and literal meanings gave way to complex
ones', the literary patriotism that Quiller-Couch and Sir Walter Raleigh
describe in their wartime criticism complicates such a clear-cut opposition.[37]
In his address to the Royal Colonial Institute on 12 December 1916, Sir
Walter Raleigh applies Edmund Burke's description of the French Revolution as a 'war of ideas' to describe the First World War. The English idea,
however, is not an 'idea' at all, it would seem. The chief characteristic of
the English 'temper', he writes, is that it has 'no theory of itself'. It is patriotic but not nationalistic:

> It is to be found not in England alone, but wherever there is a strain of English
> blood or an acceptance of English institutions ... It is everywhere in our
> trenches to-day. It is not clannish, or even national, it is essentially the lonely

temper of a man independent to the verge of melancholy. An admirable French writer of today has said that the best handbook and guide to the English temper is Defoe's romance of *Robinson Crusoe*. Crusoe is practical, but is conscious of the overshadowing presence of the things that are greater than man ... There is no danger that English thought will ever underestimate the value and meaning of the individual soul. The great English literature, it might almost be said, from Shakespeare's *Hamlet* to Browning's *The Ring and The Book*, is concerned with no other subject ... The English temper has an almost morbid dislike of all that is showy or dramatic in expression ... And the epigrams of the English temper usually take the form of understatement ... When the French troops go over the parapet to make an advance, their battle cry shouts the praises of their country. The British troops prefer to celebrate the advance in a more trivial fashion, 'This way to the early door, sixpence extra.'[38]

There is much to be said about Raleigh's understanding of Englishness in relationship to internationalism and imperialism. Raleigh's understanding of the English temper is situated within what David Simpson has delineated as a dominant tradition, beginning with Edmund Burke and continuing through E. P. Thompson, that celebrates British literary culture over and against French and German 'theory'.[39] He complicates the Burkean opposition between 'French' theory and 'English' experience, however, by drawing an alliance between a shared French and English way of thinking about *Robinson Crusoe*. The most famous French commentary on *Crusoe* was, of course, *Émile*, by Jean-Jacques Rousseau, declaimed by Burke as the most dangerous and theoretical of French writers. In this instance, however, the differences between France and England are transcended in this literary alliance, which serves as a reminder of the political alliance between France and England during the war.

While Raleigh suggests that the 'English temper' provides a kind of resistance against German imperialism and strident nationalism, his reference to Crusoe betrays the imperialist tendencies of the liberal individualism that Crusoe has represented to critics from James Joyce to Edward Said. Raleigh's and Quiller-Couch's nationalism thus share with the late-nineteenth-century liberalism of Charles Dilke, who coined the term 'Greater Britain', a complicated notion of patriotism that is at once politically anti-imperialist and culturally nationalist and expansive. Moreover, from its outset, Raleigh's literary career in England speaks to and complicates what Gauri Viswanathan has shown to be the way in which the discipline of English literature emerged in the crucible of colonialism.[40] For Raleigh had begun his career as a professor of English Literature at the Mohammedan Anglo-Oriental College, Aligarh; but by the time he returned to England due to illness, he had voiced complaints about the function of English in India. He was critical of British rule in India, of attempts to Christianise Indian culture, and of the rationalised, exam-driven, methods of learning to which the teaching of English was directed in the 'Calcutta-Mill'.[41]

A critique of modernism, or the function of sympathy in criticism

During and after the First World War, both Quiller-Couch and Raleigh sought to shape an alternative vision of English literary history against the emerging modernist conception. The modernist characterisation of Victorian writers and politics proved contentious for both men. Unlike much of the writing on Victorians that would emerge after the Second World War, projecting onto the nineteenth century generalisations about a Victorian past, Raleigh and Quiller-Couch sought to rescue Victorian modernity from being cast in terms of a 'past' that was being projected onto it. When Raleigh criticises what *we* would describe as 'modernist' approaches to literature, he finds them wanting in comparison with what *he* describes as 'the modern attitude' to literature that arose in the nineteenth century and that influenced his own approach. 'The modern attitude', according to Raleigh, 'chiefly distinguishes the nineteenth century from earlier centuries', and it arose from 'Science, Industrialism, Democracy . . . I think they could all be summed up in a word which expresses their effect on us – humanitarianism. I do not think that we love pleasure more than our ancestors, but we hate pain more.' Unlike the 'humanitarian' and 'therapeutic' perspective from which he approached literature, Raleigh's contemporaries chose to evaluate literature on the basis of specific aesthetic standards. They had become, he believed, overly concerned with distinguishing 'good' from 'bad' poetry. It was, of course, precisely that task which was ridding the emerging canon of so many Victorian poems. In particular, Raleigh takes to task Edith Sichel:

> She has recently published an amusing essay on Bad poetry . . . Mrs Hemans, for example, on sunset in the alps: I catch the mood from these verses, and I see the picture. It is not great poetry, but why should we call it Bad. It does its humble job. Obscure verses have never been a dangerous engine of revolution. Those who declare war on bores and dunces are inspired by one or other of the universal motives of war – fear, self-aggrandisement, or sport.[42]

The kind of criticism Raleigh advocated is based not so much on absolute aesthetic standards as on the understanding that literature takes its meaning from something resembling what Raymond Williams describes as a 'structure of feeling'. Raleigh saw the task of the 'literary critic', 'or rather, of those who have come to know and love some poets whose speech is not our speech, [to be] to overcome this obstacle, and to listen to them as if they belonged to our society'.[43] Like the Wordsworthian poet, Raleigh's critic is noteworthy not because of any special expertise he has as a 'literary critic' but because of his capacity to sympathetically engage with writers of the past and to help modern readers recognise themselves across the historical distance.

Quiller-Couch's most coherent response to post-war modernism and its attack on the Victorians is his collection of essays *The Poet as Citizen* (1935). Quiller-Couch was well aware of his audience's modernist aesthetic sensibility and its tendency to declare a modern break with the Victorian past. Like Raleigh, Quiller-Couch saw the task of literary criticism to be one of recreating the nation, linking the past to the present, and suturing over the historical divide the Germans were drawing in the trenches and in their scholarship. These essays contested various modernist assumptions about Victorian culture and literature, and engaged in a dialogue with Lytton Strachey, T. S. Eliot and Ezra Pound, redrawing the landscape of late nineteenth- and early twentieth-century aesthetic and political history. Connecting the essays was Quiller-Couch's commitment both to the modernity of liberalism and to literature's role in shaping British citizenship. In many respects, *The Poet as Citizen* developed some of the themes in Quiller-Couch's earlier essay 'Patriotism in literature'. Again he distinguished real patriotism from the bombastics of vulgar nationalism. The first charge to which Quiller-Couch responded was the idea that poetry is not popular. Rather than setting up an antithesis between culture and poetry on the one hand and popular national sentiment on the other, Quiller-Couch explained that poetry was deeply cherished. Much like the patriotism he had previously described as 'shy', Quiller-Couch explained, 'there is something in Poetry which makes men and women, after the age of youthful eager friendships, hide away the appeal of Poetry – and especially the emotional appeal as a whisper in their own bosoms'.[44]

In 'The cult of personality', Quiller-Couch developed his discussion of how poetry should 'serve the state'. Alarmed by the political and aesthetic trends that had taken hold since 1918, he decried the nationalism that had been driving men into 'narrow, separatist, individualist channels'. At the centre of the essay is an attack on Lytton Strachey and 'biography', a genre he identified with the emergence of the twentieth-century 'cult of personality'. Unlike the 'shy patriotism' of the poetry Quiller-Couch advocated, Lytton Strachey's writings on Victorians are typical of the kind of hero-worship that emerged with Carlyle and which 'magnifies the importance of individuals' in terms of the 'national interest'. Moreover, Strachey's essays are 'corrosive' because his emphasis on great men distorts his understanding of the Victorians:

> Well, the 'age of Queen Victoria' (if one must personify so pedantic an abstraction) certainly did not produce anything like the French Revolution. It (if we may meet this trick of personification on its own mat) even stopped the menace of its violence – the Conciergie, the Terror and its blood . . . It effected a most evident if gradual improvement in the life of what used to be called 'the poor'. But I must not be entrapped into a defence of that abstraction, 'the Victorian Age' . . . the most glorious exploits are not always the most characteristic. Sometimes a matter of less moment, an expression or a jest gives a truer insight into a man's mind than the most famous sieges.[45]

While it would take another twenty-five years for Asa Briggs to produce *Victorian People*, the definitive retort to Strachey's generalisations about the Victorian period, Quiller-Couch raised a few of the same issues as would

Briggs. For Quiller-Couch and for Briggs, Strachey's revolt against the Victorians said more about the values of the modern 'men in revolt' than it did about the nineteenth century.[46] For both, history could not be reduced to an account of the significance of the ideas or actions of individual men but could be recounted only by attending to the minute and particular circumstances in which individuals participated in 'various segments' of Victorian England.

His third essay in *The Poet as Citizen*, 'Tradition and orthodoxy', engages with T. S. Eliot's 'Tradition and the individual talent' (1920). While he concurs with Eliot's criticism of 'individualism' and 'personality', he takes issue with Eliot's orthodox conception of a 'fixed' poetic tradition and with his notion that society is so 'worm-eaten with Liberalism, the only thing possible for a person of strong convictions is to state a point of view and leave it at that'.[47] Like Strachey's modernism, Eliot's aesthetics were grounded in a wilful misrepresentation of Victorian history and politics. Defending liberalism, which Quiller-Couch defined in Arnoldian terms as a 'habit of mind . . . disengaged from formulas, party cries, vestments or "shirts" in religion or politics', he criticised Eliot for his condescension to, and his refusal to engage in conversation and debate with, his readers. His deconstruction of Eliot's conception of tradition followed from his liberal principles.

> I doubt if the tradition of any community can ever be 'formulated' – if even its minor unconscious habits can be 'formulated' save in books of etiquette, the rules of which for one generation tend to be a laughing-stock for the next . . . But tradition more vital – tradition in matters which deeply concern the moral, physical, intellectual, health of a society – is at once too various and too delicate a thing to be caught, constricted within formulas or creeds by any Church.[48]

It is here, in the liberal scepticism he expressed about the idea of such a tradition, that Quiller-Couch stepped back not only from Eliot but from Arnold and, later, from Leavis and Williams. He refused to abstract and project tradition or intellectual activity, the 'free play of the mind', into a separate cultural sphere. As he deconstructs Eliot's opposition between liberalism and tradition, he concludes by revealing them to be inextricably linked: ' "Liberalism". . . reveals itself rather as Tradition itself, throughout Literature (which is thought worth setting down and recording) the organic spirit persisting, aerating, preserving, the liberties our ancestors won and we inherit'.[49]

The Victorian canon according to Quiller-Couch

Quiller-Couch thus self-consciously wrote against the grain of the modernist divide. In his lecture 'The poetry of Thomas Hardy', he observed that 'each generation turn[s] iconoclast on its father's poetic gods. You will scarcely deny that on some of you the term "Victorian" acts as a red rag upon a young bull of the pasture.'[50] His discussion of the relevance of Hardy also offers a provocative and complex metaphor for the cultural significance of literary criticism:

> A Man may dig a trench at the end of his garden as deep as was ever dug through England by the conquest, or in 1642, or in 1660, or if you will, by the war of 1914–1918: but the seeds carry over and germinate – as the seed of Hardy has come across that ditch.

Quiller-Couch responded to the notion that modernism is a temporal rupture by conjuring a rural scene. Refiguring the trench as a ditch in a garden that is, of course, at once the nation and the literary tradition in which the nation lives, he repositions the twentieth century on a late nineteenth-century national landscape. Resisting periodisation, which he identified with the German tendency to reduce literature to a history of 'schools', 'influences', tendencies', and 'reactions', he sought to portray to his students a sense of literature 'as an organic living thing with delicate, infinitesimal roots'.

When he wrote about nineteenth-century poets and novelists, Quiller-Couch's purpose was not to set them against those of the twentieth century, but to blur the boundaries between the two centuries. The canon according to Quiller-Couch looked very different from the modernist canon that was being decided at the same moment. *The Oxford Book of Victorian Verse* (1912), edited by Quiller-Couch, is inclusive in its range, blurring the boundaries of nation and period, and providing a place for women poets, Chartist poets, minor poets – even the modernist American poet Ezra Pound – born in the nineteenth century.[51] His essays on Victorian writers collected in *Dickens and Other Victorians* (1925) map a literary landscape that seems more contemporary than that of the critics who would follow. The figures he covers – Disraeli, Gaskell, Trollope, Elizabeth Barrett Browning, and Carlyle – stand out in their dramatic difference from the canonical texts whose worth Leavis would defend in *The Great Tradition*. Quiller-Couch begins with a historical overview of 'the Victorian background' in order to set up his paired essays on Disraeli and Gaskell, two radically different figures whose commonalities help to demonstrate why 'the novel became political' as it never was before. The overview draws attention to the significance of the humanitarianism that 'dominated our literature and art in the last century'. He pays particular attention to the political and social sympathies of Shelley, Thomas Hood and William Morris, and seeks to defend early Victorian humanitarianism and its literary incarnation against charges of 'outworn sentiment'.[52]

Against the modernist critics of Elizabeth Barrett Browning, who were dismissing her as well as other Victorians seen to be writing inferior sentimental poetry, Quiller-Couch makes a fascinating argument as to why it is worth studying her poem *The Cry Of The Children*: 'a sentiment, if it works simultaneously upon a generation of great and very disparate writers, is a fact in the story of out literature – a phenomenon, at least, which makes itself an event – to be studied by you scientifically'.[53] We might read this as a moment in which Quiller-Couch speaks across the great divide of the twentieth century and in anticipation of the moment when mass culture, sentimentality and sensation fiction would be taken seriously. If, in the end, Quiller-Couch seems to have morphed into a post-modern feminist, this conclusion is perhaps not so surprising. For from the beginning, René Wellek betrayed that beneath the gentleman scholar there lurked the appeal of the Victorian poetess.

Notes

I would like to thank the following people for their comments on various drafts of this essay: Hema Chari, Madeline Detloff, James Epstein and Maria Karafilis.

1 See Elaine Hadley, 'The past is a foreign country: the neo-conservative romance with Victorian liberalism', *Yale Journal of Criticism*, 10 (1997), pp. 7–38; cf. Raphael Samuel, 'Mrs Thatcher and Victorian values', in Samuel, *Island Stories: Unravelling Britain. Theatres of Memory* (London: Verso, 1998), vol. 2, pp. 330–48.

2 Michael Wolff, 'An editorial birthday party', *Victorian Studies*, 31 (1987), p. 83; cf. James Epstein, 'Editorial' to the special issue (on 'Victorian subjects') of the *Journal of British Studies*, 34 (1995), pp. 295–6.

3 Bruce Robbins, *Secular Vocations* (London: Verso, 1993), pp. 60, 78–9. cf. Robbins, 'Presentism, pastism, professionalism', *Victorian Literature and Culture*, 27 (1999), pp. 467–63.

4 Stefan Collini, 'From "non-fiction prose" to "cultural criticism": genre and disciplinarity in Victorian studies', in Juliet John and Alice Jenkins (eds), *Rethinking Victorian Culture* (New York: St. Martins Press, 1999), pp. 13–28.

5 Robbins, *Secular Vocations*, p. 62.

6 Collini, 'From "non-fiction prose" to "cultural criticism"', p. 26.

7 Raymond Williams, *Culture and Society* (New York: Columbia University Press, 1958), p. 127.

8 A. Quiller-Couch, 'William Barnes', in *The Poet as Citizen and Other Papers* (New York: Macmillan, 1935), p. 189.

9 For critiques of the meta-narrative of modernism, see: Carol Christ, *Victorian and Modern Poetics* (Chicago, IL: University of Chicago Press, 1984), p. 140; Marjorie Perloff, 'Modernism', in Stephen Greenblatt and Giles Gunn (eds), *Redrawing the Boundaries* (New York: Modern Language Association, 1992), p. 154.

10 Robbins, *Secular Vocations*, p. 65.

11 Terry Eagleton, *An Introduction to Literary Theory* (Minneapolis: University of Minnesota Press, 1983), p. 27.

12 René Wellek, *A History of Modern Criticism*, vol. 5: *English Criticism, 1900–1950* (New Haven, CT: Yale University Press, 1986), p. 25.

13 W. K. Wimsatt and Cleanth Brooks, *Literary Criticism, A Short History* (New York: Knopf, 1957, p. ••).

14 Wellek, *History of Modern Criticism*, p. 26.

15 John Guillory, *Cultural Capital* (Chicago, IL: University of Chicago Press, 1999), p. 172.

16 *Ibid.*, p. 176.

17 Isobel Armstrong, *Victorian Poetry: Poetry, Poetics, and Politics* (New York: Routledge, 1993), p. 3.

18 Cited in F. Brittain, *Arthur Quiller-Couch: A Biographical Study of Q* (New York: Macmillan, 1948), p. 101.

19 E. M. Tillyard, *The Muse Unchained* (London: Bowes & Bowes, 1958), p. 72; on the history of English at Oxford, see: D. J. Palmer, *The Rise of English Studies* (London: Oxford University Press, 1965); Chris Baldick, *The Social Mission of English Criticism, 1848–1932* (Oxford: Clarendon Press, 1983).

20 Andreas Huyssen, 'Mass culture as woman: modernism's other', in Tania Modleski (ed.), *Studies in Entertainment: Critical Approaches to Mass Culture* (Bloomington: Indiana University Press, 1986), p. 198.

21 A. L. Rowse, *Quiller-Couch: A Portrait of Q* (London: Methuen, 1988), p. 112.

22 Q [Sir Arthur Quiller Couch], *Memoirs and Opinions: An Unfinished Autobiography*, ed. S. C. Roberts (Cambridge: Cambridge University Press, 1944), p. 103.

23 A. Quiller-Couch, 'Poor little penny dreadfuls', in *Adventures in Criticism* (London: Cassell, 1896), p. 294.

24 Franklin Court, *The Institutionalization of English Literature: The Culture and Politics of Literary Study, 1750–1900* (Stanford, CA: Stanford University Press, 1992), p. 157.

25 W. Raleigh, 'On letters and letter writers', in George Gordon (ed.), *On Writers and Writing* (London: Edward Arnold & Co., 1926), p. 35.

26 Roland Barthes, 'From work to text', in Vincent Leitch (ed.), *The Norton Anthology of Theory and Criticism* (New York: W. W. Norton & Co.), pp. 1470–5.

27 A. Quiller-Couch, *On the Art of Reading* (Cambridge: Cambridge University Press, 1920), p. 111.

28 A. Quiller-Couch, 'Inaugural address, January 29, 1913', in *On the Art of Writing* (Cambridge: Cambridge University Press, 1919), p. 17.

29 Brittain, *Quiller-Couch*, p. 103.

30 Rowse (*Q*, p. 117) points out that he was protesting against women being excluded from full membership of the university: 'he was a liberal in the matter, in which Cambridge eventually followed Oxford'.

31 Palmer, *Rise of English Studies*, pp. 144–5.

32 Rowse, *Q*, pp. 120–48.

33 *Ibid.*, p. 131.

34 A. Quiller-Couch, 'Patriotism in literature', in *Studies in Literature* (Cambridge: Cambridge University Press, 1918), p. 315.

35 *Ibid.*, p. 306.

36 *Ibid.*, p. 298.

37 For an account of I. A. Richards and F. R. Leavis at Cambridge during the First World War, see: David Simpson, 'New brooms at Fawlty Towers: Colin McCabe and Cambridge English', in Bruce Robbins (ed.), *Intellectuals: Aesthetics, Politics, Academics* (Minneapolis: University of Minnesota Press, 1990), p. 252.

38 W. Raleigh, *The War of Ideas: An Address to the Royal Colonial Institute, delivered December 12, 1916* (Oxford: Clarendon Press, 1917), pp. 12–13.

39 David Simpson, *Romanticism, Nationalism, and the Revolt Against Theory* (Chicago, IL: University of Chicago Press, 1993).

40 Gauri Viswanathan, *Masks of Conquest: Literary Study and British Rule in India* (New York: Columbia University Press, 1989).

41 Palmer, *Rise of English Studies*, pp. 118–19; cf. Court, *Institutionalization of English*, p. 157.

42 Raleigh, 'A note on criticism', in Gordon (ed.), *On Writing and Writers*, pp. 219–20.

43 *Ibid.*, p. 221; Edith Sichel's essay, 'Some suggestions about bad poetry', appeared in *Essays and Studies by Members of the English Association*, 1 (1910), pp. 136–67. Of sentimentality and vagueness in English poetry, she said (p. 139): 'it has, in this disguise or that, existed and poisoned English poetry at all times since the sixteenth century. But, of its fellow vice, vagueness, this is otherwise. For vagueness there has been no time so fertile as the first forty years of the nineteenth century, the time embracing the insipidities of keepsakes and albums, of the imitators of Byron and of the flaccid early Victorians.'

44 A. Quiller-Couch, 'The poet as citizen: ancient and modern notions', in *The Poet as Citizen and Other Papers* (Cambridge: Cambridge University Press, 1935), p. 6.

45 Quiller-Couch, 'The cult of personality', in *ibid.*, pp. 24–43.

46 Asa Briggs, *Victorian People: A Reassessment of Persons and Themes 1851–1967* (Chicago, IL: University of Chicago Press, 1955), pp. 6–7.

47 Quiller-Couch, 'Tradition and orthodoxy', in *The Poet as Citizen*, pp. 44–65.

48 *Ibid.*, p. 50.

49 *Ibid.*, p. 64.

50 A. Quiller-Couch, 'The poetry of Thomas Hardy', in *Studies in Literature* (Cambridge: Cambridge University Press, 1918), p. 188.

51 A. Quiller-Couch (ed.), *The Oxford Book of Victorian Verse* (London: Oxford University Press, 1912); this anthology was reprinted seven times down to 1948.

52 A. Quiller-Couch, *Charles Dickens and Other Victorians* (Cambridge: Cambridge University Press, 1925), p. 169.

53 *Ibid.*

5

G. M. Young and the early Victorian revival

Miles Taylor

In many respects George Malcolm Young was the father of Victorian studies. His *Victorian England: Portrait of an Age*, first published in chapter format in 1934 and then as a book in 1936,[1] has served to introduce countless scholars to the Victorian period and its culture. Although he died in 1959, Young was there in spirit in the formative years of the journal *Victorian Studies*. The first book to emerge from the *Victorian Studies'* stable – *1859: Entering an Age of Crisis* – was dedicated to Young. And as the subject expanded in the 1960s so too did Young's readership. *Portrait of an Age* went through seven paperback editions in the years 1960–73 (in 1961–64 alone it sold 32,042 copies worldwide), and in 1962 all of Young's various essays on the Victorian period were collected and published in paperback.[2] A decade later a refashioned Young emerged during the boom days of Victorian social history. In 1976 Young's *Early Victorian England* was re-issued as an Open University text-book in the UK, and in 1977 a newly annotated edition of *Portrait of An Age* appeared – lovingly, albeit critically, prepared by George Kitson Clark and featuring among its contributors several of the rising stars of the new history *from* below.[3] Historical fashions come and go, but each new wave of interest in the Victorians invariably prompts another edition of *Portrait of An Age*.[4]

In the light of his posthumous success, it is ironic that Young should once have commented that he did not want anyone to read him, but he would like someone to lecture on him.[5] Young craved fame as a stylist as much as he desired recognition as a Victorian expert. He regarded *Portrait of an Age* as his 'historic credo',[6] and he devoted as much of his career to lauding virtuoso historians as he did venerable Victorians, producing appreciations and editions of Gibbon, Macaulay, Maitland and Scott.[7] Not surprisingly, his reputation as a stylist has not endured as robustly as has his fame as a chronicler of the Victorian period. His famous dictum that 'history is not what happened, but what people felt about it when it was happening' took an early battering from E. H. Carr in 1953,[8] and never really survived the development of social history's and cultural studies' approaches to the

Victorian period. Since Young's death posterity has condescendingly extended respect to him chiefly as an authentic survivor of the Victorian period, writing 'from the inside', recalling a golden age in a manner which was both deeply nostalgic and profoundly patrician.[9]

Nowadays Young tends to be thought of as a benign Tory, a sort of Colonel Blimp of social history. This chapter offers a rather different reading both of Young and of his famous work *Portrait of An Age*. It emphasises just how radical and innovative was Young's view of the early Victorians when it first appeared. *Portrait of An Age* marked the beginning of the end of the stranglehold exerted on Victorian historiography in the 1920s and 1930s by Lytton Strachey's iconoclasm, and by the doom-and-gloom social and economic history practised by the Hammonds, and pointed instead to a more positive evaluation of the 1837–61 era. Above all, Young's work, and in particular what Stefan Collini has recently described as his 'picture of Victorian culture as one long, well-mannered inter-disciplinary seminar', helped to make the study of the Victorians the enterprise which it has remained to this day.[10]

The discussion is in three parts. First, there is a short survey of Young's life and times. Then, I look at the literary and historical context of the 1930s in which Young's work on the Victorians was produced, dealing in particular with his criticism of Strachey and other writers on the Victorians. Finally, discussion turns to Young's *Portrait of An Age*, the notion of culture that it presents and the influence of Young on Victorian studies in its early years as a scholarly endeavour.

I

George Malcolm Young was an unlikely icon for the 1960s' generation, even for its academic element. Born in 1882, Young did not begin historical writing until his middle-age.[11] He was an establishment figure, by background and by vocation. He was educated at St Paul's and then at Balliol College, Oxford, and became a fellow of All Souls in 1905. At All Souls Young flirted with Conservative collectivism and tariff reform. He was an acolyte of Viscount 'Top' Wolmer (the future third Earl Selborne), was an active member of the university's Canning Club and belonged to the Oxford Union Imperial Defence Society (of which Leo Amery was vice-president). From surviving correspondence it is clear that his political views at this stage were decidedly anti-Victorian, in so far as he thought the days of 'self-help' were over and that

> we have got to choose . . . between methods of regulation, municipal or central. That is the form in which the struggle for socialism and individualism is to be fought out. And I think by placing ourselves on the side of the former we shall be able to secure certain all-important provisions & safeguards.'[12]

Young seems to have had hopes of standing for Parliament, but a visit to South Africa in 1908, followed, on his return, by his appointment at the

Board of Education, in which he worked under the former warden of All Souls, Robert Morant, put a stop to his political aspirations.[13] In 1916 he joined the Cabinet Office, accompanied Arthur Henderson on his ill-fated mission to Russia, where he remained to witness both the Bolshevik Revolution and the subsequent civil war. In 1918 he moved on to the British Embassy in Vienna and, later, Rome, finally returning to Britain in 1919 to work briefly for the Ministry of Reconstruction.

In the mid-1920s Young retired from government service, and moved to an old farmhouse near Marlborough, in Wiltshire, where he set up home with Mona Wilson, the historical biographer and sister of Sir Arnold Wilson (the former Indian administrator and, from 1933, Conservative MP for Hitchin). From the Old Oxyard in Oare, Young devoted himself full-time to writing, turning out reviews for a catholic range of titles: from the Centre-Left *New Statesman* and *Political Quarterly* to the Centre-Right *Quarterly Review* and *Nineteenth Century*, from the avant-garde *Life and Letters* to the rather dour *Spectator*. He soon became well-known for his expertise on the Victorians, as well as on other subjects. As Rupert Hart-Davis later recalled, Young was a 'pantomath'. His studies of Gibbon, published in 1932, and of Cromwell, in 1935,[14] established his credentials as a historian; while his authoritative magazine contributions on the literary canon, from Shakespeare to Hardy, cemented his reputation as a guardian of the English language. From the early 1930s he also dabbled in local history, becoming a mainstay of the Wiltshire Archaeological and Natural History Society and an advocate of the preservation of village communities and the ancient landscape.[15] To cap it all, throughout the 1930s and 1940s Young put his formidable knowledge of the classics to good use, advising Oxford University Press on its Latin and Greek list and exchanging translations with old doyens such as Gilbert Murray and young poets such as Martyn Skinner.

So when the BBC went to war after 1940 it was no surprise that Young became a prominent part of its broadcasting offensive, publicly and behind the scenes as well. From September 1941 he served the BBC in an advisory capacity, 'on questions of language, particularly in our news bulletins'. The corporation installed a wireless in his home and he was sent listener research surveys and scripts of Home Service bulletins.[16] In April 1942 Young joined the weekly discussion panel *Freedom Forum*, alongside Harold Laski, Edward Murrow and Frederick Whyte. This 'love-making with the Left' (as Young dubbed it) lasted for a year, and Young made a dozen or so other wartime broadcasts on historical topics.[17] Within a couple of years the BBC had probably come to regret making Young a sort of Lord Chamberlain of the airwaves. In a very public attack, in June 1943, Young accused the BBC of 'the most reckless vilification of English institutions, the most grotesque distortions of English history, and the most ignorant adulation of foreign achievement'. His ire had been raised by a series of programmes: among others, an imaginary dialogue between William Wordsworth and Matthew

Arnold; a recreation of the debates of the Long Parliament (which 'made the Remonstrance sound like a Trades Union Congress'); a talk by George Orwell on the public schools; and the pro-Russian tone of many news broadcasts.[18] Despite this acrimonious episode, from which his reputation as a 'neo-Tory' and 'right-wing intellectual' undoubtedly dates,[19] Young remained one of the great and the good in post-war Britain, returning to his fellowship at All Souls in 1947, contributing another thirty talks to the BBC in the post-war decade, and serving as a trustee of the National Portrait Gallery, the British Museum and the Historical Manuscripts Commission. Having served on the wartime Scott and Uthwatt commissions on rural land-use, he then returned to serve on the Royal Commission on the Press in between 1947 and 1949.[20]

Young ended his public career as something of an embittered Tory. He regretted the waning of the British empire – 'I suppose that no nation, undefeated in war, has ever plunged so precipitately from high to low', he wrote in 1948. He campaigned hard on behalf of the 'British Society for International Understanding' – a euphemistic attempt to prop up the dominions with propaganda.[21] He also lamented the rise of the two superpowers, the democratisation of secondary education and the reform of welfare, and he managed to gripe about most of the other policies undertaken by Attlee's post-war Governments. Of Attlee himself Young had a particularly low opinion.[22] By 1953 Young was turning his hand to Conservative Central Office publications.[23] Unfortunately, much of his elderly venom was reserved not for Attlee's Labour Party, but for his own party. Young was approached to write the official life of Stanley Baldwin, whom he had known intimately. He talked extensively with his subject before the latter's death in 1947 and was given access to all the relevant private papers. However, the biography that followed dwelt on Baldwin's shortcomings as a politician, and, with a 'guilty man' flourish, singled out for special criticism his reluctance to re-arm in 1936. For Young, Baldwin's misjudgement owed more to indolence than to intelligence; but, as was recognised instantly, Young's biography itself betrayed lazy scholarship and personal invective – a sad end to two prolific decades of reviewing and writing.[24]

All of this lends credibility to the notion that Young wrote about the Victorian period from a vantage-point of post-war anxiety and nostalgia, evoking a golden age of nineteenth-century British civilisation. And there is some truth in this. In his later essays and reviews Young held up for overt admiration the respectable working-class Victorian family living on a weekly income of £3, the industrial leadership evident in the Victorian economy, the harmony which was a feature of nineteenth-century imperial relations, the masterful sincerity of Gladstone's leadership at such moments of crisis as 1879, and the diffused culture that was a feature of Victorian society from high to low.[25] In one later essay Young recalled how as a boy he had once been accosted by a mournful Kent boatman, saddened by the

news of the death of the painter Millais.[26] But if we turn our attention to
the early and mid-1930s, when Young embarked on his Victorian history,
his concerns were rather different. He was not using the Victorian period
as an ideal against which the age of austerity in Britain might be compared.
Rather he was intent on correcting the anti-Victorian bias that had become
the hallmark of so much writing about the nineteenth century. In Young's
view, four men were responsible for what he called the 'trough of deep
obscurity and ignorant contempt'[27] which passed for Victorian history in
1930: J. R. Seeley, Lytton Strachey, Aldous Huxley and Esmé Wingfield-
Stratford.

II

Young first addressed Victorian history in an article with that title published
in *Life and Letters* in 1931.[28] The pretext for the article was a review of
Esmé Wingfield-Stratford's *Victorian Tragedy*. But in the article Young
widened his focus to attack much of the conventional historiography of the
Victorian period. In particular he criticised the 'objectivity of the scientific
school [and] the flippancy and conceit of the popular school'. By the 'scientific school' Young meant J. R. Seeley and the so-called professionalisation of historical study that dated from Seeley's occupancy from 1869 of
the chair of modern history at Cambridge. Young blamed Seeley for the
'reaction against History as Literature' and the over-specialisation of
research into political and diplomatic history that had followed in his wake.
Young, perhaps mindful of his own experiences, thought diplomatic history
to be nothing more than 'what one clerk said to another', and he thought
that the contours of Victorian political history were far too well-known to
warrant further exploration. Most of his criticism, however, was directed
at the 'popular school' of Victorian history, by whom he meant Lytton
Strachey, author of *Eminent Victorians* (1918), and also Wingfield-
Stratford, perhaps better-known now for his *History of English Patriotism*
(1913), but then something of an acknowledged expert on the Victorian
period. His *Victorian Tragedy* was part of a trilogy on the Victorian years,
the publication of which was complete by 1933, a year before the first
version of Young's *Portrait of an Age*. Young's book was, in many respects,
a direct reply to Strachey and Wingfield-Stratford.

Of these two exponents of the 'popular school' of Victorian history Strachey long remained in Young's little black book. Young later claimed to
have first read Strachey's infamous debunking of the reputations of Cardinal Manning, Florence Nightingale, Thomas Arnold and General Gordon
when, back in 1919, while working as a diplomat in Russia, he borrowed
it from a colleague. As he later wrote: 'I remember handing it back with
the remark: "We are in for a bad time." . . . It seemed to me that whether
our traditional ethic was the best ethic or not, it was the only one we had,
and this new game of chipping at it with an elegant snigger . . . meant

mischief.'[29] Strachey's all-out assault on evangelicalism and humanitarian-ism, as well as his attribution of sordid and selfish motives to these four paragons of liberal virtue, offended Young deeply. This hostility towards Strachey's pseudo-Freudian personality analysis goes a long way towards explaining why so much of Young's *Portrait of an Age* is taken up with pre-senting evangelicalism and utilitarianism as a 'moral revival' rather than a mask for personal interest or psychological defects. In a similar vein, Young became a sworn foe of Aldous Huxley, whose writings in the 1920s – espe-cially *Do You What You Will* (1929) – exposed conventional Victorian public morality and religious conformity as hypocritical, and called instead for a new mystic philosophy of self-awareness and self-expression.[30] However, in the short-term it was Wingfield-Stratford's book which earned Young's sharpest historical disapproval, partly on the very reasonable grounds that *The Victorian Tragedy* was a terrible piece of scholarship, but mainly because Wingfield-Stratford so denigrated mid-Victorian intellectual culture.

The Victorian Tragedy was a silly piece of bombast, but its central argu-ment – that mid-nineteenth-century British civilisation had concentrated on material progress to the detriment of spiritual and moral development; as Wingfield-Stratford put it, 'Man, in his avidity to master things, had not even faced the necessity of mastering man' – threw down a gauntlet which Young immediately took up. Wingfield-Stratford was especially critical of the chief Victorian sages – Carlyle, Tennyson, Browning and Darwin. He summed up the mid-Victorian intellectual angst thus:

> The Victorians were, in fact, saddled with a religion that had ceased to respond to the demands of the time, they were practically bankrupt of a philosophy, for the prevailing utilitarianism was only another method for cutting theory and getting down to the task in hand . . . [Victorian science] was dangerously lop-sided and incomplete. Its most striking advances were in the direction of increasing the power of Man over things . . . But of the study of inner man, of his mind and spirit, the Victorian Age was strangely neglectful.[31]

In his 1930 review Young contradicted these claims, insisting that in the mid-Victorian years the 'clerisy' had induced 'a new spiritual orientation' and that the period as a whole had seen 'the emergence of a disinterested intelligence and the creation of organs for its exercise'. Far from being a missed opportunity, the mid-Victorian years amounted, for Young, to a 'revolution' in ideas.

Young's essay – his first extended foray into the literary scene – created something of a stir. It caught the eye of Humphrey Milford, Coleridge expert and the supremo of Oxford University Press (OUP), and he had it reprinted (with most of the derogatory references to Wingfield-Stratford carefully air-brushed out) almost immediately in an Oxford World's Classics collection.[32] Milford also turned to Young as a potential editor for a nineteenth-century survey which would complement the OUP's earlier volumes entitled *Shakespeare's England* and *Johnson's England*. Despite being warned that Young was probably not up to corralling a posse of contributors, Milford responded enthusiastically to Young's plan for a volume of essays on the Victorian age. Young drew up a contents list, in which he limited himself 'to things that could have been seen, heard, touched or smelt', deliberately eschewing 'intellectual' topics such as education – for 'that one runs off at once into a philosophic history of the age'. By April 1931, the format for a two-volume lavishly illustrated *Early Victorian England* was agreed.[33] In the end Young proved an able editor of 'E.V.E.', as it became known, assembling a team of sixteen writers who covered topics from 'work and wages' to the navy and army, through to architecture, music and drama, and on to 'charity', 'travel and holidays' (supplied by Mona Wilson), and emigration. As an epilogue, Young himself wrote what amounted to a 'philosophic history of the age': a long chapter entitled 'Portrait of an age'. In 1934 the ambitious project appeared to mostly favourable reviews.[34]

Favourable reviews there may have been, but not favourable sales. What had seemed commercially viable in the faltering economy of the spring of 1931 turned out to be a major loss in the trough of 1934. In 1936 Milford complained that he had 'lost a great deal of money over E.V.E.', and by 1937 OUP was reporting that there were still hundreds of copies still in stock, 'and hundreds of pounds outstanding'.[35] Young himself was left exhausted by editing the volume – a 'muck-heap' was how he dismissed it in 1935.[36] No doubt to restore Young's own faith, as well as OUP's balance-sheet, Milford and Young concluded another agreement, this time to bring out Young's own chapter as a separate book.[37] *Portrait of An Age* duly appeared in the autumn of 1936,[38] and, like the war economy, performed briskly, reaching its fourth impression by 1944. In 1946 the BBC's Third Programme ran a six-part series based on *Portrait of An Age* and some of the other contributions to *Early Victorian England*. Behind the scenes a young Asa Briggs helped with the additional research. Plans unfolded for a second edition of the *Portrait*, which eventually saw light of day in May 1953, in the same month that Young was awarded an honorary doctorate at Cambridge.[39] The rest, as they say, is history.

III

Or rather, the rest is culture, for the theme that recurs throughout the whole of Young's *Portrait* is that whatever material and environmental challenges were thrown at the Victorians – especially the mid-Victorians – their clerisy, or intellectual elite, was more than ready to respond. Only in the later decades of the nineteenth century did Victorian Britain fail in relation to its moral and spiritual values. This theme amounted to a complete inversion of the chronology of the Victorian years offered by Strachey or Wingfield-Stratford. The latter had seen it as all going downhill from the 1840s:

Victorian Tragedy gave way to *Victorian Sunset* and then *Victorian After-math*. Let us therefore look in more detail at the book.

Young's *Portrait of an Age* is comprised of some thirty chapters. The first three document the emergence and spread of evangelical and utilitarian ideas, showing how they were disseminated into a code, or set, of ethics. Chapters detailing population growth, the Whig reforms, Chartism and the hungry 1840s then follow, before Young offers another interlude on intel-lectual challenges and responses: tractarianism and geological science in particular, which had the effect of making evangelicalism less introverted and utilitarianism less perfectibilist. The expansion of middle-class schools and the growth of the universities diffused these new ideas for more general consumption. The 1850s were for Young a golden age of peaceful improve-ment based on a vibrant intellectual culture:

> [T]he main current of Utilitarianism was running in the channels which the great administrators had dug for it: the springs of religious feeling opened by the Evangelicals had been led over new fields which Newman, Arnold, and Carlyle – miraculous confederacy – had recovered for English thought.

Above all, Young wrote, 'the English mind was recovering its power to spec-ulate, to wonder, and to enjoy', and Carlyle, Tennyson, Dickens, Arnold, Grote and Lyell were all in their heyday, their 'disinterested intelligence' amounting to a 'religious revival'.[40] In other words, Young's early Victorian England was not the country of materialism and moral despair described by Wingfield-Stratford. Early Victorians were not the 'nightmare of Marx and Engels' creation, bred of a surfeit of Blue Books', Young told his fellow-social historian John Hammond in 1933. Indeed, mid-nineteenth-century England missed out on a *bürgerliche* culture altogether. There was no 'tra-dition or philosophy of urban life'. Young went on: 'I read the history of England from 1840+ to 1860+ as an unexpected recovery of the gentle tradition in revolt against the bourgeois way of life. By 1855 the middle classes are down and out – or scurrying to gentilize themselves in the public schools.'[41]

Thereafter, the oils on Young's *Portrait* began to run. Evolutionary ideas, the changing balance of power in Europe, artisan democracy, trades unions, agnosticism, women's suffrage and empire combined to shatter the balance between material change and intellectual leadership. Ideas remained impor-tant. Young continued for the remainder of the book to alternate between descriptive chapters on events and intellectual currents, but the provenance of the ideas had changed – they were now coming from abroad, like social-ism or imperialism – and they were emanating no longer from the clerisy, but from the new journalism and from the political agitator.[42]

'Culture' was thus a vital concept for Young. It was the connecting link between the moral and spiritual leadership provided by his heroes – Newman, Tennyson and Arnold – and those ordinary people who were most affected by the material and environmental changes of the industrial age. 'A culture is an area of inter-communication', he wrote in 1937 in a long review prompted by reading Q. D. Leavis and Compton Mackenzie, 'living and alert in all directions at once'.[43] To be sound, he argued, culture must necessarily be 'middle-brow', that is 'the high-brow elements serving as exploratory antennae, to discover and capture new ideas for the middle-brow mass to assimilate'. Peculiar to the mid-Victorian years, he suggested, was 'a far more widely diffused interest in the culture-bearers and their doings than we have known before or since . . . There was about the mid-Victorian culture . . . a certain unitary quality of doing, thinking and appreciating.' As the nineteenth century closed, that culture had dissipated, as the middle-classes had become stratified by specialist education, and the 'growing mass with no interests at all . . . had thrown up the sponge, and was becoming to all intents and purposes a proletariat'. Into this vacuum, argued Young, stepped Northcliffe and the sensationalist press. Edwardian England – 'the last fling of the Eloi before the Morlochs took command' – was thus the era when English culture failed. Wingfield-Stratford and others of his ilk had mistimed their assault by two generations.

IV

Young was not a professional historian in the modern sense of the word. He made no attempt, as Q. D. Leavis had done, to quantify and substantiate his claim that the Victorian high- or middle-brow culture was widely disseminated to the extent that a Kent river-boatman could shed a tear at the death of Millais. He relied on the *Athenaeum* – 'an inexhaustible repertory of illuminating odds & ends'[44] – for information about who was reading what and when, while he turned to the 'Blue Books' of parliamentary papers for social analysis. And he deployed concepts such as the 'clerisy' and revealed prejudices about class, sex and race which make reading him nowadays uncomfortable or simply amusing – according to taste – but certainly not enlightening. The older he became, and the more his broadcasting reputation grew, the closer he came to the stereotype of a Victorian nostalgic . But *Portrait of an Age* was a turning-point in the whole development of Victorian studies. It enshrined a version of 'Victorian culture' which had proved remarkably resistant to changing fashions. When Victorian studies – the discipline and its journal – appeared on the scene in the 1950s, Young's was one of the few recent books treating the Victorian years with any seriousness. Denunciation of Victorian culture had continued to be the trademark of much commentary in the 1930s, long after *Portrait of an Age* first appeared – the Massinghams and Sitwells making Victorian-knocking a family enterprise, aided and abetted by Bonamy Dobrée.

With the post-war decade, a thaw set in, and Young's work provided a useful bedrock for the new interest in the Victorian period evident in the work of Jerome Buckley, the Tillotsons, Walter Houghton, John Holloway and Basil Willey. All these writers were preoccupied with mind and opinion, those essential elements of Young's conception of culture. Many of these studies followed a similar path to that of Young's *Portrait of an Age*, for the most part analysing not the whole of the Victorian era, but concentrating on the early and middle decades of the reign, and singling out for particular attention the passage of thought represented by writers from the late Romantics through to Tennyson and George Eliot. Like Young, too, that generation of post-war Victorian specialists concerned itself with the transmission of ideas, hence the interest in Victorian periodical circulation and readership more generally – first revealed in Ellegård's pioneering work on the readership of the leading reviews and in Richard Altick's work on the reading public, and later of course in Houghton's famous *Wellesley Index*. Ensconced in All Souls, and in his twilight years, Young was possibly unaware of these wider developments, but without his *Portrait of An Age* it is hard to imagine the mid-twentieth century looking at the mid-nineteenth in quite the same way.

Notes

1 'Portrait of an age', in G. M. Young (ed.), *Early Victorian England, 1830–65*, 2 vols (Oxford: Oxford University Press, 1934), vol. 2, pp. 411–502; G. M. Young, *Victorian England: Portrait of An Age* (London: Oxford University Press, 1936).
2 Philip Appleman, William A. Madden and Michael Wolff (eds), *1859: Entering an Age of Crisis* (Bloomington: Indiana University Press, 1959); 'Portrait of an Age sales figures', Oxford University Press Archives, 5 March 1964, OP 1230, file 4337; G. M. Young, *Victorian Essays*, chosen and introduced by W. D. Handcock (Oxford: Oxford University Press, 1960).
3 *Portrait of an Age: Victorian England*, ed.George Kitson Clark (London: Oxford University Press, 1977).
4 The latest edition is *Portrait of An Age* (London: Phoenix Press, 2002).
5 G. M. Young, *Today and Yesterday: Collected Essays and Addresses* (London: Rupert Hart-Davis, 1948), p. 1.
6 Young to Stanley Baldwin, 15 Nov. 1938, Cambridge University Library, Baldwin Mss, vol. 174, fol. 114.
7 G. M. Young, *Gibbon* (London: P. Davies, 1932); *Speeches by Lord Macaulay: With His Minute on Indian Education*, selected, with an Introduction and notes, by G. M. Young (London: Oxford University Press, 1935); *Macaulay: Prose and Poetry*, selected by G. M. Young (London: Rupert Hart-Davis, 1952); 'Maitland', in G. M. Young, *Daylight and Champaign: Essays* (London: Rupert Hart-Davis, 1948), pp. 271–7; 'Sir Walter Scott and the historians' (1947), in G. M. Young, *Last Essays* (London: Rupert Hart-Davis, 1950), pp. 17–40.
8 E. H. Carr, 'Victorian history', *Times Literary Supplement*, 19 June 1953, p. 397.
9 John Gross, 'G. M. Young and his England', *Encounter* (March 1963), pp. 79–84; Sheldon Rothblatt, 'G. M. Young: England's historian of culture', *Victorian Studies*, 22 (1979), pp. 413–29; John Clive, 'The Victorians from

the inside: *Portrait of An Age: Victorian England*' (1978), in Clive, *Not by Fact Alone: Essays on the Writing and Reading of History* (New York: Knopf, 1989), pp. 135–45; Asa Briggs, 'G. M. Young: the age of a portrait', in A. Briggs, *Collected Essays* (Brighton: Harvester, 1985), vol. 2: *Images, Problems, Standpoints, Forecasts*, pp. 253–71.

10 Stefan Collini, 'Lament for a lost culture', *Times Literary Supplement*, 19 January 2001, pp. 3–4.

11 Unless otherwise indicated, the biographical sketch that follows is based on the entry by Lawrence Jones and E. T. Williams in the *Dictionary of National Biography, 1951–60* (Oxford: Oxford University Press, 1971), pp. 1092–4; W. D. Handcock, 'Introduction' to G. M. Young, *Victorian Essays*; G. Kitson Clark, 'G. M. Young: a biographical memoir', in G. M. Young, *Portrait of An Age*, pp. 1–8; Rupert Hart-Davis to George Lyttelton, 15 May 1956, in *The Lyttelton–Hart-Davis Letters: Correspondence of George Lyttelton and Rupert Hart-Davis, 1955–56*, ed. Rupert Hart-Davis (London: John Murray, 1978), pp. 131–4.

12 Young to Viscount Wolmer, 30 March 1907, 23 May 1907, Bodleian Library, Oxford, Selborne Papers, Mss Eng. Hist., c.1005, fols 174–6, 193–7.

13 Of Young's academic aspirations an All Souls' colleague later observed: 'He was a person of erudition, whose career would probably have been quite different if he had had a better digestion': J. L. Brieirly to Guy Chapman, 20 February 1931, OUP Archives, OP 1230, file 4337. For an even more disparaging recollection of Young at All Souls, see: A. L. Rowse, *All Souls in My Time* (London: Duckworth, 1993), pp. 23–4.

14 G. M. Young, *Charles I and Cromwell. An Essay* (London: Peter Davies, 1935).

15 G. M. Young, *The Origin of the West Saxon Kingdom* (Oxford: Oxford University Press, 1934); G. M. Young 'Introduction' to Humphrey Pakington, *English Villages and Hamlets* (London: B. T. Batsford, 1936), pp. ix–xv.

16 Director general to Young, 30 Sept 1941, BBC Written Archives, Caversham, R28/295/1.

17 Young to Brendan Bracken, 8 September [1942], *ibid.*, Young Correspondence, 910. There is a full list of Young's broadcasts in the BBC Written Archives Centre. Some were reprinted in the *Listener*, as follows: 'The art of self-government' (28 August 1941), p. 307; 'Freedom Forum: Russia and ourselves' (9 July 1942), p. 43; 'Freedom Forum: The public and the press' (30 July 1942), pp. 141–2, 150; 'Freedom Forum: After the armistice' (13 August 1942), pp. 205–7; 'Freedom Forum: What shall we do with the Germans?' (8 October 1942), pp. 461–2, 467; 'Freedom Forum: Compulsory state insurance' (21 January 1943), pp. 77–8.

18 G. M. Young, 'Some questions for the BBC', *Sunday Times*, 27 June 1943, p. 4; Young to R. W. Foot, 3 July 1943, BBC Written Archives, Young Correspondence, 910. The incident is described in Asa Briggs, *The History of Broadcasting in the United Kingdom*, vol. 3: *The War of Words* (London: Oxford University Press, 1970), pp. 54–61.

19 The verdict of Orwell: 'As I please', *Tribune*, 16 June 1944; 'Notes on nationalism' (May 1945), reprinted in *The Collected Essays, Journalism and Letters of George Orwell*, 4 vols (London: Penguin Books, 1971), vol. 3, pp. 202, 402.

20 G. M. Young, *Country and Town: A Summary of the Scott and Uthwatt Reports* (Harmondsworth: Penguin, 1943).

21 Young, *Today and Yesterday*, p. 1; cf. G. M. Young, 'Government', in Ernest Barker (ed.), *The Character of England* (Oxford: Clarendon Press, 1947), pp. 109–10; and 'Commonwealth relations', *British Survey*, 8 (July 1947), p. 10.

22 'Freedom Forum: Compulsory state insurance', *Listener*, 21 January 1943, pp. 77–8; G. M. Young, 'Rights and duties in the modern state' (1946), reprinted in *Today and Yesterday*, pp. 64–82; 'The Conservative attitude to the new world', *Listener*, 20 July 1950, pp. 92–3; Young to Archie Gordon, 7 March 1954, BBC Written Archives, Talks File 2 (1949–56), 910.

23 G. M. Young, *The Good Society* (London: NUCCA, 1953).

24 G. M. Young, *Stanley Baldwin* (London: Rupert Hart-Davis, 1952); D. C. Somervell, *Stanley Baldwin: An Examination of Some Features of Mr G. M. Young's Biography* (London: Faber & Faber, 1953); cf. Philip Williamson, *Stanley Baldwin: Conservative Leadership and National Values* (Cambridge: Cambridge University Press, 1999), pp. 6–7.

25 'If you had lived in 1860', *Listener*, 30 May 1946, pp. 703–5; 'Commonwealth relations'; 'Mr Gladstone' (1944), reprinted in *Today and Yesterday*, pp. 41–2; 'Continuity' (1949), reprinted in *Last Essays*, pp. 53–5.

26 Young, *Victorian Essays*, p. 206.

27 Young, *Mr Gladstone*, p. 4.

28 'Victorian history', *Life and Letters*, 6 (February 1931), pp. 123–45. For the same journal he had reviewed Elie Halévy's *History of the English People in the Nineteenth Century: Epilogue, 1895–1905* (1929): 'England in decline', *Life and Letters*, 3 (September 1929), which rehearsed some of the themes of his 1931 piece. On Seeley, see also G. M. Young, 'At the bar of history', in *Last Essays*, p. 70.

29 'London addresses: University College', reprinted in *Today and Yesterday*, pp. 129–30.

30 Young was not opposed to psychological explanations *per se*, but to mis-informed psychology; see his later comments on Kingsley Martin's *Magic of Monarchy*: 'Coronation literature', *London Mercury*, 15 May 1937, p. 11.

31 E. Wingfield-Stratford, *The Victorian Tragedy* (London: London: Routledge & Sons, 1930), pp. 283–4.

32 'Victorian history', in H. Milford (ed.) *Selected Modern English Essays* (London: Oxford University Press, 1932), pp. 261–77; Milford to Young, 15 December 1931, OUP Archives, Milford Letter-book, 140, fol. 666.

33 The original suggestion for a Victorian volume came from Charles Waterhouse, of the City firm Price, Waterhouse & Co.: Charles Waterhouse to Milford, 22 January 1930, OUP Archives, OP 1230, file 4337; Young to Milford, 13 March 1931, *ibid*. Young wanted to accompany the book with a series of 'source books', but the OUP was not keen.

34 *New Statesman and Nation*, 22 December 1934, p. 940. The *Times Literary Supplement* was somewhat critical, finding the selection of topics arbitrary, and wondering why the book was not called 'Dickens's England': *Times Literary Supplement*, 22 November 1934, p. 845.

35 Milford to A. S. Watt, 12 July 1937, OUP Archives, OP 1230, file 4337.

36 Young to Milford, 29 April 1935, OUP Archives, OP 1262, file 212961.

37 Milford to A. S. Watt, 15 June 1936, OUP Archives, OP 1262, file 212961. Milford claimed a 50 per cent share in the royalties, on account of having first published the 'Portrait' as a chapter in *Early Victorian England*.

38 Again the reviews were on the whole favourable, although the hastily assembled chronological table was regarded as error-strewn. Only the *Times Literary Supplement* (12 December 1936, p. 1025) remained unconvinced, commenting that 'this compressed "Portrait of An Age" makes strenuous reading'; cf. *Books*, 4 April 1937, p. 22; *New Statesman and Nation*, 12 December 1936, p. 986; and the slightly begrudging review by R. C. K. Ensor in the *Spectator*, 25 December 1936, p. 1130.

39 David Bryson to Young, 16 May 1946, BBC Written Archives Centre, G.M. Young File 1B (1943–48). Briggs and Young also worked together for the Forces Educational Unit in 1945–46: Briggs, *The History of Broadcasting in the United Kingdom* (London: Oxford University Press, 1979), vol. 4: *Sound and Vision*, pp. 809–10; OUP to Young, 17 June 1946, OUP Archives, OP 1262, file 212961; Young to Mr Cambridge, 1 May 1953, *ibid.*

40 *Portrait of An Age*, pp. 105–6; and cf. 'Sophist and Swashbuckler' and 'The faith of the grandfathers', in *Daylight and Champaign*, pp. 107–8, 250.

41 Young to Hammond, 20 January 1933 and 19 September 1933, Bodleian Library, Oxford, Hammond Papers, Mss Hammond 24, fols 73, 152–3.

42 Cf. Young, 'Ideas and beliefs of the Victorians: the Liberal mind' (1948), reprinted in *Last Essays*, p. 814.

43 'The new Cortegiano', in *Daylight and Champaign*, p. 145.

44 Young to John Hammond, 5 May 1931, Bodleian Library, Hammond Papers, Mss Hammond 23, fol. 184.

6

Culture or society?
Victorian studies, 1951–64

Martin Hewitt

I

As a scholarly enterprise, Victorian studies has a deficient sense of its own history, caught in a simple narrative which moves from Bloomsbury anti-Victorianism, through 1940s' nostalgia, the repudiations of the 1960s and the fruitless debates of the 1980s over 'Victorian values', to the interdisciplinary revivalism of the 1990s. In this environment, so the story goes, the attentions of the late Victorian and Edwardian critics gave way to decades of scholarly neglect, from which the period was only gradually and intermittently rescued, in the second half of the century, by a reaction which set in during the 1950s, a reaction which itself was subsequently challenged by the deconstructions of Marxism, feminism and eventually post-colonialism.[1]

This is a framework which needs careful examination in almost all its elements. The purpose of this chapter is to consider only one, the foundational moment of the field between 1951 and 1964. This period (roughly labelled hereafter as the 1950s) is of course significant not only for the creation of fundamental institutions and networks of the field, above all the journal *Victorian Studies*,[2] but also for the publication of all but one of the works which became its foundational texts (and the exception, G. M. Young's *Victorian England. Portrait of an Age*, appeared in a second edition in 1953 and as a popular paperback in 1960). Victorian studies has been reluctant to think in terms of foundational texts, in contrast, say, to cultural studies, which has been marked both by a very strong sense of its own scholarly development and by a willingness to interrogate the key studies out of which it evolved.[3] Nevertheless, the surveys of these years did exercise an enduring influence, furnishing interpretative motifs, defining key questions and dominating bibliographies and reading lists for thirty years. Despite the insights of works such as Richard Altick's *Victorian People and Ideas* (1973), and Geoffrey Best and J. F. C. Harrison's collective three-volume survey of Victorian England, Victorian Britain had to wait until the 1990s for a further significant effort of general reinterpretation.[4]

Three texts, Jerome Buckley's *The Victorian Temper* (1951), Walter Houghton's *The Victorian Frame of Mind* (1957) and W. L. Burn's *The Age of Equipoise* (1964) triangulate the interdisciplinary potential of this period.[5] However, alongside Buckley, the new literary historian Houghton, the synthetic examiner of mentalities, and Burn, photographer of the public face of the age, an understanding of the scholarly dynamics of the 1950s also requires a consideration of Asa Briggs, for his two essay collections, *Victorian People* (1954) and *Victorian Cities* (1963), and his widely-used textbook *The Age of Improvement* (1959), and George Kitson Clark, both for his summative *The Making of Victorian England* (1962) and a number of important earlier studies.[6] Less obviously, but none the less vitally, it also necessitates consideration of Raymond Williams's explorations of culture in the context of Victorian Britain, in a number of important essays, and two immensely influential books, *Culture and Society* (1958) and *The Long Revolution* (1961).[7]

Clearly these works had diverse and often self-consciously limited aspirations. Nevertheless, there is a striking similarity in the way in which they positioned themselves mostly as part of a concerted effort to rescue Victorian Britain from contempt and misinterpretation and to establish a new set of interpretative orthodoxies. Reviewers seem largely to have accepted these claims at face value: their talk was of remapping, debunking, new syntheses.[8] For Joseph Altholz, there had by 1963 been a 'demythologising and degeneralising process of analysis' the result of which was largely to 'dissolve traditional interpretations and to make the history of Victorian England almost unbearably complex'.[9]

II

How far can such judgements be endorsed? Despite the influence of key writings and the significance of its organisational developments, the interpretative achievements of the 1950s were perhaps much less revolutionary than they might at first seem. Such a judgement cannot be advanced without difficulty, not least because it requires a recognition that the context in which these works were produced was much more complex than their claims – and the conventional accounts of Victorian scholarship – allow.

By the 1950s the number of those remaining alive whose formative years occurred before 1901 was dwindling fast. Even so, claims that greater distance from the Victorians had finally enabled them to be rendered 'historical' were merely one manifestation of a persistent effort to 'archive' the Victorians, visible at least from the publication of Alan Bott's *Our Fathers* (1930), whose regular repetition through to the 1980s implies the continual thwarting of such ambitions. It would be hard to argue that either 1950 or the 1950s marked a genuine demographic or cultural watershed. The human survivals of Victorian England remain clear in popular works such as J. B. Leatherbrow's *Victorian Period Piece* (1954) or Ursula Bloom's

Victorian Vinaigrette (1956). As David Paul put it in a suggestive essay in *The Twentieth Century* in 1953, the Victorian period continued to resist every effort to confine it in a glass case.[10]

The Second World War made it harder to blame the Victorians for the First, and lent to works such as *Kilvert's Diary* an ease and charm which attracted many 'displaced persons', as Basil Willey put it in a much-quoted remark, 'tempted to take flight into the nineteenth century as into a promised land'.[11] Even if, as John Gardiner has argued, the forces of 'modernism' soon regrouped, they were confronted by the flowering of what Raphael Samuel has called 'retrochic'.[12] Yet to see the war as marking a decisive shift in the centre of emotional gravity of responses to the Victorians is to overestimate the hegemony of inter-war anti-Victorianism. As early as 1923, Harold Nicholson had been able to write that 'we smile today at our Victorians, not confidently, as of old, but with a shade of hesitation; a note of perplexity . . . For the tide is turning and the reaction is drawing to a close.'[13] As a judgement it was premature, but that it could be made at all alerts us to the cross-currents which marked the efforts of the 1920s and 1930s to place the Victorians: not just the graphic sloganeering of the moderns, or the cantankerous memorialising of Victorian autobiographers, but the guilty admiration of Bloomsbury and the urgent championing of the progressives.

Although G. M. Young's *Victorian England. Portrait of an Age* (1936) tends to be presented as an isolated counterblast against a prevalent anti-Victorianism, it was in reality only the most forthright, brilliant and sympathetic of a number of 1930s' surveys which tempered their critical comments with generous measures of admiration, and which rejected a monolithic Victorianism in favour of a more complex and balanced picture. As early as 1928, E. H. Dance's *The Victorian Illusion* had dismissed the idea of Victorianism as a violent over-simplification. Admittedly, Victorian 'taste' remained out of favour into the 1940s, but by 1939 – if not before – a substantial body of literature existed, with of course Young's *Portrait* at its apex, but including works such as Elliott Binns's *Religion in the Victorian Era* (1936), Amy Cruse's *The Victorians and Their Books* (1935) and *After the Victorians* (1937), and Peter Quennell's *Victorian Panorama* (1937), which presented the Victorian age as a compound of truth and doubt, of freedom of opinion and bigotry, of complacency and anxiety. If a failure, Victorian society was – even the more jaundiced Esmé Wingfield-Stratford conceded – 'one of the noblest failures'.[14]

A further indication of the limits (or at least the slowness) of the revolution in interpretation wrought in the 1950s is the appearance of studies like Clarence Decker's *The Victorian Conscience* (1952) and John Laver's *Victorian Vista* (1954) which aped in tone and coverage many texts of the 1930s. Literary treatments such as Lord Holden's *Victorian Purgatory* (1950) continued to peddle Victorian character assassination in the Stracheyite mould, while writers like William Macqueen-Pope responded with celebrations of the Victorian era which sacrificed gentle nostalgia for crotch-ety justifications.[15] And a surprising number of pre-1945 studies were reis-sued during the decade, including Cruse's *The Victorians and Their Books*, Dobrée and Batho's *The Victorians and After* (twice, in 1950 and 1962), as well as T. E. Welby's *The Victorian Romantics* (1929), Maurice Quinlan's *Victorian Prelude* (1941), and David Cecil's *Early Victorian Novelists* (1934).

Of course, most prominent of all was Young's *Portrait*, itself reissued in 1953 and 1961 (and also in 1960 as one of the first batch of OUP paperbacks).[16] By the start of the 1950s Young had become, as Geoffrey Tillotson put it, 'a name of power', his writings, 'typify[ing]' the age 'whe-ther we are historians, sociologists or literary critics'[17] – 'the one historian', remarked Briggs, 'with whom I have felt a close affinity, although not a political one'.[18] The *Portrait* continued to exasperate, for its snobbish allu-sions, its elitism and its Mandarin knowingness,[19] but it was almost cer-tainly in this period that it acquired its 'quasi-classic status',[20] and when reviewers came to assess the scholarship of the 1950s, they did so firmly in the context it had established. Hardly surprisingly, for many of the most influential ideas of the texts they were considering were drawn directly from Young's writings.[21]

III

Young was inextricably implicated in the emotionally charged debates of the inter-war period. But by carefully locating itself between the over-exaggerated recuperation of the Victorians prophesied by Humphry House in his 1948 essay 'Are the Victorians coming back?',[22] and an undiscrimi-nating Bloomsbury anti-Victorianism, the scholarship of the 1950s was able to construct a position of disinterestedness which transformed the context within which Young could be read and used.[23] It is true that this disinter-estedness was neither universal nor entirely robust. Fundamental antipathy to Victorian civilisation was not entirely dispelled, as demonstrated, for example, by the excoriating attacks in E. P. Thompson's *William Morris: Romantic to Revolutionary* (1955). Nevertheless, in a sense, the scholar-ship of the 1950s was significant less for advancing a new interpretation of Victorian Britain than for finally establishing an old one, by moving beyond Young's self-proclaimed partisanship to establish a more neutral position from which to interpret the age.

Exploiting such detachment, the writings of the 1950s and early 1960s were able to reinforce Young's overriding thesis, that Victorian Britain, notwithstanding its dramatic transformations, could best be understood as a single, if complex, subject. Central to this was a reaffirmation of the period's chronological coherence. Before 1945, 'Victorian' was conven-tionally divided, roughly equally, between 'early' and 'late', a division jus-tified by R. K. Ensor, in his volume of the Oxford History of Britain, on the grounds that 'round about 1870 occurs a watershed in English life'.[24] The period from the 1830s to the 1870s had been seen as the properly Victorian decades, and the later years as having been marked by a gradual shift to more modern patterns. By contrast, the scholarship of the 1950s inclined decisively towards more flexible tripartite divisions, either of early/mid-/late Victorian or of a 'high Victorian' age flanked by periods of emergence and decay.[25] Paradoxically, by proposing a central core merging into two eras of transition, this shift enriched perceptions of the period's integrity.

This might appear contentious. After all, partly from a conventional delicacy about the process of periodisation,[26] and partly from a desire to emphasise the dramatic changes which marked Victorian Britain, the scholarship of the 1950s generally shied away from consideration of the period as a whole: Houghton retained 1830–70, while the others homed in on variously defined central periods, sometimes acknowledging them as the core of a wider Victorian era, but often treating them as self-contained entities. Moreover, a challenge to the idea of a single Victorian period was integral to the reaction against monolithic constructions of the 'Victorian'. 'It is no more possible', Briggs observed in *Victorian People*, 'to embrace the whole of Victorian England than it was to battle against it.'[27] Even so, the three-way split, given wide currency by David Thomson's nineteenth-century volume for the Penguin *History of England*, became ubiquitous as nomenclature and as organising convention, and with it came a consensus that the early and late periods remained essentially Victorian.[28] In similar ways, the opening chapter of *The Victorian Frame of Mind* – 'The spirit of the age' – which illustrates how far 'transition' was a defining trope of the Victorians' own sense of their era, bolstered a recognition that the period could be marked both by transformation and persistence. Contemporary attempts to carve out the span from around 1880 to 1914 as a distinct period were predicated on an acceptance that those years could not yet be classed as post-Victorian, and attempts to assert any kind of fundamental caesura were likely to prompt forceful re-assertions of unity. 'The entire Victorian age was one prolonged intellectual crisis' was Altholz's response to the suggestion, made in the volume *1859: Entering an Age of Crisis*, that the year marked the onset of a new era.[29]

Alongside this chronological unity came a more synoptic approach to the period. Briggs, Burn and Kitson Clark were steeped in the literary material in a way in which historians such as E. L. Woodward were not.[30] Houghton and Buckley were widely read in the historical literature. E. P. Thompson and Williams were among a number of important scholars of the Victorian period emerging out of a teaching engagement with both literature and history. There was renewed attention to Victorian prose, not just of the cultural critics and sages, but also of writers and thinkers such as Bagehot, Smiles, Darwin and Mallock. The sense of a common enterprise amenable to shared modes of analysis – typified by John Holloway's *The Victorian Sage* (1953), but in fact characteristic of so much of the writings of the

1950s and central to the early volumes of *Victorian Studies* – established bridges across the disciplinary divide and reinforced a crucial shift in the way the interrelationships of various elements in Victorian civilisation were conceived.[31]

Prior to the 1950s there had been a tendency to defend Victorian literary figures by claiming them as anti-Victorian, standing as it were outside of Victorian culture, a tendency culminating perhaps in E. D. H. Johnson's *Alien Vision of Victorian Poetry* (1952). A decade later such distinctions seemed unnecessary and untenable. The sages were reclaimed as anti-Victorian but still *of* the Victorians: 'in almost all their criticisms', as Briggs put it, 'they accepted premises which in retrospect make them as "Victorian" as the targets of their irony or their indignation'.[32] Critics never entirely shrugged off the modernist concern that Victorian novelists and poets suffered through their 'acquiescence' in a threatening and debilitating Victorian culture,[33] but the characteristic approach came to conceive of their writings as integral to, not standing outside of, the age.[34]

Of course, installing the great Victorian critics as a central part of the Victorian condition required a more complex reconceptualisation of that condition than had been deployed hitherto. Prior to the later 1950s the cost of the rediscovery of Victorian diversity had been a degree of compartmentalisation which produced what John Clive subsequently described as a picture of Victorian England 'as an enormous playing field, with a series of teams in distinctively coloured jerseys engaged in fierce yet expertly refereed combats – Christians vs Doubters, Liberals vs Conservatives, Extroverts vs Introverts, Optimists vs Pessimists'.[35] This view produced the kind of relaxed judgements (with a genealogy back to Chesterton's 1913 *The Victorian Age in Literature*) which characterise Graham Hough's *The Last Romantics* (1949), that incompatibles were reconciled, the contradictory currents of Victorian society 'continued to live pretty comfortably together', and social and intellectual cohesion was 'not fundamentally distressed'.[36]

By the early 1960s it would have been extremely difficult to write in such a way. Perhaps historians were more inclined to see in the mid-Victorian period the kind of prosperity and stability that enabled Kitson Clark to describe it as 'a lull, a centre of indifference'.[37] But by and large Trollope and Smiles gave way to Arnold and to Clough. Earnestness escaped from hypocrisy, to be joined by accident and anxiety. What Willey had described as the 'poised uncertainty' of the mid-Victorian mind had been stripped of its poise.[38] Even Burn's notion of 'equipoise' was of an almost accidental and 'temporary balance of forces . . . struggling, pushing and shoving to better their positions'.[39] Muscular dichotomies became the rule. The achievement of Houghton, in particular, was to bring out the sense of struggle, pressure and strain in Victorian culture, to uncover the extent to which it was being pulled – and pulled taut – in a variety of contrary directions, not so much at rest as brimming with potential energy.

IV

Lionel Trilling's observation in *The Liberal Imagination* (1951) that tension is 'the proper metaphor for culture'[40] suggests the potential that these ideas offered, not just for reworking characterisations of the Victorian but for rethinking the very idea of *culture* as it applied to them. In some senses Victorian studies as a recognisable field emerged at a particularly opportune moment. As Stuart Hall has recalled, arguments within American studies, within social anthropology and, most heatedly, around the criticism of contemporary culture promulgated by F. R. Leavis and his supporters were encouraging the sense that 'culture' was the 'missing concept'.[41] Debates over culture were certainly placing on the agenda critical questions both about how the object of interdisciplinary studies might be delineated and how appropriate methodologies for such studies might be constructed. And though he was never, in any meaningful way, a 'Victorianist' it was none the less significant that a number of Raymond Williams's key interventions in these debates over the definition of culture in the 1950s and early 1960s were rooted in Victorian themes and topics.[42]

The idea of culture, not just in its narrow Arnoldian sense, had lurked around the fringes of Victorian scholarship for much of the twentieth century. In a number of his essays G. M. Young had been concerned to explore the notion of culture, and its implications for the kind of study he had attempted in the *Portrait*. 'Culture', he had remarked,

> let us always remember, is not a state but a process; a body of assumptions, judgements, tastes, and habits, constantly changing, constantly re-formulating themselves, but also constantly swerving back to gather up something which the grandfathers had dropped and the sons left lying beside the course.[43]

However, the writings of Williams, of Richard Hoggart (especially his 1957 *The Uses of Literacy*) – and indeed T. S. Eliot's earlier *Notes Towards the Definition of Culture* (1948) against which they were largely reacting – did raise exactly the kinds of questions of diversity and cohesiveness, belief and institution, that were being posed by contemporary reworkings of the Victorians, and hence the possibility that 'culture' in a new and broader conception might become a central organising concept of the field. They provided an opportunity that Victorian studies might conceive of itself as cultural history, 'more than the sum of the particular histories', but concerned rather with the 'relationships between elements in a whole way of life'.[44]

The opportunity was not taken. It may not have been considered. None of the key texts of the 1950s defined their intention in terms of portraying 'Victorian culture'. Houghton presented his object as 'those general ideas and attitudes about life which the Victorians of the middle and upper classes would have breathed in with air'.[45] Burn described his as 'certain aspects of English life and thought, certain ways of looking at things'.[46] Neither Houghton nor Burn, Briggs nor Kitson Clark attempted any sustained use of the concept, and when they did deploy it they frequently signalled their uneasiness by placing it in quotes.[47] Briggs came closest in *Victorian People*, where he represents his subjects as 'makers of social and cultural values', praising Young's discussion of culture quoted above.[48] Ultimately, however, he shied away from explicit use of culture as a unifying concept, reverting, as did the others, to alternative formulations – the 'Victorian Age', or the 'Victorian Commonwealth'. In *The Age of Improvement* and *Victorian Cities*, in fact, Briggs was surprisingly quick to revert to 'Victorianism' as his shorthand for Victorian civilisation, concentrating on values rather than broader cultural phenomena.

Why should this be? In part it was a question simply of timing. Williams's key writings, particularly in *The Long Revolution*, appeared too late to influence most of the works under discussion here. By the later 1960s the concept of culture had become much more central to Victorian studies, and Williams's work was a powerful influence on the generation of historians emerging from doctoral programmes in the early 1970s.[49] Significantly, even E. P. Thompson, a forthright critic of elements of Williams's analysis, seems to have begun to deploy the term towards the end of his writing of *The Making of the English Working Class* (1963), at least if its much greater usage in the final chapters of the book is an accurate reflection of the sequence of composition.[50]

More enduring difficulties were the continued lack of precision of the term, and the limits of the methodological innovations that were in practice derived from the discussion. Given the conceptual complexity of 'culture', neither Williams nor any of the other participants in the debate can be blamed for failing to produce definitional stability. That said, Williams's tendency to proliferate statements of definition, and his failure to distinguish different levels of meaning in use, did not help. Culture, variously deployed to mean 'the sum of the available descriptions through which societies make sense of and reflect their common experiences', 'a whole way of life', or 'the essential relation . . . between patterns learned and created in the mind and patterns communicated and made active in relationships, conventions and institutions', tended, as E. P. Thompson and Terry Eagleton among others argued, to create a meaningless conflation.[51] Nor did Williams's practice always develop his theoretical insights. *Culture and Society*, and the chapter on the 1840s in *The Long Revolution*, Williams's only 'case study' of the cultural approach, were both fairly conventional in their mode of analysis, providing summary and critique of what E. P. Thompson, not entirely without justification, dismissed as 'a set of disembodied voices',[52] or longitudinal studies of particular institutions or cultural forms, rather than the kind of integrated attention which the theoretical discussions had promised. In the early work prompted by Williams's interventions, cultural character (even when placed alongside 'structure of feeling' as a complementary concept) tended to be concerned above all with characteristic attitudes, and to treat institutions as carriers of attitudes, as text rather than process. Modes of thinking came to be

prioritised over modes of living, and processes of domination and subordi-
nation were occluded.

V

Such difficulties crucially inhibited the adoption of culture and cultural
history as the central object and mode of analysis within Victorian studies.
'Culture' at the very least could have constructed a shared object of study
for literary scholars and historians, while the idea of 'cultural history' would
have facilitated the development of distinct (and shared) modes of analysis. This shying away from culture in turn deprived the emerging field of a
central unifying focus and made the construction of a genuinely interdisciplinary enterprise considerably more difficult.

Perhaps not surprisingly, a clear sense of the focus of Victorian studies
remained elusive. The first 'Prefatory note' of *Victorian Studies* defined its
object as 'the English culture of a particular age', but the advice to contributors, included from the second issue onwards, spoke of the 'Victorian age'
rather than of Victorian culture.[53] Too often, in the surveys of the 1950s,
there was a tendency to revert to the longstanding, but unsatisfactorily open-
ended, notion of the 'Victorian age', even if bereft of the traditional capital
'A'. The dangers of the idea of the 'age' are best illustrated in the way it could
so easily be deployed in a multitude of alternative and overlapping ways: the
'age of Palmerston', the 'age of Bagehot', even, as R. B. McDowell put it in
1959, 'the age of Newman, Pusey, Keble, Stanley, Maurice and Kingsley'.[54]
Such usages suggested an almost limitless set of competing objects, and
obstructed an effective sense of period boundaries. They also obviated the
need to provide a delineation of key characteristics, relying half-heartedly on
the metonymic relationship between personal character, mind-set and
perhaps typical modes of action, and the identity of a period of time.

The anthropomorphism of this biographical approach, in particular, has
bedevilled Victorian studies. Besides the near-ubiquitous propensity to
reduce definitions of period and character to personality, it is notable, for
example, how often 'the Victorians' stands in for the Victorian, or the internal phases of the Victorian period are delimited by generational distinctions.[55] Admittedly, in some respects Buckley and Houghton did strive to
transcend the restrictions of biographical approaches, seeking wider connections and patterns, and even Briggs's *Victorian People*, despite its title
and apparent approach, had a broader ambition, its essays rarely content
with an individual case or a single reading. Even so, Briggs's individuals are
– symptomatically – often left to carry more weight than they can bear: 'To
understand the English working classes in the middle years of the century,
there is little need to go beyond Applegarth', to give but one hyperbolic
example.[56]

Apart from its reductionist tendencies, such an approach served to constrict the phenomena potentially characteristic of an age to aspects of per-

sonality, and preserved that dominant approach of inter-war scholarship (and of the work of Jacob Burkhardt and Johan Huizinga who, more than any others, defined 'cultural history' at that moment), which had identified the *zeitgeist* both as defining characteristic and fundamental object of study. It also, as Briggs's central chapter in *The Age of Improvement* demonstrated, encouraged reversion to the supposedly suspect notion of 'Victorianism' itself, as well as the skewing of emphasis from doing to thinking, from conditions or circumstances to representations or understandings of them, the tendency to empty Victorian identity of social distinction, to reduce it to a few slogans, and the privileging of certain modes of analysis, especially those devoted to the analysis of written texts and of the ideas and beliefs expressed in them. In this sense the shift Miles Taylor notes towards an anti-rationalist social history which emphasised instinct and feeling over ideology and rational thought still marked a retreat from the historians' natural attention to action and institution.[57]

The difficulties that such a shift created illuminate starkly the aridity of the ground thus prepared for interdisciplinary exchange. Witness the comment in the Preface to Buckley's *The Triumph of Time* (1966), a much more significant book than *The Victorian Temper*, and a study which illustrates the kinds of insights achievable by the sort of literary–cultural history practised by Buckley and Houghton. Taking Kitson Clark's comment in *The Making of Victorian England* (1962) that historians should 'try to disregard a little of that self-conscious, self-confident, minority who seem to have made history and certainly have normally written about it, whose voices, unless we are careful, are the only ones we are likely to hear from the past',[58] Buckley demurred.

> [T]he student of literary history or the history of ideas, working as he does with expressed thought and emotion, must necessarily, I believe, give little attention to the inarticulate majority, far less for instance, to the wordless millions than to the Matthew Arnold who perceived their condition.[59]

Literary scholars continued to find it difficult to escape from assumptions of the text, or at best the thought revealed by the text as the object of the study, and the rest as 'background' or 'context', difficulties nicely illuminated by 'The uses of context: aspects of the 1860s', an essay of Michael Wolff, then editor-in-chief of *Victorian Studies*, which appeared in that journal in 1965.[60]

Without a shared conception of an object of study which went beyond the empty notion of 'the age', or a methodological cross-fertilisation which promised to transcend existing insights, it is not surprising that the excitement at the possibilities of literary–historical exchange which marked the late 1950s and early 1960s was shadowed by a parallel sense of recoil. It is noticeable that the works of Houghton, Kitson Clark and Williams were far from comprehensively reviewed, and, where noticed, were occasionally damned with faint praise.[61] After writing *The Victorian Temper* and *The*

Victorian Frame of Mind, Buckley and Houghton went back to unim-
peachably literary topics approached in conventional ways; Briggs was
increasingly preoccupied by his history of the BBC; and while Kitson Clark
devoted himself to the ultimately revelatory task of providing Young's
Portrait with accurate references, his students turned to politics and social
policy.[62] In the early 1960s, history as a discipline showed much more interest in sociological and anthropological than in literary approaches.[63] The
scholarship of the left, including that of Williams and Thompson, either
largely shunned the Victorians altogether, or repudiated the dominant
approach of the 1950s as patrician and elitist, seeking instead to uncover
resistance and opposition of working-class sub-cultures.[64]

VI

The arguments advanced here have certainly outrun themselves, both as
analyses of the practices and achievements of a particularly scholarly
moment, and as diagnoses of problems which might help to account for the
subsequent development of Victorian studies as an interdisciplinary field.
More work is needed in depth and breadth: in depth, to generate a record
of the scholarship of this period, interviews, memoirs, critical histories, on
which a fuller account of its intellectual origins and early years could be
founded; and in breadth, to take the examination forward, to consider the
ways in which the trajectories established prior to 1964 continued to shape
the field in the years afterwards. In the absence of this work, conclusions
must be tentative.

   Nevertheless, an examination of the literature of the period suggests that
the foundational texts and institutions of Victorian studies, while underpinning the emergence of an enduring impetus towards interdisciplinary
approaches to the culture of the Victorian period, did so in ways which did
not mark as much of an interpretative or methodological revolution as they
had hoped, and occasionally claimed. These years saw the consolidation of
trends already visible in the 1930s rather than radical new approaches. They
raised the possibility of a new form of scholarly enterprise, a meaningful
cross-disciplinary approach to the culture of a historical period taken as a
coherent whole. But they were not able to capitalise on the opportunity.
Unfortunately, as Henry Sidgwick remarked in his essay 'The prophet of
culture', such a cultural approach could 'only propagate itself by shedding
the light of its sympathy liberally; by learning to love common people and
common things, to feel common interests'.[65] In this the scholarship of the
period 1951–64 ultimately fell short.

Notes

1 See Raymond Chapman, *The Victorian Debate* (London: Weidenfeld &
  Nicolson, 1968); Richard Altick, 'Victorians on the move, or " 'Tis forty years

on"', *Dickens Studies Annual*, 10 (1982–83), and most recently Francis O'Gorman, *The Victorian Novel* (Oxford: Blackwell, 2002).

2 Others include the Wellesley Index to Victorian Periodicals, the interdisciplinary seminars of George Kitson Clark at Cambridge and of Philip Collins at Leicester, the symposia on Victorian studies sponsored by the Victorian studies programme at Indiana University and the Victorian Society.

3 See, for example: Jim McGuigan, *Cultural Populism* (London: Routledge, 1992), p. 11; Stuart Hall 'Cultural studies: two paradigms', *Media, Culture and Society*, 2 (1980), pp. 57–72, Richard Johnson, 'The story so far: and further', in David Punter (ed.), *Introduction to Contemporary Cultural Studies* (London: Longman, 1986).

4 Richard D. Altick, *Victorian People and Ideas: A Companion for the Modern Reader of Victorian Literature* (New York: Norton, 1973); J. F. C. Harrison, *Early Victorian Britain, 1832–1851* (London: Fontana, 1979); and *Late Victorian Britain, 1875–1901* (London: Routledge, 1991); Geoffrey Best, *Mid-Victorian Britain, 1851–1875* (London: Weidenfeld & Nicolson, 1971). One thinks of recent works such as K. T. Hoppen's *The Mid-Victorian Generation, 1846–1886* (Oxford: Clarendon Press, 1998), as well as contributions such as David Newsome's *The Victorian World Picture* (London: John Murray, 1997), and even A. N. Wilson's *The Victorians* (London: Hutchinson, 2002).

5 Jerome Buckley, *The Victorian Temper: A Study in Literary Culture* (New York: Vintage Books, 1951); Walter E. Houghton, *The Victorian Frame of Mind, 1830–70* (Oxford: Oxford University Press, 1957); W. L. Burn, *The Age of Equipoise: A Study of the Mid-Victorian Generation* (Allen & Unwin, 1964).

6 Asa Briggs, *Victorian People: Some Reassessments of People, Institutions, and Ideas and Events, 1851–67* (London: Odhams Press, 1954); *The Age of Improvement, 1783–1867* (London: Longman, 1959); and *Victorian Cities* (London: Odhams Press, 1963); G. Kitson Clark, 'The romantic element, 1830–1850', in J. H. Plumb (ed.), *Studies in Social History: A Tribute to G. M. Trevelyan* (London: Longmans, Green & Co., 1955), pp. 209–39; and *The Making of Victorian England* (London: Methuen, 1962).

7 Raymond Williams, *Culture and Society, 1780–1950* (London: Chatto & Windus, 1958); and *The Long Revolution* (Chatto & Windus, 1960).

8 Geoffrey Tillotson in *Nineteenth Century Fiction* (1953), p. 292, J. Tumelty in *Durham University Journal*, 58 (1965–66), p. 100, W. D. Handcock, in *History* (1959), p. 274, among many others.

9 *American Historical Review*, 68 (1962–63), p. 434.

10 David Paul in *The Twentieth Century* (March, 1952), p. 253.

11 Basil Willey, *Nineteenth Century Studies* (London: Chatto & Windus, 1949), pp. 51–2.

12 John Gardiner, *The Victorians. An Age in Retrospect* (London: London & Hambledon, 2002), pp. 58–61; Raphael Samuel, *Theatres of Memory* (London; Verso, 1994), vol. 1, pp. 83–118.

13 Burn, *Equipoise*, p. 25.

14 E. Wingfield-Stratford, *The Victorian Tragedy* (London: Routledge, 1931), p. ix; see also: H. V. Routh's *Towards the Twentieth Century* (Cambridge: Cambridge University Press, 1937); and Edith Batho and Bonamy Dobree, *The Victorians and After: 1830–1914* (London: Cresset Press, 1938). For further

discussion along similar lines, see Sheldon Rothblatt, 'G. M. Young: England's historian of culture', *Victorian Studies*, 22 (1979), pp. 413–29.

15 W. Macqueen-Pope, *Back Numbers* (London: Hutchinson, 1954) and *Give Me Yesterday* (London: Hutchinson, 1957).

16 There was also G. M. Young, *Victorian Essays*, ed. W. H. Handcock (Oxford: Oxford University Press, 1962). Such issues prompted some critical attention, such as John Gross's appraisal in *Encounter*, 20 (1963), pp. 79–84.

17 Geoffrey Tillotson, *Criticism and the Nineteenth Century* (London: Athlone Press, 1951), p. 188.

18 Asa Briggs, *Collected Essays* (Brighton: Harvester, 1985), vol. 1, p. xvii.

19 See, for example, the comments in Geoffrey and Kathleen Tillotson, *Mid-Victorian Studies* (London: Athlone Press, 1965), p. 302; Humphry House, *All in Due Time* (London: Rupert Hart-Davis, 1955); G. Kitson Clark, *An Expanding Society. Britain 1830–1900* (Cambridge: Cambridge University Press, 1967), p. xiv.

20 Jose Harris, *Private Lives, Public Spirit: Britain 1870–1914* (Oxford: Oxford University Press, 1993), p. 258. See, for example, John Sutherland, 'Introduction' to Juliet John and Alice Jenkins, *Rereading Victorian Fiction* (London: Macmillan, 2000).

21 This pervasive influence is well illustrated by the various allusions to be found in Derek Beales, *England and Italy, 1859–60* (London: Nelson, 1961).

22 House, *All in Due Time*.

23 This is clearest in Burn's influential chapter 'Selective Victorianism' in the *Age of Equipoise*, but it is just as fundamental, for example, to Buckley's positioning of *The Victorian Temper*.

24 R. K. Ensor, *England, 1870–1914* (Oxford: Oxford University Press, 1936), p. 136.

25 Even Young concurred; see his article 'Mid-Victorianism', *History Today*, 1 (1951), pp. 11–17.

26 All periods were 'arbitrary and unconvincing', and contained 'historical curiosity . . . complacently within rickety frontiers', grumbled Briggs (*The Age of Improvement*, p. 1), comments echoed by Graham Hough's observation that periodisation was 'at best . . . a barren exercise': *Image and Experience. Studies in a Literary Revolution* (London: Duckworth, 1960), p. 179.

27 Briggs, *Victorian People*, 15.

28 David Thomson, *England in the Nineteenth Century* (London: Penguin, 1951).

29 *Journal of Modern History*, 33 (1961), p. 78.

30 For Briggs's attitudes see the Preface to his *Collected Essays*, vol. 2; cf the comments of Woodward, *Listener*, 14 February 1963, pp. 294, 297; for a striking example of such cross-fertilisation, see Kitson Clark, 'The romantic element'.

31 For other texts in this mould, see D. Forbes, *The Liberal Anglican Idea of History* (Cambridge: Cambridge University Press, 1952).

32 Briggs, *The Age of Improvement*, p. 432; see Philip Henderson's Introduction to his *The Letters of William Morris* (London: Longman, 1950), pp. xxv–vi.

33 For a characteristic restatement, see Mario Praz, 'The Victorian mood. A reappraisal', in Richard A. Levine (ed.), *Backgrounds to Victorian Literature* (San Francisco, CA: Chandler Publishing Co., 1967), initially published in Guy S. Metraux and François Crouzet, *The Nineteenth Century World: Readings in the History of Mankind* (London: George Allen & Unwin/UNESCO, 1963).

34 See, for example: John Wain, 'Gerard Manley Hopkins: an idiom of despera-
tion', in Wain, *Essays on Literature and Ideas* (London: Macmillan, 1964).

35 John Clive, 'More or less eminent Victorians: some trends in recent Victorian
biography', *Victorian Studies*, 2 (1958–59), p. 24.

36 Graham Hough, *The Last Romantics* (London: Duckworth, 1949), p. xi.

37 Kitson Clark, *The Making of Victorian England*, p. 43.

38 Willey, quoted by R. V. Sampson in *Victorian Studies*, 1 (1957–8), p. 76.

39 Burn, *Equipoise*, p. 82. See my 'Prologue: re-assessing *The Age of Equipoise*',
in Martin Hewitt (ed.), *An Age of Equipoise? Re-assessing Mid-Victorian Britain*
(Aldershot: Ashgate, 2000), pp. 1–31.

40 L. Trilling, *The Liberal Imagination* (London: Secker & Warburg, 1951), p. 7.

41 'Interview with Professor Stuart Hall', in Jessica Munns and Gita Rajan, *A
Cultural Studies Reader. History, Theory, Practice* (London: Longman, 1995),
p. 665; Raymond Williams, *Politics and Letters. Interviews with the New Left
Review* (London: New Left Books, 1979), p. 99. For the wider context, see
Patrick Brantlinger, *Crusoe's Footprints* (London: Routledge, 1990).

42 Williams, *Culture and Society. Coleridge to Orwell* (London: Chatto & Windus,
1958); *The Long Revolution* (London: Chatto & Windus, 1961); see also
Williams, 'The idea of culture', *Essays in Criticism*, 3 (1953), pp. 239–66;
'Culture is ordinary', in N. Mackenzie (ed.), *Conviction* (London: MacGibbon
& Kee, 1958), pp. 93–120.

43 G. M. Young, *Last Essays* (London: Rupert Hart-Davis, 1950), p. 53.

44 Williams, *The Long Revolution*, p. 63.

45 Houghton, *Victorian Frame of Mind*, pp. xiii–xiv.

46 Burn, *Equipoise*, p. 15.

47 *Ibid.*, p. 22; Briggs, *Age of Improvement*, pp. 476ff., *Victorian Cities*, pp. 43,
46, 85.

48 Briggs, *Victorian People*, p. 11.

49 As in studies such as Robert Langbaum's 'The Victorian idea of culture' published first as the Introduction to *The Victorian Age* (Chicago, IL: Academy,
1967); see the comments of Robbie Gray on the central influence of *Culture and
Society* in his review of Lloyd and Thomas, *Culture and the State*, in *Labour
History Review*, 65 (2000), p. 100.

50 Thompson acknowledged the influence of Williams in an interview in MARHO,
Visions of History (New York: Pantheon, 1984), p. 16.

51 Williams, *The Long Revolution*, p. 89; cf. *Culture and Society*, p. 325; Eagle-
ton, cited in Patrick Brantlinger, *Crusoe's Footprints*, p. 54; E. P. Thompson,
'The long revolution', *New Left Review*, 9 (May–June 1961), and *New Left
Review*, 10 (July–August 1961). For an instructive analysis along these lines see
Hall, 'Cultural studies: two paradigms'.

52 Thompson, 'The long revolution', pp. 25, 30.

53 Though 'Victorian culture' is the object of Michael Wolff's 'Victorian study: an
interdisciplinary essay', *Victorian Studies*, 8 (1964–65), pp. 59–70.

54 R. B. MacDowell, *British Conservatism, 1832–1914* (London: Faber & Faber,
1959), p. 66.

55 This approach, as with so many affirmed by these years, was itself powerfully
Victorian; for an interesting analysis, see G. U. Ellis, *Twilight on Parnassus*
(London: Michael Joseph, 1939).

56 Briggs, *Victorian People*, p. 204.

57 Miles Taylor, 'The beginnings of modern British social history?' *History Workshop Journal*, 43 (1997), pp. 155–76.
58 Kitson Clark, *The Making of Victorian England*, p. 58.
59 Buckley, *The Victorian Temper*, p. viii.
60 *Victorian Studies*, 9 (1965), Supplement, pp. 47–63. The categorisation of the Victorian bibliography of 'Economic, Political, Religious and Social Environment' itself of course raised the question of environment of what?
61 The reviewer in *Nineteenth Century Fiction*, 12 (1957–58), p. 256, thought *Victorian Frame of Mind* 'of ancillary interest to students of nineteenth century fiction', its learning deep, but its structure too rigid and inflexible.
62 Jerome H. Buckley, *Tennyson: The Growth of a Poet* (Cambridge: Harvard University Press, 1960); W. E. Houghton, *The Poetry of Clough. An Essay in Revaluation* (London: Yale University Press, 1963). This is not to say that they did not also maintain interests in more interdisciplinary work – for Houghton via the Wellesley periodicals' project, and for Buckley in the work which appeared as the *Triumph of Time*. There is a bibliography of Houghton's published work in *Victorian Periodicals' Newsletter*, 10 (1977), pp. 170–2. For some of the influence of Clark, see Taylor, 'The beginnings of modern British social history?', especially pp. 161–8.
63 See, for example, Keith Thomas, 'History and anthropology', *Past and Present*, 24 (1963), pp. 3–24, and the proceedings of the 'History, Sociology and Social Anthropology' conference reported in *Past and Present*, 27 (1964), pp. 102–8.
64 For one account of this milieu, in the English context, see Brian Harrison's Introduction to the second edition of his *Drink and the Victorians* (Keele: Keele University Press, 1994), pp. 11–18.
65 Henry Sidgwick, 'The prophet of culture', in Sidgwick, *Miscellaneous Essays and Addresses* (London: Macmillan, 1904), p. 53.

Part II
Representations

7

Industrialisation and catastrophe: the Victorian economy in British film documentary, 1930–50

Timothy Boon

Introduction: encountering catastrophe

The journalists and civil servants assembled for the press showing of *Health for the Nation*, the first documentary film by the Ministry of Health (MoH), on 19 May 1939, might have been surprised to be confronted by fourteen minutes devoted to the history of Britain since the Industrial Revolution. The audience saw sequence after sequence showing the heritage of the Victorian past: towns, transport and industries. At the fifteen-minute mark – almost half-way through the film – came the first explicit statement on health services, a sequence listing nineteenth-century and subsequent Public Health Acts. This chapter situates the film's particular historical account in relation to contemporary non-fiction films and shows how the catastrophic view of industrialisation it incorporates compares with more upbeat accounts of the period. This is a study in the kinds of representations which circulated in the public sphere, as opposed to those discussed in circles of economic historians described in David Cannadine's inspirational paper 'The present and the past in the English Industrial Revolution'.[1] Cannadine argues that the catastrophic interpretation, which ranged from Toynbee in 1884 to about 1920, began to be replaced from the time of Clapham's *Economic History of Modern Britain* in 1926, with a view that proposed that industrialisation had been much more gradual, the lives of the proletariat less wretched and the governments less culpable than the catastrophists had suggested. Arnold Toynbee wrote in catastrophic terms in conjunction with the passage that famously introduced the term 'industrial revolution', in his posthumous collection of essays of 1884:

> There were dark patches even in [Adam Smith's] age, but we now approach a darker period – a period as disastrous and terrible as any through which a nation ever passed; disastrous and terrible, because, side by side with a great increase of wealth was seen an enormous increase of pauperism; and production on a vast scale, the result of free competition, led to a rapid alienation of classes and to the degradation of a large body of producers.[2]

The etymology of the term 'industrial revolution' has been explored by Donald Coleman, who attributes its origination not to Toynbee, but to Friedrich Engels, whose first lengthy statement *The Condition of the Working Class in England* (published in German in 1845) memorably included close description of the living and working conditions of Manchester textile workers. That work, however, was not translated into English for over forty years.[3] Cannadine associates the establishment of the catastrophic account with the revival from the 1880s of the 'condition of England question', the Booth and Rowntree social surveys, and works such as Andrew Mearns's *The Bitter Cry of Outcast London*.[4] This is similar to the tradition within which Robert Colls and Philip Dodd have placed documentary film. They write of the social reporting tradition which dated from the late nineteenth century and the writings that went under the heading 'Into Unknown England', including George Sims's *How the Poor Live* (1883) and Lady Bell's *At the Works* (1907). They quote John Grierson speaking of the documentarists' need similarly 'to travel dangerously into the jungles of Middlesborough and the Clyde'.[5]

Fabian historians such as the Hammonds and the Webbs had also picked up this refrain. For these writers, as well as those less politically engaged who took up the interpretation, the Industrial Revolution was 'nasty, mean, brutish and fast', having been brought about by a series of technical inventions exploited by *laissez-faire* capitalists, and had occurred 'around 1780'.[6] This abrupt interpretation of industrialisation, when adopted for films, had the effect of eliding the industrial period with all that came after 1780, especially the Victorian age. The appeal of the catastrophic view across the political spectrum, to members of the Marxist left as well as to Fabian social historians who 'can best be described as left-wing Liberal', helps explain its pervasiveness.[7] For the period it held sway, its followers were pursuing an essentially Victorian understanding of industrialisation and its consequences.

Health for the Nation

Health for the Nation, in the version seen in May 1939, starts with dissolving scenes of English countryside accompanied by lyrical orchestral music. The first words of commentary, spoken by Ralph Richardson, are the famous lines from Shakespeare's *Richard II*: 'This precious stone set in the silver sea . . . This blessed plot, this earth, this realm, this England'.[8] The fact that the quotation was a cliché (*The Times* criticised the film for it[9]) may have had the virtue of establishing clearly the reference to nationhood. This opening made an appeal to citizenship by attaching it to established notions of literary culture and countryside, common tropes in 1930s' culture.[10] It was amplified by the remainder of the first quarter of the film, stating its thesis: the industrial development of the country. Here was an impressionistic cinematic 'English journey' accompanied by the sounds of industrial locations, introducing the coal, iron and steel districts of England and Wales, the textile industry and transport. Nine-and-a-half minutes in, the argument of the film is reprised in brief:

> For nearly 2,000 years of our history we've tilled the land: men for agriculture, men for cattle and sheep, milk and dairy, for wheat-growing, barley and oats; men for market gardening and fruit. Then came the Industrial Revolution which changed the face of the land. It changed the people too, changed them forever. From the land they had tilled for nearly 2,000 years the people moved into the houses, the attics, the basements and the cellars.

Following the caption 'The people', against the sound of a factory siren and urgently sombre music, the commentary asserts the importance of urbanisation: 'They came in their thousands, in their tens of thousands for a living, for a wage, into the city. They came in their millions into the cities.' The catastrophic interpretation is then given a forceful statement in an impressionistic sequence of panning shots of smoky industrial areas, mainly Victorian terraced housing, followed by a sequence showing a small child picking-up coal from a slag-heap, accompanied by the score at its most sombre. The caption 'The price of industry' introduces the section:

> A hundred years ago a burden lay upon the men and women and children of this country. Masses of refuse, offal and sickening filth lay among standing pools. Women and children, filthy as swine, thrive upon the garbage heap and in the puddle. Some towns were without sewers, others drained into streams converted by mill dams into stagnant pools. The cottages were old, dirty and of the smallest sort. Houses, streets, courts, lanes and streams were polluted and rendered pestilential: overcrowded, poor, under the shadow of disease. Into filthy hovels, into ill-ventilated factories and mines, was crowded the manpower, the driving force of industry: men, women and children.

The synthesis of the film, which starts in the next section, commences in 1802 with the first Factory Act, followed by the Municipal Corporations Act (1835), the Select Committee for the Regulation of Mills and Factories (1840), the creation of the Local Government Board (1871) and the establishing of the County Councils and Urban and Rural District Councils (1888 and 1894). The sequence culminates in 1919 with the foundation of the MoH. The film builds on this with a series of cases, many of them compared with the state of things in the nineteenth century, presented in impressionistic manner with sparse commentary: water supply and drainage, house-building, refuse disposal, medical services, parks, green belts, infant welfare centres, nursery schools, school milk and meals, national health insurance (a reprise of the industrial occupations from the first reel) and old-age pensions. An upbeat summary, touching on the work still to be done in improving health, gives way to dissolves between crowds of people and the English countryside. The film ends with a repeat of the Shakespearean passage from *Richard II*.

Health for the Nation, ostensibly about the health services of the country, is a film almost half of which is devoted to an account of the Industrial Revolution and its catastrophic consequences, depicted via scenes of the Victorian heritage. How did this come about? Had officials devoted too little supervision to a history-obsessed film director? Quite the contrary: the film's production was closely managed, to the extent that it can be seen as the product of agreement between its director, John Monck, and the two senior civil servants, Arthur Rucker and George North, responsible for the MoH's public relations.[11] MoH officials, who had an early and sustained wish to make a historicised film on public health services, intended the film to create in the public mind a picture of the concerns of the MoH. They were well acquainted with the documentary genre, and so proposed that the GPO Film Unit should make the film.[12] The Public Relations Committee's minutes reveal a close knowledge of documentary, showing that it was an informed and deliberate choice for officials to prefer documentary over other genres, such as the instructional and commercial alternatives. It follows that the ministers and officials would have been well aware of the documentarists' concern to depict social problems, as viewings had been arranged of, for example, *Enough to Eat?* (1936), a film about nutrition.[13] Similarly, documentary's emphasis on the industrial and working aspects of the nation's life must also have been clear to any group of people so well informed about the genre. From at least 1931, when they released their film *Industrial Britain*, the documentary film-makers had set out, as they said, to 'put the British workman on the screen as a serious figure, in contrast to the familiar light-relief treatment in British feature films'.[14]

In its turn, the GPO Film Unit commissioned a script from Monck, who submitted a brief outline in early September 1938.[15] Monck was not one of the inner circle of documentarists, but he shared both their leftist political leanings and their commitment to film-making principles established in Russia (see pp. 113–14). He had worked on Robert Flaherty's *Man of Aran* (1934) and had contributed to the social issues' newsreel *The March of Time*.[16] Like some of the documentarists, he had demonstrated a commitment to social causes, taking part with his wife, the documentary photographer Margaret Goldman, in nutritional surveys in south Wales.[17] Two weeks after North gave the go-ahead, Monck's draft script was ready.[18] Detailed discussions of nuance and coverage continued up to within six weeks of the press showing. For example, in a letter of 1 April, North stated: 'while we have nothing but praise for the bad housing shots we felt that the shots of good housing could be better, as those shown gave a rather shut-in impression'. This close collaboration on the final balance and detailed elements of the film is seen particularly in the stress on industrialisation and its effects. Given the prominence of those themes in the early drafts, it is striking to find that so great were officials' concern over the historical account of the film that North was still stressing it in January:

The only point that I need mention at the moment is that it might be brought out not only that many of our troubles are due to the industrial revolution, but also that we were the first country to work coal and iron on a large scale, the first country to have railways.

After the film was shown to the press in May 1939, it was not immediately distributed because MoH officials wished to have the film altered in response to some criticisms. Revisions were agreed by mid August, and the film was re-edited for release under the title *Forty Million People*.[19] Differences between the two versions can be seen to signify areas of sensitivity for the MoH. Although the later version is significantly shorter than *Health for the Nation*, the cuts were made at the expense of the synthetic section describing the health services, and not the opening parts discussing industry and its catastrophic effects, which were merely re-ordered.

Both the proportion of the final film devoted to industrialisation and its consequences for Victorian society, and the stress placed on them, are significant. Monck and the MoH officials shared the view, not just on the general level that present problems should be historicised, but more specifically that they were a consequence of industrialisation.

On the MoH's side we may note that the catastrophic interpretation was convenient as well as conventional. George Newman, the MoH's chief medical officer from 1919 to 1935, had stated in 1930:

> The rapid growth of the towns in industrial districts led to urbanisation of the people, and it is this which has created most of the sanitary problems of our time. The new towns were built hastily and without foresight or regard to town planning. Houses were put up regardless of soil, site, convenience, curtilage, water supply, drainage, sewage treatment – small in capacity, poor in structure, damp, unventilated, badly lighted, back to back. There was overcrowding of houses on the land and of people in the houses. There were problems of cleanliness, of feeding and of schooling; there were increased difficulties and risks in regard to infection and the incidence and the treatment of disease, all complicated and aggravated by an ever-increasing density of population.[20]

The historicity of the MoH's view was fundamental to its operation. We may speculate that if the problems of the present were understood to be the products of historical change in the past, and particularly the social changes of the Victorian period consequent on industrialisation, then officials and politicians at the MoH could evade arguments, such as those advanced by nutrition scientists and their associates, that the causes of ill-health were fundamentally those operating in the present.[21]

The historiography of industrial catastrophe in documentary films

Two earlier documentaries, made in the 1930s, embody the catastrophic interpretation of industrialisation as strongly as *Health for the Nation*: these were *The Face of Britain* (1935) and *Today We Live* (1937), both the work of Paul Rotha, one of the key figures in the documentary movement.[22] *The Face of Britain*, about which I have written at greater length elsewhere,[23] was released in 1935. It was the first documentary to make serious use of historical contextualisation – although there is no evidence that the film was the direct inspiration for *Health for the Nation*.[24] Rotha made a clear programmatic statement about the place of history in his book *Documentary Film*, written while he was making *The Face of Britain*:

> Above all, documentary must reflect the problems and realities of the present. It cannot regret the past; it is dangerous to prophecy the future. It can, and does, draw on the past in its existing heritages but it only does so to give point to a modern argument. In no sense is documentary a historical reconstruction and attempts to make it so are a failure. Rather it is contemporary fact and event expressed in relation to human associations.[25]

The point about historical reconstruction was literally so for the film-maker who, in representing the past, was obliged to shoot his material in the present; so that, for example, a modern townscape represents its Victorian self. Rotha divided *The Face of Britain* into four sections. 'Heritage of the past' paints an idyllic view of Britain's landscape and community before industrialisation. 'The smoke age' describes the impact of the industrial revolution on the land and people of Britain. The commentary asserts the catastrophist view:

> The power of steam and coal dominated the land. It gave Britain a new place in the sun. It gave her industrial, economic and political power, but at how terrible a price in the degradation and destruction of human life. And so today we endure this heritage of the Industrial Revolution, spreading its congestion of factories and slums over the face of the land, leaving for new generations the shell of a prosperous age.

'The new power', which introduces hydro-electric generation, follows, and the film ends with 'The new age', which promotes the planning of Britain, aided by the new power of electricity.

The historical account, though differently balanced, is essentially the same as Monck's in *Health for the Nation*. But, because Rotha published extensively as well as leaving a substantial archive of letters and film-production documents, it is possible to trace the genesis of this film more closely than that of Monck, and thereby to see how industrialisation became the central motif of documentary historiography. Explicit inspirations for *The Face of Britain* included J. B. Priestley's *English Journey* and the 1935 *Architectural Review* series 'The English tradition in the countryside' by the architect Arthur Eden.[26] Rotha's film shares with Priestley's book and Eden's articles a historical structure, with the Industrial Revolution as the middle term, but it did not derive simply from either. Priestley, in fact, felt sufficiently out of tune with the age in which he was writing that he stressed positive aspects of the Victorian era. For example, he held in high esteem the 'solid lumps of character', who manned the factories of the nineteenth century. He imagined a sense of working-class community that he attached nostalgically to his turn-of-the-century Bradford childhood.[27] By contrast, Eden's main focus on the Victorian period was aesthetic:

> The tragedy of the nineteenth century, in the visible world at least, was that the leaders of thought and artistic expression allowed themselves to be repelled by the grimness of the new towns ... The machine had created bad towns. Therefore the machine was bad. It could not be abolished, however, and the only course open to those who disapproved was to ... escape from the ever-present material realities into a world of make-believe of their own creation.[28]

Eden explained his term 'the world of make-believe' as the Victorian intellectuals' flight from 'the grim realities of the incomprehensible present into the known and intelligible past'; it was 'solace from the uncertainty of the changing human scene in the seemingly eternal certainties of nature'. Pugin was the chief villain here, but generally Eden, the modernist, was castigating the failure of the Victorian architectural imagination in its concentration on ornament rather than function.

But Priestley, Eden and Rotha, despite these differences of emphasis, shared the same basic historical structure. The periodisation is reminiscent of Lewis Mumford's eotechnic, palaeotechnic and neotechnic phases of the history of technology, in his *Technics and Civilisation* (1934). But Mumford's scheme was also a codification of existing historical accounts, particularly Patrick Geddes's *Cities in Evolution* (1915).[29] All these accounts made the same point: that industrialisation was the most significant event in modern history. And, because they assumed that the process was abrupt, the effect was to elide the gradual nature of social and technical change from the mid-eighteenth century and across the Victorian period which subsequent historians have emphasised.

There is, however, a source that would have been more obvious to contemporaries: that great Victorian, Karl Marx. In *Documentary Film*, Rotha quotes from Marx's *Critique of Political Economy*, that 'the mode of production in material life determines the general character of the social, political and spiritual process of life'. He moves from this to dialectic: 'The mind of the documentalist [sic] is trained best, I believe, by moving in a dialectic pattern, although it must be pointed out that this has nothing whatsoever to do with the nature of the facts contained within his subject.'[30] Leftist film-makers tended to turn to Moscow when it came to deciding how a film was to be constructed. *The Face of Britain*, and indeed *Health for the Nation*, were made following the principles of dialectical montage practised by the Soviet school, notably Sergei Eisenstein and Vsevolod Pudovkin.[31] Eisenstein had a model of Marxist dialectical montage which was part dialectical materialism, and part Hegelian dialectic, applied to the practice of film composition, as David Cook explains:

This dialectic is a way of looking at human history and experience as a per-petual conflict in which a force (*thesis*) collides with a counterforce (*anti-thesis*) to produce from their collision a wholly new phenomenon (*synthesis*) which is not the sum of the two forces but something greater than and differ-ent from them both ... Eisenstein maintained that in film editing the shot or 'montage cell,' is a thesis which when placed into juxtaposition with another shot of opposing visual content – antithesis – produces a synthesis (a synthetic idea or impression) which in turn becomes the thesis of a new dialectic as the montage sequence continues.[32]

Documentarists favoured those principles, believing them to provide a correct grammar for film-making. Rotha took up both parts of Eisenstein's commitment to dialectic – as a mode of film construction and as a mode of historical narration – although he conceded that 'by some modern authorities it is considered an out-of-date method when applied to history'.[33] This is apparently a reference to the argument of Raymond Post-gate (cited by Rotha in this section) that 'it is not possible to say that history proceeds dialectically because history, being an enormous mass of facts, is not a material which is capable of being so classified'. It is clear that it was eminently possible for film-makers on the left to take or leave various aspects of Marxist theory; to be persuaded of the truth of a dialectical outline to history but without necessarily choosing to represent the class struggle that for many was a core component. This is what we find in both Rotha's and Monck's films: in *Health for the Nation* it is the action of the Victorian (and Edwardian) State in introducing health legislation that pre-sents the synthesis; in *The Face of Britain* it is electrification. Rotha argues that 'we can see with little effort [dialectic's] possible application to the film, both in approach to subject and in technical construction'. In other words, he was more concerned to produce an account that made good *cinematic* sense than with conducting an argument in the fine detail of Marxist theory.[34]

Alternatives to catastrophe

Both *The Face of Britain* and *Health for the Nation* encapsulate a histori-cal account that is a national British history with industrialisation as the key event. This model tallies in the most general sense with Phillip Dodd's analysis in *Englishness: Politics and Culture*, in which he argues that

during 1880–1920 the conviction that English culture was to be found in the past was stabilised. The past cultural activities and attributes of the people were edited and then acknowledged, as contributions to the evolution of the English national culture which had produced the present.[35]

The two films discussed so far differed from this in the centrality given to industrialisation. They differed also in two other significant respects. First, their conception of historical process was not of the smooth transitions of

Whig history, but of the dynamic and continuing change of historical materialism.[36] As we have seen, within this view the character of the nation was both the product of the past and one that was constantly being remoulded by the dynamic of history. But the films themselves differ over the significance of *people*. The dominant visual images of Rotha's film are predominantly of English and Scottish places, and there are few shots in which people are the main focus. Monck's film, by contrast, features people and groups of people to a greater extent, as is clear in the reprise commentary quoted above. This difference can be explained in part in terms of its themes – *The Face of Britain* was 'a film of the natural and scientific planning of Britain with reference to the respective power of coal and electricity',[37] whereas *Health for the Nation* had to speak of 'the people . . . changed . . . forever' by industrialisation and its social consequences in the Victorian era.

Each film represents a distinct historiographical strand from the 'national past' purveyed by the Historical Association, which by 1918 had developed two principal political–historical stresses: one on the imperial aspect of Britain's national past, the other on Britain's standing relative to the European nations.[38] The mid-twentieth century saw many cinematic accounts of English nationhood. It is little surprise that, especially during the war, representations of Englishness had a particular currency, whether in the scarcely camouflaged nationalism of Lawrence Olivier's *Henry V* (1944), or in Humphrey Jennings's lyrical impressionism in films such as *Fires Were Started* (1943).[39] Industrialisation is a rare feature of those films. But there were two alternative traditions that bear comparison with the dominant historiography explored in this essay. One we might call the 'English genius' tradition, in which particular characteristics are ascribed to the English and their behaviour. The other is a tradition of historical pastiche, drawing attention to the differences between the Victorian past and the 'present' of the late 1930s.

England Awake! (1932) presents a conservative alternative to the films I have already discussed, and one that was much more congruent with the Historical Association's view. Co-devised by the director of British Instructional Films, Bruce Woolfe, and his board-member, the novelist and Conservative MP John Buchan, this film frames its account of national progress in the century since 1831 in terms of the pre-Victorian and Victorian officer class fulfilling its duty to the working classes. It comprises a series of 'great inventions' acted out in short vignettes: Michael Faraday and electromagnetic induction; George Stephenson and his *Rocket*; Isambard Kingdom Brunel trying to persuade non-believers of the future of steamships. This is complemented by the activities of 'courageous Englishmen' in various imperial professions in Canada, Australia, South Africa, including the contributions of British engineers to the development of those countries. Industrial products of Britain, including textiles, mechanical engineering and coal, are praised as 'the finest in the world'. A final tour of the empire concludes with the English countryside, a quotation from Shakespeare's *King John* and Edward Elgar's *Land of Hope and Glory*.[40] This picture is markedly different from that given by Rotha in *The Face of Britain*: industrialisation here is not the prime focus, but, to the extent that it does feature, it is a benediction, and the engineers are representatives of the officer class, not of the professional scientists, architects and engineers with social consciences in the final section of *The Face of Britain*.

The spirit of Shakespeare as the quintessential Englishman is also abroad in *Family Portrait* (1950), Humphrey Jennings's contribution to the Festival of Britain which, although much more sophisticated in cinematic terms and more complex in its rendition of Englishness, shares some features with Woolfe and Buchan's *England Awake!* Jennings's film gives, in impressionistic terms, a portrait of 'us', the English, presented as an amalgam of 'poetry' and 'prose', science and engineering. The Industrial Revolution features as the outcome of the 'poetry' of James Watt meeting the 'prose' of Wilkinson, the ironmaster capable of making the practical steam engine a reality. Leaving aside the difficulty of reading this as an account credible to modern eyes, we may note the similarity of the succession 'then came Trevithick . . . then came Stephenson' to the historiography of *England Awake!* The negative impact of industrialisation is conveyed in a few sentences over shots of townscapes and children playing in a slum street, familiar tropes from the other films:

> But to be honest, our matter of fact way can get the better of us. Often as the towns and population grew, the practical gifts never met the imaginative ones. And one part of us lost sight of the other. Rifts in the family we're still having to repair. We can only thank Heaven that we produced a Blake, a Shaftesbury, a Dickens to proclaim love and health and light. What a mixture of muddle and orderliness we are!

In this form, the social impact of industrialisation features scarcely any more strongly than it does in Buchan and Woolfe's view. Industrialisation here is not a key moment in English history but an instance when the English character showed its face.

Historical pastiche is seen particularly strongly in two late 1930s documentaries: Rotha's *New Worlds for Old*, made for the gas industry in 1938 and John Taylor's *The Londoners*, for the same sponsor and on behalf of the London County Council, a year later. The first of these starts with Tussaud's waxworks of Queen Victoria and several other notables. The commentary starts:

> God Save the Queen. There she was, all of her, the queen of England, complete and obvious. The world might take her or leave her; she had nothing to explain. An age of great figures; Mr Gladstone, Mr Disraeli, Mr Dickens. The wilderness of chimneys was the promised land, business was brisk, wages were rising. Confidence in the future of England had become a creed. Gas lights and gilt, an age of steel and skill in engineering which stands today.

This, accompanied by shots of smoking chimneys, the Albert Memorial and the Forth railway bridge, is soon followed by a sequence of burlesque historical enactments of gas-lit Victorian night-life, including Sherlock Holmes and a Can-Can. We can discount any suspicion that this type of historical account was favoured by Rotha because, as he says in his auto-biography, 'It was a cod film and I was in no serious mood when I wrote and made it.'[41] Taylor's film, intended to demonstrate the progressive influence of the LCC, commences with a reel of more seriously intended studio reconstructions of Victorian beggars, thieves, drunkards, prostitutes and down-and-outs, poorhouses and sewers of Dickens's London, including a dramatisation of a Sarah Gamp-like midwife visiting a labouring woman. As a foil to the progress ushered in by the LCC, this does useful work for the film. In cinematic terms it looks forward, perhaps, to the London of David Lean's *Oliver Twist* (1948).

As the catastrophist view faded from public representation, as it had done previously from professional discourse, so a space was opened up for a more technical historiography in which technical change became dominant. And it is thus that Philip Armitage and Bill Mason's *The Cornish Engine* (1948) set a new standard in the documentary representation of the industrial period. The *Monthly Film Bulletin* opined that 'scientific historians will be greatly indebted to the Shell company for sponsoring this outstanding film on the evolution of a steam engine which was wholly British in its development'.[42] In the post-war period we may detect the influence of Arthur Elton, both industrial historian and first-generation documentarist, confidently applying the craft skills of half a career in film-making to subjects remote from the social concerns that characterised the early documentary films.[43]

Conclusions

Cannadine sees the 'desire to locate the historical origins of contemporary social conditions in the Industrial Revolution' as being strongest with the Fabian school.[44] This raises specifically the work that the catastrophic account did in the 1930s. *Today We Live* (1937), produced by Rotha for the National Council for Social Service (NCSS), is about the construction of community halls, which was the NCSS's business.[45] Here, again, the film's introduction has pastoral England as a thesis that finds its antithesis in industrialisation portrayed via its Victorian architectural and social consequences, and its synthesis in a scene showing a war memorial. Rotha is here 'playing tunes' on the historical account of *The Face of Britain*. It is clearly possible to make a film about village halls without framing it in terms of the nation's social history. But Rotha makes the connection: the rolling dialectic presents the Depression of the inter-war years as the product of industrialisation and war. So, in Rotha's view, the problems of the Depression were the logical outcomes of *laissez-faire* Victorian capitalism over-

turning the stable community life of pre-industrial rural Britain. That, the
film implies, is why communities have to be rebuilt – and why you need
the NCSS to support you in the building of community halls. In the post-
war period, Monck in similar fashion reprised the catastrophic interpretation as an introduction to *Coal Crisis*, one of the films in Arthur Rank's
This Modern Age social issues' newsreel, which he directed.[46] Here the
problems of the present, as in my two main examples, are products of the
past, and specifically of industrialisation with its economic and social consequences in the Victorian scene.

This chapter started with the press showing for *Health for the Nation*.
Had anyone been surprised to find the industrial revolution featuring so
strongly here and in so many films? If they had been, there is little historical evidence of the fact. The burden of industrialisation fell across the inter-
war years as a shadow. Industrialisation – elided with the Victorian period
– and its cost were the common sense of the period. We may look elsewhere
in culture for the persistence of the catastrophic account that has been the
main concern of this chapter. Think, perhaps of Orwell, complaining in
1937 that those who ran the industrial lodging-houses visited in *The Road
to Wigan Pier* are 'part . . . of what industrialism has done for us'.[47] That
expression, like those in the films, gestures vaguely to a past that elided the
Victorian era with the whole of the post-industrial revolution period (as it
was understood at the time). From such examples we may gain an insight
into the persistence of the catastrophic view – of how, precisely, 1930s'
people historicised their lived experience.

Notes

1 D. Cannadine, 'The present and the past in the English Industrial Revolution',
   Past and Present, 103 (1984), pp. 131–42.
2 A. Toynbee, *Lectures on the Industrial Revolution in England* (London:
   Rivingtons, 1884), p. 84.
3 D. Coleman, *Myth, History and the Industrial Revolution* (London:
   Hambledon Press, 1992), pp. 1–42.
4 Cannadine, 'The present and the past', pp. 133–4.
5 R. Colls and P. Dodd, 'Representing the nation', *Screen*, 26 (1985), pp. 22–3.
6 Cannadine, 'The present and the past', pp. 135–8.
7 J. Kenyon, *The History Men: The Historical Profession in England since the
   Renaissance* (London: Weidenfeld & Nicolson, 1983), pp. 238–9.
8 This film and the circumstances around its production are treated at greater
   length in T. M. Boon, 'Films and the contestation of public health in inter-war
   Britain', unpublished PhD thesis, University of London (1999), ch. 6.
9 *The Times*, 20 May 1939, p. 10.
10 See D. Matless, *Landscape and Englishness* (London: Reaktion, 1998).
11 The main sequence of records relating to the MoH's Public Relations Committee (PRC) can be found in the Public Record Office, London (hereafter, PRO),
   MH78/147.

12 PRC, 22 June 1938. Boon, 'Films and the contestation of public health', ch. 6; for documentary see P. Swann, *The British Documentary Film Movement* (Cambridge: Cambridge University Press, 1989).

13 PRC, 15 October 1936. Boon, 'Film and the contestation of public health', chs 5–6.

14 Arts Enquiry, *The Factual Film* (Oxford: Oxford University Press, 1947), p. 47.

15 E. Hudson to A. G. Highet, 7 September 1938, PRO, INF5/57. This is the main production file for the film.

16 R. Giesler, 'John Monck' (obituary), *Independent*, 7 July 1999, 'Review 2', p. 7; R. Low, *Documentary and Educational Films of the 1930s* (London: George Allen & Unwin, 1979), p. 153. Monck was also known as John Goldman.

17 J. Monck in interview with the author, 1993 (hereafter: 'Monck interview, 1993').

18 'Production report', A. Cavalcanti to Highet, 26 Sept 1939, PRO, INF5/57.

19 G. North to J. Goldman, 19 October 1938; S. Tallents to A. Cavalcanti, 16 November 1938; S. J. Fletcher to North, 2 January 1939; North to Fletcher, 5 January 1939; North to Fletcher, 1 April 1939; North to Fletcher, 20 January 1939; K. McGregor to Fletcher, 14 August 1939, PRO, INF5/57.

20 G. Newman, *Health and Social Evolution* (London: George Allen & Unwin, 1931), pp. 76–7.

21 See, for example, G. M'Gonigle and J. Kirby, *Poverty and Public Health* (London: Gollancz, 1936).

22 The standard work on Rotha is his autobiography *Documentary Diary* (London: Secker & Warburg, 1973). It can be usefully supplemented by the introductory sections to R. Kruger and D. Petrie (eds), *A Rotha Reader* (Exeter: University of Exeter Press, 1999).

23 T. Boon, ' "The shell of a prosperous age": history, landscape and the modern in Paul Rotha's *The Face of Britain* (1935)', in C. Lawrence and A. Mayer (eds), *Regenerating England: Science, Medicine and Culture in the Interwar Years* (Amsterdam: Rodopi, 2000).

24 Monck interview, 1993.

25 P. Rotha, *Documentary Film* (London: Faber, 1936), p. 33.

26 Rotha, *Documentary Diary*, p. 102. The Rotha archive is held in the Department of Special Collections, Charles E. Young Research Library, UCLA, Los Angeles (hereafter: Rotha Archive); cf. J. B. Priestley, *English Journey* (London: Heinemann, 1934); W. A. Eden, 'The English tradition in the countryside', *Architectural Review*, 77 (1935), pp. 85–94, 142–52, 193–202. Eden qualified at the Liverpool School of Architecture, and after the war became historic buildings surveyor to the LCC. He was author of *The Process of Architectural Tradition* (London: Macmillan & Co., 1942). He died in 1975. See *The Times*, 17 April 1975, p. 18.

27 Priestley, *English Journey*, p. 378; C. Waters, 'J. B. Priestley 1894–1984: Englishness and the politics of nostalgia', in S. Pedersen and P. Mandler (eds), *After the Victorians: Private Conscience and Public Duty in Modern Britain* (London: Routledge, 1994), pp. 209–26.

28 Eden, 'English tradition in the countryside', pp. 143–4.

29 Patrick Geddes, *Cities in Evolution* (London: Williams & Norgate, 1915); L. Mumford, *Technics and Civilisation* (London: G. Routledge & Sons, 1934).

30 Rotha, *Documentary Film*, p. 234.

31 Use of the term 'thesis' in Monck's plot synopsis for *Health for the Nation* con-
firms he had learned the lesson of his trip to Moscow: undated plot synopsis,
PRO, INF5/57.

32 D. A. Cook, *A History of Narrative Film* (New York: Norton, 1981), p. 170.

33 Rotha, *Documentary Film*, pp. 234–5.

34 *Ibid.*, pp. 117–18.

35 P. Dodd, 'Englishness and the national culture', in R. Colls and P. Dodd (eds),
Englishness: Politics and Culture 1880–1920 (London: Croom Helm, 1986),
p. 22.

36 See R. Colls, 'Englishness and the political culture', in Colls and Dodd (eds),
Englishness, pp. 29–61.

37 Rotha, *Documentary Film*, p. 255.

38 K. Robbins, '*History*, the Historical Association and the "national past"',
History, 66 (1981), p. 423.

39 B. Winston, *Fires Were Started* (London: BFI Publishing, 1999); see also, for
example: A. Aldgate and J. Richards, *Britain Can Take It: The British Cinema
in the Second World War* (Oxford: Blackwell, 1986); P. Taylor (ed.), *Britain and
the Cinema in the Second World War* (London: Macmillan, 1988).

40 'Nought shall make us rue/ If England to itself do rest but true.'

41 Rotha, *Documentary Diary*, pp. 225–8; Low, *Documentary and Educational
Films*, pp. 138–9.

42 Anon., 'The Cornish engine', *Monthly Film Bulletin*, 16 (1949), p. 165.

43 See: D. J. Wended, 'Sir Arthur Hallam Rice Elton', *Dictionary of National
Biography, 1971–1980* (Oxford: Oxford University Press, 1986), pp. 287–8.

44 Cannadine, 'Present and past', pp. 135–8.

45 Rotha, *Documentary Diary*, pp. 147–9.

46 Monck interview, 1993.

47 G. Orwell, *The Road to Wigan Pier* (London: Penguin, 1989), p. 14.

8

The revival of interest in Victorian decorative art and the Victoria and Albert Museum

Anthony Burton

This chapter examines the revival of interest, during the early twentieth century, in the decorative arts of the Victorian period.[1] Their restoration to favour runs fairly closely alongside the revival of interest in Victorian architecture (for it is inherent in the idea of 'decorative arts' that they are linked in any period, *via* interior design, with architecture) and has a rather more distant connection with the revival of interest in Victorian painting. In a study of how the Victorians have been re-evaluated since 1901 the decorative arts perhaps have slightly more resonance than painting and architecture, since they can easily be seen as embodying the domestic environment of the Victorian period, as offering a representation of 'how people lived'. Unsurprisingly, however, the revival turns out to have been chiefly led by people with an interest in antiques, style and taste, rather than in social history, and this account keeps turning to the Victoria and Albert Museum as a convenient representative of such interests.

The study of any historical topic can be affected by a time-lag, an interval in which the issue, after its occurrence as a contemporary event, is forgotten or despised until, for whatever reason, it becomes historically interesting and acceptable again. With a modicum of self-consciousness, most historians, taking a relativist view, can avoid or discount this problem. But art historians, especially historians of the decorative arts, made heavy weather of it in the early twentieth century. This was because *taste* was involved. They knew that taste is transient and fickle, but wanted to believe it to be absolute. And they still do. The best-known taste guru of our generation has written of 'the conflict between my *observation* that taste changes, that values are fugitive, and my personal *conviction* that there *are* certain forms, shapes and ideas which transcend time and have a special, permanent value'.[2] Historians of the decorative arts in the early twentieth century found themselves unable to like Victorian art. They could not accept that a Victorian whatnot was merely unfashionable; they felt that it was an immoral monstrosity. Aware, however, that after a time it began to seem less monstrous, they tried to explain this change, not as a matter of fashion, but as a consequence of profound natural laws. One writer discussed the problem with James Laver of the Victoria and Albert Museum:

> He replied with what I now call Laver's Law. 'I have spent a good part of my life,' he said, 'in trying to plot the "gap in appreciation" – that is the time which must elapse before a discarded style comes into favour again. It seems to be a law of our own minds that we find the art forms of our fathers hideous, the art forms of our grandfathers amusing and those of our great-grandfathers attractive and even beautiful.'[3]

This idea of the three-generation time-lapse crops up all over the place. Writing in 1933, Fiske Kimball, an American museum curator whose speciality was the history of taste, had enough objectivity to see it as a 'commonplace', even while accepting it:

> It is a commonplace of the history of culture that each generation detests the art of its fathers, hesitantly tolerates that of its grandfathers, and takes to its bosom that of its great-grandfathers – which henceforth becomes part of the accepted canon of artistic propriety.[4]

Even Roger Fry had experienced the gap of appreciation. Dilating on the theme 'Distance lends enchantment to the view', he remarked that

> anyone who has lived long enough will have noticed that a certain distance lends a violent disgust to the view – that as we recede there comes a period of oblivion and total unconsciousness, to be succeeded when consciousness returns by the ecstasy, the nature of which we are considering.

He was considering, in a prescient article of 1919, the ecstasy that the Victorian revival might bring. He saw a few people 'hard at work collecting Victorian paper-weights, stuffed humming-birds and wax flowers', and concluded that 'we have just arrived at the point where our ignorance of life in the Victorian period is such as to allow the incurable optimism of memory to build a . . . little earthly paradise' out of its relics. He was astute enough to see that 'none of these feelings have anything to do with our aesthetic reactions to . . . objects as works of art', but he did feel that the passage of time involved a 'process of selection and elimination' that was necessary to attain historical understanding.[5] Another writer who deployed the idea, as he welcomed the displacement of 'chromium plated chairs and mathematical vases' by 'pianos tied with bunches of ribbon, and minutely carved sideboards', was Malcolm Muggeridge: 'The Victorian Age, so confident of its own greatness and solidity, had been regarded successively with horror, sniggering amusement, and now with romantic esteem.'[6]

Of course, this idea that appreciation required a time-lag to accommodate the three-stage process was nonsense, as John Summerson detected in a 1931 article acknowledging that the early Victorians had 'definitely "arrived"'. He pointed out:

For centuries people have been making new discoveries of old styles. . . . There is one curious point about this prolonged series of rediscoveries, namely, the gradually decreasing interval of time separating the period discovered from the period of discovery. More than a millennium separated the Renaissance from Rome. The Gothic revivalists looked back across half that period . . . while to-day we make museum specimens of things only eighty or a hundred years older than ourselves . . . It will not be long before we fall in love with a period only just anterior to our own, and perhaps in time we shall even begin to document, catalogue, criticise and admire the works of our own contemporaries.[7]

That time has now come. We are no longer inhibited by the time-lag of taste; yesterday's *chic* immediately becomes today's retro-*chic*. But a study of the Victorian revival in the early twentieth century must take account of the agonies which re-appraisal then wrought on at least some of those artistic people who participated in it, and who struggled with what they thought to be 'natural laws' of taste.

A related point is that revival of interest does not necessarily entail revival of esteem. The Victorian revival was not fostered only by those who had won through to the point where they were able to accept Victorian art with joy. Some of the revivalists took up Victorian art just because it was naughty, while a good deal of the motive power of the revival, as I show, was fuelled by *disapproval* of Victorian art rather than *liking* for it.

I

By the early twentieth century Victorian art had lapsed into a trough of disgust and detestation. The attitudes of the Victoria and Albert Museum conveniently illustrate this. In the nineteenth century (when, between 1857 and 1899, the museum was known as the South Kensington Museum), it did acquire some examples of the decorative art of its own period. This was really quite surprising, for it was not then usual for art museums, such as they were, to acquire contemporary material. The South Kensington Museum, however, had a particular reason for doing so. It did not acquire contemporary decorative art, as a museum might today, because it wished to document contemporary culture in a representative way. The museum's founding purpose was not just to record and preserve, but actively to change and improve Victorian decorative art objects. It was because it disapproved of the design of most contemporary British furnishings and domestic equipment that it acquired, alongside some bad pieces taken in as warnings, many good pieces deemed to manifest achieved improvement, pieces that could be regarded as salutary examples for the present and the future.

Early on, it was an article of faith for the museum that it succeeded in influencing British design. Most of the British exhibits in the Great Exhibition of 1851 had been criticised for being in lamentably bad taste, and when the museum opened in 1852 (as the Museum of Ornamental Art, at Marlborough House) it tried to show artisans, manufacturers and the public at large how it could do better. The International Exhibition in London in 1862 was thought to supply evidence of a striking improvement in the aesthetic quality of British products, and the museum, now re-launched on its present site in South Kensington, readily took credit.[8]

Yet already the museum had turned in a new direction, away from its first mission to change taste in contemporary products, to look to the past rather than the present, as museums are, perhaps inevitably, prone to do. The South Kensington Museum had collected both exemplary contemporary decorative art and decorative art from the past that was also exemplary and could be used by contemporary designers as models and precedents. It was not long before the museum's curators began to find the art of the past attractive for its own sake, and to prefer it to the art of the present.

A pivotal event occurred in the museum in 1880, when 'all modern examples of Art manufacture acquired since 1851' were banished from South Kensington to the museum's branch at Bethnal Green. The museum tried to argue that they would be more useful there, but the real agenda was that the new art, such as 'Barbedienne's bronzes and Minton's china', did not seem to fit well with the old art, 'the venerable works of Donatello, Orazio Fontana, or Bernard Palissy'. 'To the connoisseur and student of ancient art the association [of new and old] was . . . painfully repugnant'.[9] From 1880 onwards there was no Victorian art on show in the galleries at South Kensington.

When Cecil Smith became director, in 1909, he found that 'there was a rule that nothing in the galleries should be under 50 years old'.[10] The 'gap of appreciation' was thus imposed as a policy. And when the museum was extended into its new building, in 1909, and, under Smith's supervision, the new galleries were filled, there was no question of letting Victorian art back in. An earlier planning committee had made the pronouncement: 'early Victorian furniture, which no one now would desire to study except in order to avoid, may be consigned to cellars, if it must be retained at all'.[11] Smith accepted this. He did try to revive South Kensington's mission to set standards in contemporary design, but, while applying the doctrine of 1851 to the art of the 1920s, he saw no inconsistency in rejecting all the art of 1851 as a hopeless failure. In a speech in 1921 he said to a complaisant audience that 'in the museum of which he was director there was a large quantity of horrors – (laughter) – which were purchased at the 1851 Great Exhibition. They were a warning'.[12] It was not until 1952 that Victorian art was rehabilitated in the museum. The museum's view of Victorian art was widely shared by the public. As this discussion follows the revival of interest in the Victorian decorative arts, it can be seen how this was reflected at various moments in attitudes at the Victoria and Albert.

II

A turning point in the estimation of the Victorian period was Lytton Strachey's *Eminent Victorians* (1918). It was Strachey's purpose not to praise the Victorians but to mock them, and it is in a similarly disrespectful mood that the revival of interest in Victorian art began. The setting was not the Victoria and Albert Museum, but Oxford University, and the instigator seems to have been Harold Acton, who went up in 1922. Acton, brought up in exotic luxury in a villa in Florence, had already at Eton adopted the pose of an aesthete and wanted to mark himself off from the hearty Philistines who then dominated Oxford. He might have recreated himself as a Wildean aesthete, harking back to the 1890s, but he felt that the *fin de siècle*, though recently fashionable, had lost its charm, and he decided that 'the despised Early Victorians seemed to offer one solution' to his search for an image. He was not absolutely the first to rediscover the Victorians,[13] but he was noticeable.

He was accommodated in his college, Christ Church, not in the 'coveted rooms in Tom Quad, Peckwater or Canterbury', but in the 'grimly Victorian Gothic' Meadow Building, erected to the designs of the Ruskinian architects Thomas Deane & Son in 1863. From this he took his inspiration. 'I painted my rooms lemon yellow and filled them with Victorian bric-à-brac – artificial flowers and fruit and lumps of glass, a collection of paperweights imprisoning bubbles that never broke and flowers that never faded.'[14] Acton was soon imitated – both in life and in literature. Around him gathered acolytes such as Robert Byron, Brian Howard, Osbert Lancaster and Henry Yorke. In literature his rooms were memorialised as those occupied by Sebastian Flyte in Evelyn Waugh's *Brideshead Revisited* (1945), rooms which contained 'a strange jumble of objects – a harmonium in a gothic case, an elephant's foot waste-paper basket, a dome of wax fruit, two disproportionately large Sèvres vases'.[15]

While the Oxford aesthetes revelled at the time in cutting a Victorian dash, some had pangs of regret later. Henry Yorke prefaced a reminiscence with the doubting phrase 'whether we were at fault or not' when recalling that

> we collected Victorian objects, glass paperweights with coloured posies cast in them, little eternalized baskets of flowers which nothing could break, sometimes they were in the stoppers of bottles, and large piles of waxed fruits under high glass domes rarer because they were the more fragile. A number of us bought spotted dogs in china from Staffordshire, one or two had figures of the Prince Consort in the same material.

Looking back from after the Second World War, Yorke guiltily pleaded that 'it must not be assumed that because a number of us bought Victorian relics we were a weakhearted crew, nor that, though being physically weak, we compensated by exhibitionism'.[16]

But exhibitionism does seem to have been among their prime motives, along with a desire to *épater le bourgeois*. When Acton, Robert Byron and Evelyn Waugh planned an exhibition on the theme of '1840', and it was prohibited by the university authorities, that was just the effect of naughtiness they aimed to achieve. Victorianism was not the only option for the

Bright Young Things of the 1920s–1930s, as is suggested by a remark
in Waugh's novel *Vile Bodies* (1930): 'What a lot of parties', cries Adam
Fenwick Symes. 'Masked parties, Savage parties, Victorian parties, Greek
parties, Wild West parties, Russian parties, Circus parties, parties where
one had to dress as somebody else, almost naked parties in St. John's Wood
. . .'.[17] If one wanted to assume fancy dress, there were many choices, but
Victorian pastiche was certainly one of them.

After Acton's group of aesthetes had left Oxford, the Victorian craze there
simmered down somewhat. In 1930, Waugh, addressing a wider audience,
the readers of *Harper's Bazaar*, claimed (in a laborious metaphor) that it
was all over:

> The early Victorian tide in which, before luncheon, we paddled and splashed
> so gaily has washed up its wreckage and retreated, and all those glittering
> bits of shell and seaweed – the coloured glass paper weights, wax fruit, Rex
> Whistler decorations, paper lace Valentines, which we collected – have by late
> afternoon dried out very drab and disappointing.[18]

But here, surely, Waugh was writing just for effect, because elsewhere he
did as much as anyone to keep Victorianism on the boil, notably in his evocation of the fictional Victorian house 'Hetton Abbey' in *A Handful of Dust*
(1934). A specially drawn frontispiece depicts Hetton Abbey, but it is far
more powerfully characterised in Waugh's description. The house is about
to be redecorated by a modern designer, determined to install a lot of chrome
plating. Its threatened Victorian charms seem all the more precious:

> The general aspect and atmosphere of the place; the line of its battlements
> against the sky; the central clock tower where quarterly chimes disturbed all
> but the heaviest of sleepers; the ecclesiastical gloom of the great hall, its ceiling
> groined and painted in diapers of red and gold, supported on shafts of
> polished granite with vine-wreathed capitals, half-lit by day through lancet
> windows of armorial glass . . . the dining hall with its hammer-beam roof and
> pitch-pine minstrels' gallery; the bedrooms with their brass bedsteads, each
> with a frieze of Gothic text . . . all these things with which he had grown up
> were a source of constant delight and exultation to [the owner]; things of
> tender memory and proud possession.[19]

While the owner treasured his house primarily because it was his, he
went on to reflect that others might also come to esteem it, that 'opinion
would reinstate Hetton in its proper place. Already it was referred to as
"amusing", and a very civil young man had asked permission to photograph it for an architectural review'.

This last reference may well be (as will be clear shortly) a coded allusion
to John Betjeman. He, too, had been in the group of Victorian enthusiasts
at Oxford, but the problem with him was that he wrapped himself in so
many protective layers of irony and self-parody that it was difficult to be
sure what he really thought. Maurice Bowra remembered Betjeman in the
context of Oxford in the 1920s, when 'Victorianism was much in fashion,

and the more prescient aesthetes collected wax flowers, antimacassars, and Doulton images of the great queen and her consort'. But he observed that 'John went much farther in the range and depth of his knowledge' than did his fellow-*poseurs*: 'His more serious friends sometimes asked what it all meant. Was it a prolonged joke? Or did John really like the Gothic Revival, which in those days was still viewed with distaste?'[20] The answer eventually became clear: Betjeman *was* serious. In the 1920s, however, he did not admit it.

Another serious student of Victorian art and architecture was Kenneth Clark. He was up at Oxford at the right moment, but he did not play around with wax flowers and antimacassars. He wrote an academic and very influential book, *The Gothic Revival*, published in 1928. In a revised edition of 1949, Clark testified to the influence on him of Betjeman, describing him as 'one of the few original minds of our generation'.[21] But he did not say that in 1928, presumably because the aesthetes seemed still altogether frivolous.

It does not seem possible to find a direct link between the Oxford aesthetes and the Victoria and Albert Museum, though the museum did recruit a number of young men from Oxford in the 1920s. This was, in itself, an interesting sign of changed times, for during the nineteenth century the museum had kept its distance from the old universities, mindful that it had originally sprung from Prince Albert's scheme to found an alternative – industrial – university.[22] Even though Oxford graduates did come to join the museum, they seem not to have been Victorian revivalists. But, in due course, the cultural élite of London took up the Victorian revival, in a somewhat more earnest spirit than had the aesthetes. In the month of June 1931 a 'Victorian Exhibition' was staged, in aid of St Bartholomew's Hospital. This brought together much more than a few paper-weights and antimacassars. A whole house was taken over, 23A Bruton Street, in Mayfair, and each of its rooms was refurnished in the mid-Victorian manner so as to present a remarkably complete evocation of Victorian domestic life.[23] This project seems to have had no connection with the Oxford aesthetes. Its organising committee was chaired by Cecil Smith, the now-retired Victoria and Albert director, who must have changed his views about the horrors perpetrated at the 1851 Exhibition. His successor at the Victoria and Albert, Eric Maclagan, was a real art-historian, and a medievalist, but he attended the Victorian Exhibition's opening reception, and so did Trenchard Cox, who was to become director of the Victoria and Albert in 1956.[24] Cox was a lender to the exhibition, as was the Victoria and Albert itself. So this expression of interest in the Victorian period came with the stamp of approval of the Victoria and Albert and of the artistic establishment.

A review commented that the furniture, displayed in rooms that had been specially redecorated, 'radiated durability', but conjectured that 'perhaps those objects with the most permanent attraction for future generations will be the little trifles that our grandmothers themselves considered of no particular moment'. It goes on to describe silhouettes, Valentines, card-cases (of ivory, mother-of-pearl, papier-mâché, etc), daguerrotypes, knitted purses, satin shoes, buttoned boots, bell pulls, sand pictures, 'lace bobbins, and the rest of it'.[25] Inspired by the Bruton Street exhibition, the Mansard Gallery, a commercial venture at Heals furniture store in Tottenham Court Road, also mounted an exhibition of Victorian artefacts. The emphasis of both exhibitions was on bric-à-brac, but John Summerson, reviewing these exhibitions from the point of view of 'the orthodox art-historian' (and looking especially for 'serious academicism on the one hand, the latest flower of eighteenth century humanism, and, on the other hand, intensely earnest medievalism, striving to re-create in a mechanical age a sense of saintly wonder'), was able to find much to praise.[26]

The Victoria and Albert was again associated with the Victorian revival when, on 29 October 1931, it hosted a lecture on Victorian decorative art. This, entitled 'The age of euphemism', was given by the architect Harry Goodhart-Rendel, who was one of the two or three people who had done the hard work on the 1931 Victorian Exhibition. Goodhart-Rendel was a picturesque character – influential as a soldier and as a musician, as well as practising as an architect. But he was not an aesthetic *poseur*. He inherited through his upbringing a knowledge of and interest in Victorian art and architecture, and, quite impervious to fashion, expressed his pleasure in it without fear or deference to current taste. Just as the 1931 exhibition was an unabashed celebration of Victorian domestic art, so was his lecture. It was printed in *The Architect* on 6 November 1931. This journal was primarily a trade paper for practical architects, so Goodhart-Rendel's article, illustrated with wood-engravings of ornate Victorian artefacts, sits rather oddly among the reviews of neo-Georgian office blocks and *moderne* houses.

Goodhart-Rendel proceeded to give the revival another thrust forward when he delivered a series of Slade Lectures on Victorian architecture at Oxford in 1934. Nikolaus Pevsner pin-points this as a significant event, even though the lectures did not get into print until 1953.[27] The exhibitions and the lecture of 1931, and the lectures of 1934, can be seen as relatively straightforward expressions of interest in Victorian art, untainted by the mockery and attitudinising of the aesthetes.

III

A different attitude to Victorian art and design was advanced in the *Architectural Review* (*AR*). That journal, which, like *The Architect*, was aimed primarily at architects but had somewhat loftier pretensions, became during the 1930s the 'mouthpiece in England of the Modern Movement',[28] under its eccentric proprietor H. de C. Hastings and its principal writer and (from 1933) editor J. M. Richards. It is interesting that the *AR*, in promoting modern design, also drew attention to Victorian design, as a foil to it. The contrast between the two was an element in a process of persuasion. In praising the clean, geometrical lines, the functional and technical clarity, of modern movement design, the *AR* was by implication condemning the prevailing and popular neo-Georgianism. This might have led to difficulties, since most of the *AR*'s subscribers and advertisers were practitioners of neo-Georgianism. It was useful to have some other whipping-boy on which to direct hostile feeling, and high Victorian design played that role.

A significant instance occurred in the December 1935 issue. Modernism was gradually gaining approval in the 1930s, and it was hoped that the exhibition of 'British Art and Industry' at Burlington House in 1935 would help it forward. That exhibition, however, turned out 'a grotesque failure, which sent shudders down the spines of the supporters of the British modern movement'.[29] J. M. Richards tried to rally the troops with an article in the *AR*, 'Towards a rational aesthetic', which examined 'the Characteristics of Modern Design with Particular Reference to the Influence of the Machine'. The article was, predictably and appropriately, illustrated with images of electricity pylons, aeroplanes, vacuum cleaners, and so forth, but these were juxtaposed with images of despised Victorian products, and the article was preceded by a full-page 'pictorial allegory, based on products of "Art manufacture" of two generations ago'. Starting by poking fun at Victorian architecture and design, the *AR* was eventually won round by it, to the extent that in 1951 Nikolaus Pevsner, who had been one of its most committed modernists, hailed the magazine as 'altogether the principal medium from which Victorian scholarship and Victorian appreciation can be gathered'.[30]

The conversion of the *Architectural Review* was due in part to the presence on its staff, from October 1930 to January 1935, of John Betjeman. Occupying an office decorated with William Morris wallpaper, and still making a spoof out of his life and opinions, Betjeman was not as yet a wholly committed Victorian enthusiast. The uncertainty of his views comes out in his first architectural book, facetiously and ambiguously entitled *Ghastly Good Taste* (1933). The book had a historical chart demonstrating 'The growth of "good taste"' which privileged the modernist version of architectural history, showing in bold type 'the thin stream of life and vigorous influence for the good in English architecture'.[31] Yet the book also had Peter Fleetwood-Hesketh's fold-out panoramic illustration of architectural stylistic development, which seemed to convey a more relaxed and inclusive view. Anyway, Betjeman, who continued to write for it after he had left the staff, slipped into the *AR* quite a lot of coverage of Victorian design, and gradually came out as a Victorian enthusiast, deploying his considerable charm, not in mockery and parody, but in affectionate enjoyment of Victorian design. Timothy Mowl[32] detects the influence of John Piper in Betjeman's change of attitude, and proposes an article, written by Betjeman and illustrated by Piper, in the *AR* of November 1939, as the crucial moment when ideology was forgotten and sympathy took over. The title of the article was 'The seeing eye or how to like everything'.

The principal advocate of modernism among the writers at the *AR* was, from 1936, Nikolaus Pevsner, the German *emigré* scholar, who was only just beginning to establish the immense authority that he eventually attained. He and Betjeman have been seen as adversaries in the 'stylistic cold wars' of twentieth-century Britain.[33] From a post-modern perspective, Pevsner is now often regarded almost as a religious fanatic in his advocacy of modern movement architecture.[34] He believed that the modern style was not just one style among others, but the ideal, the essential, style that would eternally prevail and to which the world had inexorably been tending – an odd view for a historian. But just because he had been trained as a historian, Pevsner needed to show that the modern style had developed historically, that it had somehow arisen out of what had gone before in the nineteenth century. His book *Pioneers of the Modern Movement*, published in 1936, ingeniously identified a stream of nonconformist design in the nineteenth century – running from Paxton's Crystal Palace, through William Morris and certain arts and crafts designers – which he saw as leading to Gropius and the Bauhaus.

The paradoxical result of the Pevsnerian version of architectural history was that, as Pevsner propagandised for the modern movement, he simultaneously aroused interest in and rehabilitated considerable swathes of Victorian design. Much of Victorian design and architecture met with his disapproval, but even this, by virtue of what he did approve of, found its place in the new canonical history. As we have seen, by 1951 Pevsner could praise the *Architectural Review* for its coverage of Victorian design. And soon, after the foundation of the Victorian Society, he would become the Society's second chairman, in 1963. Betjeman may well have expected such an honour;[35] it was one of life's ironies that it went to Pevsner.

IV

History has come to depend on dates, and dates sometimes exercise a curious influence on history. The Victorian revival was helped along by centenaries. An important one came in 1934, a century after the birth of William Morris, when the Victoria and Albert put on a Centenary Exhibition. To some extent, Morris's stock had slumped, along with that of his century. One reviewer of the exhibition commented that 'Morris is not merely rather neglected by the present generation, but into the bargain persistently misinterpreted'.[36] That neglect was confronted by a member of the Victoria and Albert staff who tried to account for a 'reaction against Morris':

> Fifty years ago intelligent people may have adored such tapestries, such carpets, such furniture, but no taste, apparently, is ever so abysmally bad as that of our fathers. Morris has been treated, lately, to a good deal of that condescending

huff-snuffery so characteristic of much modern criticism. There has been some talk of 'a dull and disastrous interlude' in the history of our art, and we, who have lighted our lamps with fires brought from France and the Bantu hinterland, are invited, presumably, to pity Morris and his men, foundered in the outer and Gothic gloom.[37]

Morris was, however, big enough to surmount adverse trends. Wherein his bigness lay could be disputed: this was where misinterpretation could come in. The Introduction to the Victoria and Albert's *Catalogue of an Exhibition in Celebration of the Centenary of William Morris*, by Morris's biographer J. W. Mackail, stressed that it was Morris's artistic versatility that was being celebrated.[38] Mackail did slip in the word 'Socialist', but it was noticed that in the speech with which the exhibition was opened the Conservative politician Stanley Baldwin contrived to say nothing of Morris's politics. This infuriated some of his supporters, and they denounced the exhibition as 'an orgy of "canonisation"'.[39] Many of those who regarded Morris as a sage and a prophet, however, had little time for him as an artist. 'There was more to Morris than cretonnes and wallpapers.'[40] 'Hang the wallpapers! . . . charming and important as they are, they have distracted attention from the fact that Morris was above all a prophet; a sage.'[41] So far as the Victorian revival was concerned, Morris was a special case, transcending fashion.

Another very important centenary was to come in 1951. Before discussing it, however, it might be worth observing that, in the Victoria and Albert's rather sparse exhibition programme in the 1930s, a few Victorian subjects did feature, and seem to have been successful. An exhibition of Valentines in 1929 apparently 'found immediate favour with the public', while an exhibition of children's books, past and present, mounted with the National Book Council in 1932, was said to be 'one of the most widely popular temporary exhibitions that South Kensington has seen'.[42] Victorian pantomimes were featured in 1933. In 1936 there was an exhibition marking the death of the late Victorian sculptor Sir Alfred Gilbert: perhaps it was because his reputation was still green – 'That the late Sir Alfred Gilbert, R. A., was a genius, none can deny'[43] – that he was able to withstand the depredations of fashion.

More significant, perhaps, was the 1939 exhibition of 'Early Photography'. This was another centenary exhibition, mounted to recall that 'on the 25th of January a hundred years ago Michael Faraday announced to the public Fox Talbot's invention at the Royal Institution'.[44] There were further celebrations of that centenary, involving the Royal Photographic Society, the Royal Society of Arts and the Science Museum,[45] but the Victoria and Albert seems to have got in first. Photography was an interesting case, for it was much more easily assimilated than antimacassars and wax fruit. As one critic said, 'we have come to look on photography so largely as an almost post-Victorian development, as to forget that it is now enjoying its centenary and are ready to be amazed at the extraordinary excellence of much of the earliest work'.[46]

The Victoria and Albert's exhibition was put together by a young assistant keeper in the library, Charles Gibbs-Smith. The Victoria and Albert's library, which until 1909 combined the function of library and print department, had acquired in the nineteenth century a large corpus of photographs, mostly as documentary aids to the study of art history. It had been Gibbs-Smith's job to re-organise the collection,[47] and, because it dated back to the earliest experimental days of photography in the mid-Victorian period, he had found much that he recognised as having great historical importance.

Inevitably, the Victorian revival was stalled during hostilities, but after the war it was again Gibbs-Smith, by then head of the Victoria and Albert's education and public relations department, who put together another centenary exhibition which helped in the rehabilitation of the Victorians. As a pendant to the Festival of Britain in 1951, Gibbs-Smith supplied a show commemorating the Great Exhibition of 1851. He approached the subject primarily as a historian, but the exhibition did provide an occasion for trawling through the museum's collections, and digging out from the cellars many of the 'horrors' that had been confined there for so many years, but which now began to look interesting again. Gibbs-Smith's accompanying publication, *The Great Exhibition of 1851: A Commemorative Album* (1950), wasted no space on agonising over taste.

Alongside Gibbs-Smith's research, in which an element of piety was involved, another more rigorous and widely ranging research programme was going on in the museum. This was led by Peter Floud, keeper of the museum's circulation department, which was devoted to the creation and circulation of travelling exhibitions. His department was the only part of the museum permitted to engage with contemporary art. In addition to that, Floud wanted his department to conquer an academic field which could stand comparison with the fields which his colleagues already studied. He chose the Victorian period, which was available to be annexed as none of the other departments was interested in art after 1830. Floud inspired a small team of assistants: Elizabeth Aslin, Shirley Bury, John Lowry, Barbara Morris and Hugh Wakefield. Under Floud, these curators mounted an exhibition of 'Victorian and Edwardian Decorative Arts' in 1952. Ostensibly intended to commemorate the founding of the museum in 1852, this was turned by Floud into an opportunity to demonstrate that his department could do heavy scholarship just as effectively as any other of the Victoria and Albert departments. This exhibition was emphatically not about wax fruit and antimacassars.

Floud disparaged earlier Victorian exhibitions because they had 'consisted almost entirely of anonymous and undated material collected primarily for its picturesque or anecdotic or nostalgic appeal'. This exhibition 'only includes objects that can be authoritatively attributed to the leading Victorian and Edwardian designers'.[48] Accordingly its catalogue looked as nearly as possible like a conventional catalogue of old masters' paintings,

with biographies of the artists, bibliographical references, exhibition citations and detailed descriptions of objects.

The exhibition succeeded in raising Victorian decorative art studies to
a new level, not only by supplying scholarly apparatus, but by opening
people's eyes. The young Rayner Banham extolled the exhibition's

> eye-popping, hair-raising richness, for though the Victoria and Albert have
> sliced their history thin, they have sliced it for plums – known works by known
> masters . . . Objects rub shoulders with proper period intimacy, colour against
> colour, texture against texture, and pattern against ripe, bold, florid pattern –
> everywhere pattern. Textiles and hangings twenty feet up the walls; the floor
> nicely cluttered with furniture, massive or flimsy, staid or eccentric. But not,
> *repeat* not, pretty or whimsical or amusing.

This exhibition, said Banham, 'could be the death of the cult of fashionable Victoriana', for it reveals the 'imposing seriousness' of 'the work of
originals and innovators out of step with mass-produced taste'. 'There
begins to appear' in Victorian decorative arts, he says, 'an orderly and
consistent development'. 'The period straightens up and reveals a fairer, if
unfamiliar face.'[49]

Peter Floud died young in 1960, but his team, and others in the Victoria
and Albert, persevered with Victorian studies.[50] Some of them were founder-
members of the Victorian Society, created in 1958. Victorian decorative art
was so far rehabilitated by the 1960s that the Victoria and Albert had no
inhibitions about mounting a centenary exhibition of the 1862 International
Exhibition in London. This was not universally applauded: one critic held
to the view that Victorian art was 'a bypath in the history of art which led
directly to a wasteland of sterility'.[51] But taste was changing. The Victoria
and Albert decided that Victorian art was then sufficiently respectable for
it to deserve a permanent gallery, of which the first part opened in October
1964. It is interesting that a member of the museum's staff alluded to 'the
Victorian rooms that are now becoming a regular feature of our local
museums', and stressed that it was not the Victoria and Albert's aim to rival
them in evoking 'a "typical" Victorian ambience'. The Victoria and Albert,
as usual, claimed the aesthetic high ground, and wished 'to chart a path
through the conscious art movements of the period, concentrating on
designers and in general eschewing the typical in favour of the original and
significant'.[52]

V

This brief survey of the important moments, and the mixed motives, of the
Victorian revival has concentrated on England, it may therefore be as well
to conclude by looking farther afield. Americans were early birds in savour-
ing Victorian decorative arts, starting with bric-à-brac: 'Those of us who
enjoy the thrill of antiquing well know that the antique shops are begin-

ning to exhibit many Victorian oddities', wrote a collector in 1924.[53]
Serious interest in Victorian art developed quickly because, compared with
Europe, America had little decorative art of earlier periods. 'In a new
country the antique is a matter of mere relativity', commented a collector
as he nerved himself – 'much as I have disliked the prospect' – to write
about Victorian furniture.[54] Another wrote: 'The collector whose means are
limited finds it virtually impossible to satisfy his quantitative needs from
the field of eighteenth-century arts and crafts. He is accordingly almost
forced into investigating a larger and later domain.'[55] Academic approval
came in 1933 with an exhibition of Victorian art at the Pennsylvania
Museum of Art, Philadelphia, though a critic could not forbear from
observing that the Victorian age 'has been execrated and ridiculed as have
few artistic periods in history'.[56] An exhibition of Victorian and Edwardian
costume at the Metropolitan Museum, New York, in 1939 provoked the
more encouraging comment:

> For over a decade now there has been an increasing tendency to appreciate
> and, as a result, to preserve the furniture and other decorative arts of the
> Victorian era. This has, indeed, progressed to a point where the creation of
> pseudo-Victorian interiors is on occasion to be encountered. The revival has,
> therefore, arrived at a fashionable stage.[57]

In Europe, the pace was slower. There, nineteenth-century art could not
be associated with a revered monarch, and conveniently classified under
a term like 'Victorian' – which perhaps weakened its potential popular
appeal. In art-historical terms it was usually categorised as 'historicism' –
Historismus in German.[58] Under that title there appeared a series of important catalogues of exhibitions or museum collections in the 1960s and
1970s. These emanated from decorative art museums that had been created
in the later nineteenth century in emulation of the Victoria and Albert.
Again following the Victoria and Albert's example of 1952, they looked
back at the art of the period when they were founded. Publications from
Vienna (1964), Berlin (1973), Prague (1975), Dresden (1976) and Hamburg
(1977) were influential in rehabilitating nineteenth-century decorative art.[59]
    In explanations of historical causation, there are rarely any easy answers;
and it would certainly be rash to attribute to a museum any particular effect
on the world at large. But it does seem possible that the Victorian revival
and the Victoria and Albert Museum were connected more closely than just
by their common name.

Notes

1 For earlier accounts, see the following: Jules Lubbock, 'Victorian revival', *Architectural Review*, 163 (1978), pp. 161–7; Peter York, 'Victorian values', in his
  Modern Times (London: Futura, 1985), pp. 52–61; Clive Wainwright, 'Tell me
  what you like, and I'll tell you what you are', in *Truth, Beauty and Design:*

Victorian, Edwardian and Later Decorative Art, Exhibition Catalogue (London: Fischer Fine Art, 1986), pp. 7–14; Jonathan Penny, 'Towards the Victorian Society', *Victorian Society Annual* (1994), pp. 23–7.

2 Stephen Bayley, *Taste: The Secret Meaning of Things* (London: Faber, 1991), p. xv; for his take on the Victorian revival, see pp. 130–5.

3 Robert Wraight, *The Art Game* (London: Leslie Frewin, 1965), p. 42.

4 Fiske Kimball, 'Victorian art and Victorian taste', *Antiques* (March 1933), p. 103.

5 Roger Fry, 'The ottoman and the whatnot', *Athenaeum*, 27 June 1919, p. 529.

6 Malcolm Muggeridge, *The Thirties: 1930–1940 in Great Britain* (London: Collins Fontana, 1972 [1940]), p. 175.

7 J. N. Summerson, 'The art of the Victorians', *Country Life*, 20 June 1931, p. 791.

8 See Anthony Burton, *Vision and Accident: The Story of the Victoria and Albert Museum* (London: Victoria and Albert Publications, 1999), pp. 108–10.

9 *The Times*, 20 December 1880, Victoria and Albert Museum, National Art Library, Archive of Art and Design, Kensington, Press cuttings, September 1880–January 1882, p. 75.

10 *Westminster Gazette*, 11 September 1924, Victoria and Albert Museum, Press cuttings, October–December 1924, p. 57.

11 John Physick, *The Victoria and Albert Museum: The History of its Building* (London: Victoria and Albert Museum, 1982), p. 208.

12 *Cambridge Independent Press*, 14 October 1921, Victoria and Albert Museum, Press cuttings, 1 March 1921–6 March 1922, p. 104.

13 See Lubbock, 'Victorian revival', pp. 161–3.

14 Harold Acton, *Memoirs of an Aesthete* (London: Methuen, 1948), p. 118.

15 Evelyn Waugh, *Brideshead Revisited* (London: Penguin, 2000 [1945]), p. 33.

16 Henry Green (Yorke), *Pack My Bag: A Self-Portrait* (London: Hogarth Press, 1979), pp. 210, 217.

17 Evelyn Waugh, *Vile Bodies* (London: Penguin, 1996 [1930]), p. 104

18 Evelyn Waugh, *A Little Order: A Selection from His Journalism*, ed. Donat Gallagher (London: Eyre Methuen, 1977), pp. 19–20.

19 Evelyn Waugh, *A Handful of Dust* (London: Chapman & Hall, 1948), p. 9.

20 C. M. Bowra, *Memories 1898–1939* (London: Weidenfeld & Nicolson, 1966), pp. 166–7.

21 Kenneth Clarke, *The Gothic Revival: An Essay in the History of Taste* (New York: Scribners, 1949 [1928]), p. viii.

22 See Anthony Burton, 'Art and science applied to industry: Prince Albert's plans for South Kensington', in Franz Bosbach and Frank Büttner (eds), *Künstlerische Beziehungen zwischen England und Deutschland in der viktorianischen Epoche* (*Art in Britain and Germany in the Age of Queen Victoria and Prince Albert*), Prince Albert Studies (Munich: Saur, 1998), vol. 15, pp. 168–86.

23 See *Catalogue of the Victorian Exhibition in Aid of St. Bartholomew's Hospital, 1st June to 1st July, 1931, 23A Bruton Street, London, W1* (London: Office of the Exhibition, 1931).

24 *The Times*, 24 June 1931, Victoria and Albert Museum, Press cuttings, January–August 1931, p. 220.

25 B.B., 'Ghosts at the Victorian exhibition', *Connoisseur*, 88 (1931), pp. 58–9.

26 Summerson, 'The art of the Victorians', p. 792.

27 Nikolaus Pevsner, 'Foreword' to John Steegman, *Victorian Taste: A Study of the Arts and Architecture from 1830 to 1870* [first published in 1950 as *Consort of Taste*] (London: Nelson's University Paperbacks, 1970), pp. 5–6; H. S. Goodhart-Rendel, *English Architecture since the Regency: An Interpretation* (London: Constable, 1953).

28 J. M. Richards, *Memoirs of an Unjust Fella* (London: Weidenfeld & Nicolson, 1980), p. 122.

29 Fiona MacCarthy, *A History of British Design, 1830–1970* (London: Allen & Unwin, 1979), p. 61.

30 Nikolaus Pevsner, 'How to judge Victorian architecture', *Listener*, 19 July 1951, p. 91.

31 John Betjeman, *Ghastly Good Taste* (London: Chapman & Hall, 1933).

32 Timothy Mowl, *Stylistic Cold Wars: Betjeman versus Pevsner* (London: John Murray, 2000).

33 *Ibid.*

34 David Watkin, 'Sir Nikolaus Pevsner: a study in "historicism"', *Apollo*, 136 (1992), pp. 169–72.

35 Mowl, *Stylistic Cold Wars*, p. 146.

36 'Centenary of William Morris', *Journal of the Royal Society of Arts* (February 1934), p. 393.

37 James Wardrop, 'The William Morris Centenary Exhibition', *Apollo*, 19 (1934), pp. 206–7.

38 *Catalogue of an Exhibition in Celebration of the Centenary of William Morris: Held at the Victoria and Albert Museum, February 9–April 8* (London: Board of Education, 1934).

39 R. Page Arnott, *William Morris, the Man and the Myth* (London: Lawrence & Wishart, 1964), p. 10.

40 Esther Meynell, *Portrait of William Morris* (London: Chapman & Hall, 1947), p. 1.

41 Paul Bloomfield, *William Morris* (London: Arthur Barker, 1934), p. v.

42 'Valentines at South Kensington', *Connoisseur*, 83 (1929), p. 249; 'Children's books of the past and present', *Connoisseur*, 90 (1932), p. 413.

43 'Some current exhibitions', *Connoisseur*, 98 (1936), p. 235.

44 'Centenary of the photograph', *Connoisseur*, 103 (1939), p. 105.

45 'One hundred years of photography', *Journal of the Royal Society of Arts* (July 1939), p. 920.

46 'The early camera: an exhibition', *Architectural Review*, 85 (1939), p. 163.

47 C. H. Gibbs-Smith, 'The photograph collection of the Victoria and Albert Museum', *Museums Journal*, 36 (1936–37), pp. 46–53.

48 Victoria and Albert Museum, *Exhibition of Victorian and Edwardian Decorative Arts: Catalogue* (London: HMSO, 1952), p. 5; see also 'The small picture book', in Victoria and Albert Museum, *Victorian and Edwardian Decorative Arts* (London: HMSO, 1952).

49 Reyner Banham, 'Here's richness', *Art News and Review*, 15 November 1952, p. 3.

50 Elizabeth Aslin, *Nineteenth Century English Furniture* (London: Faber, 1962); Shirley Bury, *Victorian Electroplate* (Feltham: Hamlyn, 1971); Barbara Morris, *Victorian Embroidery* (London: H. Jenkins, 1962); Hugh Wakefield, *Nineteenth Century British Glass* (London: Faber, 1961) and *Victorian Pottery* (London:

H. Jenkins, 1962); James Laver, *Victorian Vista* (London: Hulton Press, 1954); James Laver, *The Age of Optimism* (London: Weidenfeld & Nicolson, 1966), and *Victoriana* (London: Ward Lock, 1966); Graham Reynolds, *Painters of the Victorian Scene* (London: Batsford, 1953), and *Victorian Painting* (London: Studio Vista, 1966).

51 George Savage, 'The Victorian wasteland', *Studio*, 164 (1962), p. 206.
52 Anthony Radcliffe, 'The Victoria and Albert Museum and the decorative arts of the nineteenth century', *Victorian Society Annual Report* (1966), p. 58.
53 Josephine H. Fitch, 'Some Victorian oddities', *Antiques* (December 1924), p. 316.
54 Charles Messer Stow, 'Shop talk', *Antiques* (September 1926), p. 217.
55 Sarah Foster Stovall, 'Two aspects of Victorianism', *Antiques* (November 1932), p. 171.
56 'Pennsylvania has Victorian show', *Art News*, 14 January 1933, p. 8.
57 'A special exhibition of Victorian and Edwardian dresses', *Bulletin of the Metropolitan Museum of Art*, 34 (March 1939), p. 55.
58 In the context of art history, *Historismus* means art characterised by the re-use of historical styles; it has a different meaning as applied to a historiographical method: see Michael Bentley, *Modern Historiography: An Introduction* (London: Routledge, 1999), pp. 22–3, 37.
59 *100 Jahre Österreichische Museum für angewandte Kunst. Kunstgewerbe des Historismus* exhibition catalogue (Vienna: Österreichische Museum für angewandte Kunst, 1964); *Historismus. Kunsthandwerk u. Industrie im Zeitalter d. Weltausstellgn* (Berlin: Kunstgewerbemuseum, 1973); *Historismus: Umlecké Remeslo 1860–1900* (Prague: Umleckoprumyslové Muzeum, 1975); *Kunsthandwerk und Industrieform des 19. und 20. Jahrhunderts: Historismus, Jugendstil, Bauhaus, Sachlichkeit, Sozialistischer Realismus* (Dresden: Museum für Kunsthandwerk, 1976); *Hohe Kunst zwischen Biedermeier und Jugendstil: Historismus in Hamburg und Norddeutschland*, Exhibition Catalogue (Hamburg: Museum für Kunst und Gewerbe, 1977).

9

No 'glorious assurance': the 1951 Festival of Britain looks at the Victorian past[1]

Becky E. Conekin

I

Gerald Barry, editor of the *News Chronicle* and the 1951 Festival of Britain's director-general, declared during its planning: 'One mistake we should *not* make, we should not fall into the error of supposing we were going to produce anything conclusive. In this sceptical age, the glorious assurance of the mid-Victorians would find no echo.'[2] Yet, a representation of the past which most people *would* have expected to see in the 1951 exhibitions was a display designed to mark the centenary of the Great Exhibition of 1851. The anniversary of that earlier celebration of British achievement, housed in the innovative Crystal Palace, was one of the primary justifications for the 1951 festivities.[3] First mooted by the Royal Society of Arts in 1943 to mark the centenary of 1851, the idea of an exhibition had been taken up in the autumn of 1945 by Barry in the *News Chronicle*, as well as by Sir Stafford Cripps, then president of the Board of Trade. And when the Festival officially opened on London's South Bank, on a rainy day in May, there was indeed a miniature version of the Crystal Palace, designed in glass and steel, like the original by Joseph Paxton. At either end of the 1851 Centenary Pavilion, as it was called, were slowly rotating displays, surrounded by ostrich feathers, featuring dioramas of different views of the Great Exhibition. The centrepiece was a model of the opening of the Great Exhibition featuring Queen Victoria, Prince Albert, the Princess Royal, the Prince of Wales, other royal children, as well as the queen's ministers, prelates, courtiers, gentlemen-at-arms and beefeaters. Through loudspeakers visitors were treated to the actual words spoken and the music performed at the opening ceremony on 1 May 1851.[4] Further down the Thames, the Battersea Pleasure Gardens also included a simple backdrop model of the Crystal Palace behind a fireworks stand.

But, in actuality, according to the Festival's planners, the Great Exhibition was really no more than a pretext. Stressing the centenary commemoration allowed Labour MP and Lord President of the Council Herbert

Morrison – dubbed by many 'Lord Festival' – to enlist the support of the
king and queen, who were convinced that their patronage of the 1951 exhibitions and events would demonstrate the monarchy's continuing benefac-
tion of the arts and sciences. Monarchical support in turn helped to cool
the vociferous opposition to the Festival mounted by some Conservative
politicians and the Beaverbrook press. R. A. Butler, for example, informed
Lord Woolton that were the king and queen to endorse it then the Conservative Party would have no option but to do so as well.[5]

Yet, the real proof of how little the Great Exhibition mattered to the
Festival planners is that late in the planning stages James Gardner, the co-
ordinating designer of the Battersea site, realised that there were no designs
in the Festival's blueprints for anything marking 1851. Gardner recalled in
1975: 'Everyone had forgotten that we must have something, or should
have something, about 1851.' He had been doodling one evening and came
up with the idea for a miniature Crystal Palace building, which, when he
showed it to Gerald Barry, evoked the response: ' "Oh, it's marvellous . . .
We must have that!" ' – even though there was no money budgeted for it.
'No one cared that it wasn't in the official budget', according to Gardner;
and 'this bit of nostalgia', as Gardner called it, 'was the last bit of the South
Bank show to remain standing',[7] with the exception of the Riverside Restau-
rant, the walk along the Embankment, the Royal Festival Hall, which was
a London County Council project, and the Telekinema, which became the
National Film Theatre.[8] The Tories, victors of the 1951 General Election,
announced that they were 'unwilling to become the caretaker[s] of empty
and deteriorating structures' and that they needed to make way for gardens
for the queen's coronation in 1953.[9] But, as Robert Hewison has pointed
out, the majority of the South Bank site stood empty until 1961, eventually becoming a car park in the 1990s.[10]

Charles Plouviez, the Festival of Britain's assistant to the director of exhibitions, has recently explained that 'James Gardner's little 1851 pavilion on
the South Bank was done with real affection as well as wit'. Other individuals on the Festival team also combined their 'allegiance to modernism'
with an interest in Victoriana. Peter Kneebone, a young designer who was
a member of the Festival's presentation panel, was 'madly buying Victorian
tat because it was "amusing" as well as decorative and cheap'.[11] And,
Barbara Jones, designer of the Coastline of Britain – Seaside section, on the
South Bank, and the Battersea Funfair, among others, curated a 'fringe'
exhibition of British popular and traditional art called 'Black Eyes and
Lemonade' at the Whitechapel Gallery in London's East End.[12] In that exhibition, as well as in her book *The Unsophisticated Arts*, published by the
Architectural Press in the Festival year, many of Jones's featured examples
of 'the things that people make for themselves or that are manufactured in
their taste' were from the nineteenth-century 'industrial tradition', such as
window displays, signs from shops, and delights from the seaside, fair-
grounds, canals and railways.[13] Some of the most important staff at the

Architectural Review, a major influence on the Festival's planners and architects, were promoting modernism, while simultaneously 'doing important
work on 19th century architecture and design'.[14] John Betjeman's *First and
Last Loves* (1952), delightfully illustrated by John Piper, celebrated Victorian architects and architecture, and Nikolaus Pevsner's *High Victorian
Design: A Study of the Exhibits of 1851*, published by the Architectural
Press in 1951, revealed his serious, yet ambivalent, attitude towards the
subject.[15] The 1951 Festival's typographical panel, chaired by Charles
Hasler, chose also to revive a Victorian 'Egyptian' form of lettering for use
in the exhibitions.[16] But, overall, the Festival of Britain's connection to the
Great Exhibition a century earlier was not widely celebrated in its official
events.

The Third Programme's 1851 Week

Interestingly, the British Broadcasting Corporation, unlike most of the Festival's official exhibitors, highlighted the 1951 Festival's roots in the 1851
Great Exhibition. According to Gerald Barry, the BBC had two roles to play
in the Festival. It was to 'help to create a sense of community', 'throughout the United Kingdom', by broadcasting the Festival's main events; and
it was to serve as 'a potent vehicle for expressing the national spirit' via its
wireless programming. Because they were 'part of the life-stuff of the British
people', regular BBC programmes like *The Archers* and John Arlott's cricket
test match commentaries were dubbed 'Festival of Britain Specials'.[17] In all
there were 2,700 Festival-related broadcasts,[18] some of which were programmed especially for the Festival. That perceived arbiter of middle-class
taste, the BBC's Third Programme, actually listened to by many people of
other backgrounds as well, broadcast music played at the Festival in the
summer and commissioned a new translation by Cecil Day-Lewis of *Aeneid*,
presented in twelve instalments, as well as W. H. Auden's translation of
Cocteau's *Knights of the Round Table*, and other high-brow dramatic per-
formances.[19] Yet, the Third Programme's unique contribution to the Festival celebrations was arguably its *1851 Week*, commencing on 22 April.

This well-received week of programmes was conceived by Cambridge historian Peter Laslett, who, while a junior research fellow at St John's College,
also worked as producer of BBC Talks in London. The opening announcement explained: 'During this week all the material in the Third Programme
will be taken from the year 1851. Our first broadcast is the Address delivered on the occasion of the Opening of Parliament on February 4th, 1851,
by Her Majesty Queen Victoria.'[20] Although some people found the week's
format confusing – one machine tools' apprentice reported to a Listener
Research survey that the 'atmosphere was brilliantly achieved', to such a
degree that his father 'thought that the 1851 news item was *Today in Parliament*, till mention was made of the Rt Hon. W. E. Gladstone' – a wide
array of listeners praised the week's programming as: 'a splendid idea',

according to a 'Factory Manager's wife'; 'an unqualified success', in the words of a 'Police Officer'; and 'instructive, interesting, amusing and entertaining by turns, and sometimes all at once', in the estimation of a 'Mail Order Clerk'.[21] The *1851 Week*'s offerings included:

> a dramatisation of Henry Mayhew's study of poverty in London; a reconstruction of a Philharmonic Society concert held in 1851; Victorian versions of two Light Programmes series: *Listen with Mama* and *A Pot-pourri for the Edification and Instruction of Ladies at Home* – in other words *Woman's Hour*; readings and speeches originally written by George Eliot, Thackeray, Ruskin, Berlioz, Carlyle, Browning, Disraeli, Charles Kingsley, Herbert Spencer, and Dickens.[22]

Laslett wrote in the *Radio Times* (20 April):

> Everything you will hear this week in 1951 was heard in England during 1851 ... All the musical items have been taken from concert programmes belonging to that year ... For the plays, we have chosen from the London successes of the 1851 season ... The features are likewise part and parcel of the year in question ... The news will be the news which was printed in the 1851 newspapers and the talks will be spoken versions of pronouncements made in 1851 by the eminent talkers of that generation.

His aim, he said, was 'to use the wireless to recapture the aesthetic atmosphere of the Great Exhibition year'.[23] In May 1998, in an interview with the author, Peter Laslett was adamant that the *1851 Week* was not concerned with people remembering or editorialising the past, but that 'it was letting the past address us with no intermediaries at all'. The agenda he brought as a young scholar to this *1851 Week* was clearly complex. On the one hand, there is the naïve method of letting the past speak for itself; while, on the other, Laslett did not include much material on 'ordinary lives' in mid-nineteenth century England. In fact, he was frank that the week was programmed by the educated for the educated – it was regarded not as educational programming but rather as a sort of assertion by the middle-class of the right to have access to the cultural output of their ancestors: 'it was their values we tried to represent'.[24] Nevertheless, Laslett was attempting to give his listeners a sense of the issues and concerns of that period a century earlier.[25]

Schools' contributions

Rather similarly to the *1851 Week*, the official Festival organisers and the Ministry of Education encouraged schools and teachers across the United Kingdom to plan programmes and pageants comparing 1951 to 1851.[26] A Ministry of Education Circular of December 1850 explained:

> Most schools will find in their local history, geography, arts and crafts, architecture, industries and natural history, a rich accumulation of treasures and achievements that could properly be celebrated as part of a national Festival of thankfulness and legitimate pride.[27]

Social and economic history projects were the result in most schools, focusing on the differences of life 100 years prior to the Festival. Children were broadly enlisted in acts of historical imagination imbued with a Whiggish belief in historical progress, but one which conveniently erased class conflict and the inequalities created by the Industrial Revolution. For example, in the imagined nineteenth-century there were horses rather than cars and children laboured in either urban or rural drudgery rather than enjoying the privilege of attending school. One extreme example of the erasure of controversial politics and pasts came from the award-winning school project 'Coleraine 100 Years Ago', chosen for inclusion in the Secondary Schools' Classroom Exhibition on the South Bank. This Northern Irish school's project presented 'the social, industrial and economic background of Coleraine' and contrasted it 'with that of the present day'. According to the *Belfast Telegraph:* 'Features include[d] a large-scale model of the borough years ago with a surround of social studies, painting, maps and written pamphlets'.[28] The specific stories relevant to the history of Northern Ireland and its relationship with Great Britain were entirely absent.

The official Festival exhibitions

There were nine official, government-funded, Festival of Britain exhibitions in England, Scotland, Northern Ireland and Wales, twenty-three designated arts Festivals, and a pleasure garden in London's Battersea Park. These exhibitions, planned primarily from London, included four in the metropole, the Exhibition of Industrial Power in Glasgow, the Hillside Farming Scheme in Dolhendre, Wales, and Belfast's Ulster Farm and Factory Exhibition. There were also two travelling exhibitions designed to transport miniature versions of London's South Bank exhibition to 'the provinces'. Housed on a fleet of lorries and a decommissioned aircraft carrier, these exhibitions were arranged so that 'the story told on the South Bank', which was considered 'fundamental to the expression of the Festival theme', would 'reach the main centres of population throughout the country'. The land-travelling exhibition visited Manchester and Birmingham, where it went into existing halls, as well as Leeds and Nottingham, where it had to go 'into an enormous tented structure especially built for it'.[29] The Festival ship *Campania* held the sea-travelling exhibition, and it docked, for 10–14 days, at the ports of Southampton, Dundee, Newcastle, Hull, Plymouth, Bristol, Cardiff, Belfast, Birkenhead and Glasgow, between 4 May and 6 October 1951.[30] In these varied official Festival exhibitions, evocations of the past were chosen for their appropriateness for the post-war 'New Jerusalem', an imagined world of equality. Generally, periods in history that might have seemed difficult to incorporate into a Labour-led egalitarian future, like the Victorian industrial age, were eschewed.

One exception was in Belfast, at the Ulster Farm and Factory Exhibition. There an 1851 farmstead was juxtaposed with the farmhouse and farmyard of the future. The 1851 display came in the shape of a reconstruction, authentic down to the farm implements. Here modernity had a clear and direct link to the past. The exhibition's overall message was that the farm of the future would be cleaner and easier to manage than that of the past. Based on 'building science', as it was called at the time, the buildings functioned as one complete unit, for ease in tending and feeding animals in inclement weather. The structures were designed to provide maximum ventilation and light, and the farmhouse of the future contained features, which in 1951 must have seemed very modern indeed, such as a kitchen, living-room and bedroom on the first floor and all approachable by internal and external stairways, an airy covered walkway connecting the farmhouse to the outer buildings and an uninterrupted view of the farmstead and fields from both the living-room and the balcony. The living area incorporated folding, sliding windows leading directly on to the balcony.[31] As Raphael Samuel explained in *Theatres of Memory*, 'the outside coming in was one of the architectural ideals of the period'.[32] Overall, the Ulster exhibition's agricultural display combined innovations in hygienic, convenient and affordable farm management, with all the latest modern designs for the home.

The Festival's symbiotic representations of the past and the future

Robert Hewison, one of the few people to have written in a sustained fashion about the 1951 Festival, has argued that 'the optimistic, technological vision promoted by the South Bank was at odds with the neo-romanticism associated with the prevailing ideas of Land and People'. Hewison rightly identifies that the 'the Land and the People' were 'comfortably democratic words from a lexicon of wartime propaganda that created a space within which to explore the way the nation had shaped its environment and been shaped by it'.[33] But the larger point is contentious. The Festival's imaginings of the future and the past were not 'at odds'. They were mutually re-inforcing, or symbiotic – particular renderings of the past bolstered representations of the future, and vice versa. This is clearly evident in the Belfast exhibition, but can also be identified in less overt forms in other exhibitions. Modernism has often been combined with the most traditional imaginings of Englishness or Britishness.[34]

The Festival's evocations of the past were chosen for their appropriateness in the imagined post-war New Jerusalem of equality and freedom for all. As has been seen, there *were* a few representations of the Victorian era, but generally that era was perceived as too laden with associations of capitalism, imperialism and class conflict for the immediate post-war Labour-led Festival of Britain. Victorian architecture was declared pretentious and fussy, as it had been by various critics since at least the 1880s; whereas Georgian architecture, advocated by middle-class architects and planners from the 1930s, was considered both refined *and* popular, modern yet stable.[35] In an interview in 2000, Festival architect H. T. Jim Cadbury-Brown exclaimed that, looking at the Great Exhibition, 'you can see how horrible much of the design was in 1851'.[36] Barry Curtis has argued that Victorian architecture stood accused in the post-war era of having 'brutalised' Georgian buildings by 'laissez-faire industrial capitalism', its designs reeking of 'intrusive individualism' and 'tainted from the beginning with Imperial projects'. Such associations, along with those of 'clutter, scale and gloom', made Victoriana the 'villain in the "story" of democratic design'.[37]

In broader social and cultural terms, J. B. Priestley, who broadcast the extremely popular wireless 'Postscripts' on the BBC during the Second World War, wrote in the 1930s that 'sturdy Victorian individualism' had given 'the less fortunate classes' what could only be described as 'monstrously long hours of work, miserable wages, and surroundings in which they lived like black-beetles at the back of a disused kitchen stove'. The Industrial Revolution, Priestley argued, 'had done more harm than good to the real enduring England', finding 'a green and pleasant land' and leaving behind 'a wilderness of dirty bricks'. 'It had blackened fields, poisoned rivers, ravaged the earth, and sown filth and ugliness with a lavish hand', he wrote in *English Journey* (1934). This nineteenth-century industrial England 'of coal, iron, steel, cotton, wool, [and] railways' disproportionately spoiled the midlands and the north. His overarching view of the Victorian era was expressed thus: 'It was as if the country had devoted a hundred years of its life to keeping gigantic sooty pigs. And the people who were choked by the reek of the sties did not get the bacon.'[38]

Somewhat similarly, Humphrey Jennings described the inequalities and discrepancies created by the Industrial Revolution in his film *Family Portrait*, commissioned for the 1951 Festival. But, interestingly, he referred to those inequalities as 'rifts in the family we are still having to repair'. Images of a brass band followed this statement, representing Welsh mining-village life, and the narrator informed the audience, in received English pronunciation, that 'the first locomotives in the world were Welsh'.[39] There diverse class, occupational and national histories were incorporated into a unified and simplified whole.

In the official Festival exhibitions the rendition of the past which was fitting for the post-war Labour-led world was one based on timeless traditions reminiscent of Orwell's appraisal of 'English civilisation'. Orwell wrote in 1941 that the essence of the English character was rooted in customs like an appreciation of the simple pleasures of everyday life, like 'solid breakfasts', as well as 'green fields and red pillar boxes'; 'moreover it is continuous, it stretches into the future and the past, there is something in it that persists, as in a living creature . . . And above all, it is your civilisation, it is *you*.'[40] The Festival of Britain was designed to be a 'national autobiography'[41] – the story the nation told about itself, the narrative created by the British people about the British people.[42] History with a capital 'H' was generally subjugated to the role of illustrator of greater universal truths about the British people: 'truths' like those spelt out by Orwell, such as the 'all-important English trait: the respect for constitutionalism and legality, the belief in "the law" as something above the State and above the individual'.[43]

Generally, the Festival portrayed the past, not in the sense of history as a chronicle or an analytical exploration, but rather as a series of traditions imbued with trans-class and trans-historical qualities. Tony Bennett has argued that, beginning in the mid-nineteenth century, with the discoveries made by geologists, paleantologists and anthropologists, the galleries, museums and – by extension – exhibitions, adopted an understanding of 'universal time' according to which 'the different times of geology, biology, anthropology and history were connected' in their displays.[44] Ironically, this adoption of a deep past, embedded in 'universal time', was itself the hallmark of these new disciplines founded by the Victorians. Such a sense of 'universal time', incorporating the past and the present, is identifiable in the 1951 Festival's exhibitions and events. But, building on Bennett, we need to explain *which* allegedly trans-historical and trans-class narratives were in play in the Festival's representations of 'universal time' and why the Victorian period did not figure prominently. According to Geoff Eley and Ron Suny, nations are idealised communities because they have ' "recovered" the history they need to bring diverse elements into a single whole', while they have simultaneously 'concealed the actual inequalities, exploitations, and patterns of domination and exclusion inevitably involved'.[45] Specific 'histories' are 'recovered' at particular moments in the creation and re-creation of national stories. The 1951 Festival's 'timeless' narratives presented the British people primarily as independent, freedom-loving, humble, steadfast and fair. Such notions of 'patriotism' and 'independence' had been invoked by radicals, Owenites and Chartists to construct their arguments for the extension of rights.[46] The late eighteenth century's list of the constitutive rights of English liberty included:

> Freedom from absolutism (the constitutional monarchy), freedom from arbitrary arrest, trial by jury, equality before the law . . . some limited liberty of thought, speech and of conscience, the vicarious participation in liberty (or in its semblance) afforded by the right of parliamentary opposition and by elections.[47]

By contrast, the Victorian era was perceived as one of inequality – filthy and exploitative – leading to 'rifts in the family' of the British people which, according to Humphrey Jennings, the post-war period needed to 'repair'.

Distinct from his rendition of nineteenth-century industrial England, Second World War Britain was portrayed by J. B. Priestley in terms of all of its people sharing the 'British landscape, history, political traditions and "character" '.[48] Raphael Samuel identified similar representations of Britain and Britons in 1940s films, the Directorate of Army Education brochures for soldiers, as well as in Orwell's essays, which portrayed the English as kind, modest, tolerant and sportsmanlike.[49]

The role of the past in the 1951 Festival was to illustrate how the British people were unified, yet diverse, 'cemented together' by character, tradition and ancient origins, no matter what their contemporary class position or geographical location. In the words of one of the Festival's official guide-catalogues, the exhibitions and events 'aimed to tell the story of the Land and the People – not to present a gallery of portraits'.[50] The versions of the past most relevant to the Festival were those 'already known' to the educated middle-class technocrats who organised it.[51] The Festival of Britain served to tell the stories of its time. Its time was, of course, the immediate post-war period, and, as such, the narratives most readily to hand for the Festival's planners were those told during the war.[52]

Conclusion

As we have seen, a few representations of 1851 were included in the Festival, but the Victorian era was generally perceived as too 'capitalist' and class-riven for the post-war moment. Georgian architecture, a high-brow fad of the 1930s, was presented as a past style appropriate for a new, more democratic, Britain in 1951. With the exception of a few references in Jennings's Festival film *Family Portrait*, particular pasts, especially the Victorian period and the war just ended, were also basically absent from the Festival. This is one reason why the question we should be asking is *which* pasts were represented in the Festival, rather than engaging in the now-old argument as to whether Britishness was (and is) backward-looking or forward-looking.[53] Sarah Benton's contention that, at the end of the Second World War, with Labour in power, 'it was part of the contradictory nature of inventing new Britain that alongside the myth of founding a new society was the myth of the ancestor' is convincing.[54] Surely, in the immediate post-war period, if not always, representations of Britain and Britishness were 'Janus-faced', looking simultaneously to the past and to the future for explanations of who and what they were.[55] Unlike for the BBC or the Ministry of Education, the Great Exhibition and the Victorian era more generally did not loom large in the Festival's official exhibitions. And, yet, the 1951 Festival of Britain did embrace the Victorian sense of 'universal time' in its full complexity. Most obviously, it incorporated the Victorians' bold belief in technological progress and the future, cleverly combining this with a sense of an appropriate and often 'ancient' past.

Notes

1 This chapter is a revised version of chapter 4 of my book on the Festival, *'The Autobiography of a Nation': The 1951 Festival of Britain* (Manchester: Manchester University Press, 2003). I wish to thank Manchester University Press for allowing me to publish this revision here. In addition, for their helpful suggestions relating to this material, I would like to thank: Geoff Eley, Peter Mandler,

Charles Plouviez, Sonya Rose, Adam Tooze and James Vernon. I would also like to acknowledge the support of the London College of Fashion in the form of a part-time research fellowship, a post I have happily held since 1998. The initial research for the larger project of which this is a part was funded by the (American) Social Science Research Council, and I would like, finally, to thank the SSRC, and especially the then Director of the Western Europe Programme Kenton Worcester, whom I now have the pleasure of calling a friend.

2 Gerald Barry, as quoted in Michael Frayn's 'Festival', in Michael Sissons and Philip French (eds), *The Age of Austerity, 1945–1951* (Harmondsworth: Penguin, 1964), pp. 330–52, at 336.

3 See, for example, Bevis Hillier, 'Introduction' to Mary Banham and Bevis Hillier (eds), *A Tonic to the Nation: The Festival of Britain, 1951* (London: Thames & Hudson, 1976), pp. 10–17, at 12.

4 '1851 Centenary Pavilion', in Ian Cox, *The South Bank Exhibition: A Guide to the Story it Tells* (London: HMSO, 1951), p. 85; and T. W. Hendrick, 'The achievements of "Cockade"', in Banham and Hillier (eds), *Tonic to the Nation*, pp. 163–4; see also Anon., '1851 Centenary Pavilion', *Architectural Review*, 109 (1951), p. 266.

5 See, for example: Hillier, Introduction' to Banham and Hillier (eds), *Tonic to the Nation*, pp. 13–14; Frayn, 'Festival', p. 341; Robert Hewison, *Culture and Consensus: England, Art and Politics since 1940* (London: Methuen, 1997), p. 58; and Butler to Woolton, 18 May 1950, Conservative Party Archive, Festival of Britain, Additional File II, as quoted by Richard A. J. Weight, '"Pale stood Albion": the promotion of national culture in Britain, 1939–56', unpublished PhD thesis, University of London, 1995, p. 143.

6 James Gardner (1975), quoted in Hillier's 'Introduction' to Banham and Hillier (eds), *Tonic to the Nation*, p. 12.

7 James Gardner, 'Pleasure gardens, Battersea Park: Battersea pleasures', in Banham and Hillier (eds), *Tonic to the Nation*, p. 118.

8 Hewison, *Culture and Consensus*, p. 65.

9 David Eccles, Conservative Minister of Works, 1951, quoted by Hewison in *Culture and Consensus*, p. 65.

10 Hewison, *Culture and Consensus*, p. 65.

11 Charles Plouviez, electronic mail message to the author, 4 August 2002.

12 *Ibid.*; Barbara Jones, 'Popular arts', in Banham and Hillier (eds), *Tonic to the Nation*, pp. 129–32.

13 Barbara Jones, *The Unsophisticated Arts* (London: Architectural Press, 1951), pp. 9–10.

14 Plouviez, 4 August 2002.

15 John Betjeman, *First and Last Loves* (London: John Murray, 1952); and Nikolaus Pevsner, *High Victorian Design: A Study of the Exhibits of 1851* (London: Architectural Press, 1951).

16 For more on this, see: Paul Rennie, 'Fat faces all around: lettering and the Festival style', in Elain Harwood and Alan Powers (eds), 'Festival of Britain', *Twentieth Century Architecture* (special issue), 5 (2001), pp. 109–16; Charles Hasler, 'Festival lettering', in Banham and Hillier (eds), *Tonic to the Nation*, pp. 114–15.

17 Gerald Barry, *Radio Times*, 27 April 1951, p. 5; see also Weight, '"Pale stood Albion"', p. 152.

18 Frayn, 'Festival', p. 349.

19 Humphrey Carpenter, *The Envy of the World: Fifty Years of the BBC Third Programme and Radio 3, 1946–1996* (London: Weidenfeld & Nicolson, 1996), pp. 107–8.
20 'Talks: 1851 Week', BBC Written Archives Centre, Caversham, R51/131/1–2.
21 'Talks: 1851 Week', 5 June 1951, BBC Written Archives Centre, R9/9/15, quoted in Carpenter, *The Envy*, p. 109. According to Carpenter (*The Envy*, p. 109), 'a Listener Research survey into the "character" of the Third's audience, completed in the spring of 1953', revealed that, in the *Economist*'s words, ' "the Third Programme has a far bigger market among the supposedly philistine than among the cultured" ', with a larger number than imagined of 'poorly educated people' listening at least once a week.
22 Carpenter, *The Envy*, p. 108.
23 Peter Laslett, *Radio Times*, 20 April 1951, quoted by Carpenter, *The Envy*, p. 108.
24 Dr Peter Laslett, Trinity College, Cambridge, in interview with the author, 26 May 1998. Dr Laslett did, however, subsequently say that, of course, there was editorialising involved in 1851, when *The Times*, which was the key source of this week of programming, selected what would be published.
25 Laslett later saw the *1851 Week* as a prefiguration of his three talks on the Third Programme in March and April, 1960, which focused on 'the social order before the coming of industry', and ultimately resulted in his book *The World We Have Lost* (London: Methuen, 1965), a key text in early British social history (Laslett interview, and quoted by Carpenter, *The Envy*, p. 191).
26 Ministry of Education, Circular 231 (15 December 1950), ED 142/4, PRO, London.
27 *Ibid.*, p. 2.
28 'Coleraine 100 years ago: intermediate schools' exhibition opened by the minister', *Belfast Telegraph*, 5 April 1951, p. 3.
29 *The Official Book of the Festival of Britain 1951* (London: HMSO, 1951), p. 62.
30 *The Festival of Britain*, pp. 62–3.
31 'The Festival', *Architects' Journal*, 114 (July 1951), p. 116; *1951 Exhibition Ulster Farm and Factory, Belfast, Northern Ireland*, Festival of Britain Catalogue (London: HMSO, 1951).
32 Raphael Samuel, *Theatres of Memory*, vol. 1: *Past and Present in Contemporary Culture* (London: Verso, 1994), p. 52.
33 Hewison, *Culture and Consensus*, p. 59.
34 See, for example, Bill Schwarz, 'Englishness and the paradox of modernity', *New Formations*, 1 (1987), p. 152.
35 Peter Mandler, *The Fall and Rise of the Stately Home* (London: Yale University Press, 1997), p. 330; Barry Curtis, 'One continuous interwoven story (The Festival of Britain)', *Block*, 11 (1985–86), p. 51.
36 H. T. Cadbury-Brown, ' "A good time-and-a-half was had by all" ', in Harwood and Powers (eds), 'Festival of Britain', *Twentieth Century Architecture*, 5 (2001), p. 60.
37 Curtis, 'One continuous interwoven story', pp. 51–2.
38 J. B. Priestley, *English Journey* (London: Heinemann, 1984 [1934]), pp. 298–300.
39 Humphrey Jennings, *Family Portrait 1951: A Film on the Theme of the Festival of Britain, 1951* (Wessex Film, 1951).

40 George Orwell, *The Lion and the Unicorn: Socialism and the English Genius* (London: Penguin Books, 1970 [1941]). Unfortunately, Orwell wrote of England and Englishness rather than of Britain and Britishness.

41 *The Official Book of the Festival of Britain, 1951*, p. 66.

42 As Raphael Samuel has written, 'traditions . . . are not inherited: they are a name given to something which is constantly being made': *Theatres of Memory*, vol. 2: *Island Stories: Unravelling Britain* (London: Verso, 1998), p. 275.

43 Orwell, *The Lion and the Unicorn*, p. 44.

44 Tony Bennett, *The Birth of the Museum: History, Theory, Politics* (London: Routledge, 1995), p. 39.

45 Geoff Eley and Ronald Grigor Suny, 'Introduction: from the moment of social history to the work of cultural representation', in Eley and Suny (eds), *Becoming National: A Reader* (Oxford: Oxford University Press, 1996), p. 24; the authors, of course, acknowledge their indebtedness to Benedict Anderson.

46 E. P. Thompson, *The Making of the English Working Class* (New York: Vintage Books, 1966), pp. 78–9; see also: Gareth Stedman Jones, 'Rethinking Chartism', in Stedman Jones, *Languages of Class: Studies in English Working Class History 1832–1982* (Cambridge: Cambridge University Press, 1983), pp. 90–178; Hugh Cunningham, 'The language of patriotism, 1750–1914', *History Workshop Journal*, 12 (1981), pp. 13–21.

47 Thompson, *Making of the English Working Class*, pp. 78–9.

48 Sian Nicholas, *The Echo of War: Home Front Propaganda and the Wartime BBC, 1939–1945* (Manchester: Manchester University Press, 1996), p. 233.

49 Samuel, *Theatres of Memory*, vol. 1, p. 218.

50 A. D. Hippisley Cox, 'The seaside', in Ian Cox, *Festival Ship* Campania: *A Guide to the Story it Tells* (London: HMSO, 1951), p. 31.

51 Bennett, *Birth of the Museum*, p. 147.

52 Ministry of Information, quoted by Nicholas, *Echo of War*, pp. 2, 229.

53 Hewison, for example, argues that 'the optimistic, technological vision promoted by the South Bank was at odds with the neo-romanticism associated with the prevailing ideas of Land and People': *Culture and Consensus*, p. 59. For one of the founding texts in this debate, see Patrick Wright, *On Living in an Old Country* (London: Verso, 1985).

54 Sarah Benton, 'The 1945 "republic"', *History Workshop Journal*, 43 (1997), p. 253.

55 Tom Nairn, *The Break-up of Britain* (London: New Left Books, 1977), pp. 329–63.

10

The BBC and the Victorians

James Thompson

I

This chapter examines the ways in which the BBC has portrayed the Victorian period through its programming since the 1920s. The BBC is a major cultural institution whose output reaches an audience of millions. In his study *Theatres of Memory*, the late Raphael Samuel wrote that 'in the present day television ought to have pride of place in any attempt to map the unofficial sources of historical knowledge'.[1] Whether through factual programmes or period dramas, the BBC has done much to shape popular perceptions of the Victorian period. Broadcasting throughout the twentieth century constituted the closest to a common culture Britain has ever had. A particular interest attaches to the role of the BBC in moulding views of the Victorian past. The creation of the BBC owed much to characteristically late nineteenth-century concerns. Its conception of public service broadcasting might be seen as itself deeply Victorian. Sir John Reith, director-general between 1923 and 1938, and widely regarded as the corporation's founding father, has been seen as a relic of Victorianism. 'Reithian' has certainly acquired connotations of earnest improvement often identified with the Victorian period. Under Reith, the BBC was often cast as the last bulwark of Victorianism.

In an important article, Dan LeMahieu claimed that 'Reith never suffered the disillusion with nineteenth century values which characterised so many of his contemporaries'.[2] Throughout the 1920s, Reith articulated and defended a notion of public service deeply rooted in the values of late nineteenth-century Britain. In his book *Broadcast Over Britain*, he elaborated a notion of culture which firmly emphasised its more *improving* features.[3] The purpose of the BBC was not to pander to existing taste, but to improve it. Reith set great store by the emergence of 'a new and mighty weight of public opinion' fostered by the disinterested output of the national broadcaster.[4] Under his leadership, the BBC took seriously its commitment to the 'public interest'. This was conceived with reference to the requirements of the general community rather than those of particular interests, but also in terms of the need to develop and elevate a common culture which would bind the nation together. The origin and nature of the Reithian commitment to 'public service' are important in understanding the ways in which the BBC has told the story of the Victorian period.

There are many difficulties to surmount in considering the portrayal of the Victorian age by the BBC. The BBC has never been a monolithic organisation pursuing a consistent historiographical line. Over the last eighty years it has broadcast a huge variety of programmes concerned in some manner with the period 1837–1901, ranging from fairly austere historical analysis destined for a small minority to big-budget costume drama aimed at a primetime audience. Many original programmes, on both radio and television, do not survive. The BBC's output has never been restricted to broadcasting. It has been responsible for many publications, from magazines to books, and now boasts some of Europe's most popular websites.[5] This multimedia presence makes it difficult to generalise about its cultural impact. The approach adopted here is to focus on programmes and publications that seem most significant in shaping attitudes to the Victorians, and to locate such output in the wider context of BBC programming.

The rest of this chapter falls into three sections. In the first, attention is devoted to factual programming, especially to major series on both radio and television, dedicated to the Victorian era. In the second, the focus moves to costume drama, clearly the most popular means of representing the past available to the BBC. The final section returns to some of the questions raised in this introduction about the relationship between the BBC's corporate self-image and its narration of the nation's history.

II

In the relationship between the BBC and the Victorians, anniversaries have loomed large. The coverage provided in 1951 and in 2001 is considered below, but it is worth emphasising that anniversaries have always provided occasions for revisiting the past. In May 1938, the centenary of the emergence of Chartism was marked by a programme written by Jimmie Miller (Ewan MacColl) and produced by John Pudney. This broadcast reflected the particular character of Manchester programmes in that period, equally apparent in Olive Shapley's *The Classic Soil*, comparing Manchester in the 1840s and 1940s.[6]

No study of the BBC and the Victorians can ignore the major radio series broadcast in 1948 that became the volume *Ideas and Beliefs of the Victorians*.[7] This series lasted over four months, consisting of 57 talks and 26 readings.[8] In his multi-volume history of broadcasting, Asa Briggs argued that *Ideas and Beliefs* suggested that 'time was ripe for a reassessment of the Victorians'.[9] John Gardiner has portrayed the 1940s as a period of scholarly re-assessment of the Victorians, and that is the context in which the series should be seen.[10] As the *Radio Times* announced, 'the series will examine the assumptions of the Victorian Age, appraise its ideas, and re-assess its controversies in the belief that such an examination will shed light on the urgent issues of today'.[11] The series was much concerned with what it called 'the "working out" of Victorian ideas', and particularly the relationship of the collectivism of the 1940s to the nineteenth-century past. Its focus was very much on intellectual or, in some cases, cultural history, embodying a conception of Victorianism as primarily a set of ideas or attitudes. Reflecting the Third Programme at its most serious, this was undoubtedly an instance of public service broadcasting. The combination of speaker and channel could create a strong sense of connection with the Victorian past – never more so than during an introductory discussion featuring G. M. Trevelyan, Bertrand Russell, Lord David Cecil and Christopher Dawson. There was here an almost palpable sense of connectedness to the past. However, the perspective offered in the series as a whole was more complex.

The shape of *Ideas and Beliefs* was influenced by the desire to re-assess the Victorian age's 'controversies'.[12] There was also, though, a clear intention to produce 'an historic revaluation of the Victorian age'. After the series had been broadcast, Harman Grisewood, controller of the Third Programme, wrote a memo to the production team in which he suggested that the series was 'somewhat "Victorian" in its massive large-scale design and in the conscientious, diligent care that was bestowed upon the detail', before remarking that 'as [of] the Victorian age itself, I am sorry it is over'.[13] The series was conceived as part of a re-evaluation of the Victorians and their rehabilitation from the forces of Stracheyism. In drawing up suggestions for the final discussion, W. N. Newton, assistant director of BBC Talks, asked 'why there has been (as shown in this series) such a marked change in our attitude to the early Victorians since the 1920s'.[14] This background was very apparent in some of the broadcasts. Trevelyan observed approvingly that 'the BBC has chosen the time for this series well', claiming that 'the period of reaction is over . . . the era of dispassionate historical valuation has begun'.[15] A review of the series in *The Times*, preserved in the BBC's archives, describes the series as 'the climax of a reaction against the idea of Victorian England which prevailed twenty years ago and was inseparably associated with Lytton Strachey'.[16]

The protracted process of research, interviews and discussion that lay behind the series was reflected in certain guiding assumptions. It was noted that broadcasts could not be confined strictly to the years 1837–1901. Grisewood suggested that 1832–1914 made more sense as a period.[17] There was evidently a distinct awareness of change as having marked the period. Jean Rowntree, a former Talks' producer who did most of the background research for the series, proposed that 1850–1875 might provide the best cross-section, if such was wanted.[18] Grisewood objected to G. M. Young's

Portrait of an Age on the grounds that it underestimated the element of change.[19] The series that was eventually broadcast certainly displayed an attention to variety within its period. This was apparent from the very first programme.

G. M. Trevelyan began by asserting that he had 'no intention of trying to epitomise the ideas and beliefs of the Victorian era, for they were various and mutually contradictory'. He described the Victorian age as one characterised primarily by 'constant change, variety and self-criticism'.[20] The variety and ubiquitous change of the Victorian period were repeatedly emphasised in the talks. Dawson closed the introductory discussion by claiming that 'the paradox of Victorianism is that for half a century it has been a by-word for all that is stuffy and conventional and reactionary; whereas in actual fact it was a great revolutionary age'.[21] This stress on the modernity of the Victorians recurred in a number of the talks. Humphry House noted the 'acute sense of modernity' common to both Macaulay and Dickens.[22] The modernity of the Victorians was, however, defined in interesting ways, for some speakers portrayed the early Victorians as closer than their late-Victorian grandchildren to the world of the 1940s.

Divisions within 'the Victorian age' were repeatedly emphasised in the talks, particularly the differences between early and late Victorians. The dividing line was commonly taken to be around 1870. K. B. Smellie, reader in public administration at the London School of Economics, suggested that 'instead of speaking of the Victorian age from 1837 to 1901 it would better mark the forces at play if we were to speak of a nineteenth century which began in 1832 and a twentieth century which began in 1870'.[23] Contributors differed in their evaluation of those two periods. Rosalie Glynn Grylls, in her talk on the emancipation of women, emphasised the accomplishments of the period, arguing that 'by the end of the reign of Queen Victoria . . . common sense had taken over from sensibility'.[24] There was, however, a more general tendency in the talks to regard the earlier Victorians as the greater and, at least for some, the more relevant. Richard Crossman offered the most strident version of this perspective, suggesting that 'the later Victorians, like their Edwardian successors, seem so remote from our age', whereas 'the Victorians of the 1830s and 1850s are as close to me as Plato, who is . . . as close as anybody could be today'.[25] If the relative merits of the sub-periods within the Victorian age were disputed, the existence of such divisions was more generally accepted. E. L. Woodward put the point well, noting that 'there was not one Victorian age, there were at least three'.[26]

The architecture of the series, and of the book, was revealing. It began with a number of talks on 'the idea of progress'. Trevelyan, inevitably, discoursed on 'Macaulay and the sense of optimism'; stressing both the reality of material progress, drawing upon the work of John Clapham, and its conditional nature for the Victorians.[27] Humphry House adumbrated 'the mood of doubt' with special reference to Dickens and Ruskin, while Laski portrayed the Fabian Society as typical of 'the Indian summer of Victorian England'.[28]

The set pieces of Victorian religious controversy received extended consideration in the second series of talks. Evangelicalism, nonconformity and tractarianism were discussed at length. Jean Rowntree urged, in a memo that may have reflected her discussions with Noel Annan, that 'the single topic that seems to me of the most outstanding importance . . . is Victorian Evangelicalism'.[29] The relationship between evangelicalism and the subsequent crisis of belief evident in many subsequent studies of the late Victorians, notably Annan himself on Leslie Stephen or Martin Wiener on Wallas,[30] is evident in the organisation of the talks. Apart from Annan, the consultant who seems to have impressed Rowntree most was Jacob Bronowski, who advised that science occupy 'a major place under the heading of the challenge to religion'.[31] Victorian science was consequently integral to the talks dealing with the relationship between man and nature. Attention was given to the significance of geological discoveries in undermining the plausibility of a literal reading of the Bible, as well as to the celebrated achievements of Victorian naturalists. A contrast may be drawn between this 1940s' portrait of the Victorians and that provided in 2001. While Victorian science was much discussed on the centenary of Victoria's death, the character of Victorian religion received less coverage. The centrality of religion to *Ideas and Beliefs* was indicative of a very different view of the Victorian period than that propagated at the turn of the twentieth century. It was the relationship between science and religion that received scrutiny in 1948 rather than simply the technological foundations of twenty-first-century life.

A number of talks were given illustrating the unfolding of 'the liberal idea', including two on the emancipation of women. In the discussions that led to the series, there was a repeated emphasis on the contemporary relevance of the Victorian period. In an important memo, George Barnes, the originator of the series, described the purpose of the talks as being 'to enquire into the beliefs, assumptions and aspirations of our grandfathers, the manner in which they changed and the legacy we have inherited', in the belief that 'such an enquiry will do more to promote thought on our present discontents than yet another attempt to measure them'.[32] Such concerns were manifest in the talks on the liberal idea. The broadcasts on the working out of Victorian ideas also focused heavily on issues of state intervention and personal responsibility, taking in questions of the family and of sex along the way. It was perhaps in these two sets of talks that the concerns of the 1940s were most obviously apparent. In the talks on empire, it was the colonial separatists who were celebrated as 'the first to foresee the modern Commonwealth'.[33] In contrast, late Victorian imperialism was castigated by Cobban as a kind of 'bastard imperialism', 'nationalism writ large', which was destined to prove 'a temporary phenomenon' because 'there was *no* British nation'.[34] In fact, while Davidson's emphasis on modest conceptions of empire reflected the temper of the late 1940s, Cobban's emphasis on the multinational diversity of the British Isles had a tone more usually identified with the 1970s.

The talks about the Victorians and sex reflected the developments of the post-Victorian era. While the social historian H. L. Beales emphasised the combination of prudery and prostitution, the psychoanalyst Edward Glover celebrated the insights of Sigmund Freud in 'at last letting in light into dark places'.[35] His Freudianism offered an obvious diagnosis of anti-Victorianism, which he characterised as the obverse of ancestor worship, arguing that 'until the Edwardians die off we cannot expect to be objective about the Victorians'. He insisted, with reference in particular to Thackeray and Dickens, that 'the most weighty and popular Victorians were themselves violently anti-Victorian'. He closed with the claim that 'the spirit of those progressive Victorians who fought against the sexual obscurantism of their own times reached its finest expression in the work of Freud'.[36]

In its published form *Ideas and Beliefs* consisted of the talks given in radio broadcasts but omitted the twenty-six readings on subjects as diverse as Victorian prosperity and William James on the new psychology. Jean Rowntree had characterised the advantage of broadcasting as its ability to reveal 'what [the Victorians] said of themselves'.[37] This notion was developed in the *1851 Week* broadcast in 1951, the year that marked both the fiftieth anniversary of Victoria's death and the centenary of the Great Exhibition. The aim was to produce a week of broadcasts on the Third Programme taken directly from the music, plays, literature and news of 1851. Originally conceived by Peter Laslett, this was a striking and well-received attempt at recreating 'the aesthetic atmosphere of the year of the Great Exhibition'.[38]

Laslett set out the guiding principles of the *1851 Week* in a memo to Grisewood. These were, firstly, that 'the year 1851 should be allowed to speak for itself' ('1850 and 1852 are out'), and, secondly, that 'we should not hesitate to cut or to improvise whenever we feel that twentieth century audiences would prefer us to do so'. It was not self-evident that the desire to please the audience of 1951 was compatible with the presentation of the 'aesthetic atmosphere' of 1851. There were also, of course, historical questions about the representativeness and the editing of the chosen items. The selection policy indicates the perspective applied to these problems. In dealing with the talks, Laslett proposed that 'our policy of selecting for our implied contrast between 1851 and 1951' suggested that 'we are deliberately searching for material which will illustrate the attitude of our great-grandfathers to the problems which concern us most closely'. The ultimate aim was 'to select from the literature just those items which . . . would have been broadcast as wireless talks (preferably as Third Programme talks) if the wireless had existed in 1851'.[39] Awareness of the demands of radio as a medium could have consequences for the ambition to recreate the past on its own terms.

The tensions were perhaps most apparent over the question of music. It was evidently the intention of the co-ordinators of the week that a real sense should be conveyed of typical Victorian music-making. The music department accepted this, and put together a concert for each night of the week, but clearly chafed at the notion of recreating too closely Victorian concerts. In a letter to Harman Grisewood, the controller of the Third Programme, Sir Steuart Wilson, the head of music, observed that 'we should have to avoid altogether some of the most characteristic Victoriana, which would be quite intolerable to modern listeners'.[40] Laslett was strongly committed to revealing 'the indelible impression of everything hanging together in some mysterious way because it all belongs to the same date'.[41] He argued that here was something novel which radio alone could provide, namely the opportunity to live for a week in 1851. Evidently, within the music department there was less enthusiasm for the prospect of residence in 1851.

1851 Week was an innovative and exciting venture, which provoked, according to Listener Research, a largely positive response.[42] Serious effort was put into conveying the news of the period, as though it were news rather than history. The selection of news items was governed by consideration of topicality with reference to both 1851 and 1951, as is apparent in Laslett's recommendation of Dickens on railway strikes. *The Listener* suggested that a report on 'colonial self-government' based on parliamentary debates about the Seventh Kaffir War in South Africa 'provided an interesting contrast with present-day notions of colonial policy'.[43] There was, though, running through *1851 Week* a genuine commitment to offering listeners an encounter with the attitudes and arguments of a century ago. As the director general put it in a memo to the controller of the Third Programme: 'Integrity is everything. Be stern. If only it is genuine it will be memorable.'[44]

In 1951 attention was given by the BBC to the centenary of the Great Exhibition. This coverage lay mainly outside of *1851 Week*, which was programmed on the assumption that the exhibition would receive more than adequate coverage elsewhere. In 2001, Victorian technical achievement loomed large. There were, of course, commemorative programmes on both radio and television, but books were also published and web pages written. Among these, the popularity of *What the Victorians Did For Us*, a light-hearted tour of the Victorian legacy stands out. This whirlwind guide to Victorian achievements, presented by Adam Hart-Davis, was 'a celebration of . . . unparalleled growth and development'. In the book of the series, Hart-Davis remarked that 'the Victorian age laid the foundations for our own; indeed, much of the world we live in is Victorian'.[45] In its portrayal of science and religion, this was essentially a story of scientific progress, as its title suggested. There were clearly episodes to regret – British policy in China in 1839 was described 'as a disgraceful piece of gunboat diplomacy' – but the dominant impression given of the Victorian period is one of expansive accomplishment, growing wealth and the ceaseless codification of life.

Victorian fun received much attention, along with the increase of what Victorians would have called 'ease'. It was the growth of industrial wealth, 'a new stratum of society', that provided the theme for much of the series. This was a fairly heroic view of nineteenth-century capitalism, in which 'the industrial revolution made it possible for anyone with enough drive and business acumen to acquire vast amounts of money'.[46]

While *What the Victorians Did For Us* was a cult success, the prestige history series of recent times was undoubtedly Simon Schama's *A History of Britain*. This was a vast enterprise, in terms of both its temporal sweep and its sheer length on the small screen. It was avowedly interpretive in its approach and thematic in its organisation. The published third volume deals with the years 1776–2000 under the rubric 'The fate of empire'. Empire provides the primary focus for this 'frankly interpretative reading of modern British history', which is described as an attempt 'to bring together imperial and domestic history, trying at all times to look at the importance of India, in particular'.[47]

The Victorians occupied a significant place in this narrative, and one Victorian in particular loomed very large, namely the queen herself. This was undoubtedly the Victorians with Victoria at the centre. It was also the Victoria and Albert story in what at times verged on a portrait of the marriage as much as of an age. The attention given in the series to Victoria follows the grain of recent historiography, much of which has been concerned with the difficulties of representing a sovereign who was also a wife. There are, of course, difficulties in putting Victoria centre-stage, not least in dealing with the political history of the time. Domestic politics was presented largely through the time-honoured Punch-and-Judy show of Gladstone versus Disraeli. The seamless story-telling so prized by television does, of course, demand ruthless selection. After Chartism and the Great Exhibition, much of the population awaited their next walk-on-parts with the revival of the 'condition of England' question in the 1880s.

This is not, however, to present *A History of Britain* as simply history from the winner's point of view. It was, undoubtedly, in some ways, a progressive's account, but certainly its picture of the Victorians offered something a good deal more complex than simple affirmation. The opening image of the Victorian episodes was of the monarch at the Great Exhibition, but Schama's 1840s are very much the 'hungry 1840s', especially, and tragically, in Ireland. While mid-Victorian prosperity healed many of the wounds of industrialisation, it was presented as both a vast and an uneasy achievement. Echoing the concerns of some of the contributors to *Ideas and Beliefs*, Schama insists that 'whatever else might be said about the Victorians, it is impossible to accuse them of complacency'.[48] The image of the Crystal Palace is used to highlight the linked phenomena of economic growth and consumer spectacle, but the chapter closes with Reginald Richardson, former Chartist, campaigning against the despoilation of the landscape.[49] The rise of industry is not incompatible with – indeed, it seems for Schama to reinforce – a yearning for the countryside. If the Victorian age marks the emergence of British modernity, it was a modernity in which town and country were interlinked.

The Victorian age portrayed in *A History of Britain* is fraught with tension, but it was a tension which gave rise to extraordinary creativity, whether artistic, industrial or administrative. However, for Schama, there was a dark side to metropolitan achievement, namely the empire. The chapters on empire argue that, for all the talk of civilising the natives, British policies favouring metropolitan exports had grave consequences for the empire. This is made most apparent in the analysis of famine in India. Schama suggests that the turn towards 'neo-feudal exoticism' after 1857 embodied 'an extraordinary self-deception'. The turn towards ornamentalism is linked to 'the way in which late Victorian Britain – or some of its most powerful spokesmen – reacted to their industrial society'.[50] This diagnosis of the late Victorian empire renders the baroque hierarchy of the Raj as a refuge from industrial reality. The echoes here of Wiener's portrait of the decline of the industrial spirit are as evident as those of Cain and Hopkins's account of British imperialism. The symbiosis of town and city in British modernity, evoked earlier in *A History of Britain*, contrasts with the rapacious neo-feudalism evident in Schama's imperial narrative of 'how the good ship "Victoria" ran aground'.[51]

Simon Schama's *A History of Britain* was much lauded for its narrative drive and popularising vigour. For all their success, however, it has not been the BBC's factual programmes that have projected the Victorians to the widest audience. That title goes to costume drama, and to that genre I now turn.

III

Costume drama attracts large audiences and provokes strong feelings. Since the late 1930s, the serial adaptation of a classic novel has been a mainstay of the schedules. Such programmes have projected images of the Victorians into millions of households over many years. These programmes have often garnered large audiences, but have also generated much discussion. Debate has focused particularly on adaptations as purveyors of nostalgia to a nation infatuated with its 'heritage'. As the concern of this section is with representations of the Victorian past in BBC costume dramas, some general remarks are required about the patterns and character of period drama before more specific themes are tackled. Particular attention is paid to adaptations of Dickens and Trollope and of Thackeray's *Vanity Fair*.

Much commentary on period drama has addressed its preoccupation with surface accuracy.[52] Considerable effort has traditionally been expended on the details of costumes and interiors; and the oddities of this concern with verisimilitude have often been pointed out. A familiar litany of criticisms has emerged, which notes that all dresses are new, all clothes either pristine or ragged, and all teeth implausibly white.[53] It is clearly the case that a certain look became central to the BBC's tradition of serialised classics. As Gerald Davies, set designer of the 1987 *Vanity Fair*, suggested, 'the audience have an expectation of these things and we are aware of that'. He argued that 'they expect the past to be slightly glamorised, a golden age and very appealing, and you are actually using that within the design'.[54] This style is not, of course, the only one available, as recent adaptations of Dickens suggest. Fashions change, as Andrew Davies's dark and broadly satirical 1998 version of *Vanity Fair* demonstrates. The lushness of many dramas set in Victorian England is apparent, but recognition of this should not obscure the different tone evident in some adaptations of the work of Dickens, Hardy or Charlotte Brontë.

The quantity of drama set in the Victorian period broadcast by the BBC in its history is considerable. Even so, the same relatively small number of novels and novelists have tended to dominate that output. There are some trends evident, notably the increased prominence of Hardy since the 1970s, but generally continuity more than change is apparent. The continuing popularity of Dickens is simply the most striking of these. If the same novelists have predominated over time, much the same can be said about the novels. There are some surprises here, though. Despite, or perhaps because of, its high critical reputation, *Hard Times* was a long time in coming to the screen. Television has also tended to fight shy of *Middlemarch*, perhaps put off by Virginia Woolf's daunting description of the book as 'one of the few in English for grown-ups'. Given the Sunday tea-time slot traditionally occupied by classic novel serialisations, and the intended family audience, notions of accessibility did have an impact on patterns of adaptation. Early works of Dickens have proved more popular than his later writings, though in recent years this has changed, along with the timing of broadcasts, as the sexual content of adaptations – and not only those by Andrew Davies – has increased.

Some common generalisations about patterns of adaptation require qualification. Television has always prized human interest, and the idea of adaptations as up-market soap-opera goes back at least to the enormous success of *The Forsyte Saga* in 1967. This is far from surprising. Some novels concerned with politics, notably *Felix Holt*, have not proved congenial to television, but it would be possible to argue that the absence of politics from the period drama has been exaggerated.[55] Some adaptations, like *The Pallisers*, met with a mixed reception, but it is their very existence that is perhaps more noteworthy. The focus of *The Pallisers* was, admittedly, very much the private lives of public figures. Its relationship to Trollope's novels and its contemporary reception are addressed below, but the valid observation that the political content of Victorian novels has often been reduced in the journey from page to screen should not be confused with the claim that party politics has been entirely absent from the period drama. The condition-of-England issue was repeatedly examined by Victorian novelists.

Social criticism has had a powerful presence in some adaptations of Dickens. While Gaskell's *Wives and Daughters* recently hit the small screen, *North and South* was dramatised to considerable acclaim in the late 1960s.[56]

The cosiness of the period drama, particularly in its Sunday tea-time years, has been much criticised. There is, undoubtedly, some justification for this criticism, and it is reflected in the scheduling of what was generally intended to be family viewing.[57] It is worth recalling, though, that the furore generated by the murder of Nancy in the BBC's 1962 version of *Oliver Twist* extended even to parliamentary debate. The competition for audiences provoked by the advent of commercial broadcasting has been cited in explaining departures from the earlier tradition of family values and textual fidelity.[58] Reithian certainties were undoubtedly modified by the emergence of competition, but their demise can be exaggerated – the idea of textual fidelity was never straightforward or uncontested. The 1964 adaptation of *Martin Chuzzlewit* included an opening argument between the Chuzzlewit brothers that is absent from the book; yet it is clear that the makers of the 1987 version of *Vanity Fair* upheld the importance of textual fidelity.[59] For my purposes, the extensive debate about translating novels to the screen is less germane than is the notion of period drama as heritage television.[60] This is approached by examining the composite picture of the Victorian past propagated through the literary adaptation.

It is, of course, a treacherous task. The variety described earlier, and explored below, prohibits easy generalisation. It is possible, though, to make some meaningful remarks. The first is about the *look* of the Victorian period in costume dramas, which has tended to be lovingly furnished and radiantly lit, though this can be overplayed. In recent years, in particular, dramatisations of later Dickens's works have been positively crepuscular. The attention given to houses, interiors and costumes has sometimes presented the Victorian past as a kind of pageant, consisting primarily of the replacement of one frock by another. It was the extraordinary success of *The Forsyte Saga* that did most to establish the prevailing lushness of period adaptation. The second point is about technology in adaptations of Victorian novels. Train journeys are nearly as common as engagements. While the horse-drawn carriage dominates the televisual world of Austen, it is the railway carriage, often as the opening shot, that predominates in televisual Victoriana. The transition was nicely exemplified by the start of the 1993 *Middlemarch* in which Tertius Lydgate observes the construction of the railways and remarks: 'Look! The future!'[61] While it was conventional wisdom in the mid-nineteenth century that railways were, along with the telegraph, emblematic of the march of progress, it has become a powerful signifier of the Victorian past. The appearance of the London Underground at the start of Iain Softley's 1997 film of *The Wings of the Dove* updates the familiar Victorian steam-driven train, striking a more modern note.

There is a persistent tension in Victorian costume drama between distance and immediacy. The widespread emphasis on the well-upholstered Victorianism of period drama has been matched by complaints that the emotional landscape portrayed has been modernised to satisfy the requirements of a contemporary audience. This charge was apparent in criticism of the 1974 serial *The Pallisers*, as well as of more recent adaptations such as the 1998 version of *Vanity Fair*, celebrated in *Radio Times* as a pioneering example of girl power.[62] The most recent examples of the genre, such as the 2001 *The Way We Live Now*, have been presented as distinctly modern. Comparisons between Melmotte and Robert Maxwell, the newspaper tycoon, abounded both in the press and on television. This tendency is apparent also in drama set in the Victorian period but based on recently published historical novels. The prime example of this is, undoubtedly, *Tipping the Velvet*, in which the 'Other Victorians' were portrayed with a novel explicitness. This evoked a metropolitan world of music halls and same-sex relationships little glimpsed within the traditions of the classic novel adaptation. Recent historiography has done much to recover the cultures of same-sex relationships in late nineteenth-century London, moving beyond a fixation with the operatic demise of Oscar Wilde.[63] These are, however, difficult themes to treat televisually without recourse to anachronism.

The complexities of the Victorians on the BBC are nicely exemplified by the career of Dickens. As the currency of the adjective 'Dickensian' suggests, images derived from Dickens have done much to colour perceptions of the Victorian past. This is a subject which has received considerable coverage, and is treated here only briefly. John Gardiner has rightly drawn attention to the different faces of Dickens on radio and television.[64] Bransby Williams, the music-hall veteran and Victorian, was performing his Dickensian monologues on radio, and then on television, as late as 1946. Here it was the Dickens of Christmas and Dingley Dell, as immortalised on the £10 note, which predominated. There is, of course, a darker Dickens, apparent in his social criticism, whose critical stock has risen since the 1940s. Through melodrama and sentimentality, Dickens combines evocation of good cheer, often identified with a passing older England, and lurid portrayals of the dust-heap excesses of nineteenth-century capitalism. Interpretations of the films made by David Lean in the post-Second World War period have tended, following Raphael Samuel, to locate them at a radical moment in which the vestiges of Victorian squalor were banished by letting in the light of the future, as Pip famously does at the close of Lean's *Great Expectations*. Yet, it is often claimed, by the 1960s Dickens had been subsumed within the packaged Victorianism of the theme pub. Samuel argued that even notionally radical readings of Dickens, like Christine Edzard's 1987 film of *Little Dorrit*, were prevented by their realist preoccupation with surface details from conveying the melodramatic vibrancy and critical power of the originals.[65] From the late 1970s, it was the late works of

Dickens, often encrusted with dirt, that were appearing more regularly on television. Granada's 1977 *Hard Times* and the BBC's 1985 *Bleak House* were important examples of this. In introducing his 1994 adaptation of *Martin Chuzzlewit*, it was the 1985 *Bleak House* to which David Lodge particularly appealed. *Martin Chuzzlewit* was a production presented by its makers as a far cry from the 'heritage' feel of the previous year's *Middlemarch*.[66] The more psychological and non-naturalistic Dickens invoked in post-war literary criticism has been apparent in more recent adaptations, such as Tony Marchant's 1999 *Great Expectations* or the 1998 version of *Our Mutual Friend*.

Dickens has often been celebrated, most canonically by Eisenstein, as a uniquely visual novelist.[67] Recent literary criticism has been correspondingly interested in the relationship between theatre and the novel, and in the role of illustration in nineteenth-century fiction.[68] These issues are well illustrated by the complex career of *Vanity Fair* on television. The novel has been dramatised four times by the BBC, most recently in Andrew Davies's controversial 1998 version. *Vanity Fair* was initially published in serial form in 1847–48. The novel is, of course, set in the 1810s, and this does present some initial questions for adaptations. It is after all far from reverential in its recreation of the 1810s, just as it is so often sharply satirical in tone. Joyce Hawkins, costume designer for the 1987 adaptation, observed that she had not used Thackeray's illustrations 'because they were wrong'.[69] This does, of course, raise the question of Thackeray's purpose in setting the novel thirty or so years before his time of writing. It seems strange to see the novel as purely historical, as though Thackeray was ingenuously creating a world which had been safely superseded by mid-Victorian morality. The playfulness apparent in the novel is hardly captured by an obsession with the number of buttons on regimental jackets. Thackeray calls the fight between Figs and Cuff 'the last charge of the Guard', only to note that 'it *would* have been, only Waterloo had not yet taken place'.[70] In Andrew Davies's 1998 version, deliberate anachronism became central to the whole design, with Natasha Little playing Becky Sharp as though still starring in *This Life*.

The popularity of the novels of Dickens and of Thackeray's *Vanity Fair* as sources for television is scarcely surprising. Trollope's presence on the small screen is perhaps more so. The subject matter of both *The Pallisers* and *The Barchester Chronicles* does not seem obviously suited to the demands of television. The broadcasting of Simon Raven's *The Pallisers* in 1974 was widely regarded as an attempt to recreate the success of *The Forsyte Saga*, but it was equally widely regarded by the press as a failure to do so. Michael Ratcliffe rightly observed in *The Times* that 'there was no visual tradition of Trollope', and he regarded the first episode as 'anonymous, lavish and dull'.[71] Roy Hattersley in *The Listener* attacked the serial for its failure to covey the sombreness of Victorian life, and for its inclusion of references to sex.[72] Raymond Williams contrasted the genuine relationship possible with the bourgeois world of *The Forsyte Saga* with the aristocratic remoteness apparent in *The Pallisers*.[73] Audience figures were far from sensational, though loyal viewers challenged the strictures of the press. In many respects, *The Pallisers* indicates that the heritage fascination with lost glamour does not guarantee popular success without a more direct relationship to characters. However grand the houses, a sense of connectedness with the characters and an interest in the plot are as necessary for costume drama as for any other kind of drama.

In some respects the milieu of *The Barchester Chronicles* might appear even less likely to win audience approval than the high-powered world of *The Pallisers*. Yet the serial proved notably the more successful. Peter Ackroyd called it 'a cosy subject treated in a cosy manner' but wondered whether, as during the Second World War, 'our present recession will work wonders for *The Barchester Chronicles*'.[74] Alan Plater's adaptation was described in the *Radio Times* as 'highly topical'. The presence of Nigel Hawthorne, essentially reprising his role in *Yes, Minister*, may have added to this impression. The 'modernisers' of the serial, Mrs Proudie and Obadiah Slope, were compared unfavourably to the 'young left wingers' of *The Warden*. They were 'more dogmatic and self-righteous and monetarist' than their counterparts in the earlier novel.[75] The highlighting of contemporary relevance in the 2001 version of *The Way We Live Now* emerges as of a piece with traditions of dramatising Trollope for television. It was, of course, no longer monetarists, but the 1980s in general, and Robert Maxwell in particular, that became the target. The relationship, though, differed. In *The Barchester Chronicles*, local resistance to centralising modernisation is portrayed sympathetically, but the analogy with the 1980s takes some making. In *The Way We Live Now*, David Suchet's Melmotte amounted at times to an impersonation of Maxwell. Assertion of continuity, or parallels, between then and now were noticeably more overt.

IV

This chapter has surveyed the complex relationship between the BBC and the Victorians across an extensive period and a variety of genres. BBC productions have contributed significantly to both academic and more popular evaluations of the Victorian period. The BBC was, through *Ideas and Beliefs*, in the vanguard of the professional 'revaluation' of the Victorian age. In its early years, it was arguably better disposed to the nineteenth century than to the world of Stracheyite Bloomsbury, though, precisely because of this, it may also have been more closely aligned to broader currents of public opinion than to the aesthetes of WC1. It has, though, also created resonant images of the Victorian age, from its period adaptations to such original series as *The Onedin Line*. The impact of such representations on popular perceptions is both complex and elusive. Audience researchers asked viewers of *The Onedin Line* whether they made connections between the programme and the industrial unrest of the 1970s. The answer, in the main, was 'No'.[76] Cruder versions of the 'heritage' argument have tended to read off audience reaction from their interpretation of the product concerned, supported by the existence of visitor centres and historical theme parks. The commodification of the past and the existence of the 'heritage' industry are undeniable, but care is required in generalising about popular perceptions on what is somewhat slender evidence. This chapter has preferred the more manageable task of examining the BBC's production of images of the Victorians. The relationship it has revealed is complex, but it is perhaps that very complexity, rather than the flatness suggested by some critics of the heritage industry, which deserves greater acknowledgement than it has tended to receive.

Notes

1 R. Samuel, *Theatres of Memory*, vol. 1: *Past and Present in Contemporary Culture* (London: Verso, 1994), p. 13.
2 D. L. LeMahieu, 'John Reith, 1889–1971: entrepreneur of collectivism', in S. Pedersen and P. Mandler (eds), *After the Victorians: Private Conscience and Public Duty in Modern Britain. Essays in Memory of John Clive* (London: Routledge, 1994), p. 192.
3 J. Reith, *Broadcast Over Britain* (London: Hodder & Stoughton, 1924), p. 34.
4 J. Reith, 'Memorandum of information on the scope and conduct of the Broadcasting service' (1925), p. 3, quoted in P. Scannell and D. Cardiff, *A Social History of Broadcasting*, vol. 1: *Serving the Nation* (Oxford: Blackwell, 1991), pp. 8–9.
5 *Observer*, 8 December 2002, p. 1.
6 Scannell and Cardiff, *Social History of Broadcasting*, pp. 333–56.
7 Noel Annan et al., *Ideas and Beliefs of the Victorians: An Historic Revaluation of the Victorian Age* (London: Sylvan Press, 1949).
8 *Ibid.*, p. 11.
9 A. Briggs, *The History of Broadcasting in the United Kingdom*, vol. 4: *Sound and Vision* (Oxford: Oxford University Press, 1979), p. 67.
10 J. Gardiner, *The Victorians: An Age in Retrospect* (London: London & Hambledon, 2002), pp. 59–60, 172–9.
11 BBC Written Archives Centre, Caversham, R 51/254/1.
12 Annan et al., *Ideas and Beliefs*, p. 12.
13 Grisewood to Laslett, 4 June 1948, BBC Written Archives Centre, R 51/254/1.
14 *Ibid.*, Memo by W. N. Newton, 3 May 1948.
15 Annan et al., *Ideas and Beliefs*, p. 15.
16 *The Times*, 29 May 1948, p. 5.
17 Memo by Grisewood, 7 May 1947, BBC Written Archives Centre, R51/254/1.
18 *Ibid.*, Memo by Rowntree to Barnes and Grisewood, 4 August 1947.
19 *Ibid.*, Memo by Grisewood, 4 May 1947.
20 Annan et al., *Ideas and Beliefs*, pp. 15–16.
21 *Ibid.*, p. 27.
22 *Ibid.*, p. 73.

23 *Ibid.*, p. 294.
24 *Ibid.*, p. 260.
25 *Ibid.*, pp. 423, 435.
26 *Ibid.*, p. 53.
27 *Ibid.*, pp. 50–1.
28 *Ibid.*, p. 78.
29 Memo from Rowntree to Barnes and Grisewood, 21 May 1947, BBC Written Archives Centre, R51/254/1.
30 Noel Annan, *Leslie Stephen: His Thought and Character in Relation to His Time* (London: MacGibbon & Kee, 1951); Martin Wiener, *Between Two Worlds: The Political Thought of Graham Wallas* (Oxford: Clarendon Press, 1971).
31 Memo by Rowntree, 27 June 1947, BBC Written Archives Centre, R51/254/1.
32 *Ibid.*, Memo by G. Barnes, 17 September 1947.
33 Annan *et al.*, *Ideas and Beliefs*, p. 323.
34 *Ibid.*, pp. 328–9.
35 *Ibid.*, p. 359.
36 *Ibid.*, pp. 359, 361, 364.
37 Memo by Rowntree, 21 May 1947, BBC Written Archives Centre, R51/254/1.
38 *Ibid.*, Laslett, 'Report of preliminary research', 11 November 1950, R51/131/1.
39 *Ibid.*
40 *Ibid.*, Head of music to controller of the Third Programme, 22 October 1950.
41 *Radio Times*, 20 April 1951, p. 6.
42 H. Carpenter, *The Envy of the World: Fifty Years of the BBC Third Programme and Radio 3* (London: Weidenfeld & Nicolson, 1996), pp. 108–9.
43 *Listener*, 3 May 1951.
44 Director-general to controller of the Third Programme, 18 December 1950, BBC Written Archives Centre, R51/131/1.
45 A. Hart-Davis, *What the Victorians Did For Us* (London: BBC, 2001), pp. 7–9.
46 *Ibid.*, pp. 72, 155, 176.
47 S. Schama, *A History of Britain*, vol. 3: *The Fate of Empire 1776–2000* (London: BBC, 2002), p. 9.
48 *Ibid.*, pp. 172–3.
49 *Ibid.*, p. 193.
50 *Ibid.*, p. 346.
51 *Ibid.*, p. 269.
52 These issues are explored in R. Giddings, K. Selby and C. Wensley, *Screening the Novel: The Theory and Practice of Literary Dramatisation* (Basingstoke: Macmillan, 1990).
53 R. Giddings and K. Selby, *The Classic Serial on Television and Radio* (Basingstoke: Palgrave, 2001).
54 Giddings, Selby and Wensley, *Screening the Novel*, p. 154.
55 For an analysis of serial drama as part of the heritage industry, see J. Rice and C. Saunders, 'Consuming *Middlemarch*: the construction and consumption of nostalgia in Stamford', in D. Cartmell, I. Q. Hunter, H. Klaye and I. Whelehan (eds), *Pulping Fictions: Consuming Culture Across the Literature/Media Divide* (London: Pluto Press, 1996), pp. 85–98.
56 Raymond Williams wrote: 'It is as if some part of the BBC, some part of England, turns with particular readiness to the years before 1900: with nostalgia, of course, as we shall see in *The Forsyte Saga*; but also with interest, with

a connection to that history of the industrial revolution, the class war, the struggle for democracy, which is so clearly unfinished but which can be looked at, carefully and seriously, if there is a bonnet of two about': *Listener*, 12 September 1968, p. 347.

57 Much costume drama was shown outside of the Sunday slot: see Giddings and Selby, *Classic Serial*, p. 26.

58 *Ibid.*, pp. 22–30.

59 *Radio Times*, 5 November 1994, pp. 26–30.

60 As early as 1974, Michael Ratcliffe was noting that 'costume drama is under attack' and that Hugh Whitemore's *Outrage* was charged with 'being too glossy, too clean': *The Times*, 2 May 1974, p. 13.

61 See Giddings and Selby, *Classic Serial*, p. 92.

62 *The Times*, 21 January 1974, p. 7; *Radio Times*, 31 October 1998, pp. 24–8; the front cover read, 'Girl power – if you don't know a woman like Becky Sharp you'll want to'.

63 The literature here is considerable: a pioneering study was J. Weeks, *Sex, Politics and Society: The Regulation of Sexuality since 1800* (London: Longman, 1989), chs 5–6. On *fin-de-siècle* London, see J. Walkowitz, *City of Dreadful Delight: Narratives of Sexual Danger in Victorian London* (London: Virago, 1992).

64 Gardiner, *The Victorians*, pp. 161–81.

65 Samuel, *Theatres of Memory*, p. 402.

66 *Radio Times*, 5 November 1994, p. 28.

67 S. Eisenstein, 'Dickens, Griffith, and the film today', in his *Film Form: Essays in Film Theory*, ed. and trans. J. Leyda (London: Dennis Dobson, 1949), pp. 195–255.

68 These trends are reflected in, for instance, J. O. Jordan (ed.), *The Cambridge Companion to Charles Dickens* (Cambridge: Cambridge University Press, 2001).

69 Giddings, Selby and Wensley, *Screening the Novel*, p. 110.

70 W. M. Thackeray, *Vanity Fair*, ed. J. Carey (London: Penguin, 2001), p. 53.

71 *The Times*, 21 January 1974, p. 7.

72 *Listener*, 25 July 1974, pp. 105–7.

73 *Listener*, 31 January 1974, p. 155.

74 *The Times*, 11 November 1982, p. 10.

75 *Radio Times*, 6 November 1982, pp. 84–90.

76 A. Briggs, *The History of Broadcasting in the United Kingdom*, vol. 5: *Competition* (Oxford: Oxford University Press, 1995), p. 945.

11

Theme-park Victoriana

John Gardiner

Theme-park history and the Victorians

In 2001 the Victoria and Albert Museum hosted an exhibition that set out to show 'the Victorians as they saw themselves – as the inventors of the modern world'.[1] A somewhat Whiggish scheme, one might think; but, a century on from the demise of Queen Victoria, it was felt that there was a need for a reminder of how the Victorians 'invented' modern Britons.[2] And though the curators used all the conventional trappings of museum display in 'The Victorian Vision' – carefully captioned paintings, documents and artefacts encased by glass – a more visceral claim to connection with the Victorians was also extended, with buttons that could be pressed to summon machinery into action, headphones to be donned in order to hear the voices of Florence Nightingale, William Gladstone and music-hall performers, and whole walls turned into cinema screens for Victorian street scenes. 'Exhibition design', commented its designer John Outram, 'is a bit like theatre design, a show to draw the visitor in.'[3]

There are elements here of what might be called a 'theme-park' approach to the Victorians. This is a view of history in museums, visitor attractions and shops that foregrounds the interactive and the commercial, favours sensory input and atmosphere above the dryly factual, and elevates private and local experience beyond the traditional narratives of national history. Its manifestations are the museum display, the contents of the museum gift shop, the antique and the imitation period object. Bracketed together as they sometimes are under the term 'heritage industry' (a phrase coined by Robert Hewison in the 1980s), these characteristics and manifestations have been the site of fierce debate among historians and cultural critics for the last twenty years.[4] Aspects of these characteristics and manifestations, and this debate, are explored in the course of this chapter. Meanwhile, it may be useful to outline some of the implications of according the Victorians 'theme-park' treatment.

One implication, pertinent to what is to follow, is that the search for a uniquely *Victorian* strand within 'heritage' is in some respects an artificial exercise. 'Heritage', writes David Lowenthal, a leading scholar on the subject, 'is not an inquiry into the past but a celebration of it . . . tailored to present-day purposes'.[5] We might infer from this that theme-park Victoriana embodies a relationship with the past rather than a systematic attempt to reflect the Victorian period as a scholarly, nuanced whole. Here is the past as a site of nostalgia and atmosphere, where the *frisson* of 'olden times' often seems to be more potent than excitement generated by conscious connection with a particular age, and is as applicable to the Victorians as it is to, say, the Second World War. A stroll around any 'Past Times' shop (the chain was founded in 1986) or the large gift shop at the Victoria and Albert Museum will confirm how comfortably imitation Victoriana nestles alongside arte- facts from other periods when it is being sold to the public.

This tendency to collapse different historical periods within a generalised view of the national 'heritage' has been underpinned by the success of organisations such as the National Trust (founded in 1895) and English Heritage (founded in 1983) – savers and restorers, respectively, of Tyntesfield in Somerset (discussed below) and the Albert Memorial.[6] But the rhetoric of conservation, as the names of these two organisations suggest, has essentially been a matter of English and/or national pride – the past as a homogeneous whole, in which it has become increasingly unthink- able (and impolitic) to acknowledge the greater claims of any specific period.[7] Those organisations have benefited from influential connections, substantial governmental assistance and widespread public support. (By the end of the twentieth century the National Trust had achieved the dazzling feat of a membership in excess of 2 million.)[8] Smaller organisations such as the Victorian Society (founded in 1958) have done sterling work in raising the profile of Victorian architecture, but when it comes to raising money they have found public generosity to run less deep. The unsuccess- ful bid to save Euston Arch in 1962 was one notable setback for the society.[9]

If this tendency to submerge the Victorians within a generalised view of the national heritage may seem detrimental to a nuanced engagement with them, we might none the less withhold some of our pessimism. For a further implication of theme-park attitudes to history is that they embody a post- war trend that has been broadly beneficial to our appreciation of the Vic- torians. This relates to the generational animus that was so marked a feature of the intellectual reaction against the Victorians in the early twentieth century. When, according to the *Oxford English Dictionary*, Ezra Pound coined the term 'Victoriana' in 1918, he used it to attack rather than to cel- ebrate the past. 'For most of us', he declared, 'the odour of defunct Victo- riana is so unpleasant . . . that we are content to leave the past where we find it'.[10] There was, as Anthony Burton shows in chapter 8 of this volume, a certain following for Victoriana among Oxford aesthetes like Harold Acton and Henry Yorke in the 1920s, but it was not really until after the Second World War that Victoriana – and the Victorians in general – were able to escape the shadow of Stracheyan sniping.[11] For Asa Briggs the

Festival of Britain, with its echoes of 1851, was a key moment in the intellectual rehabilitation of Victoriana.[12]

Generational hostility to the Victorians has fallen away completely since the 1950s and 1960s. Here we should not forget the demographic aspect of changing attitudes to the Victorians, and the fact that the last cohort of people who could reasonably have been called 'Victorian' by upbringing was passing away during the third quarter of the twentieth century – think, for example, of the deaths of George VI (1952), Winston Churchill (1965), Clement Attlee (1967) and Bertrand Russell (1970). These are only high-profile demises; everywhere, in those years, the last Victorians were dying out. From the perspective of the fully fledged 'heritage industry' of the 1980s and 1990s, the waning of generational animus has anticipated and complemented the integration of the Victorians within a generalised vision of the national heritage. According the Victorians theme-park treatment has therefore, for all its conceptual shortcomings, underlined their emotional proximity to the present.

The remainder of this chapter looks at three aspects of theme-park Victoriana – the rediscovery of alternative histories; interacting with the past; and the commercial dimension to the 'selling' of the Victorians – before returning briefly to consider the debate among scholars about the benefits and drawbacks of theme-park history.

Whose heritage?

An important social development underpinning theme-park Victoriana since the 1970s has been the growth in the number of museums and museum-goers. Between 1971 and 1987 the number of museums in the United Kingdom doubled to 2,131, and by 2001 that figure had increased to over 2,500 museums.[13] Very few of them, of course, were museums uniquely dedicated to the Victorian period, but it is significant that those with substantial holdings of Victoriana, such as the Victoria and Albert Museum, could enjoy well in excess of a million visits annually by the turn of the millennium.[14] What drew visitors in such large numbers? In part, perhaps, it was the result of deep-rooted changes within perceptions of history and how it should be reflected within museums.[15] And, ironically, where the Victorians were concerned, this echoed a move away from a recognisably 'Victorian' (in the sense of neo-Arnoldian) attitude to museums that had largely held sway until the Second World War. In 1949, for example, Sir John Forsdyke, director of the British Museum, stated that 'the first duty of a museum is . . . to demonstrate the truth of things', adding that in national museums, truth 'is the paramount consideration, for these institutions are the ultimate authorities in matters of fact that rest upon material evidence'.[16]

That mid-twentieth century voice, urbane and assured, now seems rather dated. Forsdyke's certainty that exhibits can demonstrate 'truth' jars against sensibilities weaned on post-modernism, while his implicit faith in a manageable relationship between museums and their public – one based on the exchange of fact-based knowledge – sits oddly alongside our experience of the varied ways in which we use the past. Here we have been profoundly influenced by the rise, since the 1960s and 1970s, of linguistic theory and of social and economic history.[17] As late as 1944 G. M. Trevelyan was able to comment (somewhat wryly) that social history was 'history with the politics left out'. A generation later social history was something closer to history with the ordinary people put back in. With initiatives like the History Workshop movement from the late 1960s, people began to reclaim and rewrite history with greater attention given to language, region and everyday experience.[18] Equally, the ways in which our memory of the Victorians (and other periods) have been manipulated or even 'invented' has been one of the most powerful legacies of recent scholarship.[19]

To what extent did these changes affect the emergence of a theme-park approach to the Victorians? While inevitably avoiding the more theoretical aspects of professional academic practice, schools and libraries were the places where regional and family history was pushed to the fore. Projects for children might typically include researching the history of a local Victorian building, such as their own school, or a brewery, mill or church. Places like the Centre for Kentish Studies at Maidstone also testify to the strength of interest in local history. In the year 1997–98 over 8,000 people drew on its resources, which include Kent's electoral registers from 1832, census returns from 1841 to 1891, wills and inventories up to 1858, and records of local regiments.[20] Public libraries and county record offices have grown used to accommodating a daily stream of visitors eager to consult census figures and to trace ancestors. Most of these census returns (stored on microfilm) are, of course, Victorian in origin, as befits an age obsessed with statistics.[21]

Museums have also come round to privileging local Victorian history. Small museums, lacking extensive collections, have always tended to emphasise local connections. Larger museums have not necessarily been so fast. The Birmingham Museum and Art Gallery, with its fine collection of pre-Raphaelites, for many years restricted municipal pride to its connection with figures like Sir Edward Burne-Jones. It was not really until after the Second World War that Birmingham grew fully sensitive to its industrial past. Perhaps it needed post-industrial distance to lend enchantment. 'The relics of the near past are the archaeology of the future', Trenchard Cox reflected in 1949, 'and all records of the Industrial Revolution will soon be lost unless they are preserved in some technical museum.'[22] Cox's own Birmingham Museum was soon to do something like this. The museum today makes great play of its 100–foot-long Industrial Hall, replete with locally manufactured ceramics, glass, metalwork and carved ivory. Elsewhere in Birmingham, the canals that once acted as lifelines to local industries, many miles of which had been closed by the 1960s, have been restored since the 1980s and made open to public navigation.

This re-instatement of alternative pasts, those based on regional and working-class histories, has become one of the most notable features of theme-park Victoriana. Several of these tourist attractions are discussed below in a slightly different context, but here it is worth noting a few examples. At the Ironbridge Gorge in Shropshire, opened in 1973, an entire Victorian town, called Blists Hill, has been recreated with brick-and-tile works, blast furnaces, iron foundry, tinsmith and blacksmith. The brick-and-tile works, blast furnaces and tinsmith are all indicated in current publicity as 'original' features of the site. Prouder still of their 'living' connection with the past are two industrial museums in Sheffield, Abbeydale Industrial Hamlet (opened in 1970) and Kelham Island Museum (opened in 1982). Kelham Island employs genuine 'little mesters' (craftsmen in cutlery, silverware and tool-making) and boasts the country's only surviving example of the Bessemer steel converter (crucial for Sheffield's manufacture between 1865 and 1975). Saltaire, near Bradford, gradually restored to its Victorian self since the 1970s, is a similar example of esteem for local industrial history. The ambivalence of the town's status as an emblem of a lost way of life, however, was signalled by its designation as a 'world heritage site' by UNESCO in December 2001.[23] (Ironic, too, is the fact that its '1853 Gallery' has became celebrated for housing not Victorian paintings but those of a later Bradford native, David Hockney.)

These somewhat wistful post-industrial perspectives on local heritage, felt no doubt all the more keenly in the north during the 1980s–1990s, exemplify the way in which theme-park Victoriana has been used to help stage a quiet act of historical revisionism. No longer is it presumed, as it was until the Second World War, that national heritage is the tale of kings, queens, great battles and general progress.[24] Gone is the mild condescension towards the provinces on the part of luminaries such as Sir John Forsdyke, who talked about national museums as the ultimate repositories of historical 'truth'. The passing away of this neo-Arnoldian hierarchy of museums is not to be much lamented. And it is not to be much lamented because it has widened and invigorated our potential connection with the Victorians. The death of a 'Victorian' attitude to museum display does not necessarily signal the death of the Victorian past.[25] Resurgent in recent years have been local pride and an appreciation of the craftsmanship and sheer drudgery that made Victorian society what it was.

Interacting with the past

Part of the revolution in school practice after the Second World War was a mounting emphasis on historical empathy.[26] This was the result of the decline of earlier educational practices such as learning about the lives of inspirational Victorian heroes and imperialists.[27] Drum-and-trumpet history of this kind, perhaps unsurprisingly, declined in the wake of war and the unravelling of empire. So, too, were new intellectual and social trends on the ascendant. In the 1960s, writes Raphael Samuel, 'teachers were encouraged to think of themselves as "educationalists" rather than specialists; to see their role as an enabling rather than a didactic one, and their subjects as adjuncts to the acquirement of cognitive skills'.[28] In such a climate children were taught that imagining their way into the past was more important than learning dates and names. Margaret Thatcher and Kenneth Baker famously tried to reassert the centrality of facts and figures in the Education Act of 1988. Yet, although story-telling about famous Victorians has enjoyed something of a renaissance at the turn of the millennium, the legacy of post-war individualism has so far proved to be ineradicable.[29]

This individualism has filtered powerfully into the National Curriculum since the 1990s, where personal experience is privileged to an unprecedented degree. Younger children have taken part in activities like 'Doing the Victorians', which involves playing such roles as the Victorian servant or maid, while 'A Day in the life of a Victorian school' has had children sitting on benches, slates in their hands, ready for lessons.[30] By the age of 14 pupils are expected to have a broad knowledge of nineteenth-century imperialism and industrialisation, and their impact on indigenous races and different social classes, respectively.[31] It is difficult to imagine children prior to the Second World War being taught about the Victorians with quite such political correctness.

The relevance of all this to theme-park Victoriana is that a close link has been encouraged between schools and museums, in which there is continuity between acting out aspects of Victorian life and interacting with either real or imitation Victoriana. Many museums now have education officers and museums send out information or exercise packs to schools in advance of organised trips. Kelham Island Museum actively advertises exhibits in which younger children can be 'processed like steel' as being suitable for particular year-groupings within the National Curriculum.[32] Likewise, the interactive Nicholas Nickleby-style schoolroom at the Charles Dickens Centre in Rochester complements activities such as 'A day in the life of a Victorian school', while 'Doing the Victorians' is echoed, at York Castle Museum, by the 'real-life experience' of walking down 'a genuine Victorian cobbled street' to 'call at the Victorian police station'.[33] Victoriana, meanwhile, goes out to schools as well. 'Cost of coach travel prohibitive?' asks the Macclesfield Heritage Centre. 'Then let a visit from our education staff put the zing into your topic with an array of unusual Victorian artefacts.'[34]

Perhaps the most thorough of all interactive experiences, however, is to be found at Blists Hill, Ironbridge Gorge. Its own promotional description in 2002 ran:

Blists Hill is one of the largest open air museums in Britain. A small Victorian town has been created above thirty acres of woodland walks on the banks of the Shropshire Canal. The top of the town has a bank, grocer's shop, chemist, printing shop, bakers and sweetshop, while the back streets are busy with small offices, works and factories including a working foundry and iron rolling mill. Cottage gardens and smallholdings thrive and refreshment is always available at the New Inn Victorian pub and the Forest Glen Pavilion tea rooms. Victorian souvenirs on sale include cast-iron, copperware and plaster mouldings made on site, as well as traditional sweets, chemist recipes and freshly baked buns. Costumed staff give a warm welcome and a serious insight into how life was lived in Victorian times.[35]

Blists Hill offers 'have-a-go' events in which participants can 'get a real flavour of working life as it was more than one hundred years ago'. The options available over one weekend in April 2002 included participation in making bricks, weaving rugs, printing, plaiting leather and grooming horses.

A different kind of interactive experience has focused on the atmosphere generated by Victoriana in time-capsule form. The most famous of such time-capsules was Osborne House, Queen's Victoria's beloved residence on the Isle of Wight. Here, not for the first time, the Victorians anticipated twentieth-century observers in their attitude to 'heritage'.[36] Queen Victoria ordered that parts of Osborne House were to be left exactly as they were when Prince Albert died in 1861. And so, in the closing decades of the nineteenth century, servants at Osborne House were forced to go through an unwittingly elaborate dress-rehearsal for the 'heritage industry' of today, setting out hot water and clothes each morning for a Victorian paterfamilias who would not be there to shave or dress. As early as the First World War, when Osborne House was used as a military convalescents' hospital, Robert Graves enjoyed sleeping in the royal nursery, playing on the royal billiards table and even drinking some of the Rhine wines laid down by Prince Albert.[37] There is interaction, one is tempted to reflect, and interaction. Present-day visitors to Osborne House tend to be much more reverential towards the Victoriana that surrounds them.

Osborne House is not the only Victorian residence in which time has been allowed to stand still. Calke Abbey near Derby was acquired by the National Trust in 1985 in a state of great decay, and since then only 'essential' repair works have been undertaken to the house. This can be explained partly by the vagaries of finance, but also by a 'heritage' aesthetic that prizes the 'authenticity' of decay. 'Collections of birds, paintings, ornaments and family photographs dating from [the Victorian] period and earlier sit amongst peeling wall paper and paint', one guide comments with clear enthusiasm, 'seeming to wait for the family to return.'[38]

More remarkable still was the purchase by the National Trust in 2002 (with public and government aid), at a cost of £24m, of Tyntesfield in Somerset, described by the journalist Maev Kennedy as 'the last great unaltered Victorian mansion and estate'.[39] Commissioned by William Gibbs (the guano entrepreneur), in 1875, and built in a fantastical mock-Gothic style, the house remained within the family until 2001. It includes a rich collection of Victoriana, with original carpets and wallpapers, a kitchen stocked with nineteenth-century cutlery and crockery, innumerable decorative items, ornately carved mantelpieces and even a mock-Gothic chapel. As Mark Girouard points out, the Victoriana has been supplemented by later additions, and much has been 'banished to bedrooms, corridors, attics and cellars'.[40] Theme-park Victoriana often thrives off artefacts that have survived by chance, or, as here, by the waning fortunes of stately home owners who have not had the money to cast off antiquity.[41] Yet we may be sure that it will be these very corridors and cellars that attract much attention when Tyntesfield is opened to the public.

Another facet of theme-park Victoriana has been the way in which certain buildings and landscapes have been venerated on account of their supposed 'link' with the past. The 'blue plaque' scheme, currently overseen by English Heritage, has always given a prominent place to Victorians. The houses of Macaulay, Carlyle and Gladstone were accorded plaques in 1903, 1907 and 1908, respectively, the Gladstone plaque suggesting by the rapidity of its appearance (he had died only a decade earlier) an overhang from the Victorian age of hero-worship.[42] A less 'heroic' figure like Wilde had to wait until the centenary of his birth, 1954, for a plaque to appear on his Chelsea home; but then Matthew Arnold, too, had to wait until 1954 before one of his houses was accorded 'heritage' treatment. The logic of the blue plaque scheme is, no doubt, somewhat arcane; but it has nevertheless bequeathed to us a peppering of blue lozenges across the country.[43] 'Plaques don't just honour the great figures of the past', comments English Heritage. 'They celebrate a personal connection with an actual building and transform bricks and mortar into living history.'[44]

This echoes the way in which we can feel 'haunted' by the Victorians when we visit their homes or the landscapes they inhabited.[45] This seems particularly the case where the individuals in question were creative artists supposedly inspired by a sense of place – one thinks of the connection (played up by tourist boards) between Hardy and Dorset, or Elgar and the Malverns.[46] Lucasta Miller, meanwhile, has shown that tremendous interest was taken in the relationship between the windswept Yorkshire moors and the mythically tragic existence of the Brontë sisters.[47] At any rate, that was how Elizabeth Gaskell chose to portray Charlotte in her 1857 biography, seeking to emphasise her provincial naivety as a way of disarming the criticism that no polite mid-Victorian novelist could have written such passionate novels. But the image stuck. Haworth Parsonage opened as a museum in 1928, and continues to house clothes, writing implements, household objects and other fairly unsensational items, all nevertheless invested with a special 'charge' to Brontë lovers. One visitor described how, in 1976, after gaining permission momentarily to don Emily's shawl, she felt the hands of its long-dead owner pressing on her.[48]

Buying and selling the past

Visitors to Haworth Parsonage can take home items that will commemorate their experience of Brontë country. These come in the guise of tea-towels, ashtrays, biscuits and soap on sale in the gift shop. A similar situation exists in most museums today, such that the absence of a gift shop might be considered almost tantamount to professional ineptitude. Elsewhere, when entrepreneurs can play up historical connections, tours are offered. 'Dickens tours' of Rochester and London are offered, for example, tracing places visited by the author and depicted in the novels. Stranger by far is the lucrative 'heritage industry' that since the 1960s has developed out of tours of the murder sites of Jack the Ripper in London's East End. A host of companies compete here for an apparently inexhaustible market of tourists, while the tour culture itself has become a contentious issue. In 2001 a Tower Hamlets' councillor reported complaints from residents that the swarm of Ripper-hunters was threatening to turn the area into 'a zoo or circus'.[49]

Museum gift shops and 'heritage' tours have evolved in response to the important commercial dimension within theme-park Victoriana. This contrasts markedly with earlier attitudes to Victorian memorabilia. 'Victoriana', as we have seen, initially tended to carry a pejorative connotation – it was the detritus of antiquity, the emblem of all that was faded and constricted. In *Lady Chatterley's Lover* (1928), for example, D. H. Lawrence has Connie discover an intricate Victorian utility box. 'The thing was wonderfully made and contrived', Lawrence writes, 'excellent craftsmanship of the best Victorian order. But somehow it was monstrous . . . It had a peculiar soullessness.'[50] Lawrence's feelings were echoed in the 1930s by commentators like John Steegman, who argued that refined taste had collapsed amid the ostentatious Mammon worship of the Victorian period. That was still Steegman's overall feeling in his *Consort of Taste*, published, perhaps pointedly, on the eve of the Festival of Britain. The Victorians, he argued, had privileged personal whim above objective aesthetic criteria established by a taste-making elite.[51]

It was not until the 1950s and 1960s that Victoriana began to be fully rehabilitated.[52] Acquirers of Victoriana benefited in these years from the passing away of the last generation of Victorians, which allowed an influx of memorabilia to be available cheaply on the Portobello Road (awash with Victorian clothes, jewellery and furniture during the 1960s) and in auction-rooms.[53] This commercialisation of Victoriana was sustained, in turn, by the consumer boom that encouraged a culture of greater expenditure; by the waning of intellectual prejudice against the Victorians after the 1950s; and by the way in which Victoriana was beginning to fall within the now generally agreed remit of 'antique'. According to antiques expert Judith Miller, by the 1970s, the old definition of the antique (anything pre-1840) was softening to accommodate items over 100 years old.[54] Since then, the shortening of the threshold of nostalgia – that span of time that intervenes before something becomes categorised as 'heritage' – has made Victoriana seem even more antique.[55]

Since the 1950s Victoriana of all sorts has fetched remarkable prices at auction. By the mid-1990s, for instance, a 3-inch-tall late Victorian brass photograph frame was costing the collector up to £35; an early Victorian wall clock with a rosewood case, up to £550; and rarer items, such as a set of six Royal Doulton ceramic napkin rings (styled after Dickens's characters), up to £700.[56] Many of these items are displayed in homes that themselves have been renovated in 'period' style, as advocated by such magazines as *Period Living* and *BBC Homes and Antiques*. For Victorian-style renovations, this might mean anything from 'arts and crafts' rusticity, all carved wood and Morris fabrics, to an imitation of the bourgeois domesticity against which that movement reacted, all heavily brocaded curtains and cluttered mantelpieces.[57] Theme-park Victoriana has literally allowed the nineteenth century to return home.

Conclusion

This re-instatement of the nineteenth century within the home has been a crucial characteristic of theme-park Victoriana. With its egalitarian, interactive and commercial emphases, the 'heritage industry' has enabled people to engage with the Victorians in ways that would have been unrecognisable to pre-1945 generations, or, indeed, to the Victorians themselves. This may or may not have been beneficial to our historical sense. As I have noted, the 'heritage industry' has been a site of deep controversy among scholars.[58] Arguments continue to rage at the start of the twenty-first century. They have, never the less, moved on in certain respects since the first salvos were fired in the mid-1980s. Then historians seemed to be reacting partly against the era of Thatcherite 'Victorian values', conflating her suspect use of history with the nostalgia they identified all around them. Some saw the 'heritage industry' as a reflection of listlessness in Britain following the demise of post-war consensus: 'We need the fierce spirit of renewal', Robert Hewison urged in 1987, 'we must live in the future tense not the past.'[59]

Such polemics have since died down, but troublesome issues remain. For all the historical revisionism that has been consolidated by theme-park Victoriana – the renewed emphasis on local, family and working-class histories, the importance of empathy, the preservation of much Victorian memorabilia – it is worrying to some that factual background tends to be given a lower priority than personal engagement. It might be argued that the widening gap between empathy and an objective framework within which this might be pondered will damage future generations' understanding of the Victorians. Yet, as David Lowenthal argues, 'heritage' is more a personal relationship with the past than a nuanced attempt to portray its intricacies; we should not expect theme-park Victoriana, even with education officers in museums, to embody the latest or most detailed scholarship.

Mixed sentiments of this sort are intrinsic to theme-park Victoriana, and might be well illustrated by a final example. In 1999 a television series called *The 1900 House* ran on Channel 4. This followed the fortunes of a modern middle-class family living for three months in a painstakingly reproduced late Victorian house. The regular crises involved not the progress of the Boer War or the rise of the Labour Party, but mixing the correct cake recipe or fitting into a corset. Here was theme-park Victoriana at its height: private rather than public history, hands-on connection with the past, commercial awareness (there was an accompanying book,[60] and advertising breaks during the programmes). Vicarious the family's experience of Victoriana may have been; but, our own experience as viewers was more vicarious still. This underlines a challenging ambivalence about theme-park Victoriana. For in privileging the imaginary above the actual, it suggests both whimsical nostalgia and a shrewd scepticism about the ability of historical narratives – the stories we tell ourselves about the past – ultimately to resonate in anything other than imaginative terms.[61]

Notes

1 'The Victorian Vision', Victoria and Albert Museum publicity pamphlet, 2001; see also John M. MacKenzie (ed.), *The Victorian Vision: Inventing New Britain* (London: Victoria and Albert Publications, 2001).

2 Cf. Matthew Sweet, *Inventing the Victorians* (London: Faber, 2001).

3 'Interview: John Outram', *Country Life*, 29 March 2001, pp. 96–7.

4 Among the extensive literature, see especially: David Lowenthal, *The Past Is a Foreign Country* (Cambridge: Cambridge University Press, 1985), and *The Heritage Crusade and the Spoils of History* (Cambridge: Cambridge University Press, 1998); Patrick Wright, *On Living in an Old Country* (London: Verso, 1985); Robert Hewison, *The Heritage Industry: Britain in a Climate of Decline* (London: Methuen, 1987); David Cannadine, 'The past in the present', in Lesley M. Smith (ed.), *The Making of Britain: Echoes of Greatness* (London: London Weekend Television, 1988), pp. 9–20; Raphael Samuel, *Theatres of Memory*, vol. 1: *Past and Present in Contemporary Culture* (London: Verso, 1994).

5 Lowenthal, *Heritage Crusade*, p. x.

6 Chris Brooks (ed.), *The Albert Memorial. The Prince Consort National Memorial: Its History, Contexts and Conservation* (London: Yale University Press, 2000).

7 John Major, likewise, set up the Department of National Heritage after his electoral victory in 1992. Stefan Collini suggests that this may have corresponded to a Europe-wide bid to foster 'public memory' in an age of mounting anxiety about national identity. With the prospect of European integration, the emphasis on national heritage (and its possible impact on how we relate the Victorians to an overall scheme of national history) seems, if anything, set to become more pronounced: Stefan Collini, *English Pasts: Essays in History and Culture* (Oxford: Oxford University Press, 1999), p. 39.

8 Peter Mandler, *The Fall and Rise of the Stately Home* (London: Yale University Press, 1997), p. 411; David Cannadine, 'Conservation: the National Trust and the national heritage', in his *In Churchill's Shadow: Confronting the Past in Modern Britain* (London: Allen Lane, 2002), p. 224.

9 Samuel, *Theatres*, vol. 1, pp. 125–7.

10 Ezra Pound in *Future* (October 1918), cited in *The Oxford English Dictionary Supplement* (Oxford: Oxford University Press, 1982), p. 1159.

11 Richard D. Altick, 'Eminent Victorianism: what Lytton Strachey hath wrought', *The American Scholar*, 64 (1995), pp. 81–9.

12 Asa Briggs, *Victorian Things* (Harmondsworth: Penguin, 1990), pp. 12–13; cf. chapter 9 by Becky Conekin, this volume.

13 Richard Weight, *Patriots: National Identity in Britain, 1940–2000* (London: Macmillan, 2002), p. 578; *Whitaker's Almanack 2002* (London: Stationery Office, 2001), p. 594.

14 Precise figures, respectively, for the years 1999–2000 and 2000–2001: 1,265,123 and 1,342,079, Victoria and Albert Museum, *Annual Report* (London: Victoria and Albert Museum, 2001).

15 A more prosaic, but no less important, factor may be the widespread abolition of entry fees for museums. The Victoria and Albert Museum dropped its entry fee in December 2001, and by the summer of 2002 attendance figures had risen by 157 per cent: Michael White, 'Museum visits soar after entry fees are scrapped', *Guardian*, 9 August 2002, p. 2.

16 RSA, 'The functions of a national museum', in J. Forsdyke (ed.), *Museums in Modern Life* (London: Royal Society of Arts, 1949), p. 2.

17 Histories of historiography are legion, but see for example: Richard J. Evans, *In Defence of History* (London: Granta, 1997); Michael Bentley, *Modern Historiography: An Introduction* (London: Routledge, 1998); Arthur Marwick, *The New Nature of History: Knowledge, Evidence, Language* (Basingstoke: Palgrave, 2001); David Cannadine (ed.), *What Is History Now?* (Basingstoke: Palgrave, 2002).

18 For an overview of relevant historiography, see Rohan McWilliam, *Popular Politics in Nineteenth-Century England* (London: Routledge, 1998).

19 The seminal work on 'invented traditions' remains Eric Hobsbawm and Terence Ranger (eds), *The Invention of Tradition* (Cambridge: Cambridge University Press, 1983).

20 Centre for Kentish Studies website: www.kent.gov.uk/e&l/artslib/archives/archcks.html.

21 On the nineteenth-century craze for statistics, see Asa Briggs, *Victorian Things*; G. M. Young, *Portrait of an Age: Victorian England*, 2nd edn (London: Oxford University Press, 1953), pp. 28–9.

22 Trenchard Cox, 'The provincial museum', in Forsdyke (ed.), *Museums*, p. 20.

23 David Ward, 'World heritage honour for revolutionary mills', *Guardian*, 15 December 2001, p. 14. Also accorded 'world heritage site' status at this time were two older industrial complexes: Derwent Valley, Derbyshire, and New Lanark, Scotland.

24 For an overview of arguments about what constituted British history (especially in schools) in the 1980s and 1990s, see: Raphael Samuel, *Theatres of Memory*, vol. 2: *Island Stories: Unravelling Britain* (London: Verso, 1998), pp. 197–229.

25 For some recent perspectives on the Victorians and display, see: Paul Greenhalgh, *Ephemeral Vistas: The Expositions Universelles, Great Exhibitions and World's Fairs, 1851–1939* (Manchester: Manchester University Press, 1988); Thomas Richards, *The Commodity Culture of Victorian England* (London: Verso, 1991); Annie E. Coombes, *Reinventing Africa: Museums, Material Culture and Popular Imagination in Late Victorian and Edwardian England* (London: Yale University Press, 1994); Judith Roof, 'Display cases', in John Kucich and Dianne F. Sadoff (eds), *Victorian Afterlife: Postmodern Culture Rewrites the Nineteenth Century* (Minneapolis: University of Minnesota Press, 2001), pp. 101–21; Pamela Pilbeam, *Madame Tussaud and the History of Waxworks* (London: Hambledon & London, 2003).

26 On school practice in general, see chapter 12, by Eric Evans, this volume.

27 For an example of such a book designed for schoolchildren, see G. H. Blore, *Victorian Worthies: Sixteen Biographies* (London: Oxford University, 1920); for the broader pedagogical context, see Valerie E. Chancellor, *History for Their Masters: Opinion in the English History Textbook, 1800–1914* (Bath: Adams & Dart, 1970).

28 Samuel, *Theatres*, vol. 2, p. 216.

29 In October 2002 Prince Charles convened a conference on the teaching of English and history in schools. Attended by Niall Ferguson, David Starkey and Simon Schama – all prominent historians within the public eye – they reflected a united front in attacking post-war trends in history teaching. 'Historical "process" is desiccated, tedious, pointless', argued Starkey. 'Abolish the monstrous monotone of textbooks', cajoled Schama, 'it's far better to read children pages of Carlyle and Gibbon.' Schama's own take on the Victorians in his BBC *History of Britain* programmes (2002), though recognisably in the tradition of Carlyle and Gibbon for drama, subtlety and wit, did nevertheless suggest an 'un-Victorian' view of the nineteenth century, criticising the imperial ethos in India and Ireland, and exploring social life in Britain through the experience of women. For the conference, see *Daily Telegraph*, 7 October 2002, p. 22.

30 Samuel, *Theatres*, vol. 1, p. 280.

31 History guidelines in *The National Curriculum* (London: Department for Education, 1995).

32 In this case children up to Year 4, corresponding to roughly midway through Key Stage 2 (7–11-year-olds) of the National Curriculum. Kelham Island Museum website: www.simt.co.uk/kel1.

33 York Castle Museum website: www.york.castle.museum.

34 Macclesfield Museums and Heritage Centre website: www.silk-macclesfield.org.uk.

35 Ironbridge website: www.ironbridge.org.uk.

36 On the Victorians and 'heritage', see Mark Girouard, *The Return to Camelot: Chivalry and the English Gentleman* (London: Yale University Press, 1981); Lowenthal, *The Past Is a Foreign Country*, pp. 96–105; Mandler, *Fall and Rise*, pp. 21–69.

37 Robert Graves, *Goodbye to All That* (Harmondsworth: Penguin, 1960 [1929]), p. 206.

38 Calke Abbey website: www.derbyshireuk.net/dhouse2.html.

39 Maev Kennedy, 'Heritage campaign saves Victorian treasure trove', *Guardian*, 19 June 2002, p. 5.

40 Mark Girouard, 'House of secrets', *Saga Magazine* (September 2002), p. 72. By the time of writing, Tyntesfield had not been opened to the public.
41 On the declining fortunes of Victoriana in stately homes, see Mandler, *Fall and Rise*, especially pp. 278–95.
42 On the Victorians and hero-worship see: Walter E. Houghton, *The Victorian Frame of Mind, 1830–1870* (New Haven: Yale University Press, 1957), pp. 305–40; David Newsome, *The Victorian World Picture: Perceptions and Introspections in an Age of Change* (London: John Murray, 1997), pp. 154–64.
43 The current criterion for English Heritage blue plaques is that they must commemorate persons of recognised public and professional significance within their field; moreover, a plaque cannot appear until twenty-five years after the person's death or until the centenary of the person's birth (whichever is the earlier).
44 English Heritage website: www.english-heritage.org.uk.
45 Richard Holmes has written eloquently on the subject, with direct reference to Robert Louis Stevenson, in his *Footsteps: Adventures of a Romantic Biographer* (London: Hodder & Stoughton, 1985).
46 On the early origins of the Hardy–Dorset 'heritage industry', see Sweet, *Inventing the Victorians*, pp. 31–7. The Elgar 'heritage industry' has yet to be documented fully, but see Ken Russell's 1962 film *Elgar* (which prominently features the Malverns) and his 2002 *South Bank Show* remake, which ends with a shot of the actor playing Elgar cycling through present-day Worcester, and of Russell conversing with a statue of Elgar recently erected in the high street.
47 Lucasta Miller, *The Brontë Myth* (London: Jonathan Cape, 2001); on Brontë 'heritage', see especially pp. 98–108.
48 *Ibid.*, p. 101.
49 'Ripper tours spark anger in East End', BBC News website (27 October 2001).
50 D. H. Lawrence, *Lady Chatterley's Lover* (Harmondsworth: Penguin, 1994 [1932]), p. 148.
51 John Steegman, *The Rule of Taste from George I to George IV* (London: Macmillan, 1936), and *Consort of Taste* (London: Sidgwick & Jackson, 1950).
52 See, for example, Violet Ward, *Victoriana: A Collector's Guide* (London: G. Bell & Sons, 1960); Peter May, *Collecting Victoriana* (London: Arco, 1965); James Laver, *Victoriana* (London: Ward Lock, 1966); Guy Williams, *Collecting Victoriana* (London: Corgi, 1970).
53 Samuel, *Theatres*, vol. 1, pp. 92, 96–8, 152; Asa Briggs, *The Age of Improvement, 1783–1867* (London: Longman, 1979), p. 471.
54 Judith Miller (ed.), *Miller's Antiques Encyclopedia* (London: Mitchell Beazley, 1998), p. 10.
55 On the shortening threshold of nostalgia, see Lowenthal, *Heritage Crusade*, especially pp. 17–19.
56 Madeleine Marsh (ed.), *Miller's Collectables Price Guide* (London: Reed International, 1995), pp. 110, 113, 316.
57 On the Victorian 'look', see Samuel, *Theatres*, vol. 1, pp. 51–135.
58 See the works cited in note 4, above.
59 Hewison, *Heritage Industry*, p. 146.
60 Mark McCrum and Matthew Sturgis, *1900 House* (London: Channel 4, 1999).
61 On this theme see Kucich and Sadoff, *Victorian Afterlife*.

12

The Victorians at school: the Victorian era in the twentieth-century curriculum

Eric Evans

I

'Now, what I want is, Facts. Teach these boys and girls nothing but Facts. Facts alone are wanted in life. Plant nothing else, and root out everything else.'
(Dickens, *Hard Times*)[1]

Thus, Thomas Gradgrind, the fictional creation of Charles Dickens and patron of the kind of elementary school which his creator attacked as providing mere information at the expense of understanding. This chapter examines the 'facts' about the Victorians which twentieth-century children were encouraged to absorb and considers to what extent those facts aided understanding of Victorian society and values.

Whiggish Victorians learned their own progressive lessons about the long reign through which they lived. They cloaked themselves in the comforting unity of progress, characterised by the move towards inclusive representative political systems, and by industrial leadership, commercial supremacy and extensive, though high-minded and even self-sacrificing, imperial control. Historians have rightly unpicked each of these pretensions, but this is not to deny that Victorian contemporaries felt them to be central to their existence. As Colin Matthew observed:

Many who lived in the nineteenth century hoped that they were establishing patterns of life and standards of behaviour that would condition the development of the world generally, for, though bewildered by the pace of change, the Victorians had a high view of the world-role of the United Kingdom.[2]

Early twentieth-century pupils were expected to absorb a similar view. They traced 'our emerging national story' teleologically. An imperial power, in the making from the Anglo-Saxon period onwards, reached its grand imperial climax in late Victorian Britain. A Board of Education Circular of 1905 indicated that the study of history should be employed to enable children to 'learn about their nationality which distinguishes them from the other people of other countries'. Children in elementary schools should be told stories: 'The lives of great men and women, carefully selected from all stations in life, will furnish the most impressive examples of obedience, loyalty, courage, strenuous effort, serviceableness, indeed of all the qualities which make for good citizenship'.[3]

Queen Victoria herself was regularly presented as a symbol of national continuity. The Raleigh 'History Readers', published in the later 1890s, described Victoria as 'the descendant of the Saxon chiefs who settled in Wessex more than fourteen centuries ago':

> She represents the growth of our people from very small beginnings to its present world wide power: and all who know the history of our country feel a thrill of pride and joy when they think of its wonderful past and its prosperous present, with all of which our royal family has been so closely associated. When we sing 'God Save the Queen', we think not only of the queen but of the people whose past and present life she represents. For the time we forget parties, and we remember that, after all, we are one nation, closely related in blood and community of interest.[4]

The changing public image of Victoria over the course of her reign was veiled from impressionable minds. Children did not learn about the transition from *ingénue* to fecund matriarch and on to the grieving, non-functioning, non-working monarch of the 1860s. The Victorian story revealed her only as the 'splendid, public and popular' figure who celebrated Golden and Diamond Jubilees in 1887 and 1897.

The queen was the focus for more than just monarchical continuity. History teaching, which occupied a growing place in the school curriculum from the 1880s onwards, inculcated lessons about identity and citizenship. In venerating the memory of Victoria, Edwardian children were to see her as a symbol of British nationhood. The queen headed a *special* nation. This was Victoriolatry rampant. History as a lesson in citizenship taught that the Victorians bequeathed a unique legacy to their successors. As the Board of Education explained in its *Suggestions for the Consideration of Teachers and Others in the Work of the Public Elementary Schools*:

> All boys and girls in Great Britain have, by the mere fact of birth, certain rights and duties which some day or other they will exercise, and it is the province of history to trace how those rights and duties arise [. . .]
>   It is important that from the history lessons they should learn something about the nationality which distinguishes them from the people of other countries. They cannot understand this, however, unless they are taught how the British nation grew up and how the mother country in her turn has founded daughter countries beyond the seas. The broad facts of this growth when properly handled ought to form a stirring theme full of interest to even young citizens of the British Empire.[5]

Those 'young citizens' were much more likely to be presented with what J. R. Seeley called 'the bombastic' interpretation of empire, 'lost in wonder and ecstasy at its immense dimensions, and at the energy and heroism which presumably have gone to the making of it'. The alternative, 'pessimistic', school – an empire 'founded in aggression and rapacity, as useless and burdensome, a kind of excrescence upon England' – received little rehearsal.[6] Typical were the concluding words of H. C. Mackinder's influential textbook *Our Island Story*: 'The little kingdom made by Alfred the Great has spread until the British Peace now reigns over one-fifth of the world.' This was published five months before the outbreak of the First World War.[7]

Victoria's status as queen–empress after 1876 reinforced the imperial message. In some hands it became transcendent. Vital to the special *otherness* of Victoria was the fact that the queen–empress was not a queen–autocrat. In contrast to her regnant European relatives, Victoria seemed the symbol of her people's liberties rather than the apparently immovable barrier to their achievement. England was specially favoured in its constitutional monarchy. Since she was a hereditary monarch, Victoria had no special interests to serve beyond those of her people as a whole. In school readers, the position was articulated without reservation or awkward caveat.

Finally, Victoria was a woman. That might seem a difficulty in the awakening of children to a sense of history through stories of male heroes whose military and naval exploits, and exciting deeds of derring-do, advanced the cause of empire. The queen, though, had other virtues. This focus of constitutional veneration was a mother nine times over. School readers dutifully made the obvious link. Children were taught that

> Family life, after all, lies at the root of all society, and no political life is sound which is not founded upon the family virtues of the nation. No man can rule others well till he has ruled himself, and become a Constitutional Sovereign, and not a tyrant in his own household.

Girls were told that they 'must be always grateful for the example of what a true woman's influence on the world can be'.[8]

Edwardian children, then, were presented with the most potent images of the Victorian age as the apogee of imperial grandeur. Those images derived disproportionately from the last twenty years of the queen's reign and they took on a distinctively personal and imperial hue. Even the humblest British citizen could claim, firstly, distinctive political liberties and, secondly, membership of the largest, proudest and most beneficent empire the world had ever seen. Empire was about belonging, and history was about informing ordinary people that they, too, belonged.

II

The Fisher Education Act of 1918 was one of the last pieces of legislation associated with the progressive consensus. In raising the minimum school-leaving age to 14, and in seeking to eliminate divisive distinctions between elementary and secondary schools, H. A. L. Fisher was trying to rectify what he saw as 'a continual wastage of ability [and] of character', created by a system which saw so many pupils leave at the age of 10, 11 or 12.[9] Adverse economic circumstances for much of the two decades that followed would shortly clip progressive wings, although there was reason to believe that history would continue its flourishing pre-war development as a school subject. True, the Board of Education was issuing warnings that pupils did not have sufficient knowledge of key events and outstanding individuals. It recommended that pupils be given an 'alphabet' of thirty-two dates to remedy this defect.[10] Of these only four were Victorian, or near-Victorian: the 1832 Reform Act; the publication of *Origin of Species* in 1859; the Franco-Prussian War of 1870; and the death of Victoria in 1901.

In contrast to this, university historians saw it as a key function of their work to write school textbooks.[11] The chairman of the Historical Association's examinations committee suggested in 1928 that 'the great advance that has been made in history teaching in English schools during the last thirty years or so is due in no small part to the influence of university historians'.[12] The Historical Association itself, founded in 1906, also played a significant part.[13]

Few pupils in elementary schools followed a systematic history course and, if they did, they did so for only an hour or two a week. However, the numbers entering for School Certificate examination increased substantially – from about 25,000 in 1919 to 55,000 by 1927, when some 88 per cent of pupils took history as one of their certificate subjects.[14] Between one-third and one-half of all Higher School Certificate candidates offered history as one of their matriculation subjects, though the proportion tended to decline in the later 1930s. The proportion of predominantly northern candidates offering history as a qualifying subject for the Joint Matriculation Board's Higher School Certificate Examinations stood at 33 per cent in 1919, rose to 45.6 per cent by 1934, fell back to 32 per cent early in the Second World War and stood at 27 per cent (3,405 candidates in all) in 1950, the last year of the pre-GCE system.[15]

The utilitarian value of the study of history, still frequently stressed, now worked to reduce the importance of the Victorian period. The emphasis prior to 1914 was on Victorian history as a means of heightening a sense of identity, of inculcating love of country and of celebrating imperial achievements. Post-war emphases shifted towards helping pupils to understand both the horrors of war and the means of avoiding destructive mass conflict in the future. H. A. L. Fisher recommended in 1927 that the League of Nations be taught in history lessons.[16] Some textbooks had already anticipated him, although the results could be incongruous. Harry Cooper's *How the Empire Was Won* concluded with a chapter on the League of Nations. In the immediately preceding chapter, 'The intermingled peoples', he had informed his readers of 'chocolate-skinned people in Upper Burmah who still practise marriage by capture' and 'people who have a coco-nut every

morning for breakfast – and climb the tree to get it – as regularly as others
fry ham and eggs'. Pupils were warned that empires can fall as well as rise,
and that some 'second-rate nations of Europe' were once 'vast world-
empires'. Cooper's was a moral message:

> [E]mpire, like greatness in general, is not dominion, it is service. The things
> which hold the empire together, the things which redeem the occasional stains
> in its past history, the things which give security against the only perils that
> Britain has need to fear, are the doing of justice, and the loving of mercy, and
> the walking with humbleness before God.[17]

As the nation faced up to the renewal of conflict in 1940, the distinguished Tudor historian J. D. Mackie summed up the prevailing mood:

> Ever since 1919 the very idea of war has been most unpopular [. . .]
>   The warriors who returned from what they had thought was a crusade . . .
> themselves had had enough of fighting . . . Anxious to maintain peace at all
> costs, the public found the leaders it wished for, because in every walk of
> life, in every trade and profession, authority passed, in large measure, to the
> non-combatants.[18]

Mackie was concerned that too many historians had shifted their focus to
the very recent past. 'In these days of enlightenment', he sardonically noted,
'the old has seemed less worthy of study than it used to be.' Thus, he argued,
too many students failed to understand that constitutions and nations were
intrinsically fragile entities that needed to be nurtured by understanding of
long-term factors and causes which excessive concentration on twentieth-
century history obscures.[19]

Mackie also noted that concentration on 'the economic interpretation of
history' had gained unwonted popularity after 1919 'as a reasonable thing
in contrast to "political history" which concerned itself with foolish ambitions and wasteful wars'. Furthermore, the empire was increasingly seen as
'suspect'. There 'seems to be a school of thought which attributes our every
action to low motives – usually economic – and takes no account of the
value with which an empire has been won, or of the benefits it has conferred upon great peoples'. Pupils in the inter-war period had, in Mackie's
view, been short-changed. The irony was that the League of Nations, which
many pupils had studied in some depth, had now been exposed as impo-
tent, while what Mackie called 'our empire', allegedly 'founded upon injus-
tice and maintained by incompetence, is the sole bar between the rule of
reason and the rule of force'.[20]

The stirring deeds of Victorian adventurers received much less prominence than they had prior to 1914. Political history defaulted to (in the term
of one educationist[21]) a discredited 'politico-militaro-dynastic' emphasis.
The expansion in the number of history classes taught in the inter-war
period outran the supply of history teachers. It has been estimated that more

than half of England's secondary-school history teachers in the late 1920s had not been professionally trained.[22] Board of Education inspectors, visiting London elementary schools in 1927, conceded that pupils' knowledge of chronology was stronger than it had been 10–15 years earlier. However, it remained unsatisfactory: 'knowledge of historical facts (persons and events) is deficient', syllabi were overloaded[23] and out-dated textbooks were in widespread use.

Textbooks, whether for elementary or secondary schools, tended to trace British history over the period from the Roman or Anglo-Saxon settlements to the outbreak of the First World War or perhaps a little beyond. They were text-heavy; maps, time charts and portraits were the only usual leavening. The Victorian era did not receive special treatment. The mode was narrative, albeit with an occasional assertively moral commentary. In one text which gave 'the Victorian age' two chapters out of its total of twenty-five, the queen was asserted to be 'a popular monarch, and remained so throughout her long reign . . . she won respect for [the monarchy] by the whole manner of her life'.[24] Another, originally published in 1910 but regularly reprinted and updated in the inter-war period, arranged most of its chapters according to regnal periods. The reign of Victoria was assigned seventy pages in a book which ran to 581, and would have occupied less but for the text's strong concentration on imperial and, to a lesser extent, foreign policy.[25]

Examinations were increasingly seen as a problem. In a complaint which has been echoed in every decade since, Fisher, writing in 1917, noted as a 'grave defect of our present scheme of secondary school life' the 'distracting tangle of examinations'. He hoped, vainly, to relieve 'our schools of this incubus'.[26] C. H. K. Marten, chairman of the Historical Association's examinations committee, argued in 1928 that the School Certificate examination had for a year – 'sometimes two years' – become 'the dominating factor in the history curriculum'. The Oxford and Cambridge Schools Examination Board required students to study British history from 1714 to 1878 and European history from 1815 to 1871. The London Examination Board's most modern selection would see candidates making an outline study of British and European history from 1783 to 1914. British history was taken to include 'Colonial'.[27]

Examination questions were also criticised as overly 'political' and unlikely to engage pupils' interest. One female teacher from Bexhill complained that her charges, while they might very well be 'extremely interested in Disraeli', would flinch from ' "estimating his influence on English political ideas" because English political ideas were not yet familiar to them'. Although a question on the social and economic history of the nineteenth century would, in theory, be welcome, those posed were unfeasibly broad. How might a candidate, asked to '[g]ive some account of the chief developments in the nature and organisation of British commerce and industry since the middle of the nineteenth century', effectively organise and deploy relevant information and understanding in the twenty-three minutes allowed, on average, for an answer.[28] How indeed?

Another teacher criticised the excess of political detail necessitated by JMB syllabi, especially those covering the nineteenth century where the emphasis was on ministries, foreign relations and political reform. This teacher was concerned about the selection for examination of what he called a 'list of minor characters'. For the broader Victorian period, these comprised Adam Smith, Wilberforce, Cobbett, Owen, Bentham, Shaftesbury, Canning, Rowland Hill, O'Connell, the prince consort, Dalhousie, Florence Nightingale, Darwin, Plimsoll, Salisbury and Chamberlain.

Candidates had to grapple both with a narrow interpretation of what constituted Victorian history and a lack of certainty about which topics might 'come up' on the examination paper. School Certificate candidates in 1924 were faced with only eight questions on English history 1714–1902 (albeit extended by three 'either/or' formulations in the same broad area). A chronological black hole opened up between the quaint requirement to '[b]alance the gains and losses to this country resulting from the period of war with Revolutionary France and Napoleon' and the injunction to '[n]arrate briefly the chief events in the parliamentary struggle between Disraeli and Gladstone'.[29]

The Victorian period rarely received detailed attention in the chronological scurries recommended to teachers by the Board of Education.[30] The main exception to this concerned the empire in the late Victorian period. How much information children actually absorbed is, of course, unknowable, although critics of fact-led history were numerous. One conducted an experiment during the Second World War on almost 400 service recruits designed to elicit how much information about the past they could recall. Among those not educated beyond elementary school level, only 18 per cent could make even a vague approximation as to when 'England and Scotland [were] united under one crown'; the same percentage could give 'any good reasons out of the past for the South of Ireland's ill-feeling towards us'.

It is perhaps significant that very few questions were asked directly on British nineteenth-century history; again the concentration was on the empire, and those questions received the strongest responses. Thus 54 per cent of elementary and 73 per cent of secondary educated respondents could identify the 'part of the Empire' associated with Cecil Rhodes; 64 per cent and 76 per cent, respectively, could name 'to whom Canada belonged before we acquired it'. The only other question in that part of the test which had a higher recognition factor was on Queen Elizabeth, who was correctly identified as the ruler of England at the time of the Armada by 74 per cent of elementary- and 88 per cent of secondary-school-educated respondents. By contrast, only 39 per cent of the elementary-school-educated could place the Indian Mutiny, the Reformation and the Crusades in the correct chronological order.[31]

III

The reorganisation of primary and secondary education under the Butler Education Act of 1944 seems to have made surprisingly little difference to the quality of education in historical studies. The Norwood Report, the Act's precursor, continued to recommend history's importance in citizenship education and it gave teachers considerable scope in syllabus design. It suggested, however, that it would not be appropriate for pupils to handle the late Victorian period and the twentieth century until the age of 15, by which time they would be able fully to appreciate that they were 'citizen[s] of the United Kingdom'.[32]

For able pupils passing the 11+ examination, of course, the opportunity to progress to university now lay open. Public examinations, re-organised into General Certificate of Education Ordinary (O) and Advanced (A) levels from 1951, continued to demand much the same as their School Certificate predecessors. Typically, O-level candidates were required to answer 5 or 6 questions from those set on periods, which could be restricted to British or to European history. A social and economic history syllabus was available which required students to explain, for example, how Gladstone tried to solve the problem of Irish discontent, to '[d]escribe the development of the iron and steel industry in the nineteenth century' or to 'give a short account of the Great Exhibition of 1851 and estimate its importance'.[33]

At A-level, candidates sat two (sometimes three) three-hour papers, nearly always one on British and one on European history. In the 1950s, the JMB still felt it necessary to spell out what 'British economic history, 1700–1914' comprised (a fair number of social history topics like 'reform of factory conditions' and 'changes in conditions and standards of living', as it turned out), but orthodox, and usually dynasty-driven, British political history syllabi were assumed to be self-explanatory. Teachers had to infer from the scrutiny of past papers that British history 1815–1914 concentrated on high policy in both domestic and foreign affairs. The twelve questions on the 1955 paper, from which pupils had to attempt four, had nine in this category. Two of the other three – on education and late nineteenth-century agriculture – had so few takers that the examiners' report ignored them. The third, asking how far the Chartist movement was a failure, was now considered as surrogate high politics. The examiners, though, were not impressed: 'Very few answered the question set but [instead] explained the reasons for the rise and fall of Chartism.'[34]

By the 1960s, history was losing its distinctive place in the syllabus of many secondary-modern and new comprehensive schools, as both topic work and a broader 'humanities' curriculum alike became fashionable.[35] The advent of the new Certificate of Secondary Education for less-able pupils in the mid-1960s provided only limited reassurance for progressive teachers. Those studying the Victorian period were invited to concentrate on 'social and economic history' since that was deemed to present 'more accessible' content. In practice, economic history hardly featured and social history barely touched on social structure. Topics favoured in the examination were 'social conditions' – usually of factory children before 1833 – 'the poor law' (much more was known about the 1834 Act than about the diversity of implementation and experiences to which it gave rise) and 'education' (usually in terms of legislative highlights). As Martin Booth noted:

> Such papers, designed as they were for the majority of examination youngsters, were a reflection of the belief that memorization and recall of knowledge were all that most 16–year-olds could cope with; they simply had not the mental capacity for engaging in historical thinking of a higher order.[36]

Gradgrind's writ, evidently, still ran. The Historical Association's journal *Teaching History*, founded in 1969, aimed to inform teachers about the potential of imaginative history lessons as an antidote to 'the unpopularity of traditional school history in the age of comprehensive education'.[37]

Several history teachers also complained about excessive concentration on national history. One argued that, since 'the supreme reality' was no longer the British constitution, syllabi running from Magna Carta through to '1832, 1867 and 1884' had lost their salience. Teaching less of the Victorians would help children understand that Britain was but a small nation in an increasingly complex world. Education as citizenship, it seemed, now demanded more contemporary world history. Only thus could historical studies continue as 'the very seed ground of the adolescent's understanding of society'.[38]

Concentration on British history also inhibited proper understanding. Even if children 'in stable and reasonably developed societies' could be encouraged to develop 'a strong patriotic interest', national studies were likely to encourage 'an attitude of contemptuous superiority to any nations which fall outside their own pattern of development'. By the late 1970s, Her Majesty's Inspectors were advocating a broad and balanced curriculum grounded in the skills of evidence evaluation and the understanding of the perspectives of people in the past. No specific content was prescribed, but it was recommended that students be given a framework of world, British and local studies.[39]

The culmination of reaction to chronologically determined, 'fact-driven', history came in 1972 with the establishing of the so-called Schools' Council History Project (SHP). This aimed to liberate pupils from the tyranny of memory over comprehension and thus, or so it was argued, from a subject which had become 'excruciatingly, dangerously, dull, and what is more, of little apparent relevance to pupils'.[40] The Victorian period had no purchase; after all, Queen Victoria had been dead for more than sixty years. The SHP's answer to 'relevance' was to encourage pupils to work directly with the historical evidence. A little outline knowledge of developments in medicine in the Victorian period was required for a long-term 'study in development'. However, only the earliest Victorian years were represented, as 'Britain

1815–51, – one of the four options as 'depth studies'. It attracted relatively few takers; the 'American west' rapidly established itself as the market leader.[41]

IV

In 1960, David Eccles, minister of education in the Macmillan Government, bemoaned the fact that Parliament hardly ever discussed 'what is taught to the 7 million boys and girls in the maintained schools'. 'Of course', he continued, 'Parliament would never attempt to dictate the curriculum.'[42] Developments in 'skills-led', 'child-centred' and 'experiential' learning during the 1960s–1970s led to radical re-appraisal when the Conservatives were returned to power under Margaret Thatcher. Keith Joseph, in a startling address to the Historical Association in 1984, conceded the importance of historical skills but stressed the centrality of content and a chronological map, especially of British history, if the subject was to have the impact expected of it.[43] The Education Act (1988) established a National Curriculum for state schools and set up subject-specific working groups to specify the content and skills appropriate to pupils of different ages.

The History working group's proposals were not aimed at increasing the profile of Victorian history in state schools. A trite and unreflective anti-imperialism among teachers also played a part. Content central for Edwardian children now became deeply suspect. One teacher opined that the proposed option 'The British Empire at its zenith, 1877–1905' would be widely avoided by progressive teachers, given its 'xenophobic connotations'.[44] A leading historian of Victorian Britain and critic of Thatcherism stressed the importance of grand narratives but the need for fresh perspectives. The British empire should be presented not in terms of what he called the 'grab for Africa' but in terms of its domestic impact: 'The high point of this story might be . . . the inter-war years, when investment in Empire reached an all-time peak, when Empire trade accounted (in 1937) for some 70% of Britain's imports'.[45]

In the event, the two-penny coloured formulations of the History Working Group were rapidly reduced to penny-plain because of extreme content overload. The slimming down of the National Curriculum overall in 1994 led to the removal of the compulsory Key Stage 4 (14–16) for History.[46] Some study of the Victorian period, however, remained compulsory in the guise of a unit normally studied towards the end of Key Stage 3 (11–14). Its blandly chronological title, 'Britain 1750–1900', is misleading. Pupils studied themes, with emphasis on 'the expansion of trade and colonisation', 'industrialisation' and 'political changes'. No named individuals had to be studied, which gave rise to splenetic outbursts in the right-wing press. Instead, the Qualifications and Curriculum Authority (QCA) offered guidance both on people who might be profitably studied and on key themes to enhance historical understanding.

The QCA's list was bizarre. If students learned about the impact of industrialisation on cultural developments, the named individuals considered relevant included William Hogarth (1697–1764), alongside Jane Austen, J. M. W. Turner and Gustav Holst (1874–1934). The only 'high-Victorians' on the list were Dickens, George Eliot, Henry Wood and the quaintly-named 'William Gilbert and Arthur Sullivan'. The 'political leaders' nominated as worthy of particular study were Queen Victoria, Robert Peel, William Gladstone and Benjamin Disraeli. 'Reformers' such as William Wilberforce, the Nigerian ex-slave, anti-slavery campaigner and iconic autobiographer Olaudiah Equiano, John Howard and 'Elizabeth Garret [sic]' were also listed.[47]

Guidance was given on questions considered appropriate for pupils of differing ability. This, too, had its idiosyncrasies. It is far from clear, for example, why the unit entitled 'The franchise', covering pressure for parliamentary reform from 1815 to 1928, should have as its subtitle 'why did it take so much longer for British women to get the vote?'[48] In the case of at least one-third of adult males, of course, it did not.

If teachers made use of the new opportunities presented by CD-ROM in this unit their pupils could make three 'investigations' related to 'the British empire', 'Industry and people' and 'People, protest and government'. In the first, the key questions were: 'Did slaves themselves abolish slavery?' and 'Did India benefit from British rule?' In the second they were: 'Did nineteenth-century factory reformers really care about the workers?' and 'Why was there a public health crisis in the nineteenth century?' The third investigation prompted: 'Does Chartism deserve its reputation as a failure?' and 'How democratic was Victorian Britain?'[49] These resources gave opportunity for teenagers to acquire considerable basic knowledge about the Victorian period. However, the emphasis remained firmly on enquiry skills.

The main focus of an optional unit on the British empire was on how, by 1900, 'Britain controlled nearly half the world'. In place of the admiration intended to be evinced at the start of the twentieth century, pupils in the 1990s were to be taught about the importance of war, trade and exploration, respectively, in the development of empire. They were expected to consider whether contemporary visual representations of key imperial 'events' were likely to be accurate or plausible. They could also enquire how and why, in the early twentieth century, annual celebrations of Empire Day were held throughout Britain.

Under the National Curriculum, therefore, children in England and Wales *did* 'do the Victorians', albeit folded into a longer time-frame designed to emphasise the importance of the Industrial Revolution and the British empire. The emphasis was on broad understanding rather than on detailed knowledge, and on themes rather than chronology. Key aspects of the Victorian age – notably both the centrality and the divisiveness of religion, foreign policy unrelated to empire, and pretty much the whole of political life other than pressure for parliamentary reform – received scant attention.

Arguably, also, both the selection and the presentation of illustrative content were unduly influenced by late twentieth-century sensibilities and political correctness.

Against this, children were encouraged genuinely to *understand* aspects of the Victorian age and, in particular, how the Victorians differed from inhabitants of contemporary Britain. In the series of four well-illustrated books entitled 'Life in Victorian Britain', designed for pupils at the top end of junior school (Key Stage 2), the author provides an accessible and effective introduction to domestic life, work, schools, leisure and sport. A feature of this series, and of others, was an emphasis on portraits, photographs, written contemporary sources and the oral testimony of folk born towards the end of the Victorian era. Probably for the first time, at least for school education in general, children could experience some ordinary Victorians, as it were, speaking to them.[50]

Beyond the age of 14 the study of history was not compulsory. It was also, in a damning phrase, declared to be 'a reading subject' and thus – in what passed for conventional pedagogical wisdom – not suitable for less able pupils. Teachers, fearful of the impact of poor results on government league tables, treated history warily.[51] Few 16-year-olds preparing for the General Certificate of Secondary Education (GCSE) examination, introduced in 1988, encountered the Victorians at all: no syllabus concentrated on nineteenth-century political history. Many teachers were dissuaded from entering their candidates for examination on the social and economic history of industrial Britain since so much of the syllabus content had been covered in Key Stage 3. The number of takers for the SHP's depth study on Britain 1815–51 dwindled alarmingly.[52]

The Victorian age fared rather better at A-level. In many syllabi from the 1980s and 1990s, candidates were entered for examination on a long period but prepared in detail on only a portion of it, since teachers knew that the range of questions would offer those pupils adequate choice. One such option, run by the Oxford and Cambridge Schools Examination Board until 2001, required candidates to answer three questions, covering 1689–1980, from a choice of thirty-six. Candidates concentrated their efforts overwhelmingly on the period 1815–80.

The OCSEB did not restrict itself to central political themes, although candidates did. Thus a question in 2001 asked candidates to 'choose any one English novelist writing in the nineteenth century. Examine his, or her, importance as a source of information about English society at the time.' It was attempted by fewer than ten candidates. Scarcely more popular were questions on the Oxford movement or on the validity of the term 'Great Depression' to describe British economic performance in the last quarter of the nineteenth century. By contrast, questions about the extent to which Chartism had failed by 1848, why a Reform Act was passed in 1867 and whether, on the evidence of his career from 1868 to 1886, Gladstone was a 'great national figure' but a poor party leader were all immensely popular,

despite the fact – at least in this last case – that almost no candidate explicitly set up any criteria by which a great national figure or a party leader
could be judged.[53] Political history and foreign policy remained the staples
of A-level Victorian history.

'Curriculum 2000' represented the biggest change to A-level studies in
fifty years. A-level history was modularised, candidates taking six units,
each predominantly skills-led. While candidates had to study some British
history, this could be – and was for the very many students concentrating
on European history in the first half of the twentieth century – restricted to
one unit. Study of the dictatorships of Hitler, Mussolini and Stalin was wor-
ryingly prevalent. Victorian history nevertheless retained more than a toe-
hold. The atomisation of study, however, made it even more likely that
students would study familiar 'highlights', such as the Chartists, parliamentary reform or the ministries of Gladstone and Disraeli. Only the
requirement to study the process of change over a period of at least 100
years – a new feature of the criteria governing the construction of history
specifications – compelled examination of content in novel ways. Award-
ing bodies selected what they hoped would be popular themes to help pupils
understand the process of change. Edexcel offered two examination options
grounded in the nineteenth century: 'Representation and democracy in
Britain, 1830–1931' and 'The State and the poor in Britain, 1830–1939'.[54]
OCR offered an option on Ireland from the Act of Union to the Partition.

Textbooks supporting these and other predominantly Victorian options
were of surprisingly high quality. Publishers insisted on 'designer busy-ness'
and many proscribed large numbers of words on a page. However, authors
generally showed themselves aware of recent scholarship and made
attempts to integrate its findings into their books. In addition to the now-
obligatory visual materials, specimen questions and hints on writing
answers of different types, and remarkably up-to-date bibliographical references were provided.[55] The themes covered remained orthodox, although
with significant shifts. In comparison with their early twentieth-century
counterparts, twenty-first-century students would encounter less material
on the empire, and very little on imperial heroes such as General Gordon.
They would learn little about Queen Victoria herself.

V

The essence of 'Victorianism' is difficult to capture. Victoria's reign lasted
for more than sixty years, and historians jib at reconstructing a coherent
'Victorian era', let alone passing it on to the young in assimilable form. The
world of the Chartists and the Opium Wars was so fundamentally different from that of the Labour Representation Committee and the Second Boer
War as to mock any generalising uniformity. It is true that Melbourne and
Salisbury, Victoria's first and final prime ministers, happened to be shrewd
and cynical aristocrats, but that is only a superficial – and anyway a

misleading – continuity set in a sea of swirling change. It is asking a great deal of a fragmented and loosely structured education system that it should capture the Victorian age's essence and present it in coherent form to schoolchildren.

Not surprisingly, what the young have learned about the Victorians has changed over time. Throughout the twentieth century, however, 'Victorianism' has been dressed in distorting garb. Prior to 1914 the emphasis was on imperial mission, regal symbolism and British 'exceptionalism'. Since 1918, Victorian life has tended to be presented with an overly political slant, through key ministries and 'struggles for reform' – for able and older pupils – or as a series of poorly contextualised social vignettes – education, work and social life – for less able and younger pupils. Little serious attempt has been made to portray the diversity and complexity of 'Victorian values'.

Few twentieth-century pupils gained any understanding of the centrality of religion in Victorian public and private life. Few learned about the reasons for, and the importance of, civic pride. Even fewer understood the importance of public spiritedness, mutuality, citizenship, trust, high seriousness and the overall ethic of service as represented in the huge number of social organisations – charitable societies, mechanics' institutes, friendly societies, trades unions and the rest – which expanded and flourished in the Victorian era. In a contemporary society dominated by the bubble reputation of celebrity, by value defaulting to mere wealth, and in a State which can no longer construe the meaning of 'public virtue', this lack of historical understanding amounts almost to criminal negligence. It may also help to explain why late twentieth-century politicians do not appreciate why teaching 'citizenship' was once considered the natural province of the historian. Perhaps, in truth, the Victorians are now farther away even than historians think.

Notes

1 Charles Dickens, *Hard Times* [1853] (London: Penguin, 1969), p. 47.

2 Colin Matthew, *The Nineteenth Century: The British Isles, 1815–1901* (Oxford: 2000), p. 37.

3 P. Harnett, 'Heroes and heroines: exploring a nation's past. The history curriculum in state primary schools in the twentieth century', *History of Education Society Bulletin*, 62 (1998), p. 85.

4 S. Heathorn, *For Home, Country and Race: Constructing Gender, Class and Englishness in the Elementary School, 1880–1914* (Toronto: University of Toronto Press, 2000), p. 41; see also Peter Yeandle's unpublished paper 'Imperialism, Englishness and the elementary-school history lesson, c.1880–1914' (a revised version of a paper presented at the British Island Stories Conference at King's Manor, York, April 2002), and his 'Writing and rewriting a narrative for the nation', unpublished MA thesis, University of Lancaster, 2001, pp. 38–53. I am heavily indebted to Mr Yeandle for the argument in this section of the paper.

5 *Parliamentary Papers*, vol. 60 (1905), pp. 61–4.

6 J. R. Seeley, *The Expansion of England*, 2nd edn (London: Macmillan, 1895), pp. 340–1.
7 H. C. Mackinder, *Our Island Story* (London: George Philip & Son, 1914), p. 320.
8 Quoted in Heathorn, *For Home, Country and Race*, p. 82.
9 *Hansard*, 5th series, vol. 104 (13 March 1918), col. 392.
10 D. Sylvester, 'History teaching, 1900–93', in H. Bourdillon (ed.), *Teaching History* (London: Routledge, 1994), p. 10.
11 V. E. Chancellor, *History for Their Masters* (Bath: Adams & Dart, 1970), pp. 1–17, 106, 119; W. E. Marsden, *The School Textbook: Geography, History and Social Studies* (London: Woburn Press, 2001), p. 37.
12 C. H. K. Marten, 'The first school examination and the teaching of history', *History*, 13 (1928), p. 24.
13 B. J. Elliott, 'An early failure of curriculum reform: history teaching in England, 1918–40', *Journal of Educational Administration and History*, 12 (1980), p. 40. The commitment of senior academics to the development of school examination syllabi was a pronounced feature of the first half of the twentieth century. Of the forty academics listed as examiners of matriculation subjects in 1905, twenty-one were full professors: *Calendar of the Joint Matriculation Board* (Manchester: JMB, 1905), Preface.
14 Marten, 'The first school examination', p. 18.
15 J. A. Petch, *Fifty Years of Examining: Joint Matriculation Board, 1903–53* (London: Harrap, 1953), p. 121.
16 P. Harnett, 'Heroes and heroines', p. 87.
17 H. Cooper, *How the Empire Grew* (London: RTS, 1920), pp. 130, 135.
18 J. D. Mackie, 'The teaching of history and war', *History*, 35 (1940), p. 133.
19 *Ibid.*, p. 139.
20 *Ibid.*, pp. 137, 139, 142.
21 A. C. F. Beales, *A Guide to the Teaching of History in Schools* (London: University of London Press, 1937), quoted in Marsden, *The School Textbook*, p. 42.
22 Elliott, 'An early failure of curriculum reform', p. 44.
23 J. A. White 'The Board of Education report on the teaching of history in London', *History*, 12 (1928), p. 322.
24 R. Jones, *The English People: A Junior History* (London: J. M. Dent, 1928), p. 164.
25 J. E. Morris, *Great Britain and Ireland: A History for the Lower Forms* (Cambridge: Cambridge University Press, 1922), p. 480.
26 *Hansard*, 5th series, vol. 92 (19 April 1917), col. 1907.
27 Marten, 'The first school examination', pp. 18, 21.
28 *Ibid.*, pp. 20–1.
29 *Syllabus of the Matriculation Examination conducted by the Joint Board of the Universities of Manchester, Liverpool, Leeds, Sheffield and Birmingham* (Manchester: JMB, 1924), p. 22; *ibid.* (1934), pp. 32–3. School Certificate examinations followed a broadly similar pattern across the country. The Oxford and Cambridge Schools Examination Board, for example, offered at School Certificate level four chronologically unequal 'English history outlines' papers in the early 1940s: 878–1485; 1485–1714; 1714–1852; and 1815–1919. The Higher School Certificate comprised optional 'outlines' papers in English and European

history, together with a choice from six 'special subjects'. Three of these were: 'The Chartist movement'; 'Economic history' and 'English colonial history 1660–1867': H. McNicol, *History, Heritage and Environment* (London: Faber & Faber, 1946), p. 171.

30 *Handbook of Suggestions for the Consideration of Teachers and Others Concerned in the Work of Public Elementary Schools* (London: Board of Education, 1937), p. 413.

31 H. McNicol, *History, Heritage and Environment*, pp. 177–86. It is worth noting that the Armada was often taught as part of the history of England's acquisition of empire.

32 S. M. Toyne, 'History and the Norwood report', *History*, 29 (1944), pp. 68–71; see also B. J. Elliott, 'The impact of the Second World War upon history teaching in Britain', *Journal of Educational Administration and History*, 26 (1994), pp. 153–63.

33 The examples above, which are typical, are taken from the Joint Matriculation Board, *Regulations and Syllabuses 1955* (Manchester: JMB, 1955).

34 *Ibid.*

35 Sylvester, 'History teaching', p. 14.

36 M. Booth, 'Ages and concepts: a critique of the Piagetian approach to history teaching', in C. Portal (ed.), *The History Curriculum for Teachers* (London: Falmer Press, 1987), p. 23.

37 J. B. Coltham, *The Development of Thinking and the Learning of History* (Historical Association: London, 1971), p. 44.

38 E. E. Y. Hales, 'School history in the melting pot', *History Today*, 16 (1966), pp. 202–9.

39 *Curriculum 11–16* (HMI: London, 1977). See also J. Slater, 'History in the National Curriculum: the final report of the history working group', in R. Aldrich (ed.), *History in the National Curriculum* (London: Kogan Page, 1991), pp. 8–38. HMI reinforced its key messages in *History in the Primary and Secondary Years: An HMI View* (London: DES, 1985). Strongly influenced by SHP's methodology, it urged teachers to encourage pupils' active learning while offering little but generalities about historical content.

40 Mary Price, 'History in danger', *History*, 53 (1968), p. 344.

41 Schools History Project developed an extensive and, in some cases, highly polemical literature. Many teachers found the new approach anathema: see *Schools Council Projects on History Teaching: A New Look at History* (London: Holmes McDougall, 1976); D. Shemilt, *History 13–16: Evaluation Study* (London; Holmes McDougall, 1980); S. F. Lang, 'The sacred cow history project', *Times Educational Supplement*, 4 April 1986, pp. 27–8.

42 *Hansard*, 5th series, vol. 620 (21 March 1960), cols 51–2; see also G. McCulloch, 'Curriculum history in England and New Zealand', in I. Goodson (ed.), *International Perspectives in Curriculum History* (London, 1986), p. 299.

43 Keith Joseph, 'Why teach history in school?', *The Historian*, 6 (1984), 10–12.

44 P. Goalen, 'Only connect . . .', *History Workshop Journal*, 29 (1990), p. 112.

45 R. Samuel, 'Grand narratives', *ibid.*, p. 129.

46 The story of the emergence of National Curriculum history is expertly told in R. Phillips, *History Teaching, Nationhood and the State: A Study in Educational Politics* (London: Cassell, 1998), especially pp. 53–134.

47 Updated advice is provided for teachers on the National Curriculum website: www.nc.net.

48 *History: A Scheme of Work for Key Stage 3* (London: QCA, 2000).

49 Ben Walsh and Karen Brookfield, *Britain 1750–1900* (London: British Library Marketing and Publishing Office, 2000).

50 R. Rees, *The Victorians at School*; *The Victorians at Work*; *The Victorians at Home*; and *The Victorians at Play* (Oxford: Heinemann, 1995).

51 The general trend of entries for both GCSE and A-level history was downwards. Almost 248,000 GCSE candidates took history in 1995; this had declined to 220,456 by 2001. At A-level, 46,698 candidates in 1992 had dwindled to 43,796 by 1995 and to 39,443 by 2001, the last year of 'old-style' A-levels. Statistics available from the QCA: www.qca.org.uk.

52 In 2002, for example, of 17,507 candidates entered for the Edexcel syllabus 1328 (Schools History Project) only 592 students (3.4 per cent) took the nineteenth-century Britain option compared with 8,584 for the American west and 8,331 for Nazi Germany.

53 *OCR Examination Paper 5749: English History, 1689–1980* (Cambridge: OCR, 2001). Comments on the relative popularity, and relative success, of the various questions, can be found in the accompanying examiners' report.

54 *Edexcel Advanced GCE in History* (Sept. 2000) (London: Edexcel Foundation, 2000), p. 28.

55 From a very large selection, see particularly: M. Scott-Baumann, *Years of Expansion: British History, 1815–1914*, 2nd edn (Oxford: Hodder & Stoughton, 2002), E. J. Evans, *The Birth of Modern Britain, 1780–1914* (Longman: London, 1997); M. Lynch, *An Introduction to Nineteenth-Century British History* (Oxford: Heinemann, 1999); Bob Whitfield, *The Extension of the Franchise, 1832–1931* (Oxford: Heinemann, 2001); Duncan Watts, *Tories, Unionists and Conservatives, 1815–1914* (London: Hodder & Stoughton, 2002).

Part III
Revisions

13

Victorian studies in the digital age

Patrick Leary

On Sunday 31 March 1901, census enumerators fanned out across England and Wales, knocking on doors. On Wednesday 2 January 2002, the Public Record Office proudly unveiled its ambitious effort to make the results of that census available to the general public worldwide over the internet. This digitised portrait of England and Wales at the end of Victoria's reign was designed to enable visitors to search the entire database of 32 million entries by a variety of terms and to call up scanned images of the actual pages of the enumerators' books. At nine o'clock that morning the website opened and the visitors started arriving – and within hours it had all come crashing down. Over 1 million visitors, most of them descendants of the Victorians who had warily opened their doors to the enumerators on that Sunday a century earlier, had arrived at the site by electronic proxy all at the same time and had tried to find their ancestors in the census. Expecting the new site to be a popular destination for genealogists, the PRO had designed the system to handle some 1 million 'hits', or individual attempts to log on; had that system been able to accommodate all of the visitors that day, simultaneously clamouring to use the census, it would have logged about 32 million hits. The site quickly went offline – where it stayed, while the technicians tinkered, the public complained and questions were raised in Parliament.[1]

After many months the 1901 census did eventually go back online, and is already proving to be a fine resource for amateur and professional researchers alike. But that ignominious, though thankfully temporary, catastrophe served as a vivid reminder of both the promise and the unpredictability of online and electronic resources. Already the range of such resources either available or in development is too large to be encompassed by a brief survey; and the volatility of the marketplace in which they operate, and which scholars often share with interested members of the public, makes any static picture a mere snapshot of a rapidly changing scene. Yet even the sampling offered here may suffice to give a clearer notion of how digital applications have changed and are changing the way we locate, use, and share nineteenth-century evidence, and how, to an extent undreamt of only a few years ago, our relationship to the Victorian period – indeed, to the past itself – has come to be mediated by digital technology.

Digital beginnings: mainframes to desktops

The census makes a natural startingpoint for a survey of the impact of digital technology on Victorian Studies, for it is emblematic of the beginnings of one emerging information society and the applications of computers to its study by another. The nineteenth-century censuses represented part of a revolution in the way information was gathered, organised, used and shared in the nineteenth century, and the quantity and consistency of those and other records attracted modern historians eager to make use of the new capabilities offered by the first mainframe computers.[2] The vast quantity of routinely gathered and, for the most part, consistently organised records amassed by the Victorians was a natural fit with the computer's ability to make rapid calculations based on large quantities of records that could be coded into distinct fields. While such early work as that of Deane and Cole on modern British economic statistics was accomplished without electronic aid,[3] the labour involved in even small-scale projects could be enormously costly and time-consuming, particularly for studies that involved the linking of data among records in such a way as to track individual people, events, places, and so on, through related sets of documents. Before the advent in the 1960s of mainframe computers, matching a personal name in one record to any occurrences of the same name in hundreds or thousands of other records could only be done by physically checking each of those records against the first one, and then beginning anew for the next name. The new-found ability to use 80-column punch cards – themselves nineteenth-century products, descendants of Joseph Jacquard and Charles Babbage – to record and manipulate data represented a huge saving in cost and time, and historians of the nineteenth century were not slow to take advantage of it.[4] Michael Anderson's influential 1971 work on family structure in nineteenth-century Lancashire, the rich variety of source materials including a 2 per cent sampling of the 1851 census, was one of a number of studies to demonstrate the usefulness of the kind of statistical analysis that had become possible with these new tools.[5]

The mainframe computer thus represented a tremendous advance over manual techniques of sorting, exploring and presenting data. In the late 1960s, political scientist Norman Nie developed the *Statistical Package for the Social Sciences* (*SPSS*), which, while challenging to use, lessened the need for extensive programming skills and remains one of the most popular software programmes for these purposes. By the early 1970s, historians L. Burr Litchfield and Howard Chudacoff at Brown University were using *SPSS* with data coded from nineteenth-century censuses taken in Stockport,

Lancashire (1841 and 1851), and in other cities, to teach undergraduates
the basics of using quantitative methods to explore social, urban, demographic and family history.[6] But while quantitative historians working with
Victorian data continued to refine their techniques throughout the 1970s –
Wrigley and Schofield's *Population History of England 1541–1871* (1981)[7]
represented one of the great accomplishments of this era – the technology
involved in the process remained clumsy, expensive, tedious, demanding
and often fragile. Mainframe users will vividly recall the queues for 'jobs'
at computer centres, long hours at the keypunch machine, the catastrophe
of dropping a stack of punch cards or having cards jam during processing,
and the frustration of poring over stack upon stack of dot-matrix printouts
in search of a programming error.[8] Magnetic tape eventually did away with
the punch card, but it was the arrival of the desktop personal computer
(PC) in 1980 that signalled the beginning of a truly revolutionary advance
in the ability of historians to efficiently manipulate large quantities of data.

The increase in desktop computing speed, memory and storage capacity,
with the concomitant increase in the sophistication of computational and
database software, had by the mid-1980s drawn many more historians to
explore the potential of these new tools. While economic and demographic
research has continued to be the main focus of many quantitative
historians – with such results as Joel Mokyr's analysis of the Irish famine
and Robert Woods's recent magisterial study of the demography of
Victorian England and Wales – an increasingly wide variety of topics in
Victorian social, political and cultural history has proven amenable to
investigation by such means.[9] K. D. M. Snell and Paul S. Ell were able to
analyse thousands of variables, drawn from the 1851 census of religious
worship, to map the patterns of Victorian religious activity by region.[10] The
analysis of Victorian poll-books by such historians as John Phillips, R. J.
Morris, and Frank O'Gorman has transformed our understanding of
the impact of the Reform Act of 1832.[11] Publishing historian Simon Eliot
used Stationers' Company records and trade publications to compose the
first overall picture of the patterns of growth in the nineteenth-century publishing industry and the changing proportions of different kinds of books
published over the course of the period.[12] The integration of spatial data
with census, vital registration and electoral data is the hallmark of the Great
Britain Historical GIS Project under Humphrey Southall. Begun in 1994,
the project seeks to record the shifting boundaries of registration districts
and to correlate these with (primarily) nineteenth-century trends in mortality, social structure, electoral behaviour and many other areas.[13] So ubiquitous has the technology become that these examples represent just a few
of the many recent applications of computers to the task of untangling the
strands of change over the course of the nineteenth century – applications
that, as R. J. Morris argued penetratingly in a 1995 essay, have subtly
shifted the grounds of the approach of historians to such matters as the
pace of industrialisation and the impact of reform, and which continue to

raise important methodological issues.[14] Although data entry remains costly, as desktop PCs have developed at once greater power and ease of use, many Victorianists well outside the rubric of 'quantitative history' have been emboldened to integrate databases and statistical tables of many kinds into their own projects, as well as to make use of an expanding variety of textual materials now available in electronic form.

Electronic resources for Victorian research

With the emergence of the internet and the web as a global network in the 1990s, the range of electronic resources for historical and literary research, and for teaching about the Victorian period, has grown exponentially. To be sure, the collapse of the 'dot com bubble' in 2001 cooled many of the more utopian enthusiasms, and the tightening of the world economy added new fiscal restraints that made large-scale electronic projects a harder sell both within and beyond the academic world. But just as the building of railway infrastructure in Victorian Britain continued to grow in importance after the railway boom of the 1840s had dissolved in a flurry of scandal and bankruptcy, so has the digital revolution continued to transform the way historians and literary scholars alike pursue research, teaching and community. Listing all of these resources here would be impracticable, though even a glance at some of the more useful of them suggests that such tools have become indispensable to Victorian research of many kinds.

One of the most important but least heralded trends of the past decade has been the appearance of searchable electronic catalogues, bibliographies, location registers and collection descriptions; these have made an enormous difference in the speed and thoroughness with which Victorianists go about finding the books, periodicals, newspapers and manuscripts necessary for their research. Quite apart from the major library catalogues like OCLC's (Online Computer Library Center) WorldCat (and such union catalogues as the USA's *LIBCAT* and the UK's *COPAC*), there has been a welcome boom in electronic bibliographical resources specific to nineteenth-century Britain. Both of the two major bibliographies of work in the field are now available in this form. The *Cumulative Bibliography of Victorian Studies*, compiled at the University of Alberta, familiar to many scholars in its printed form, has been re-christened the *Victorian Database* and comes in both CD-ROM and online versions, covering books and articles published since 1945.[15] In 2002, the journal *Victorian Studies* began to make its annual bibliography available, to subscribers and non-subscribers alike, as *Victorian Bibliography Online*.[16] Though of course broader than either of these, the electronic version of the venerable *Royal Historical Society Bibliography* is of special interest for its inclusion of many specialised historical journals, and can easily be searched by time-period covered. After having published a CD-ROM version with Oxford University Press (OUP), the Historical Society took the unusual and widely welcomed decision to make the whole available online to the public at no charge, a decision made possible by OUP's permission and by a range of funding sources.[17] Over the past few years the full texts of an increasing number of articles in scholarly journals such as *Victorian Studies* have been made searchable and retrievable online through such subscription services as Project Muse, EBSCO and JSTOR.

The *Nineteenth Century Short Title Catalogue* (*NSTC*) on CD-ROM integrates 1.5 million records from eight major US and UK libraries, including the British Library and the Library of Congress, to provide an unrivalled window into nineteenth-century print culture. Despite some limitations – Welsh books are seriously under-represented and differently catalogued entries for the same volumes can be misleading – the NSTC none the less makes it possible not simply to find titles of particular nineteenth-century books and pamphlets on various subjects but to gauge the kinds and quantity of literature that the age produced at different times and in different places.[18] The ability to search the whole of a text electronically has added a vastly important new dimension to familiar works of reference, such as the index to the House of Commons *Parliamentary Papers* on CD-ROM. The search engine of the CD-ROM version of the *Wellesley Index to Victorian Periodicals* makes indispensable an already important resource by reducing the need for the painstaking page-by-page scan for articles on particular subjects that has for years marked the earliest stage of many a research project. Though not updated by the publisher since then, the 1999 CD-ROM includes many corrections and additions to the five-volume printed edition.[19] Outside of the 'magic circle' of the forty-five major periodicals indexed by the *Wellesley* lies a largely unmapped territory, making *Poole's Index to Periodical Literature*, for all its annoying idiosyncrasies, a necessary port of call for researchers. Now compounded with other related indexes into a subscription online service and re-christened *19th-Century Masterfile*, it offers a wide array of citations of Anglo-American periodicals. For basic bibliographical information on the era's staggeringly numerous serial titles – periodicals and newspapers alike – one must turn to John North's magisterial ongoing project, the *Waterloo Directory*, the electronic incarnation of which allows one to range easily across its ten volumes and more than 25,000 entries in search of titles, subjects and places, and the names of people (editors, publishers, contributors) associated with those often fugitive publications.[20]

Victorian newspapers are an essential but notoriously elusive source for many aspects of nineteenth-century life. Out of thousands of titles and millions of copies, many have not survived; few among those that have survived are readily accessible, and even in the case of well-known newspapers the prospect of creeping through the surviving wilderness of closely printed un-indexed prose via microfilm has daunted many a hardy researcher. One of the most exciting and far-reaching developments in Victorian studies in the twenty-first century will be the opening up by electronic means of the hitherto largely unexplored contents of nineteenth-century newspapers and periodicals, made possible by improvements in the efficiency of text scanning and in the accuracy of optical character recognition. We are now only beginning to make the first inroads into this vast *terra incognita* of print with two competing electronic editions of the nineteenth-century *Times* of London, one of them searchable with an online version of the old *Palmer's Index*, the other offering direct searches of the actual text of the newspaper.[21] Both ProQuest and Gale Research, two companies associated with these *Times* products as well as a range of other digitisation projects, have expressed an interest in further coverage of nineteenth-century serials, while pilot projects like the Internet Library of Early Journals and the British Library's Online Newspaper Archive give a hint of the resources in this area that we can hope will one day soon be open to researchers.[22]

Such progress is far from inevitable, but projects of this kind have demonstrated that the sufficiently dedicated application of current technology has the potential to release researchers forever from the wearying tyranny of microfilm, the often prohibitive cost of long sessions in the reading room of the British Library Newspaper Library in Colindale, and the frustration of visually scanning endless columns of nineteenth-century newsprint for names, at the same time bringing into view as never before the hidden universe of Victorian journalism.

Locating and using nineteenth-century manuscript materials has always relied on the dedication of skilled archivists and the catalogues they have created, and this has never been more true than today. Thanks to years of work to put those catalogue descriptions online in searchable form, it is getting easier and faster to find letters, reports and other documents, many of them in small local repositories. The website of the National Register of Arabives remains the first part of call for manuscript searches, and many related projects have followed its lead. The most immediate challenge over the next few years will be to link all of these together seamlessly. Yet these meta-catalogues can be only as useful as the institutional catalogues that comprise them, and the progress of detailed cataloguing and digitisation of manuscript holdings is necessarily uneven, varying from one institution to another. As of this writing it is not yet possible, for instance, to find any detailed listing or index of the papers of Blackwood's, the powerful nineteenth-century publishers, in the online catalogues of the National Library of Scotland. In the University of Southampton's system, by contrast, not only are 100,000 items in the Duke of Wellington's Papers meticulously described, but the distant researcher can browse and search this entire index and pull up, in many cases, full transcripts of individual letters.[23] The *Charles Darwin Correspondence Project Online* database at Cambridge,[24] to name but one other example, sets a similarly high standard for such resources. A number of specialised guides to the locations of manuscripts are also coming online. The indispensable *Location Register of English Literary Manuscripts and Letters: Eighteenth and Nineteenth Centuries*, which grew out of the programme established in the early 1980s to create a centralised register of literary manuscripts, was fully incorporated into the RLG union catalogue in 2000, and in the USA is accessible from RLG's Eureka. The *Artists' Papers Register*, which contains location information for the papers of many Victorian artists, was created by the Association of Art Historians at Leeds and is now hosted in electronic form by the National Register of Archives. The Mundus Gateway[25] offers a location guide to missionary-related holdings in the repositories, many of which are particularly rich in nineteenth-century materials.

The Victorians and the web

Today, when the *World Wide Web* is so ubiquitous in the Anglophone world that it sometimes seems as if a website exists for everything and everyone, it is astonishing to reflect on how few years have elapsed since the internet – with its exciting new graphical interface, the web – was inhabited almost exclusively by people in universities exchanging messages and working in comparative isolation on a variety of non-profit projects. Yet even now most of the websites that serve the Victorian studies community continue to reflect the distinctive visions of dedicated individual webmasters, most of them associated with universities, rather than the broader aims of commercial or institutional initiatives. George Landow's widely praised and hugely informative Victorian Web is one such site, to whose encyclopaedic riches no brief summary can do ample justice.[26] A distinguished literary scholar and pioneer in the theory and development of hypertext in the humanities, Landow brought to the construction of the Victorian Web many years of experience at Brown University's Institute for Research in Information and Scholarship in developing hypermedia documents for teaching Victorian literature. The website draws together thousands of carefully hyperlinked documents, contributed by a number of historians and literary scholars that helpfully summarise the significance of a host of Victorian writers, artists, events and preoccupations, and includes many e-texts of secondary works on the nineteenth century and scans of their illustrations. Currently funded by the University Scholars Programme of the University of Singapore, this extraordinary teaching and reference tool also hosts an online publishing programme of enormous potential utility, offering authors of out-of-print scholarly texts in Victorian studies the opportunity, though still retaining copyright, to give their works a new life, and new readers through online versions available at and hyperlinked with the Victorian Web itself.

A very different but complementary set of web pages is the Victoria Research Web (VRW), which brings together a host of practical information of use to working scholars, educators, students and researchers of all kinds in planning and carrying out their explorations of the period. The site began as a set of browser bookmarks and notes assembled in the course of my studies and researches as a postgraduate student at Indiana University, and has since expanded as both a portal to other useful sites (links to all the resources mentioned in this article, and many more, mention of which is precluded by considerations of space, will be found there) and as a repository of advice and information gleaned from my own experience and also contributed by other scholars. Sections supply the visitor with guides to archival, library and bibliographical resources, links to syllabi for a wide variety of courses in Victorian history and literature, contact information for scholarly journals, Victorian studies organisations and discussion lists, information for planning research trips, and links to reviews of scholarly books in the field. Increasingly, the VRW is also becoming a modest publishing medium for short topical bibliographies, works in progress and research guides contributed by scholars.

Electronic texts of many kinds have formed a huge growth industry in humanities computing for many years now, a growth accelerated by the prospect of making such texts available through the web, and by the affordability of the basic hardware and software required. Texts of Victorian literary works can be found online in bewildering profusion, varying enormously in the editorial care with which they have been created. Most such texts, while adequate to the needs of casual readers, remain inappropriate for classroom or scholarly use. Setting a high standard in this respect is the Victorian Women Writers Project (VWWP) begun in 1995 under the direction of Perry Willett at Indiana University. Using the widely tested Standardised General Markup Language (SGML) developed as a flexible encoding system that makes possible sophisticated textual analysis, the VWWP has made freely available over 150 out-of-print and often inaccessible works by Victorian women writers as different as Harriet Martineau, Catherine Booth and Eliza Lynn Linton.[27] A model for other e-text projects in the field, the VWWP offers unprecedentedly wide access to a virtual collection that no physical collection could hope to rival.

Websites devoted to individual Victorian authors and featuring e-texts of their works are widely available online, many of them reflecting an extraordinary amount of devoted effort on the part of their creators. The most astounding of these goes back to the very beginnings of the web in the early 1990s and draws on the unique strengths of the medium to create a comprehensive edition that seeks to overcome the limitations of the traditional codex. The work of a team led by renowned literary historian Jerome McGann, the Dante Gabriel Rossetti Archive is a hypermedia edition of the textual and pictorial works of one of the most versatile and creative minds of the Victorian period.[28] McGann has conceived the project as a 'working laboratory' that invites interpretive interchange about the nature of textuality, and aims ultimately to reproduce the whole of Rossetti's extensive body of work. Based at the pioneering Institute for Advanced Technology in the Humanities at the University of Virginia, the Rossetti Archive already represents an impressive and thought-provoking achievement.

Of the dozens of other fine websites on Victorian themes a handful of titles will have to serve to indicate some of the wealth of information published in this most accessible of modern media. Online explorations of Victorian London are the aims of two ambitious projects. The *Monuments and Dust* website, the inspiration of Michael Levenson of the University of Virginia, aims to enlist scholars around the world to contribute materials about nineteenth-century London, and boasts such features as a 'virtual reality' simulation of the Crystal Palace's structure, dynamic population and mortality data-sets, and an online version of Blanchard Jerrold and Gustave Doré's *London: A Pilgrimage.*[29] For *The Dictionary of Victorian London*, aimed at both scholars and general readers, librarian Lee Jackson has assembled a wide variety of hard-to-find documents, many of them in full text, organised by subject.[30] Ralph R. Frerichs of UCLA's department of epidemiology has explored in fascinating detail the dramatic career of the legendary John Snow in this richly informative multimedia site that illuminates issues in Victorian public health, while historian of science John van Whye has assembled a guide to Victorian phrenology based on his doctoral research at Cambridge.[31] Mitsuharu Matsuoka's continually updated Gaskell Web assembles a vast variety of texts by and about Elizabeth Gaskell in one of the earliest and fullest single-author Victorian sites to appear online. Robert Schwartz's online booklet introduces students to the power of historical GIS methods through an exploration of railways and population change in industrialising England.[32] These and similar web-based projects reflect the energy, the erudition and the public spiritedness that Victorianists from many disciplines continue to bring to the building and maintenance of online resources.

Victorianists and online community

Electronic discussion lists came into their own in the early 1990s, when Eric Thomas in Paris made widely available the Listserv mail distribution software he had designed for what was then the BITNET network. With the vast popularity of email, discussion lists quickly came into their own as routine parts of everyday give-and-take for many thousands of users worldwide. Several lists in related disciplines – like the H-ALBION list for British history, SHARP-L for students of publishing history and H-WOMEN for women's history – feature occasional contributions about the Victorian period, while a growing number of specialised lists focus on individual authors and topics that fall within the period. Two rival Trollope lists, for example, offer different approaches to that novelist, while DICKNS-L offers a lively and erudite discussion of matters Dickensian. Several single-author lists, such as those for George Eliot and Lewis Carroll, have migrated to web-based services like Yahoo!Groups, where they welcome scholarly specialists and general readers alike, and a number of such lists sponsor group-reads of Victorian fiction with a weekly discussion of each instalment.

The largest and most active list for all those interested in the period is VICTORIA, founded in February 1993 and currently hosting a shifting membership of about 2,000 subscribers from some thirty-eight countries. Those subscribers represent a cross-section of the Victorian studies community: Victorianists in English departments predominate, although there are a good many academic historians as well, as well as independent scholars and interested amateurs of all kinds. Scholarly lists have sometimes been likened to an academic conference that runs twenty-four hours a day and never ends, a nightmarish notion if ever there was one. But in fact that analogy is not particularly apt: the ordinary run of messages on VICTORIA reflects a much less formal exchange of ideas, information and opinions, one much closer to the sort of thing once found in the nineteenth-century volumes of *Notes and Queries*. And like the astoundingly diverse array of topics that makes browsing through a mid-century volume of that periodical's semi-annual indices such a fascinating exercise, the content of the list defies easy summary.

Postings arrive in subscribers' mailboxes at a rate of a dozen to as many as forty a day, and ranging in content from the practical ('Where can I find a listing of all the nineteenth-century Anglican bishops?') to the speculative ('What concrete purposes, if any, did Victorian "fiction with a purpose" actually serve?'). Inevitably, given the constant influx of new subscribers, some topics routinely reappear: the popular old myths about ruffles on piano legs and lying back and thinking of England seem to need debunking every year or two, for instance, and various list-members are happy to oblige. But the bread-and-butter of daily discourse on VICTORIA are the research query and reply, which come in many varieties from people working on all sorts of projects. At their best, these exchanges function not as a substitute for going to the library to look things up but rather as a way of working through and framing aspects of research in collaboration with other scholars. For while the format of the list's content does not resemble that of an academic conference, it does serve some of the same purposes, particularly in enabling connections between people working along similar lines, or whose interests dovetail in various ways. Retired and independent scholars, people working on dissertations or books far away from their home campuses, and those teaching in campuses on which they are the only Victorianists, especially, find that a list like VICTORIA can be a kind of lifeline to current developments in the field. Given the limited funding available for attending conferences, involvement in this online community provides an important means of overcoming the kinds of isolation – hierarchical, geographic, cultural – that everyone working in the field experiences from time to time.

The varied membership of the list brings to the discussion a comparable range of research questions. Editors of various Victorian texts, for example, have called on the list's help in tracking down allusions and quotations; biographers have sought assistance in locating materials; and historical novelists frequently ask for help in purging their stories of various anachronisms. The acknowledgments pages of an increasing number of scholarly books bear witness to the extraordinary daily generosity of list-members in sharing with one another information, resources and ideas through this medium. At a time when toll-gates are going up all over the online world, restricting access to scholarly information to paying customers, these non-commercial arenas for information exchange grow correspondingly more vital to the health of the scholarly enterprise. More than anywhere else, connections made online have played an important role in fostering collaboration, including the building of the kinds of non-profit, openly accessible projects that are such a necessary counterweight to the commercial enclosure occurring elsewhere on the web.

Perhaps most importantly, VICTORIA has from the beginning provided a place to compare experiences, ideas, strategies and problems that bear on the challenge of teaching Victorian studies, with results that have proven, and continue to prove, of real utility in the classroom. Even the routine notices of the kind traditionally carried in the back pages of journals – the calls for papers and articles, announcements of jobs, grants and workshops – often take on a new character because of the immediacy and global range of the medium. Our collective sense of what is happening in our field – grounded, of course, in our reading of books and reviews and our attendance at traditional conferences – is steadily enriched by the tidal flow of this daily infusion of mail. The usefulness of these and other exchanges extends beyond the particular discussions that gave rise to them. Each posting ever sent to VICTORIA is accessible in its online archives – some 80,000 messages in all, and of course growing every day. Searchable in a variety of ways, this archive constitutes an extraordinary resource for research of many kinds and, incidentally, a fascinating record of many of the field's preoccupations over the past several years. If we were to draw a Darntonian communication circuit diagram to show how information circulates within the discipline, it would look very different today than it would have looked ten years ago, largely because of the role of lists like VICTORIA.[33]

Conclusion

As varied and impressive as are the many digital resources created by and available to Victorianists over the past several years, incidents like the 1901 census debacle remind us of the fragility of even the most stoutly supported and thoughtfully designed projects. The continued survival of many resources remains highly vulnerable to changes in funding priorities, individual and institutional commitment, and the acquisition budgets of university libraries. Small web-based projects, particularly, require ongoing maintenance and constant updating to maintain their viability, yet all too often the end of the funding period or a change in personnel leaves such sites orphaned and in decay.[34] The last few years have made clear that the progress of IT applications in the humanities is not the linear series of triumphs imagined in the heady days of the mid-1990s, when the 'universal library' sometimes seemed just around the corner, and earnest advocates urged their colleagues into cyberspace with missionary zeal.[35] Yet to leave behind such Whiggish presumptions is also to recognise that the undeniably enormous potential of such applications can be brought to fruition only through continued trial and error and the willingness of Victorian specialists to get involved in helping to bring these resources to our work, our students and the wider public.

Notes

1 *Guardian*, 3 January 2002, p. 5; 'Census website goes offline', BBC News Online, 8 January 2002. Issues about the stability and accuracy of the online census (www.census.pro.gov.uk), including the questions raised in Parliament, were covered in detail by the Federation of Family History Societies at their website: www.ffhs.org.uk.

2 M. Steig, 'The nineteenth-century information revolution', *Journal of Library History*, 15 (winter 1980), pp. 22–52.

3 Phyllis Deane and W. A. Cole, *British Economic Growth, 1688–1959: Trends and Structure* (Cambridge: Cambridge Universty Press, 1962).

4 An article that neatly marks this transition is Ian Winchester, 'The linkage of historical records by man and computer: techniques and problems', *Journal of Interdisciplinary History*, 1 (autumn 1970), pp. 107–24. There is, of course, a vast literature from roughly the 1970s onwards dealing with quantitative methodologies in history, from ongoing debates about 'cliometrics' to handbooks and specialist studies. For one particularly useful survey of the state of computer usage in history and history teaching at the beginning of the internet era, see R. Middleton and P. Wardley, 'Information technology in economic and social history: the computer as philosopher's stone, or Pandora's box?' *Economic History Review*, 43 (1990), pp. 667–96.

5 M. Anderson, *Family Structure in Nineteenth-Century Lancashire* (Cambridge: Cambridge University Press, 1971).

6 R. B. Litchfield published the results of his own work with the Stockport census as 'The family and the mill: cotton mill work, family work patterns and fertility in mid-Victorian Stockport', in Anthony Wohl (ed.), *The Victorian Family: Structures and Stresses* (London: Croom Helm, 1978); Litchfield and Chudacoff later marketed the course materials they had developed as the 'Comparative cities teaching package'.

7 E. A. Wrigley and R. S. Schofield, *The Population History of England 1541–1871: A Reconstruction* (Cambridge: Cambridge University Press, 1981).

8 The techniques involved during this era, and particularly the emphasis on the pre-coding of data, were reflected in E. Shorter's popular 1971 handbook *The Historian and the Computer* (New York: Prentice-Hall). The book included among its sample codebooks the one used by L. Lees in analysing data from the censuses of 1851 and 1861, material that would find its way into her *Exiles of Erin: Irish Migrants in Victorian London* (Ithaca, NY: Cornell University Press, 1979).

9 J. Mokyr, *Why Ireland Starved: A Quantitative and Analytical History of the Irish Economy, 1800–1850* (London: Allen & Unwin, 1983); R. Woods, *The Demography of Victorian England and Wales* (Cambridge: Cambridge University Press, 2000).

10 K. D. M. Snell and P. S. Ell, *Rival Jerusalems: The Geography of Victorian Religion* (Cambridge: Cambridge University Press, 2000).

11 J. Phillips, *The Great Reform Bill in the Boroughs: English Electoral Behavior, 1818–1841* (Oxford: Oxford University Press, 1992); F. O'Gorman, *Voters, Patrons and Parties: The Unreformed Electoral System in Hanoverian England, 1734–1832* (Oxford: Oxford University Press, 1989); R. J. Morris, *Class, Sect and Party: The Making of the British Middle Class: Leeds, 1820–50* (Manchester: Manchester University Press, 1990).

12 S. Eliot, *Some Patterns and Trends in British Publishing, 1800–1919* (London: Bibliographical Society, 1994).

13 Great Britain Historical GIS Project, available: www.geog.port.ac.uk/gbhgis.

14 R. J. Morris, 'Computers and the subversion of British history', *Journal of British Studies*, 34 (October 1995), pp. 503–28.

15 *Victorian Database*, available: www.victoriandatabase.com/index.cfm.

16 *Victorian Bibliography Online*, available: www.iupjournals.org/vicbib.

17 I. W. Archer, 'Royal Historical Society Bibliography', *History Today* (August 2002), pp. 5–6; the online version can be found at www.rhs.ac.uk/bibl.

18 The *Nineteenth Century Short Title Catalogue* (*NSTC*) (Newcastle upon Tyne: Avero Publications, Ltd, 1996 and 2002) consists of series 1 and 2, covering records for 1801–70, and series 3, for 1871–1919; the latter series featuring improved searching capability. Simon Eliot has written about the promise and the limitations of using the *NSTC* (series 1 and 2) for quantitative research in publishing history in a two-part article: 'Patterns and trends and the *NSTC*: some initial observations', *Publishing History*, 42 (autumn 1997), pp. 79–104, and 43 (spring 1998), pp. 71–112.

19 Walter Houghton (ed.), *Wellesley Index to Victorian Periodicals, 1824–1900 on CD-ROM* (London: Routledge, 1999); corrections and additions to *Wellesley* continue to be published in the *Victorian Periodicals Review*.

20 John S. North (ed.), *The Waterloo Directory of English Newspapers and Periodicals, 1800–1900*, 10 vols (Waterloo, Ontario: North Waterloo Academic Press, 1986–98). The *Directory* is available both as a CD-ROM (1994) and in an online edition (2001) at www.victorianperiodicals.com.

21 The first of these is *Palmer's Full-Text Online* at Historical Newspapers from Chadwyck-Healey, now owned by ProQuest: history.chadwyck.co.uk; the second is *The Times* Digital Archive 1785–1985 from the Gale Group: www.galegroup.com/Times.

22 Internet Library of Early Journals: www.bodley.ox.ac.uk/ilej; British Library Online Newspaper Archive: www.uk.olivesoftware.com.

23 Wellington Papers Database: www.archives.lib.soton.ac.uk/wellington.shtml

24 *Charles Darwin Correspondence Online* database: www.darwin.lib.cam.ac.uk.

25 Mundus: Gateway to Missionary Collections in the United Kingdom: www.mundus.ac.uk.

26 The Victorian Web: www.victorianweb.org; Victoria Research Web: victorianresearch.org.

27 Victorian Women Writers Project: www.indiana.edu/~letrs/vwwp.

28 The Complete Writings and Pictures of Dante Gabriel Rossetti: www.iath.virginia.edu/rossetti/index.html.

29 *Monuments and Dust: The Culture of Victorian London*: www.iath.virginia.edu/mhc.

30 The *Dictionary of Victorian London*: www.victorianlondon.org.
31 John Snow: www.ph.ucla.edu/epi/snow.html; *History of Phrenology on the Web*: pages.britishlibrary.net/phrenology.
32 The Gaskell Web: lang.nagoya-u.ac.jp/~matsuoka/Gaskell.html; *Railways and Population Change in Industrializing England*: www.mtholyoke.edu/courses/rschwart/rail/intro_hist_gis.htm.
33 See Robert Darnton's seminal essay 'What is the history of the book?' in his *The Kiss of Lamourette: Reflections in Cultural History* (New York: W. W. Norton, 1990), pp. 111–12.
34 For a recent study of such 'link rot', see J. Markwell and D. W. Brooks, 'Broken links: the ephemeral nature of educational WWW hyperlinks', *Journal of Science and Education and Technology*, 11 (2002), pp. 105–8.
35 This advocatory tone characterises much of the writing of the time about such resources; for an example addressed to a Victorianist audience, see Patrick Leary, 'Babbage's children: Victorian studies resources on the internet', *Victorians Institute Journal*, 23 (1995), pp. 11–26.

14

Victorian studies in North America

Christopher Kent

Victorian studies in North America has been much more the creation of literary scholars than of historians. This is due partly to disciplinary demographics – quite simply, many more North American scholars specialise in nineteenth-century English literature than in nineteenth-century British history. History departments, though typically smaller than English departments, have a far larger potential remit. Britain was once considered a field in which any self-respecting history department would have more than one specialist – a Tudor–Stuart historian being the first priority, since the period was considered to constitute the official 'pre-history' of the United States. Student demand for classes in that area was also sustained by the perception of aspiring lawyers, one not discouraged by historians, that they would help get them into law school, since here lay the foundations of the American legal system. Second priority was usually the nineteenth century, since here was Britain at the apogee of its power – this was 'Britain's century', to quote the title of a recent textbook on the period by the American (by birth) historian W. D. Rubinstein.[1] The twentieth century being in that same sense America's century – or at least the century of the United States – nineteenth-century British history arguably held a privilege somewhat akin to that which the history of Greece held for imperial Rome. The hegemonic experience of the predecessor should have particular interest for its successor. But the special status of British history in the USA, like the celebrated 'special relationship' between the two nations in the realms of power and diplomacy, is not what it was. The privilege of British history is eroded by the ever-increasing ethnic diversity of the USA and the demand for historians who can meet its needs and interests. Nearly fifty years ago I attended a public high school near New York City where Gilbert and Sullivan were performed annually and the yearbook's name was *Jabberwock*. The sense, however attenuated, in which British history might be deemed 'my history' by a student of Anglo-Saxon ethnicity is not there for an increasing number of students, the more so as a university education has become less and less an elite experience. Not that ethnicity wholly deter-

mines choice of field for either its students or its teachers. It is central to
the ethos and rationale of the discipline of history that it should not: for-
tunately, for many who come to history, and especially for those who go
on to become professional historians, it does not.

The case of Canada might be expected to differ from that of the United
States. After all, Victoria and Regina are the capital cities of two western
provinces, while between them lies the province of Alberta, commemorating the duly feminised prince consort. And Queen Victoria's great-great-
granddaughter is Canada's monarch today. But even in Canada the privilege
of British history is declining, as is evident at the University of Toronto,
once the North American powerhouse of the field. Thirty years ago it had
four historians of nineteenth-century Britain: today it has one. Similar cultural and ethnic factors are at play in Canada and the USA. The historical
resonance of those Victorian city and provincial names for most Cana-
dians is not much greater than that of such royal place-names as Georgia,
Carolina, Virginia and Maryland, or Georgetown, Charleston and
Williamsburg, for Americans. The button marked 'Victorian values' would
not have the political potency in North America that it had in Britain when
Mrs Thatcher punched it a few years ago. On the other hand, BBC and ITV
adaptations of Victorian novels such as *The Way We Live Now*, *Our
Mutual Friend* and *Daniel Deronda*, to mention some recent examples, have
projected versions and visions of Victorian culture more widely in North
America than Victorian scholars could ever dream of doing, and for this
scholars are grateful, since my own experience suggests that student
interest in classes on the Victorian period probably owes more to movies
and television than to ethnicity. Hollywood has also contributed to this
consciousness, notably with Stanley Kubrick's *Barry Lyndon*, Roman
Polanski's *Tess* and Francis Ford Coppola's *Dracula*. The very word 'Victorian' has remarkable power quite independent of its monarchical associations, though in the annals of iconhood few faces outrank that familiarly
forbidding one so vividly evoked recently by Judi Dench in *The Queen and
Mr Brown*. Perhaps the commonest associations of the term relate to
authority, prohibition and repression – the Stracheyan legacy. However, in
North America it does not carry the same freight of material hardship that
it bears still in Britain, where the leader of the Labour Party could respond
to Mrs Thatcher's celebration of Victorian values by declaring that the
ruling values of Victorian Britain were 'cruelty, misery, drudgery, squalor
and ignorance'.[2]

A visit to the website of the Victorian Society in America reveals that
the word has considerable resonance beyond academic circles – reassuring,
'old-fashioned' associations in which nostalgia plays an important part.
(Although the name Victoria turns up only rarely in my class lists, I wonder
whether it does not have some occult connection, through the queen's
beloved Highlands, with Heather, that archetypal 'preppie' name.) In short,
Victorian is a valuable cultural and commercial – think of 'Victoria's Secret'

lingerie – franchise. Not the least interesting of its aspects for the historian is that it is a creation of the very century when historicism first flowered. The term 'Victorian' was in circulation well before Queen Victoria died, her longevity, celebrated by two jubilees, and the rise of journalism, that great school of instant history, being two important factors in their auto-historicism. It is not sufficiently appreciated, when we are being so knowing about 'the Victorians' at their expense, that they knew a lot about being knowing about themselves.

I

What are we doing with the Victorian franchise? How goes the scholarly enterprise of Victorian studies? As an international project, it owes much to North America. *Victorian Studies*, the field's senior journal, was founded over forty-five years ago by Michael Wolff and several colleagues at Indiana University. It triggered a boom which saw a number of Victorian studies' societies, programmes and publications spring into existence, all of them still flourishing today with more recent additions. Another vital North American contribution was Walter Houghton's monumental *Wellesley Index to Victorian Periodicals*, which successfully mobilised a remarkable interdisciplinary team of scholars to break the code of anonymity in Victorian higher journalism long before the 'author function' became a critical buzzword. This in turn gave rise to the Research Society for Victorian Periodicals (RSVP), another Michael Wolff initiative, which continues to explore and publicise the extraordinary wealth of Victorian magazines, newspapers and reviews through its annual conferences and its inter-disciplinary journal *Victorian Periodicals Review*. The Victorian periodicals project is currently being taken to new levels of exhaustiveness and tech-nological sophistication by John North of the University of Waterloo with his remarkable *Waterloo Directory of Nineteenth-Century UK Newspapers and Periodicals*. Having captured some 3,900 Irish periodicals and 7,300 Scottish, North and his teams of researchers are now in pursuit of the more than 125,000 different titles that he estimates were published in England during the nineteenth century: 10,350 of these, at last report, are available in ten very stout volumes totalling 7,350 pages – and, more significantly, in CD-ROM format with index, date, key-word and Boolean search capa-bilities. 'Carlylean' seems the appropriate word to convey the heroic char-acter of North's achievements, not to mention his ambitions. Their potential value for Victorian studies is only just beginning to be appreciated. More-over, these journals are widely available through the amazingly rich hold-ings of North America's public and university libraries, some of which have Victorian periodicals not accessible in Britain itself.

North America also contains a number of rich manuscript collections in the Victorian period: Yale, Princeton, Harvard, New York Public Library, the University of Texas, the University of British Columbia are some of the better known locations. In such luxurious settings as the Huntington Library in Los Angeles, the J. P. Morgan Library in New York City or the Newberry Library in Chicago, Victorian scholars can still benefit from the Anglophilia once *de rigueur* among mega-rich American businessmen who laundered their wealth and reputations through splendid collections and endowments. Not unconnected with these great collections is the fact that North America has long been at the forefront of publishing original Victorian literary and historical sources. Thus the heroic project of publishing Thomas Carlyle's complete correspondence proceeds steadily, with the twenty-ninth volume now out from the University of North Carolina Press.[3] Its editorial team is appropriately international. At Queen's University in Kingston, Ontario, the Disraeli Project has now seen the publication of the sixth volume of the correspondence of Benjamin Disraeli, each one superbly edited and annotated by the team led by M. G. Wiebe.[4] At the University of Toronto Press, lead publisher of the *Wellesley Index*, the publication of the complete works of John Stuart Mill was completed not long ago, a decades-long project directed by the late John Robson.[5] Not the least of its achievements was the recovery of Mill's extensive periodical publications. Among a number of other North American publication projects in the Victorian period which deserve mention here are R. H. Super's scholarly edition of the complete works of Matthew Arnold with the University of Michigan Press[6] and the collected letters of William Morris edited by Norman Kelvin and published by Princeton University Press.[7] In the unglamorous and under-acknowledged work of scholarly editorship in Victorian studies North America has certainly pulled its weight. Its university presses have committed resources to these costly, long-running projects without which Victorian studies would be greatly impoverished. Under the current fashion regime, the privilege extended to certain canonical authors by such projects makes them vulnerable to criticism or, at least, to scepticism. On the other hand, they may well outlast the present vogue. Meanwhile, over a dozen North American journals strive to represent cutting-edge scholarship, and a number of university presses are very receptive to Victorian studies, as are several commercial presses, notably Routledge with its strong North American presence and its near-monopoly of the high theory market. Like Routledge, the university presses of Oxford and Cambridge maintain largely autonomous publishing operations in North America.

II

Another feature of Victorian studies in North America is its multiplicity of scholarly organisations, several of which are regional and intended to overcome the geography of a continent across which are scattered 1,000 or more institutions of higher education in which Victorian scholars are likely to be found. The strength of attendance at their peripatetic annual conferences testifies to the irreplaceable value of face-to-face contact in the age of cyberspace and virtuality. Such are the Victorian Studies Association of Western Canada, founded in 1972, the Victorian Studies Association of the Western United States (1995), the Midwest Victorian Studies Association (1977), the Northeast Victorian Studies Association (1975), the Victorian Studies Association of Ontario (1968), the newly founded Eastern Canadian Victorian Studies Association, and the Canadian umbrella organisation the Network of Victorian Studies Associations (2001). In addition to these, the previously mentioned RSVP, with its strong international membership, frequently holds its annual conference in the UK, and plans to meet in Ghent, Belgium, in 2004. Then there are the Victorians Institute (1971), the Dickens Project at the University of California (1981), the CUNY Victorian Seminar (1984), the Interdisciplinary Nineteenth-Century Studies Association (1979), the Monuments and Dust project on the culture of Victorian London (1995), centred at the University of Virginia but meeting in London, and the Dickens Society of America (1995), all holding annual conferences, with several publishing journals or proceedings. There is currently talk of yet another society, a proposed North American Victorian Studies Association, as an umbrella organisation.

Viewed from the continental perspective, the institutional strength and scholarly resources of Victorian studies are remarkable. However the engagement of each individual scholar with this enterprise is unique, and just as there was no such person as 'the average Victorian' so too is the average Victorianist a fiction. What follows is a necessarily idiosyncratic ground-level view of Victorian studies over the last few decades. I began attending Victorian studies conferences over thirty years ago, drawn by an interest in the history of ideas, where much of the best work was done by scholars in Victorian literature, and in the uses of the novel to cultural and social history. I had taken a degree in history and literature at the University of Toronto in a programme that was interdisciplinary only in a rudimentary – additive – sense: students were required to take a large number of classes in the honours programmes of both the history and the English department, but no attempt was made to integrate them. There was, however, a benefit to this approach: one was exposed to the disciplinary unself-consciousness of both disciplines, a salutary, if initially puzzling, experience for anyone curious about the sociology – or ethnology – of knowledge. It gave me a sense of being both an insider and an outsider in each discipline, holding a sort of dual-citizenship. I decided to do a doctorate in history at the newly founded University of Sussex, drawn there by its serious commitment to interdisciplinary scholarship, and emerged a duly accredited British historian – period: nineteenth century; sub-discipline: intellectual history. It was best to situate oneself within the traditional grid, for job-seeking purposes at least. Disciplines offer jobs; inter-disciplines do not. Such at least was the case in the late 1960s for historians, and it is largely the case still in North America.

Victorian studies, as represented by its societies, conferences and journals, was from the start dominated by English literature scholars, with a considerably smaller number of historians, including a sprinkling of art and music historians. The relationship between the two disciplines was complementary in a traditional way. Victorian studies meant in a sense viewing 'Victorian Britain', a clearly delineated space and time, from the perspectives of two clearly delineated and separate disciplines. The combined effect would be rather like binocular vision, giving greater depth. This literature–history partnership commonly took the form of a division of intellectual labour – one of the most compelling justifications for separate disciplines, after all – in terms of canon and context. For literature specialists, a commitment to Victorian studies was in some respects a rejection of the New Criticism's orthodoxy, which was dedicated to strengthening the autonomy and identity of the discipline by raising the academic study of literature to the status of a science with its own distinctive objectives and specialised techniques. A central element of the New Criticism's agenda was escaping history. An autonomous discipline needed autonomous objects of analysis, free from the trammels of time – enduring masterpieces whose distinctive features did not need to be contextualised to be recognised and appreciated. The emphasis on context central to Victorian studies was an implicit challenge to that particular disciplinary ideology. For historians, by contrast, Victorian studies did not imply quite such a disciplinary disruption. Indeed, they could, and did, view it rather complacently as a case of literary scholars seeing the light and summoning the historians' invaluable assistance. The literature folk tended still to cleave to their canonical deities, Dickens, George Eliot, Tennyson *et al.*, with perhaps slightly greater attention than usual to the 'Victorian prose' authors like Carlyle, Ruskin and Arnold, whose work so undeniably addressed the distinctive characteristics of their own time. The job of the historian in the inter-disciplinary partnership was to fill in the 'background' and provide those interesting 'facts' with which they were so famously obsessed, and to which the literature people could confidently moor their authors. Although members of the minority discipline in this partnership, historians were treated with the utmost cordiality. We were welcomed – as, for example, I was by a literature scholar who told me after my paper that he always enjoyed listening to historians 'because I always learn something new from them'.

Non-canonical authors were a different matter. As a historian, one had a sense that by dealing with these figures literary scholars somehow felt themselves to be undermining the dignity of their profession – and perhaps impairing their own prospects for professional recognition. In this respect the new critical ideology was being deferred to, since non-canonical works by definition lacked the timeless merits which justified their being studied without the assistance of history. Consequently such works were best left to historians. I once attempted to elevate this impression to the dignity of theory, labelling it 'the bologna thesis'. The corpus of literature resembles a cow in that its parts when cut up occupy a hierarchy similar that occupied by fillets, prime ribs, New York strips, etc., in the meat trade. And just as those parts of the animal that cannot be made presentable are ground up and turned into hamburger or sausage, such too is the fate of non-canonical literature. If the butchers in this crass analogy are the literary scholars, the sausage-makers are the historians. G. W. M. Reynolds, Edmund Yates, Rhoda Broughton and Mary Braddon cannot stand alone for posterity. Their work is best ground up, spiced, stretched, preserved and made edible – in the scholarly sense – by the addition of facts. Indeed their humble novels could even be put to useful work, being full of valuable information about the minutiae and the taken-for-granted of Victorian, mainly middle-class, existence that industrious historians could glean from them. A fascinating and neglected monument to this approach to Victorian literature is Myron Brightfield's *Victorian England in its Novels*.[8] This four-volume work by a literary historian of huge industriousness and selflessness, is the product of the author's doggedly ploughing through hundreds of forgotten Victorian yellowbacks – my 'bologna' literature – collected by Michael Sadleir and subsequently purchased by the UCLA library, where they offer a standing justification to any Victorianist in need of an academic excuse for visiting Los Angeles. Brightfield gives us a treasure trove of snippets from these novels, assembled under thematic chapters and sub-headings – for example chapter 10, 'The path to the altar', includes fourteen sub-headings such as 'The demerits of men', 'Flirts and witches', 'Fallen women', 'The double standard', and so on, each illustrated by nuggets of text drawn mainly from authors as little known as Mrs Harriet Smythies or Hawley Smart. As for the slight, if engaging, authorial text that ties them together, it is as far from the discourse of today's new historicism as it is possible to imagine. And it must have been an even greater affront to the values of the New Criticism under whose hegemony it was compiled. Photo-reproduced direct from typescript, Brightfield's work was apparently deemed barely worthy of the dignity of publication.

Those volumes deserve rediscovery today. Canon-busting is all the rage. Minor Victorian novelists, especially women, now receive unprecedented critical attention. Sausage is now on the best academic menus – it is gourmet sausage. The *charcutiers* are the new historicists of literature studies, and the value-added is not so much fact as theory. Historians should be pleased with this apparent move towards the concerns of their own discipline. Actually, not entirely. Historicism, almost as much as history itself, is a protean word which for historians means something almost directly opposed to what it means in current literary scholarship. For historians it refers mainly to the one, arguably the only, big theory their discipline has ever developed, one that could almost be called the founding and enabling ideology of the modern historical profession. According to historicism, the past admits of being recovered and understood, to a very significant degree, in and for itself and on its own terms. The word used to mean something similar in the discipline of literature. In fact its initial drive for disciplinary independence was largely grounded in historicism, the tools and values of the historical science being applied to the study of literature. In reaction, the New Criticism made historicism a term rather of abuse, since its agenda for achieving disciplinary autonomy and scientific status, as noted earlier, entailed throwing off the humiliating tutelage of history. Now, however, literary scholars embrace a confident 'new historicism' which seems bent on mastering history.

III

Some scholarly Rip Van Winkle re-awakening after thirty years in the midst of a typical Victorian studies conference of today might, on glancing at the programme, leap to the conclusion that Victorian studies has been taken over by historians. But after listening to the papers he might well come to a different conclusion – that history had been taken over by English literature. The convergence of literary and historical scholarship has not been due solely to developments in the discipline of the former. The practice of history has changed in ways that have made it more familiar to literature specialists, making it look more like something they can do themselves. When our Van Winkle had fallen asleep the ascendant sub-discipline in history was social history, resonating with the populist mood of the 1960s and afire with zeal to recover the history of the neglected masses and give voice to the inarticulate. One victim of this trend was intellectual history, a distinctively North American sub-discipline that had strong links with both literature and philosophy. Its traditional concerns were now being stigmatised as elitist, and some practitioners even feared its demise. But the social history boom began to flag in the 1970s. Its social scientific credentials were always somewhat tenuous: it was ill at ease with theory – and with statistics, despite its concern with the masses. Its links with sociology, its 'natural' cognate discipline, remained weak, and it was the soft science of cultural anthropology that seemed to offer it the most promising methods of recovering past individual experience. Social history also had a certain relationship with Marxism. Preoccupied with class as its privileged analytical category, it was *marxisant* even in North America, where its practitioners did not usually consider themselves Marxists. Its commitment to the liberationist meta-narrative of modernism made it vulnerable to postmodernist critique. It tried to remain aloof from the intellectual turmoil associated with structuralism and the advent of post-modernism, but post-modernism's challenge to class as a master category cut particularly closely to the bone for historians of Victorian Britain, the world's first industrial society and the strategic location in which Marx and Engels spent most of their lives. However, social historians in North America tended to be less heavily invested in the fate of the proletariat than were their British counterparts. On the other hand, they were at the forefront of history's prolonged resistance to Michel Foucault in the name of resisting theory – and nasty French practices in general – not realising that Foucault was himself in flight from theory, and they indignantly rebuffed his claims to be doing history.

Coming to terms with Foucault has taken historians three decades, a change of generation, a significant shift in gender balance and the emergence of a newly dominant sub-discipline which is something of an amalgam of social and intellectual history – cultural history. Our latter day Rip Van Winkle, who probably would not have heard of Foucault when he fell asleep, would be exposed more to his influence than his name, utterance of which it is still considered slightly bad form among historians. The students of the 1980s who referred to Foucault as 'the F-word' in mock deference to their scandalised elders are now professors themselves, and have so far internalised many of his insights as to now take them almost for granted. Our awakened sleeper will, of course, have been struck by something else – the majority of the paper-givers at the conference are women, who in the historical profession at least have generally been more receptive to heterodoxies and were among the first to appreciate the uses of Foucault. Feminist scholars, familiar from personal experience with margins and limits – the operations of power that define and maintain them, and the tactics of existence and resistance of those so situated – were better able to appreciate the force of insights dismissed by other eyes as paranoia. A notable example of this can be found in the work of Judith Walkowitz.[9] Her *Prostitution and Society* (1980), one of the most original and influential works in Victorian history of the last few decades, is the work of a social historian attempting to reconcile the claims of class and gender analysis with the aid of Foucault's tools for analysing the technologies of state power as applied to the Contagious Diseases Acts and Lock hospitals. The Foucauldian presence, though shadowy, is crucial. It is more explicit in her *City of Dreadful Delight* (1992), an outstanding example of the new cultural history; here the policing of female bodies in urban spaces is developed as a central theme with considerable theoretical sophistication, but without the loss of narrative drive which, historians fear – and with good reason – is too often theory's price. Another notable Victorian historian whose trajectory illustrates the sub-disciplinary shifts within the profession is Martin Wiener, who came to cultural history from intellectual history.[10] His *English Culture and the Decline of the Industrial Spirit* (1981) won him the distinction, rare and coveted among historians, of having his name attached to a controversial thesis – the 'Wiener thesis', attributing Britain's decline from its mid-Victorian industrial supremacy to the fatal attractions of aristocratic culture for its business elites. Wiener has subsequently gone on to the study of Victorian crime and policing, an area in which the impact of Foucault's work is unavoidable.

It might be taken as a sign of closer inter-disciplinary bonds in Victorian studies that certain common terms are increasingly found in the discourses of historians and literary scholars: 'discourse' itself is one, and 'narrative' is another. Among historians their use is evidence of another notable development of recent years – a heightened disciplinary consciousness marked by a sharp rise in yet another sub-discipline: historiography. Until recently historians prided themselves on the unself-consciousness of the discipline they loved to call the craft of history. This attitude, suspicious of theory as profitless navel contemplation, is nicely captured by the distinguished Marxist historian Eric Hobsbawm's observation that the carpenter who thinks about every hammer stroke will end up bending a lot of nails. The advent of Foucault & Co. has heightened historians' awareness of theoretical issues and of the need to formulate more explicitly just what it is that historians do, and do not. Catering to this need has provided increased employment to intellectual historians. Another figure who has changed the inter-disciplinary climate for history and literature is Hayden White, who, like Foucault though in a different way, seemed to threaten the identity of history by defying the disciplinary boundaries that defined it. A duly accredited mediaevalist and intellectual historian, White could not be so easily dismissed as an interloper. He once sourly observed that a discipline is 'largely constituted by what it forbids its practitioners to do . . . and none is more hedged about by taboos than professional historiography'.[11] He knew whereof he spoke, having broken its greatest taboo by boldly exploring and expanding the common ground occupied by history and literature and saying things that sounded to some ears like 'history and fiction are the same thing'. Shunned, as a result, by his own discipline, he was welcomed by others, particularly literature, which granted him refugee status, then honourary citizenship.

What historians did not want to hear from White literature scholars were eager to listen to, since their discipline was in an imperial mood. As the high theories of structuralism crumbled with late modernism and the Berlin Wall, 'History' seemed to be on the move: what better moment to join it? The very ambiguities of that protean word – which Foucault tried to escape by using words like 'archaeology' and 'genealogy' – have always been among its chief assets: capital H-as-in-Hegel History, history as the past, history as subject and history as discipline offer rich rhetorical resources. Even the poverty of theory which once made history an object of scorn now signalled an opportunity. The new historicism opened vast new territories to the talents of the discipline of literature. 'Where's the problem?' the committed inter-disciplinarian might ask. Victorian studies is surely all about inter-disciplinarity: perhaps it *is* even an inter-discipline. Does it matter that non-historians are doing history, especially given an apparent shortage of history department Victorianists? Turf wars and boundary police are surely antithetical to true scholarship. Historians have long been aware that they have no intellectual property rights or professional monopoly in history. Anyone can claim to do it: everybody is in it, and making it. Historians have always shunned professional arcana and exclusive terminology: 'whiggism' is practically their only term of art. Loosely meaning presentism, whiggism is the favourite heresy of the non-professional historian.

IV

Surely the most successful example of inter-disciplinarity is that of women's studies and its offspring, gender studies. Our re-awakened Rip Van Winkle would be amazed by the dramatic increase in the breadth and sophistication of Victorian scholarship in this area over the past thirty years. As a universalising ideology, feminism is inherently inter-disciplinary. In the history of sexuality and gender the presence of Foucault is again impossible to avoid, and here the Victorian period enjoys a peculiar privilege. His phrase 'We Other Victorians', an allusion to Steven Marcus's pioneering study of Victorian pornography, reminds us that the enormous resonance of the word 'Victorian' extends beyond the English-speaking world – even to France[12] – and reminds us too of the crucial role that, with all its accumulated baggage, it continues to play in the self-congratulatory, and self-deceiving, narrative of liberation that we have constructed for ourselves over the past century.[13]

While it is not easy to identify the distinctiveness of the North American contribution to this area of Victorian studies, except perhaps that it bears fewer marks of disentanglement from Marxism than does its British counterpart, the quantity and quality of that contribution has been particularly noteworthy, and has been made largely by women scholars. Works by Mary Poovey and Elaine Showalter come to mind as examples of historicist literary scholarship.[14] A reciprocal example of a historian heavily indebted to the theoretical insights of literary scholars is Kali Israel's innovative study of Emilia Dilke.[15] Moreover, it is under the sponsorship and inspiration of feminist literary scholars that the study of Victorian masculinity has moved beyond its traditional preoccupation with the public school and is now attaining new levels of sophistication. The work of Eve Kosofsky Sedgwick and Regenia Gagnier deserves mention in this regard.[16] An historian who has for some time been recognised as among the most theoretically astute, and readable, analysts of Victorian culture and sexuality is Peter Bailey.[17]

Having liberated the informal empire of Victorian sexuality, scholarship has more recently been turning its attention to the formal empire of Victorian Britain, which is now being resurrected and re-liberated in the name of post-colonialism. This is perhaps the most striking recent development in Victorian studies, and one where North America, particularly the USA, has made a distinctive contribution. Here, too, the contribution of literary scholars has been notably greater than that of historians, and the new historicism has shown itself to least advantage. Imperial history was once a respected sub-department of British history, fairly well represented in Canada where it provided a sort of official national pre-history, but it became marginalised by nationalist sentiment and by the pressure of social history which dismissed it as an un-edifyingly retrograde drum-and-trumpet affair. In the USA, Victorian imperial history had power-political resonances for a nation becoming, like it or not, Britain's successor in world power and position. In Britain itself, where imperial history had been represented as a largely one-way transaction of power and influence, academic (but not popular) interest waned with the empire itself. But with the advent of post-modernity the empire, as the saying goes, struck back.

The history of post-colonialism is an important chapter in the history of the present and a striking example of the Janus face of historicism. Literary scholars have been quickest to respond to its appeal – Patrick Brantlinger and Anne McClintock are two influential examples – perhaps because relevance has always been a less problematical notion for them than for historians, of whose work in this vein Douglas Lorimer's and Howard Malchow's provide interestingly contrasting examples.[18] Relevance draws the attention of students, no small consideration, by demonstrating utility. Henry Rider Haggard may seem like some time-imprisoned hack, but *She*, appropriately read, can serve as a window into the nightmare fantasies of Victorian imperialism and racism (not to mention sexism), the knowing post-Freudian dissection of which may partially, at least, assuage a sensitive student's guilt about the world hegemony of today's USA: 'We weren't the first; they were worse, and at least I feel bad about it.' Of course no serious scholar would deal so crudely with Rider Haggard, in print; but what goes on in the classroom and in the minds of students bears thinking about. The danger of this kind of historicising is presentist complacency – 'the enormous condescension of posterity', in E. P. Thompson's memorable phrase – that relieves us of the difficult duty of seeking difference, rather than a comforting sameness, in the past. The kind of relevance it offers may not be all that constructive. Historians' suspicion of the term 'relevance' is largely a resistance to the notion that history can have predictive power or offer formulaic lessons, both of which encourage the search for sameness. Homogenising and reifying terms like 'imperialism' and 'colonialism', however unavoidable, tend to encourage that search, particularly when driven by a form of historicism that is fixated on the present and the self-imposed duty to judge the past. All who teach British history in North America will testify to the remarkable student demand for Irish history, which reflects the way in which Irishness has been so constructed that all can partake of it, convivially on St Patrick's Day, that great ecumenical holiday, tragically in the memory of the Irish Famine which confers the historically valued claims of victimhood on all who keep it green.[19] Attempts to explain its occurrence in terms other than of oppression and exploitation become affronts to memory, which becomes a privileged form of history in this process, one in which professional historians are made particularly aware of their lack of privilege.[20] Among the most interesting and active areas to which post-modernism has directed historiographical studies is popular memory and the politics of commemoration as history-making forces. It has proved to be a notably successful site of inter-disciplinary activity, bringing art history, psychology and political studies, among others, into the mix. Here of course the Victorian period offers fertile ground.

While the good-thinginess of inter-disciplinarity is a commonplace of Victorian studies' celebration, the merits of disciplinarity must always be kept in mind – all the more so today with the emergence, in the space vacated by Marxism, of the flourishing enterprise of cultural studies, employing a number of the old firm's more agile personnel, and sharing many of its intellectual characteristics, such as the belief that scholarship should embody criticism of the present, materialist preferences in its explanatory strategies, a strong taste for the language of theory and large inter-disciplinary ambitions. The retreat of Marxism has given new respectability to inter-disciplinarity, especially in administrative circles, where its economies are particularly eye-catching.[21] Traditional disciplines are expensive and resistant to 'rationalisation'. Cultural studies presenting itself as a free-standing inter-discipline looks to the academic bureaucrat like an all-purpose Swiss-army knife, and in some of the newly accredited universities that have proliferated in the last decade or so it has been institutionalised to the point of supplanting history and other traditional departments. Cultural studies has not been formally institutionalised to quite the same extent in North America, which has not seen the same new university boom. Victorianists should perhaps view it has a particularly suitable subject for their historicising interests, since Victorian Britain is a privileged site for cultural studies as it was for Marxism. Raymond Williams's *Culture and Society* and *The Long Revolution*, its founding texts, are centrally concerned with Victorian Britain and the great Victorian intellectuals who were, as Stefan Collini reminds us, inter-disciplinary and even anti-disciplinary thinkers *avant la lettre*.[22]

V

If, as increasingly seems the case in North America, Victorian history is to be done by literature scholars, they should perhaps become better acquainted with what professional historians consider the distinctive merits of their discipline. The ethos of this discipline requires them to seek an abundance of evidence from as many disparate sources as possible, and all know the temptations of infinite deferral that this can entail. The pleasures of ingenuity for the historian come particularly in research, in discovering new and pertinent information in new or unlikely places. The pleasures of ingenuity for the literary scholar, or such is my impression, seem to lie in devising new ways of interrogating a privileged text. The new historicism seems often to be taking history *to* the text rather than from it, that history too often having come rather naïvely from some convenient 'authority'. Historical agency may then be conferred on the text, contextualised by such question-begging formulas as 'the cultural work performed by' the text in question. All too often the new historicism fails to perform the primary task of the historian, to tell us something new. One has a certain sense that both sides of the street are being worked. On one side the convenient historian is taken as an unproblematical source of facts; on the other side, once these have been obtained, anyone can do history. Hayden White's valuable insights into the literary creativity and figuration of historical writing have been taken as showing that history and literature, looking the same, must be the same. It may well be that in Derrida's ontology 'there is no outside the text', but for most historians the research, with its techniques and ethos on which they base their self-identity, is most definitely 'outside the text' in the ordinary sense of those words. It is done at the archival site where the imaginative act of encountering new evidence of the past on its own strange terms – the defining act of historians' historicism – is performed. If some of the historiographical attention currently lavished on the rhetoric of historical writing were directed to analysing the complex processes of historical research, the differences between the new historicism and historians' history, and the latter's distinctive merits, might be better appreciated to the benefit of Victorian studies in North America and elsewhere.

Notes

1 W. D. Rubinstein, *Britain's Century: A Political and Social History, 1815–1905* (London: Arnold, 1998).
2 Raphael Samuel, 'Mrs Thatcher's return to Victorian values', in T. C. Smout (ed.), *Victorian Values* (Oxford: Oxford University Press, 1992), p. 13.
3 *The Collected Letters of Thomas and Jane Welsh Carlyle* (Durham, NC: Duke University Press, 1970–), general ed. Charles Richard Sanders.
4 *Benjamin Disraeli: Letters*, ed. J. A. W. Gunn *et al.* (Toronto: University of Toronto Press, 1982–).
5 *The Collected Works of John Stuart Mill*, ed. John M. Robson *et al.* (Toronto: University of Toronto Press, 1963–).
6 *The Complete Prose Works of Matthew Arnold*, ed. R. H. Super, 11 vols (Ann Arbor, MI: University of Michigan Press, 1960–77).
7 *The Collected Letters of William Morris*, ed. Norman Kelvin, 4 vols (Princeton, NJ: Princeton University Press, 1983–96).
8 Myron Brightfield, *Victorian England in its Novels (1840–1870)* (Los Angeles: University of California Library, 1968).
9 Judith Walkowitz, *Prostitution and Victorian Society: Women, Class and the State* (Cambridge: Cambridge University Press, 1980); *City of Dreadful Delight: Narratives of Sexual Danger in Late-Victorian London* (London: Virago, 1992).
10 Martin J. Wiener, *English Culture and the Decline of the Industrial Spirit, 1850–1980* (Cambridge: Cambridge University Press, 1981); *Reconstructing the Criminal: English Culture, Law and Policy, 1830–1914* (Cambridge: Cambridge University Press, 1990).
11 Hayden White, *Tropics of Discourse: Essays in Cultural Criticism* (Baltimore, MD: Johns Hopkins University Press, 1978), p. 126.
12 Michel Foucault, *The History of Sexuality*, vol 1: *An Introduction* (New York: Pantheon Books, 1978), pp. 3–13. Stephen Marcus, *The Other Victorians: A Study of Sexuality and Pornography in Mid-Nineteenth-Century England* (New York: Basic Books, 1966).

13 Robert Mighall, 'Vampires and Victorians: Count Dracula and the return of the repressive hypothesis', in Gary Day (ed.), *Varieties of Victorianism: The Uses of a Past* (Basingstoke: Palgrave, 1998), pp. 236–49.

14 Mary Poovey, *Uneven Developments: The Ideological Work of Gender in Mid-Victorian England* (Chicago, IL: University of Chicago Press, 1988); Elaine Showalter, *Sexual Anarchy: Gender and Culture at the Fin de Siècle* (New York: Viking, 1990).

15 Kali Israel, *Names and Stories: Emilia Dilke and Victorian Culture* (New York: Oxford University Press, 1999).

16 Reginia Gagnier, *Idylls of the Market Place: Oscar Wilde and the Victorian Public* (Stanford, CA: Stanford University Press, 1986); Eve Kosofsky Sedgwick, *Between Men: English Literature and Male Homosocial Desire* (New York: Columbia University Press, 1985).

17 Peter Bailey, *Popular Culture and Performance in the Victorian City* (Cambridge: Cambridge University Press, 1998).

18 Patrick Brantlinger, *Rule of Darkness: British Literature and Imperialism, 1830–1914* (Ithaca, NY: Cornell University Press, 1988); Anne McClintock, *Imperial Leather: Race Gender and Sexuality in the Colonial Contest* (New York: Routledge, 1995); Douglas A. Lorimer, *Colour, Class, and the Victorians: English Attitudes to the Negro in the Mid-Nineteenth Century* (Leicester: Leicester University Press, 1978); Howard L. Malchow, *Gothic Images of Race in Nineteenth Century Britain* (Stanford, CA: Stanford University Press, 1996).

19 Ian Buruma, 'The joys and perils of victimhood', *New York Review of Books*, 8 April 1999, pp. 4–9; Mike Cronin and Daryl Adair, *The Wearing of the Green: A History of St Patrick's Day* (New York: Routledge, 2002).

20 'It may be time for Famine historians to abandon the emotional high ground and regain their objectivity, deferring empathy to the reader as the ultimate arbiter of emotion', writes Melissa Fegan in *Literature and the Irish Famine, 1845–1918* (Oxford: Oxford University Press, 2002), pp. 3–4; see also Kevin O'Neill, 'The star spangled shamrock: memory and meaning in Irish America', in Ian McBride (ed.), *History and Memory in Modern Ireland* (Cambridge: Cambridge University Press, 2001). The chief centres for the burgeoning field of Irish Studies in North America are Notre Dame University and Boston College.

21 Joe Moran, *Interdisciplinarity* (London: Routledge, 2002), p. 183.

22 Stefan Collini, 'From "non-fiction prose" to "cultural criticism": genre and disciplinarity in Victorian studies', in Juliet John and Alice Jenkins (eds), *Rethinking Victorian Culture* (Basingstoke: Macmillan, 2000), pp. 25–7.

15

The state of Victorian studies in Australia and New Zealand

Miles Fairburn

I

As the term 'Victorian studies' is vague and elusive, perhaps the best place to start discussion of the state of the genre in the Antipodes is to look at the practices of its self-declared adherents. The Australasian Victorian Studies Association, the only group of its kind in the region, provides us with the clearest idea of what these practices are. Although comparatively small in membership, the association has been able to generate commitment sufficient to hold conferences every year since its foundation in 1975, and to produce its own peer-reviewed journal, the *Australasian Victorian Studies Journal*, without a break since 1995.

The journal tells us a good deal about the meaning of Victorian studies in Australasia, notably in regard to its contributions and contributors. Almost all its contributions are on British topics; very few on those of New Zealand and Australia. The topics, moreover, are restricted to certain areas of mid- and late nineteenth-century British high culture – poetry, novels, periodicals, sculptures and paintings – not political theory, science, theology, law, social theory, let alone *mentalités* (the social history of ideas). Moreover, most of its contributors are art historians, cultural studies people, and *lettrists*; only a small minority are historians of any sort, let alone historians of colonial New Zealand and Australia.[1]

New Zealand and Australia are not unique in some of these respects. Commenting on the state of Victorian studies in Britain, Miles Taylor has complained that it has lost its way because the historians of ideas and social historians have deserted the field, leaving it to be colonised by the practitioners of English literature.[2] In New Zealand and Australia things are different. Here, unlike in Britain, Victorian studies has always been dominated by non-historians. Here, Victorian studies has almost no local content; in Britain most of the content is local. Thus, whereas in Britain Victorian studies may have lost its way, in Australasia it has never really been on the way except as a study of British 'high culture' in which historians take little part.

Victorian studies specialists are not responsible for this state of affairs; rather it is the historians, not historians in general but specifically historians of nineteenth-century New Zealand and Australia. With some exceptions, the latter do not regard themselves as practitioners of Victorian studies, and take surprisingly little interest in the Victorian cultural and intellectual heritage of their respective societies. Except for a post-structuralist niche, the subject is quite unfashionable.

The linguistic usages of Antipodean historians – their naming practices, to be precise – are revealing in this regard. When referring to the last two-thirds of the nineteenth century in New Zealand or Australia, they have no convention of labelling it 'the Victorian era' or 'the Victorian age'. As a general rule, they do not think that something designated 'Victorian' has much relevance to what they do unless it explicitly refers to the place – the region, or colony, and later the state – of Victoria in Australia. If asked a question about some aspect of the 'Victorian period' in reference to Australian or New Zealand history, they would find the question somewhat puzzling and seek its clarification. The meaning of the label would be clear to them in relation to British history but not, as a rule, to that of Australia and New Zealand. Accordingly, it is quite uncommon for the label to feature in their job descriptions, publications, their titles of courses and theses.[3] Far more common is the term 'colonial era', a label that the ensuing discussion shows to have diverse connotations, many of them strongly negative.

Antipodean historians' indifference to the local Victorian intellectual and cultural heritage takes many forms. One can be seen in their colloquia and special essay collections on generic topics. Some of the more favoured topics have been gender history, women's history, race relations, Irish immigration, Scots' immigration, the environment and, in New Zealand's case, the Treaty of Waitangi. But, so far as can be determined, conference themes and essay collections have never covered the *generic* subject of Victorian intellectual and cultural influences in New Zealand and Australia.[4] A salient case in point is the 2001 conference round on both sides of the Tasman. In contrast to their British counterparts, historians of New Zealand and Australia did not display interest in commemorating local Victorians and Victorianism. Thus, no consideration was given to the possibility when the New Zealand Historical Association organised its annual conference at my own university in December 2001. The 'Victorian age' is yours, not ours, apparently. It belongs to you, not to us.

The aloofness of Antipodean historians towards their Victorian intellectual and cultural heritage can also be seen in the reference books they produce on Australian and New Zealand history. Take *The Oxford Companion to Australian History* (1999).[5] Edited by three of Australia's most distinguished historians, the *Companion* is a most useful guide to the richness of Australian history. At the same time, its inclusions and exclusions tell us a good deal about the preoccupations and fashions of Australian historians. The *Companion* has a substantial number of entries on 'Aboriginal history' and 'Women's history', and an entry on each of 'Nationalism', 'Radical nationalism', and 'National identity' – interesting distinctions perhaps not obvious to the outsider. Yet if we wanted to find out something about Australia's Victorian heritage we would be rather disappointed. Few entries deal specifically with the content and influence of imported mid- and late nineteenth-century British ideas and *mentalités*. There is no entry under 'Victorians' or 'Victoria' (excepting the place). The several entries on religion say very little about nineteenth-century theological debates or popular ideas about religion. The entry on 'Heritage' is entirely devoted to the rise of the modern conservation movement in relation to historic urban buildings and sites. The entry on 'British–Australian relations' is all about constitutional and political relations. It makes no reference to the intellectual and the cultural background. The entry on 'History of ideas' is equally unhelpful: its focus is on the history of Australian ideas, with the noteworthy qualification:'Attempts to assess Australian ideas as such have been few.'[6]

The thinness of the genre is manifested as well in general surveys of the history of culture which otherwise are comprehensive and useful. A typical Australian example is John Rickard's *Australia: A Cultural History*.[7] Although Rickard acknowledges that certain cultural baggage was carried by nineteenth-century British migrants to Australia, he does not unpack the baggage in detail or see it as particularly important. A typical New Zealand example is Peter Gibbons's survey chapter on culture for the highly authoritative *Oxford History of New Zealand*. At the outset Gibbons states that 'European New Zealanders, both immigrants and locally born, were equipped with a stock of British ideas.'[8] Although he regards those ideas as highly influential (though in a negative rather than a positive sense, it should be noted), we learn little about their content in the rest of the chapter.

II

It would be quite wrong, however, to give the impression that Antipodean historians have completely neglected Victorian studies. There are some notable exceptions, divisible into two basic types: those in the fashionable vein (cultural history in the post-structuralist style, otherwise known as 'discourse analysis'); and those in the unfashionable fields (traditional intellectual history and social history of ideas).

As is the case outside of the Antipodes, post-structuralist studies of the history of thought in the Victorian era have enjoyed considerable vogue in Australia and New Zealand.[9] The subject matter in either case consists mainly of the reforms by the nineteenth-century colonial state of such things as education, health, medicine, labour conditions, welfare, prisons, and so on. The studies follow a formula. They start by showing how the reforms were engineered by figures proclaiming they were acting in the name of humanitarianism, efficiency and progress. The studies then proceed to assert that underlying the reforms was an insidious oppressive objective: namely, to impose prescriptive ideologies on subordinate people to turn them into compliant subjects. Sometimes, however, the studies are of the prescriptive ideologies themselves, whether propagated by state agencies or by leading public intellectuals. Besides flashing the appropriate Foucauldian recognition signals (by using such terms as 'sites', 'contestation', 'discourse', 'genealogy of ideas'), the studies possess two distinguishing characteristics. One is to assume that a prescriptive ideology succeeds in attaining its underlying objective – that what makes the subordinate elements subordinate is that they have assimilated the prescriptive ideology. The other is to assume that the subordinate elements none the less have agency and thus can and do 'contest' the dominant ideology. Such studies, although of interest when Foucauldian ideas first came into vogue, have never overcome their inherent weaknesses. For one thing, the two assumptions are taken as givens by post-structuralists and are thus seldom exposed to empirical testing. The consequence is that the post-structuralist approach to the history of Victorian thought is an epistemic dead-end: the low value placed on empirical testing and theoretical coherence is hardly conducive to the growth of knowledge. Paradoxically, then, the fashionable nature of the post-structuralist approach to the history of Victorian thought in Australia and New Zealand has not helped the genre at all.

By contrast, there has been some growth of knowledge in the unfashionable – traditional – fields in the genre. Here the pioneering work was done by George Nadel's *Australia's Colonial Culture* (1957). Nadel traced the early history of certain intellectual institutions imported from nineteenth-century Britain – notably libraries, book-selling, mechanics' institutes and learned societies – and argued that they were responsible for transplanting the high culture of the metropolitan society to a much greater extent than expected.[10] John Hirst, an Australian historian, pushed Nadel's point further, maintaining that it was British working-class immigrants who brought friendly societies and mechanics' institutes to Australia, that the values and beliefs of those institutions spread to other classes, exercising greater influence than the home-grown ideology of 'mateship' and the 'legend of the bush' which historical orthodoxy claims were at the core Australian tradition.[11] The New Zealand historian Erik Olssen has taken a line similar to Hirst's, maintaining that the values of British artisans who immigrated to New Zealand in the late nineteenth century were fed into the protective legislation passed by the reformist Liberal Government of 1891–1912, and thus became embedded in the New Zealand tradition.[12] The New Zealand welfare historian David Thomson has recently put forward the very interesting argument that the highly charged concepts of 'pauperism' and 'self-help', inherited from Victorian Britain, shaped state action in nineteenth-century New Zealand in paradoxical ways: the negative connotations of 'pauperism' deterred the State from replicating the

English system of poor relief, while the positive connotations of 'self-help' legitimised novel state interventions to create property-owning opportunities and so prevent the working classes from falling into poverty.[13]

As well as studies with big themes in the traditional fields, there have been those with more specialist interest. Notable examples are Jill Roe's book on the theosophy movement in Australia; Stuart MacIntyre's biographical study of the evolution of Australian liberalism from the classical stage to second-wave liberalism in *A Colonial Liberalism*; Mark McKenna's *The Captive Republic*, which traces the history of republican ideas in Australia; a study by Mark Francis of views about the role of governors; and recent research by historians of science on the reception of Darwinism in both New Zealand and Australia.[14]

Biographies also have touched on the Victorian intellectual and cultural heritage. Among the more prominent examples are J. A. La Nauze's monumental biography of the Australian statesmen Alfred Deakin and Keith Sinclair's account of William Pember Reeves, the New Zealand Fabian and later director of the London School of Economics.[15]

Yet works in the traditional fields have been relatively few and far between. Moreover, it would be foolish to pretend that even the best works on New Zealand and Australia are as important as those produced on Victorian England by the likes of Boyd Hilton, Frank Turner and Stefan Collini. Lastly, sometimes the few major works have methodological problems – problems made possible by the lack of critical standards, the product of the inchoate state of the genre.

An example of such a work is James Belich's *The New Zealand Wars and the Victorian Interpretation of Racial Conflict*, widely acclaimed for the primacy it gives to the role of ideas and to the Maori agency.[16] Belich argues that in the wars of the 1840s–1860s Maori won most of the battles even though they were outnumbered and outgunned by the British. The reason for Maori military success was that they outsmarted the imperial foe with a strategy based on highly innovative and effective techniques of trench warfare; indeed, they invented trench warfare. Europeans, however, had racial preconceptions that made them quite incapable of observing the Maori achievement. They brought with them from Britain an all-pervading racial ideology, derived from proto-social Darwinist doctrines, claiming that indigenous peoples lacked the 'higher mental faculties' and thus were innately incapable of innovative and strategic thinking.

Belich's argument is commendably bold and sweeping. Yet he takes for granted that the racial ideology was pervasive instead of advancing empirical evidence in support of the contention; questions have been asked about the representativeness of his depiction of mid-century Victorian racial doctrines;[17] and his crucial claim, that the pervasive racial ideology prevented Europeans from recognising the Maori achievement and its basis, is contradicted by his own use of their testimonies. The evidence he cites for Maori victories being the product of clever and innovatory tactics of trench warfare consists of observations by European eyewitnesses – it was what *they* saw and recorded![18] Either an all-pervading racial ideology blinded Europeans to the Maori achievement or it did not.

III

It is perhaps surprising that Antipodean historians have distanced themselves from the intellectual and cultural side of their Victorian heritage: both Australia and New Zealand were highly dependent on Britain in the Victorian era. Britain was their major source of trade, investment capital, immigrants, technology, and political and constitutional forms. Indeed, New Zealand probably possessed the purest Victorian heritage of any settler society, given that its European population numbered only about 2,000 when it was annexed by Britain in 1840 and that most of its colonisation occurred from the 1850s to the 1880s. (Australia had an earlier start, having been annexed in 1788, and thus had a more varied foundational culture.) Historians have long acknowledged the importance of such links and have studied them closely and extensively. The intellectual and cultural links must have been equally important. So why have those links and their local adaptations not been studied with the same attention?

Another reason why this distance is surprising is the extraordinary popularity of the heritage movement, not just with the populace at large but among academic historians. Indeed, on both sides of the Tasman it has led history departments to establish courses on public history which include large components on the heritage value of buildings and monuments, and the other physical remains of the Victorian era in the new world. Keen interest in heritage has led academic historians to produce many illustrated histories of cities and towns covering the nineteenth century that focus in detail on changes in their physical layout, in land-use patterns, architectural styles and on engineering solutions to environmental problems.[19] One would have expected historians to be curious about the minds of the people who built and occupied these spaces; yet this has not happened. Acute interest in the physical side of the Victorian past has not developed into an interest in the intellectual.

Related to this, the remnants of the Victorian past are littered everywhere in both Australia and New Zealand. It is impossible not to bump into them every day and be reminded of the era they represent. They are expressed not only in the architectural style of old buildings and in monuments (commemorating famous imperial as well as colonial heroes and events), but in the names of towns, regions, buildings, natural landmarks, voluntary organisations, learned institutions, business firms and streets.[20] The signs, too, are evident in the categories that David Lowenthal refers to in his well-known work *The Past Is a Foreign Country*,[21] including antiques, old books, nineteenth-century paintings, vocabulary, television and film costume dramas, museum and library collections, genealogies, family heirlooms, diaries and letters in private hands, cemeteries, parks, gardens and plant collections, long-established exotic street-trees, and so on. The biggest sign, perhaps, is the extraordinary transformation of the natural landscape, if not the entire ecological system, a landscape transformation that gives another dimension to Simon Schama's notion about the way in which the natural landscape is conceived in human terms.[22] But these ever-present reminders of everyday life in the Victorian past have not stimulated Antipodean historians to give high priority to the investigation of what the famous idealist philosopher of history R. G. Collingwood discussed as the thought inside the event.[23]

Lastly, we would expect them to have taken greater interest in the intellectual history of Victorian Australasian society, given the prestige of the generic sub-disciplines of the history of ideas and the history of *mentalités*, which are well-known in Australian and New Zealand universities. Although some of the experts in colonial history are parochial, certainly not all are. At least some have read the key books in the history of ideas and the social history of ideas. They thus would have read – or at least be aware of – the classic works on the history of political theory such as J. G. A. Pocock's *The Machiavellian Moment* and Quentin Skinner's contextualist *The Foundations of Modern Political Thought*. They would also have become acquainted with the foundational *annaliste* works on *mentalités* such as Lucien Febvre's attempt in *The Age of Unbelief in the Sixteenth Century* to demonstrate that it was structurally impossible for Rabelais to have been an atheist; and micro-histories in the Geertzian mode like Carlo Ginzburg's *The Cheese and the Worms*. They might also have come into contact with some of the leading works on Victorian cultural and intellectual history, such as V. A. C. Gatrell's on social attitudes to hanging, Stefan Collini's on public moralists, Jonathan Rose's on the intellectual life of the working classes, among others.[24] Why, then, is it that these sub-disciplines – intellectual history and the history of *mentalités* – have exercised little influence on the historiography of nineteenth-century New Zealand and Australia?

It can be argued, of course, that at least some of the formative ideas transplanted from Britain to colonial Australia and New Zealand were not Victorian but pre-Victorian in origin. To that extent, the neglect by New Zealand and Australian historians of their *Victorian* ideational heritage is explicable. A salient example is Edward Gibbon Wakefield's theory of systematic colonisation: supposedly exercising a marked influence on the development of New Zealand from 1840 (but less so on Australia), Wakefield's theory was conceived and produced prior to Victoria's reign – in fact, one historian claims that its underlying assumptions are traceable to the eighteenth-century 'Enlightenment'.[25] Another example is afforded by the prevailing ideas about appropriate gender roles in colonial New Zealand and Australia: although prevalent during the Victorian era, their origins are traced by one influential study to Evangelical thought in the late eighteenth and early nineteenth centuries.[26] A further example is the notion that contact with Europeans had a 'fatal impact' on indigenous peoples: that notion ostensibly played the primary role in the British decision to annex New Zealand in 1840, and came out of the British humanitarian movement, which peaked in the 1830s, and so can be considered only partly Victorian.[27] A final example applies to the specific case of Australia: there has been a long-running debate over the claim that the most important of its formative ideas of a popular kind were brought by its convict population during the heyday of transportation from 1788 to 1840.[28]

But though some of the key ideas of nineteenth-century Australia and New Zealand were (or may have been) pre-Victorian, others – probably the bulk – were certainly not. Thus we must search for other explanations for the fragmentary state of the historical literature on Victorian intellectual and cultural influences in the trans-Tasman world. These are advanced in what follows. Although they are conjectures based on an amateur sociology of knowledge, they do have some inherent plausibility.

IV

One such explanation is what can be called the 'pragmatic myth' of New Zealand and Australian history. According to this myth, colonial (white) New Zealanders and Australians were dominated by a pragmatic way of thinking and therefore were inherently incapable of being deeply influenced by ideologies, Victorian or otherwise. Although they often flirted with different sorts of theories, these were 'fads', ultimately having minimal effect on their behaviour, especially when it counted and when core areas of self-interest were at stake. What made them into pragmatists was their occupation of a new environment where they were presented with novel problems demanding highly specific solutions, and where in consequence fixed principles and preconceptions were a liability, and successful adaptation depended on common sense and fostered highly concrete, practical, open and flexible ways of thinking.

The pragmatic myth of Australian and New Zealand history has a long pedigree in the historiography and has been used primarily to explain the content of state interventions during the phases of radical reform, most notably from the 1890s to the First World War. Its most overt expression perhaps is *Le Socialisme sans doctrines* written by Albert Métin, a French visitor to Australasia who was struck by the paradox that the labour movements of Australasia were the driving force behind the growth of its States but were unmotivated by ideology, socialist or otherwise.[29] It can also be seen in such classics as J. B. Condliffe's economic history, *New Zealand in the Making* (1936), and W. K. Hancock's *Australia* (1930), that emphasise the 'practical' motives and intentions of labour reformers.[30] Many historians have rejected the pragmatic myth, at least in part, especially the more theoretically oriented among them, including those familiar with the cultural turn in history. One famous historian in the traditional mode represents a key exception to the pattern – Manning Clark, whose multi-volume epic general history of Australia takes the ideologies of Protestantism, Catholicism and Marxism as the prime movers of the principal actors.[31] Even so, the myth exercises considerable though unconscious sway in traditional modes of history.[32]

The second reason why the study of locally produced Victorian ideas has never taken off is a more obvious one: it is that neither society has produced adequate source material for such a study since neither gave rise in the nineteenth century to thinkers of the calibre of Carlyle, Ruskin, Darwin, J. S. Mill, Matthew Arnold, T. H. Green *et al.* Antipodean historians are reluctant to admit this point, for fear of appearing to display what has been called the 'colonial cringe'. But the point is none the less true and it would be silly to pretend otherwise. This is not to say that the trans-Tasman Victorian world failed to produce any thinkers at all; on the contrary, it produced many whose ideas deserve to be studied in the appropriate social and ideational contexts, the most numerous being amateur and gentlemen scientists and naturalists, ethnographers and so on. As much as they deserve to be studied, however, they and their ideas are hardly capable of sustaining a major research programme engaging a large body of scholars. What promises to be a far more promising research programme, if the work to date is anything to go by, is the study of the *reception* in the Antipodes of major ideas imported from Britain and their adaptation to local circumstances.[33]

On top of this, several trends in the historical discipline in Australasian universities have stunted the genre's development. The popularity of nineteenth-century British history has markedly diminished. The rise of cultural studies and its penetration of history departments has tended to debase much cultural history, diverting it into off-the-wall hermeneutics and dealing with such topics as surfing, women's conveniences in Napier, freakshows and Zandow the Strongman. In addition, despite its respectability, the history of ideas, which never constituted a major field, has fared badly in recent years, as epitomised by the closure of the History of Ideas Unit at the Australian National University following the death of its director, Eugene Kamenka.

Also stifling the growth of the genre are the nationalistic orientations of historians in the two countries. Although it is impossible to give a precise date for the origins of this trait, perhaps the first general history of Australia that significantly affected it is W. K. Hancock's *Australia* (1930), its counterpart in New Zealand being W. B. Sutch's *The Quest for Security* (1942).[34] It is a convention, of course, for historiographies to take the nation state as the primary unit of study, to highlight certain events and actors in the history of the nation state as its sources of identity, and to celebrate implicitly or explicitly at least some of these events and actors. The modern historiography of New Zealand and Australia goes further. Its key point of reference is a highly affirmative view of the growth of nationhood. It is abnormally concerned with finding, tracing, explaining and emphasising all the elements that indicate a movement away from a relationship of dependence with the metropolitan society not just in a constitutional sense, but in terms of foreign policy, politics, social arrangements, economic structure and culture. Dependence is bad and independence is good. The country's history progresses when it diverges in some way from the metropolitan society, and regresses when it stops diverging or, worse still, takes a convergent course. Although both New Zealand and Australian history are seen as having made overall progress in these terms, the process is none the less something of an endless struggle that is more successful in some periods than in others.

In this nationalist version of Antipodean history, the modern metropolitan society is represented by the USA. But in past time, of course, the role of the evil empire was played by Britain. Consequently, Antipodean historians tend to disapprove (or at least do not explicitly approve) of the close links that existed between the Australasian colonies and Britain in the Victorian period, to regard them as regrettable signs of immaturity ('tied to the mother country's apron strings') out of which both countries thankfully grew. On economic, foreign policy and political matters, the disapproval is frequently combined with sophisticated arguments that this or that colony maximised the advantages of the close relationship or that the relationship was in the colony's best interests. But it is impossible to think of any modern work, even the most sophisticated, that actually celebrates the British connection – this is unheard of. On cultural matters, moreover, the British connection is seldom seen as having any redeeming qualities at all. The prevailing assumption is that British culture was hegemonic, the progenitor of a provincial and derivative culture in Australia or New Zealand, a sickly imitation of the original, inauthentic and not worth taking seriously, something out of which we have thankfully now grown.[35]

This brings us to the final factor that has fostered disdain for Victorian ideas. Despite the immense appeal of specific aspects of the Victoria era, the overall reputation of the Victorian period in Australia and New Zealand among the educated is at its nadir. Paradoxically, a love for television costume drama, genealogy and the architecture of the colonial era co-exists with a great deal of Victorian-bashing. A small range of things is valued, especially the artefacts, but others, notably the ideas, are the subject of condemnation and ridicule. The Victorian past in certain respects is regarded with nostalgia; yet if we want to raise a laugh or to evoke self-righteous indignation in a class or at a conference, the mention of a Victorian foible can be relied on to do the trick. In Australasia, as in Britain since Lytton Strachey, the Victorian period is associated with moral hypocrisy, an extreme and arid puritanism, and all sorts of fuddy-duddy values and peculiar customs. But in Australasia the rejection of Victorianism seems to have gone further. Whereas in Britain an extensive debate was generated by Margaret Thatcher's 1983 plea for the revival of the Victorian virtues, in Australia and New Zealand such a debate has never taken place, and would be unimaginable since the colonial past and thus Victorianism as a whole are vilified for creating the modern sins of racism, colonialism and sexism – in particular, for establishing the ideas that motivated the agents of the sins.

The Australian historian Geoffrey Blainey in 1983 coined the term, 'black arm-band history' to characterise this guilt-laden view of Australia's colonial past; but it applies also to New Zealand, perhaps to an even greater extent. To be sure, in Britain racism, colonialism and sexism are also regarded with opprobrium. But in the trans-Tasman world the opprobrium carries greater political weight. For one thing, Australia and New Zealand have an image of themselves as progressive and advanced societies, a self-image central to their sense of national identity, which for over a century has given them a sense of superiority over the old world. For another, as they are smaller and newer societies, they have fewer vested interests capable of resisting fashionable ideologies, with the consequence that radical movements protesting against past injustices tend to have greater influence and attract more sympathy.[36] Lastly, unlike Britain which has granted independence to its indigenous minorities – the Irish, the Welsh and the Scots – Australia and New Zealand still hold their indigenous peoples – Aborigines and Maoris – in what looks like subjugation, a matter about which they are extremely sensitive, given that it contradicts their self-image as 'social laboratories of the world'.

V

In sum, the history of elite and popular ideas in the Victorian era is the poor relation of Australian and New Zealand historiography. It is far less developed than are traditional historical sub-disciplines (political, constitutional, military and economic history), and, with the exception of the post-structuralist variant, it has been overshadowed by the newer historical sub-disciplines (including social history and the history of sport, gender, women and race relations). In order for it to grow, a shift in disciplinary fashions is required, a shift that places greater importance on the study of ideas, especially folk ideas, in their own historical context. Also required is greater attention to the problems of method. The notion of what constitutes the history of ideas in the northern hemisphere is less appropriate in Australia and New Zealand, where major thinkers in the nineteenth century were few but sub-literary ideas – folk ideas – were abundant. In this situation the best method would seem to be some sort of mix of two different genres of the history of ideas: one, the social history of ideas or *mentalités*; and the other, intellectual history, preferably with a strongly contextualised focus as conceived and practised by the Cambridge school.

Notes

1 This is confirmed by the latest list of paid-up members of the Association posted on its website (accessed August 2002); of the 54, none is identified as a professional historian: www.uq.net.au/avsa/register.html#top.

2 Miles Taylor, 'Bring back the 19th century' (review of Richard Price's *British Society 1680–1888*), *London Review of Books*, 22 June 2000, pp. 32–3.

3 Among the exceptions are J. Miller, *Early Victorian New Zealand: A Study of Racial Tension and Social Attitudes 1839–1852*, 2nd edn (Wellington: Oxford University Press, 1974 [1958]); J. C. Beaglehole, 'Victorian heritage', *Political Science*, 4 (1952), pp. 29–37.

4 In using 'generic' I am excluding forums and essay collections on highly specialised topics. Although conferences on highly specialised subjects related to the history of ideas have taken place over the last two or so decades, there have been a few of these. It should be emphasised that the comments above exclude historians of nineteenth-century Britain working in universities in Australia and New Zealand: they have held several conferences on their area over the last few decades.

5 G. Davison, J. Hirst and S. McIntyre (eds), *The Oxford Companion to Australian History* (Melbourne: Oxford University Press, 1999).

6 *Ibid.*, pp. 335–6.

7 J. Rickard, *Australia: A Cultural History*, 2nd edn (New York: Longman, 1996).

8 P. Gibbons, 'The climate of opinion', in W. H. Oliver (ed.), *The Oxford History of New Zealand* (Auckland: Oxford University Press, 1981), p. 302.

9 E.g. L. T. Smith, *Decolonising Methodologies: Research and Indigenous Peoples* (Dunedin: University of Otago Press, 1999); E. Papps and M. Olssen, *Doctoring, Childbirth and Regulating Midwifery in New Zealand: A Foucauldian Perspective* (Palmerston North: Dunmore Press, 1997); K. Neumann, N. Thomas and Hilary Erikson (eds), *Quicksands: Foundational Histories in Australia and Aotearoa New Zealand* (Sydney: University of New South Wales Press, 1999); J. Damousi, *Depraved and Disorderly: Female Convicts, Sexuality and Gender in Colonial Australia* (Melbourne: Cambridge University Press, 1997); J. Mathews, *Good and Mad Women: The Historical Construction of Femininity in Twentieth Century Australia* (Sydney: Allen & Unwin, 1984); S. Garton, *Medicine and Madness: A Social History of Insanity in New South Wales, 1880–1940* (Sydney: New South Wales University Press, 1988); J. Pratt, *Punishment in a Perfect Society: The New Zealand Penal System 1840–1939* (Wellington: Victoria University Press, 1992); M. Crotty, *Making the Australian Male: Middle-Class Masculinity 1870–1920* (Melbourne: Melbourne University Press, 2001).

10 G. Nadel, *Australia's Colonial Culture: Ideas, Men and Institutions in mid-Nineteenth Century Eastern Australia* (Melbourne: F. W. Cheshire, 1957).

11 See e.g. J. Hirst, 'Keeping colonial history colonial: the Hartz thesis revisited', *Historical Studies*, 21 (1984), pp. 85–104; see also his *Australia's Democracy: A Short History* (Sydney: Allen & Unwin, 2002).

12 E. Olssen, *Building the New World: Work, Politics and Society in Caversham 1880s–1920s* (Auckland: Auckland University Press, 1995).

13 D. Thomson, *A World without Welfare: New Zealand's Colonial Experiment* (Auckland: Auckland University Press, 1998).

14 Jill Roe, *Beyond Belief: Theosophy in Australia, 1879–1939* (Kensington: New South Wales University Press, 1986); S. MacIntyre, *A Colonial Liberalism: The Lost World of Three Victorian Visionaries* (South Melbourne: Oxford University Press, 1991); M. McKenna, *The Captive Republic: A History of Republicanism in Australia 1788–1996* (Cambridge: Cambridge University Press, 1996); M. Francis, *Governors and Settlers: Images of Authority in the British Colonies, 1820–60* (Christchurch: Canterbury University Press, 1992); R. L. Numbers and J. Stenhouse (eds), *Disseminating Darwinism: The Role of Place, Race, Religion and Gender* (New York: Cambridge University Press, 1999).

15 J. A. La Nauze, *Alfred Deakin: A Biography*, 2 vols (Carlton: Melbourne University Press, 1965); Keith Sinclair, *William Pember Reeves: New Zealand Fabian* (Oxford: Clarendon Press, 1965).

16 J. Belich, *The New Zealand Wars and the Victorian Interpretation of Racial Conflict* (Auckland: Auckland University Press, 1986).

17 See review by M. Francis of *The New Zealand Wars* in *Political Science*, 40 (1988), pp. 88–90, and J. Stenhouse, '"A disappearing race before we came here"', *New Zealand Journal of History*, 30 (1996), pp. 124–40.

18 E.g. Belich, *New Zealand Wars*: 'Most of the concealed positions, in the words of a naval officer who inspected the *pa* after the Maori abandoned it two months later, were "rifle pits of a ingenious and novel construction, so that it is impossible to fire into them from the outside"' (p. 98); 'In November 1860 a colonist wrote: "It is now apparent that the natives have it in their power to protract this unhappy war as they please . . . [they] are too clever tacticians to meet us on open ground"' (p. 114); 'Inside, the redoubt was less a fortification than a killing ground, as soldiers who inspected the redoubt after the battle attested. "Those who were in this morning for the first time say they never saw such a place in their life, and that you might as well drive a lot of men into a sheep pen and shoot them down as let them assault a place like that"' (p. 187); see also pp. 162, 185.

19 E.g. G. Rice, *Christchurch Changing: An Illustrated History* (Christchurch: Canterbury University Press, 1999).

20 Studies of the naming of the natural landscape have so far largely been by postmodernist historians who interpret it as another form of colonisation; see G. Byrnes, *Boundary Markers: Land Surveying and the Colonisation of New Zealand* (Wellington: Bridget Williams Books, 2001); and Paul Carter, *The Road to Botany Bay: An Exploration of Landscape and History* (New York: Knopf, 1988).

21 David Lowenthal, *The Past Is a Foreign Country* (Cambridge: Cambridge University Press, 1985).

22 For landscape transformation, see e.g. A. W. Crosby, *Ecological Imperialism: The Biological Expansion of Europe, 900–1900* (Cambridge: Cambridge University Press, 1990); Tim Flannery, *The Future Eaters: An Ecological History of the Australian Lands and People* (Port Melbourne: Reeds, 1994); S. Schama, *Landscape and Memory* (New York: Knopf, 1995).

23 R. G. Collingwood, *The Idea of History* (Oxford: Clarendon Press, 1946).

24 V. A. C. Gatrell, *The Hanging Tree: Execution and the English People 1770–1868* (Oxford: Oxford University Press, 1994); S. Collini, *Public Moralists: Political Thought and Intellectual Life in Britain, 1850–1930* (Oxford: Clarendon Press, 1991); J. Rose, *The Intellectual Life of the British Working Classes* (New Haven, CT: Yale University Press, 2001).

25 E. Olssen, 'Mr Wakefield and New Zealand as an experiment in post-Enlightenment practice', *New Zealand Journal of History*, 31 (1997), pp. 197–218.

26 L. Davidoff and C. Hall, *Family Fortunes: Men and Women of the English Middle Class 1780–1850* (London: Hutchison, 1987).

27 See e.g. K. Sinclair, 'Why are race relations in New Zealand better than in South Africa, South Australia or South Dakota?', *New Zealand Journal of History*, 5 (1971), pp. 121–7.

28 Seminal here is R. Ward, *The Australian Legend*, 2nd edn (Melbourne: Oxford University Press, 1977 [1958]).

29 Albert Métin, *Le Socialisme sans doctrines* (Paris: F. Alcan, 1908); this was translated as *Socialism Without Doctrine* (Chippendale: Alternative Publishing Company, 1977).

30 J. B. Condliffe, *New Zealand in the Making* (London: Allen & Unwin, 1963); W. K. Hancock, *Australia* (Brisbane: Jacaranda Press, 1961).

31 C. M. H. Clark, *A History of Australia*, 6 vols (Carlton: Melbourne University Press, 1961–87).

32 M. Freeden, *Ideologies and Political Theory* (Oxford: Clarendon Press, 1998), p. 18, rightly notes that the decisions of so-called pragmatic actors are culturally constrained. Their decisions are limited by certain beliefs about what is possible and by certain values that constitute and order their preferences.

33 For New Zealand, see: J. Stenhouse, ' "A disappearing race" ' and his ' "The wretched gorilla damnification of humanity": the "battle" between science and religion over evolution in nineteenth-century New Zealand', *New Zealand Journal of History*, 18 (1984), pp. 143–62. In Australia much has been done on the reception of Chartism: see e.g. Michael Roe, *Quest for Authority in Eastern Australia, 1835–1851* (Parkville: Melbourne University Press, 1965).

34 Hancock, *Australia*; W. B. Sutch, *The Quest for Security* (Harmondsworth: Penguin, 1942). Historiographical discussions of Australian nationalism include: Frank Farrell, *Themes in Australian History: Questions, Issues and Interpretations in an Evolving Historiography* (Kensington: New South Wales University Press, 1990), ch. 4; Luke Trainor, *British Imperialism and Australian Nationalism: Manipulation, Conflict and Compromise in the Late Nineteenth Century* (Sydney: Cambridge University Press, 1994), pp. 166–71; Stuart McIntyre, 'Australia and the empire', in Robin Winks (ed.), *The Oxford History of the British Empire*, vol. 5: *Historiography* (Oxford: Clarendon Press, 1999), pp. 166–73.

35 See e.g. G. Serle, *From Deserts the Prophets Come: The Creative Spirit in Australia 1788–1972* (Melbourne: Heinemann, 1973); and J. Belich, *Paradise Reforged: A History of the New Zealanders from the 1880s to the Year 2000* (Auckland: Allen Lane, 2001).

36 In New Zealand protest by Maori led the Government in 1975 to establish the Waitangi Tribunal, the equivalent of a permanent truth and justice commission, to investigate crown violations of Maori rights, its brief being extended in 1985 to cover Maori grievances from the beginning of the colonial era in 1840. Protest by women about their injustices has been even more effective, to the point that at the time of writing the prime minister, the governor-general, the chief justice and the CEOs of some of the largest corporations are women. Historians have played a major part in raising consciousness about these matters.

16

Victorian studies in the UK

Helen Rogers

To survey the field of Victorian studies in the UK is a daunting prospect. Encompassing an ever-expanding range of topics and straddling disciplines across the humanities and the social sciences, and reaching into the sciences, the field's boundaries stretch into a hazy distance. Faced with profuse and varied growth, it is tempting to renounce the ambition of mapping out the entire territory and to retreat to one's own small plot. And, indeed, one of the curious features of Victorian studies is just such a collective reluctance to step back and take in the wider view. In recent decades, as Martin Hewitt, a fellow-contributor to this volume, has contended, there has been a remarkable absence of reflection on and interrogation of the Victorian studies project.[1] This critical neglect may stem less from a refusal to appraise or re-assess than it does from a resistance to define and hence prescribe the object of study – 'the Victorian' – either as period or concept. This reluctance was voiced loudly and fervently in 2000 at the founding meeting of the British Association for Victorian Studies (BAVS), where it was agreed unanimously that the period should be defined loosely as 'the long nineteenth century': without any founding texts or fixed dogma, Victorian studies in the UK would be, to switch metaphors, a broad church. The argument of this chapter, while it appreciates the ecumenical spirit that has inspired such a diverse congregation, is that in refusing to debate the object of study we are in fact missing opportunities for dialogue and exchange. Sometimes it can be helpful to sing from the same hymn-sheet.

I

First, some caveats. Given the international dialogue and co-operation that has characterised the field since the formation of the journal of *Victorian Studies*, at Indiana University in 1957, the idea of a national variant is in many ways anomalous. The explosion of post-colonial studies in the last few decades has changed dramatically the focus of Victorian studies, as scholars have sought to deconstruct and decentre the 'metropole' and to re-examine its relationship with the purported 'periphery'.[2] It has become axiomatic that we cannot survey Victorian Britain without investigating how the 'nation' was forged, the connections between its component parts, or its position within the world. Nowhere has this enquiry been more necessary than in the relationship between Ireland and the UK. As in the case of the Society for the Study of Nineteenth-Century Ireland, formed in 1994, many scholars choose to pursue their analysis within the context of Irish studies rather than Victorian studies, with its imperialist connotations.[3] With the resurgence in the histories of colonialism and empire, it is arguably Britain's relationship with Europe that is now the more neglected area of study.

From an institutional perspective, the trajectory of Victorian studies in the UK has differed from those in North America and Australasia, and its development continues to be uneven. In comparison with the long-running journals and associations in those regions, the UK saw the setting up of a major academic periodical – the *Journal of Victorian Culture* – only in 1996, and it was not until 2000 that a national association (BAVS) and an annual conference were formed.[4] Always a popular topic in schools, Victorian Britain is now singled out for particular attention at Key Stage 2 of the National Curriculum (Years 7–11) at which children examine 'the impact of significant individuals, events and changes in work and transport on the lives of men, women and children from different sections of society'.[5] Likewise, Victorian studies thrives at postgraduate level, taught mostly on an inter-disciplinary basis or in collaboration between departments.[6] Modules on Victorian society, literature and culture form a staple part of undergraduate degrees in history, literature, history of art and cultural studies. Though influenced by inter-disciplinary studies of the period, undergraduate teaching takes place overwhelmingly within the traditional academic disciplinary structure of UK universities. Despite the cross-disciplinary participation in the Victorian studies project, this traditional academic framework continues to impact on the kind of research undertaken by scholars in the field.

Most assessments of Victorian studies begin with a paean to the virtues of inter-disciplinarity and this has been one of its main attractions for students and researchers. The field generates exchange between specialists and lay-persons across the disciplines, and in the many different sites at which the period is encountered and interpreted, including museums, galleries and heritage centres. Hosted by the Science Museum, and with its emphasis on things, sights and space as well as on people, identity and place, the 'Locating the Victorians' conference (2001) materially embodied those ambitions. The *Journal of Victorian Culture* exemplifies the vitality and eclecticism of scholarship, encouraging debate over method and interpretation in the 'Roundtable' section. Over the last thirty years or so, the field has embraced new areas of enquiry that are now firmly embedded in the curriculum, particularly the history of women and gender relations, and the study of non-canonical literature and popular culture: indeed, it can be argued that inter-disciplinarity was a necessary pre-condition for the development of topics that were poorly served by traditional disciplinary sources and procedures. The emergence of 'new' subjects of enquiry – the Victorian woman, the working-class writer, the music-hall audience, the subjects of empire – has impressed on us the diversity of Victorian culture and identity, while disciplinary exchange has alerted us to aspects of that culture, hitherto obscured: the spectacle of the science lecture, or the theatricality of the pulpit, for examples.[7]

For all the benefits that can be reaped, there are problems with inter-disciplinarity, and these are likely to be foregrounded in the next few years. Though eclecticism is celebrated as a feature of Victorian studies, in practice it masks the hegemony of literary studies.[8] While literary topics are over-represented in journals, essay collections and conferences, dialogue between the component branches of the field is often attenuated as historians of politics, the economy, art and science choose to publish elsewhere.[9] Many scholars are sceptical of the usefulness of the term 'Victorian', in terms of periodisation and ideological connotation; for some it smacks of antiquarianism. Among historians, there is a marked preference for teaching and writing on aspects of the 'long nineteenth century', or parts of it, rather than on the Victorian age *per se*. The term has always been more favoured by literature departments where it is used to indicate an area of specialism, but even here there have been calls for its abandonment.

While literary studies has been the dominant partner within the Victorian studies project, cultural history has been its preferred methodology, but even that term, like inter-disciplinarity, conceals very different interests and forms of engagement. Overwhelmingly, the work that has found a hearing within Victorian studies has been concerned with the discursive construction of identity and, increasingly, its performative aspects, often in self-conscious dialogue with or critique of the 'linguistic turn'.[10] Some topics lend themselves to such enquiry better than others. The research by historians that has been most influential within Victorian scholarship has been on the operation of public discourses, for example on empire, sexuality and politics, and it is also in respect of those topics that there has been some of the most fruitful inter-disciplinary exchange. Work by historians on the languages of radicalism, for instance, has renewed literary interest in working-class and subaltern writing, and has generated a lively investigation of the literary and theatrical modes of radicalism.[11] While there have been detailed examinations of the discursive construction (and especially the gendered meanings) of 'skill', 'trade' and 'professionalism', there has been much less analysis of the experience of work or the operations of business and industry.[12] Indeed, in recent years *experience* has been as much the subject of epistemological deconstruction as it has of historical enquiry, and studies of the everyday experiences of family, community and even of public insti-

tutions like hospitals and schools are more likely to be published in the
social history journals than in those of Victorian studies.[13]

Recent preoccupations within Victorian studies are exemplified by a succession of titles published over the last decade compiling essays by predominantly literary scholars: *Rewriting the Victorians* (1992); *Victorian
Identities* (1996); *Writing and Victorianism* (1997); *Varieties of Victorianism* (1998); and *Rethinking Victorian Culture* (2000).[14] Each challenges the
notion of a homogenous Victorian culture. Informed by cultural theory, and
especially by post-structuralism, these volumes self-consciously interrogate
traditional conceptions of culture, knowledge and discipline. We are invited
to 'play' with the Victorians, and, increasingly, to see the Victorians
themselves as playful.[15] But even as some scholars encourage us to see the
Victorians as post-modernists *avant la lettre*, cannily anticipating
twentieth-century critiques of modernity, there are indications of a retreat
from theory and a return to a modified form of disciplinarity.[16] While the
move can be detected across the humanities and social sciences, it is most
evident within literary studies where it is sometimes connected with the
so-called 'ethical turn'.[17] In part a reaction against, in part development
on, the political criticism of the late twentieth century which focused, often
exclusively, on the ideological construction of morals and morality, the
'ethical turn' is characterised by a sympathetic reconsideration of ethical
criticism and an engagement with moral philosophy. To date, much of this
debate has been conducted at the abstract rather than the applied level, and
it remains to be seen what implications it will have for research and teaching in Victorian studies. There are, however, signs of a renewed interest in
the ethical criticism produced by literary figures, such as Matthew Arnold,
Henry James and even F. R. Leavis, as well as of a return to the literary
text in the investigation of ethical issues.[18] It seems that a re-assessment of
liberal humanism and even its re-instatement may be pending.

All the essay collections noted above are marked by a reluctance to define,
and thus to set limits to, either 'the Victorian' or 'Victorianism'. They reveal
the diversity of Victorian culture and yet give very little sense of the dynamic
processes and trends within that culture. In the 1990s, the essay collection
rather than the general study became the main vehicle for Victorian studies,
a form that is not best suited to such analysis. But, as Hewitt contends, if
Victorian studies is to have viability as an object of study, it 'needs to sustain
an attention to the connections and connectedness of Victorian culture and
society, and offer over-arching formulations of these which can set or at
least contextualise and draw into relation new agendas for research'.[19] Currently, the field lacks 'a recognized common scholarship' or 'a coherent
historiography' that, Hewitt suggests, could offer 'bold interpretative
re-assessments' of the pioneering studies of the 1950s and 1960s, a body
of work that strove to reveal the complexities and contradictions of
Victorian culture while at the same time identifying its distinctive features.
As Asa Briggs observed, 'a fair appraisal of the Victorian Commonwealth

demands a knowledge of historiography as well as of history'.[20] If Victorian studies is not to be eclipsed by the renaissance in eighteenth-century studies and the increasing popularity of earlier periods, due in no small part to innovative television programming in archaeology and history, it needs to produce public intellectuals who can rival the likes of Linda Colley and Roy Porter, whose magisterial narratives of eighteenth-century Britain have made revisionist historiography accessible to the general reader.[21] In the year of Victoria's death, that role fell to journalists rather than academics: witness Adam Hart Davis's energetic *What the Victorians Did for Us* and Matthew Sweet's *Inventing the Victorians*.[22] Overviews of the period, however, demand persistent attention to the question of periodisation, to which recent Victorian scholars have been averse.

II

'Nobody takes 1837–1901 seriously', Richard Price contends provocatively.[23] As Asa Briggs admitted in his seminal essay 'Victorianism', 'there never was one single "Victorian Commonwealth" beginning in 1837 and ending in 1901'; and most scholars, following Briggs, have tended to concentrate on a period within the reign.[24] It is not simply that scholars like Price have found alternative forms of periodisation to the reign more convincing; it is rather that many have chosen to investigate a specific cultural moment in favour of analysing change over time and the composition of so-called 'grand narratives'.[25] In many studies the term 'Victorian' is not defined, and even where it appears in the title it is often used merely as a synonym for 'the nineteenth century'.

While historians have long been sceptical of the terms 'Victorian' and 'Victorianism', a number of literary scholars, too, have begun to express doubts. In an essay on late-nineteenth-century republicanism, John Lucas contends that the terms 'are all too frequently employed in ways that are chronologically indefensible, historically dubious, intellectually confusing and ideologically unacceptable'.[26] While for some, like Lucas, the term 'Victorian' excludes those who dissented from orthodox and loyalist political culture, there is another tendency to invest the descriptor with a set of values that is all too easily read as 'dominant', *pace* 'bourgeois' or 'middle class'. Isobel Armstrong has argued forcefully that even more problematical than periodisation is the tendency for 'Victorian' to become 'an insidiously homogenizing and deeply unhistorical term'. As she eloquently proposes: 'There were no typical Victorians. Nor were there "other" Victorians asserting a mirror image of the "true" figures of the time, just as there was no counter-culture in opposition to the dominant.'[27] Despite these reservations, Armstrong does seek to identify the characteristic features of the era:

> It is rather a shame that the only term that would suit the fractured and diverse 'long' nineteenth century, 'early modern,' has been quietly and cannily appro-

priated to replace the outmoded terms, 'Elizabethan' or 'Renaissance.' 'Antemodern' for the years 1790–1914 is the best I can do.[28]

Armstrong's conviction that the period marked the onset of modernity is one shared by many Victorianists, particularly in literary studies. Conversely, this view has been challenged by scholars in other disciplines, Price for instance. It is remarkable that the very different narratives of modernity and modernisation constructed within the component disciplines of Victorian studies have scarcely been brought into dialogue, let alone interrogated.[29]

It is perhaps surprising that it is scholars at the literary end of Victorian studies who appear most wedded to the association of the period with 'the modern', for it is within this area of the discipline that post-structuralist and post-modernist critiques of teleological paradigms and grand narratives have been most influential. As the editors of *Rethinking Victorian Culture* contend, their volume 'is predicated on the assumption that the history of modern culture is paradoxically Victorian'.[30] The Victorian period is important within cultural history, they claim, precisely because this was the society that first began to reflect self-consciously on 'the idea of culture as a category'. Just as Raymond Williams postulated that the industrial and democratic revolutions of the long nineteenth century were connected with a revolution in communication, these editors trace a simultaneous 'cultural revolution'.[31] Their introduction of this term highlights the very different interpretations of the period in the 'historical' and 'literary' ends of the field:

> The radical changes in the social, political and economic structures of nineteenth century Britain make this dislocation [of the relationship between 'high' and 'popular' culture] unsurprising if not predictable. Industrialization, the Reform Bills, the increase in literacy, and changes to the legal and economic structure of the nation are just some of the momentous historical developments which began or gathered pace in the early nineteenth century; these changes, and the shift in attitudes which attend them, have led some to regard this era as the beginning of a 'modern' era. Quieter perhaps than the social, political and economic revolutions of the nineteenth century, but no less formative in the creation of a 'modern' state, was the cultural revolution which enabled more and more people to gain access to 'culture'.[32]

The narrative depicted here is dependent on a long-standing historiography that equates the Victorian age with the Industrial Revolution and the rise of modern class-structured society – a narrative which has been interrogated within all fields of historical enquiry.

Dispelling the myth of 'the distinctiveness of "Victorian" England and its role as the axis of modern English history' has been the objective of Richard Price, as elaborated in his compelling study *British Society 1680–1880*. He observes, perceptively, that the idea of the nineteenth century as an age of 'transition to modernity' originated in the confident sense of many Victorians that they were the progenitors of progress. Such a self-congratulatory

myth can no longer withstand the weight of historical revisionism.[33] For a
start, the idea that this was the age of the 'Industrial Revolution', still
omnipresent in so many accounts, rumbling like a volcano, its aftershocks
wrenching society apart, has been shaken by more than a generation of
research demonstrating that economic growth was relatively faster for much
of the eighteenth century than it was during the nineteenth, and that production continued to be geared not by the factory but by the traditional
sources of power, technique and labour, certainly until the later decades of
the nineteenth century.[34]

   Nor can the 'rise of the middle class' be seen in any straightforward sense
as either the cause or the effect of industrialisation and modernisation since,
among many reasons, the landed classes were responsible for much commercial and industrial innovation, while retaining effective control over
government into the twentieth century, a point made forty years ago by
Kitson Clark.[35] Many would now concur with Price that it 'was the weak-
ness of the industrial middle class that formed the overriding reality of
Victorian England, not their strength'.[36] Yet, within Victorian studies, the
perception of the period as 'the middle-class century' persists. Acknowledging the entrepreneurship of the landed classes and their hold over government, Robin Gilmour concludes that the middle classes were

> the chief agents and beneficiaries of modernity . . . the parvenus who trans-
> formed a 'feudal' society into a 'modern state', [who stamped] Victorian
> culture with the values that had inspired their emergence: hard work, energy,
> self-help, individualism, earnestness, domesticity.[37]

While J. B. Bullen argues that 'the network of middle-class influence [was]
more extensive than previously supposed, serving everywhere to determine
the very epistemology of the culture itself and to affect the nature of identity and self-definition', we should be careful not to assume that the cultural elite spoke for a unified and self-conscious middle class.[38] The frenetic
debate over self-culture and improvement may be indicative more of cultural anxiety than of authority.

   If the landed classes were bourgeois long before the middle classes, so
too were many so-called 'Victorian values' evident long before Victoria
came to the throne. To take but one example, Victorian culture has long
been associated with the cultivation of the domestic ideal. More recently
feminist scholars have argued that the early nineteenth-century middle class
defined itself against aristocratic debauchery and working-class delinquency
by proclaiming the virtues of domesticity.[39] Nonetheless, the identification
of domesticity with the Victorian middle class is increasingly challenged. As
Nancy Armstrong has shown, the bourgeois family was prefigured in late
eighteenth- and early nineteenth-century conduct books and novels.[40] In her
sensitive exploration of the lives and sensibilities of gentry folk, Amanda
Vickery has demonstrated that the cult of domestic propriety was alive and
well in Georgian England, long before the middle and working classes began

to aspire to a 'separate spheres' ideal.[41] Both studies could be used to support Price's contention that 'Victorian England makes little sense *except as a stage within a broader period that stretched from the late seventeenth century to the late eighteenth*'.[42]

Intellectual historians have also begun to free themselves from the 'mind forg'd manacles' of the Industrial Revolution, and they increasingly emphasise the long *durée*. In a recent essay Mark Bevir explains how the work of the Sussex school, led by John Burrow and Donald Winch, should challenge us 'to move from a narrow focus on Queen Victoria's reign to a long view stretching from 1750–1950'. When we wish to 'survey an era, we should avoid reifying any one way of splitting time or of clumping thinkers as if it had a definite beginning, a monolithic content, or a precise end', Bevir advises. Usefully, he challenges us to explore 'the long intellectual history of the nineteenth century' – and we might extend this to include all aspects of its history – 'as a series of over-lapping beginnings, contents, and endings'.[43] The complex relationships that intellectual historians are now tracing between Enlightenment, Romanticism, evangelicalism and liberalism complicate our understanding of the sources and meanings of nineteenth-century conceptions of individualism, and especially of the role of political economy, the old bugbear of Victorian historiography.

There is much to recommend Bevir's suggestion that we consider periodisation in terms of overlapping beginnings, contents and endings, rather than as fixed blocks of time. Nevertheless, this would require us to foreground much more closely the dynamics of historical continuity and change. In particular, it seems time for a renewed discussion of the term 'revolution', one used quite carefully and cautiously, it should be remembered, by an earlier generation of historians.[44] Seeking to explore the forces of continuity as much as those of change, it could be argued that historians have become too cautious, overlooking the sense of profound transformation and cultural shock experienced and expressed by contemporaries. By comparison, there has been a tendency in literary studies to interpret almost every event and text, and even the most conservative voices, in terms of crisis or revolution. In a recent discussion of the 'boundaries of period', Hewitt has contended that moments of transition are rarely those of revolution, but are rather of reformation or transformation. The significance of such changes should be assessed not just in the moment of innovation but in their diffusion, while resistance to change might characterise a period as much as the challenge of the new.[45]

In assessing the coherence of the Victorian period, we might then ask, in what ways does it make sense to talk of the 1830s and 1840s as revolutionary, in terms of radical changes in politics, culture and sensibility; or is the notion of cultural revolution in need of reconceptualistion? To point to one example: the pervasiveness and persistence in nineteenth-century society of what has been termed the 'melodramatic imagination' might be interpreted as evidence of a dynamic continuity in popular traditions, rather than as an element of a 'residual culture' that is increasingly overwhelmed by the emergent forms of realism and empiricism.[46] (Indeed, it may be time for a reappraisal of Raymond Williams's tacitly teleological categories of the residual, the emergent and the dominant that have characterised so much thinking about nineteenth-century culture.)[47] Perhaps, then, developments in nineteenth-century popular traditions are also part of the long *durée* and the truly revolutionary developments occur towards the end of the century with the development of mass-commodification and consumption, the emergence of an *avant-garde* that self-consciously sought to separate itself from mass culture, and the specialisation of knowledge. Such an analysis would be compatible with Price's argument that it is the late nineteenth century that should be seen as the real turning point, when steam power and factory production became ascendant, along with a mass consumer market, when organised labour and political parties began to take their modern shape and the slow process of political democratisation was cranked up a gear.[48]

And yet, *contra* Price, it is, perhaps after all, the Victorians' sense that they were modern which constitutes one of the distinctive features of their culture. As Jose Harris has argued, the Victorians had very different conceptions of what constituted – and how much they valued – 'the modern'. While cautioning against stereotyping and homogenizing Victorian sensibilities, she notes an important distinction between early and late constructions of the term: early Victorians sought 'mainly to distinguish "modern" from "classical" (or "medieval") times', while by the 1870s 'the modern' referred specifically to the contemporary; to 'the way we live now'. Where early Victorians tended to conceive progress in terms of continuity with past traditions, by the late nineteenth century their successors saw themselves at the dawn of a new age, witnessing the birth of 'the New Woman', a new 'race' or a new 'nation'.[49] Harris is concerned mainly with delineating the character of late Victorian and Edwardian Britain, but her careful comparison of the changing perceptions of progress and society might be extended to consider changing mentalities across the reign.

III

One of the ways in which we might think productively about the Victorian preoccupation with 'the modern', and indeed the more general sense of cultural awareness and self-reflection in the period, is to analyse how, and the extent to which, identity, both personal and collective, was connected with Victoria and her reign. Which Britons came to see themselves or the nation as 'Victorian', and when? What might this identity mean for those who rejected it, as well as for those who embraced it? At what point – and why – did those outside Britain and even beyond the empire (witness the USA) begin to describe themselves or their culture as Victorian? In his discussion of 'Victorianism', Briggs cites what is reputedly the first adjectival usage of

'Victorian' in 1851; but, as was pointed out in the Introduction, no study has traced the etymology, diffusion or popularity of the term.[50]

To understand oneself, one's culture or one's forebears as 'Victorian' implies some connection between the monarch and society. In the light of the questions above it may pay dividends to give more attention to Victoria, or, more particularly, to her subjects' views of the queen and her reign. It is remarkable that many of the principal studies of the 1970s and 1980s made at most only passing reference to the monarchy.[51] By contrast, the 1990s saw a prodigious growth in studies of the monarchy, inspired by David Cannadine's pioneering essay on the monarchy and 'the invention of tradition', and in biographies, precipitated by Dorothy Thompson's *Queen Victoria: Gender and Power*.[52]

Though interest in the monarchy has been revived, its meanings for British subjects are only now becoming the focus of investigation. That is paradoxical, for while the construction of the Victorian subject and subjectivity, especially in terms of class, gender and race, has been a – if not the – central preoccupation of recent scholarship, the constitutional aspects of subjecthood have been almost entirely overlooked.[53] The *Journal of British Studies* special issue on 'Victorian subjects', for example, did not consider how all inhabitants of Britain and its colonies were subjects of Victoria; an identity from which they could not opt out.[54] The dynamics of constitutional monarchy are omitted from the recent and important cultural history of the Reform Act of 1867 by Catherine Hall, Keith McClelland and Jane Rendall, which examines the formation of new political subjects within the context of colonial and imperial, as well as domestic, politics. Despite its title, *Defining the Victorian Nation*, the book does not reflect on how the nation was redefined as specifically 'Victorian'.[55]

The growing literature on empire, patriotism and republicanism offers insights on some of the more resolute opinions in favour of and against the monarchy, exemplified by Richard Williams's impressive examination of the often turbulent currents of veneration and repudiation of royalty throughout the reign.[56] It is probable, though, that there was a range of less trenchant views or explicitly ideological forms of identification. On the occasion of Victoria's death, for instance, many of her subjects may have looked back on and re-assessed their own lives, at least in part, in relation to hers; and her death may well have prompted a surge in autobiographical writing.[57] Others were already turning their back on the Victorians, a process of detachment that led Lytton Strachey to his *Eminent Victorians*. Yet while Strachey disowned his reputable forebears, he disavowed much that was 'Victorian' in himself. As William Lubenow argues in chapter 1 of this volume, he was as much an 'eminent Victorian' as a Bloomsbury modern. Similarly, in their analysis of the British intelligentsia in the first half of the twentieth century, Susan Pedersen and Peter Mandler have detected 'a quintessentially "Victorian" tendency to link private behaviour to public morality'.[58] When and why people stopped seeing themselves or others as

'Victorian' are questions as intriguing and open as that of when they began to see themselves in that guise. So perhaps, after all, we should take seriously 1837–1901. The reign ought not to define our sense of period, but it should at least inform it. If 1837 provides a meaningful endpoint for a historian of the eighteenth century, as it does also for Linda Colley, then it must be time for those of the nineteenth century to give it some consideration.

IV

There are many ways in which we might explore the questions and issues outlined above. Over recent decades we have acknowledged, and indeed revelled in, the varieties of Victorianism and the many faces of the Victorians; perhaps it is now time to recognise more fully the differences among students of the Victorian period. Just because scholars elsewhere are considering a return to disciplinarity is no reason to abandon the Victorian studies project; but it must surely require us to examine that project more critically. It matters less whether we find the label 'Victorian' a help or a hindrance than that we establish fora where such issues can be rigorously debated, if not finally settled. We need to foreground and bring into dialogue the critical debates that are taking place within different areas of the field and, just as importantly, to engage with significant intellectual developments in the study of other periods. Above all, we need to be less timid in our analysis of the dynamics of continuity and change across the society, culture and economy. To define is not to prescribe.

Notes

1 Martin Hewitt, 'Victorian studies: problems and prospects?', *Journal of Victorian Culture*, 6 (2001), p. 143.
2 Edward Said, *Culture and Imperialism* (London: Chatto & Windus, 1993); Robert Young, *Colonial Desire: Hybridity in Theory, Culture and Race* (London: Routledge, 1995); Ian Baucom, *Out of Place: Englishness, Empire and the Locations of Identity* (Princeton, NJ: Princeton University Press, 1999); Catherine Hall, *Civilising Subjects: Metropole and Colony in the English Imagination 1830–1867* (Cambridge: Polity Press, 2002).
3 See the Society's website at qub.ac.uk/english/socs/ssnci.html.
4 The BAVS website is at www.qub.ac.uk/en/socs/bavs/bavs/html.
5 The National Curriculum website is at www.nc.uk.net.
6 The increasing popularity of Victorian studies is evident in the proliferation of post-graduate courses since the 1990s: Leicester (1966); Birkbeck (*c*.1980); Nottingham (1992); Leeds, Trinity and All Saints (1994); Lancaster (1996); Anglia Polytechnic University (1998); St David's, Lampeter (1998); Huddersfield (2000); Royal Holloway (2000); Exeter (2001); Kent (2002); Manchester (2004). Only Lampeter runs an undergraduate programme.

7 Notable examples include: Martha Vicinus (ed.), *Suffer and Be Still: Women in the Victorian Age* (Bloomington: Indiana University Press, 1972); David Vincent, *Bread, Knowledge and Freedom: A Study of Nineteenth-Century Autobiography* (London: Methuen, 1982); Anne McClintock, *Imperial Leather: Race, Gender and Sexuality in the Colonial Context* (London: Routledge, 1995); Alison Winter, *Mesmerized: Powers of the Mind in Victorian Britain* (Chicago, IL: University of Chicago Press, 1998); Martin Hewitt (ed.), 'Platform culture in nineteenth-century Britain' (special edition), *Nineteenth-Century Prose*, 29 (2002).

8 A survey of the disciplinary provenance of the current BAVS membership reveals the following affiliations: English (142); history (47); theatre/drama (13); art (8); media/cultural studies (7); women's studies (1); theology (1); dance (1); unaccounted (44); a total of 264: see *Yearbook and Directory of Members* (BAVS, 2002).

9 Hewitt found ('Victorian studies', pp. 145–6) that in the 1990s two-thirds of the essays in *Victorian Studies* were on literary topics.

10 See Patrick Joyce, *Visions of the People: Industrial England and the Question of Class, 1840–1914* (Cambridge: Cambridge University Press, 1991); Mary Poovey, *Making a Social Body: British Cultural Formation, 1830–1864* (Chicago, IL: University of Chicago Press, 1995); Peter Bailey, *Popular Culture and Performance in the Victorian City* (Cambridge: Cambridge University Press, 1998).

11 See Gareth Stedman Jones, *Languages of Class: Studies in English Working-Class Culture, 1932–1982* (Cambridge: Cambridge University Press, 1983); Helen Rogers, *Women and the People: Authority, Authorship and the Radical Tradition in Nineteenth-Century England* (Aldershot: Ashgate, 2000); Florence Boos (ed.), 'The poetics of the working classes' (special edition), *Victorian Poetry* 39 (Summer 2001).

12 Patrick Joyce (ed.), *The Historical Meanings of Work* (Cambridge: Cambridge University Press, 1987); Sonya Rose, *Limited Livelihoods: Gender and Class in Nineteenth-Century England* (Berkeley: University of California Press, 1992); Deborah Valenze, *The First Industrial Woman* (Oxford: Oxford University Press, 1995).

13 For the debate on 'experience', see Keith Jenkins (ed.), *The Postmodern History Reader* (London: Routledge, 1997), pp. 313–83; for exceptions, see Ellen Ross, *Love and Toil: Motherhood in Outcast London, 1870–1918* (Oxford: Oxford University Press, 1993), and Anna Davin, *Growing Up Poor: Home, School and Street in London 1870–1914* (London: Rivers Oram, 1996).

14 Linda M. Shires (ed.), *Rewriting the Victorians: Theory, History and the Politics of Gender* (London: Routledge, 1992); Ruth Robbins and Julian Wolfreys (eds), *Victorian Identities: Social and Cultural Formations in Nineteenth-Century Literature* (Basingstoke: Macmillan, 1996); J. B. Bullen (ed.), *Writing and Victorianism* (London: Longman, 1997); Gary Day (ed.), *Varieties of Victorianism: The Uses of the Past* (Basingstoke: Macmillan, 1998); Juliet John and Alice Jenkins (eds), *Rethinking Victorian Culture* (Basingstoke: Macmillan, 2000). For two earlier attempts to deconstruct and historicise 'Victorian values', see James Walvin, *Victorian Values* (London: Andre Deutsch, 1987) Gordon Marsden (ed.), *Victorian Values: Personalities and Perspectives in Nineteenth Century Society* (London: Longman, 1990).

15 See Robbins and Wolfreys, *Victorian Identities*, p. 1; and John Schad, *Victorians in Theory: From Derrida to Browning* (Manchester: Manchester University Press, 1999). Locating the 'post-modern' in the 'Victorian' has been a feature of considerable scholarship in the USA: see George Levine, 'Victorian studies', in Stephen Greenblatt and Giles Gunn (eds), *Redrawing the Boundaries: The Transformation of English and American Literary Studies* (New York: Modern Languages Association, 1992), pp. 130–53.

16 Robert Eaglestone, *Ethical Criticism: Reading After Levinas* (Edinburgh: Edinburgh University Press, 1997); Martin McQuillan, G. MacDonald, R. Purves and S. Thomson (eds), *Post-Theory: New Directions in Criticism* (Edinburgh: Edinburgh University Press, 1999); Todd Davies and Kenneth Womack, *Mapping the Ethical Turn: A Reader in Ethics, Culture, and Literary Theory* (Charlottesville: University of Virginia Press, 2001).

17 Nancy Armstrong, 'Confessions of an ex-historicist', unpublished paper, Liverpool John Moores University, 2002.

18 See the Introduction to Jane Adamson, Richard Freadman and David Parker (eds), *Renegotiating Ethics in Literature, Philosophy and Theory* (Cambridge: Cambridge University Press, 1998), especially the essay (pp. 65–83) by Lisabeth During: 'The concept of dread: sympathy and ethics in *Daniel Deronda*'.

19 Hewitt, 'Victorian studies', pp. 142–3 and p. 152; see also Martin Hewitt (ed.), *An Age of Equipoise? Reassessing Mid-Victorian Britain* (Aldershot: Ashgate, 2000).

20 Asa Briggs, 'Victorianism', in *The Age of Improvement, 1783–1867* (London: Longman, 1963), pp. 447–8.

21 Linda Colley, *Britons: Forging the Nation 1707–1837* (London: Pimlico, 1994); Roy Porter, *Enlightenment* (London: Penguin, 2000).

22 Adam Hart-Davis, *What the Victorians Did for Us* (London: Headline, 2001); Matthew Sweet, *Inventing the Victorians* (London: Faber & Faber 2001).

23 Richard Price, 'Does the notion of Victorian England make sense?' in Derek Fraser (ed.), *Cities, Class and Communication: Essays in Honour of Asa Briggs* (London: Harvester Wheatsheaf, 1990), p. 153.

24 See Briggs, *Age of Improvement*, p. 448. For one of the few recent general surveys, see Theodore Hoppen, *The Mid-Victorian Generation, 1846–1886* (Oxford: Clarendon Press, 1998).

25 This approach is exemplified by Judith Walkowitz's influential study *City of Dreadful Delight: Narratives of Sexual Danger in Late-Victorian London* (London: Virago, 1992) in which the author resisted 'a traditional historical narrative' in order to investigate the multiple and contested responses to the Ripper murders (p. 10).

26 John Lucas, 'Republican versus Victorian: radical writing in the later years of the nineteenth century', in John and Jenkins (eds), *Rethinking Victorian Culture*, p. 29.

27 Isobel Armstrong, 'When is a Victorian poet not a Victorian poet? Poetry and the politics of subjectivity in the long nineteenth century', *Victorian Studies*, 43 (2001), p. 280; see also Dorothy Thompson's reviews of Carolly Erickson, *Her Little Majesty* (1997), and Margaret Homans and Adrienne Munch (eds), *Remaking Queen Victoria* (1997), *Victorian Studies*, 42 (1998), p. 139.

28 Armstrong, 'When is a Victorian poet not a Victorian poet?' p. 280.

29 One attempt to focus such questions was the conference 'The Victorians and Modernity' held at Trinity and All Saints, Leeds, in 1997.

30 John and Jenkins (eds), *Rethinking Victorian Culture*, p. 5.

31 Williams's conception of a democratic revolution and the revolution in communication has of course been deeply influential. See especially his *The Long Revolution* (London: Chatto & Windus, 1961).

32 John and Jenkins (eds), *Rethinking Victorian Culture*, pp. 3–5.

33 Price, 'Does the notion of Victorian England make sense?' pp. 153–4; for an extended exposition of the argument, see Price, *British Society 1680–1880: Dynamism, Containment and Change* (Cambridge: Cambridge University Press, 1999).

34 Price, *British Society*, pp. 17–51; for some of the most influential work in this extensive field, see: Raphael Samuel, 'The workshop of the world: steam-power and hand-technology in mid-Victorian Britain', *History Workshop Journal*, 3 (1977), pp. 6–72; Maxine Berg, *The Age of Manufactures 1700–1820* (London: Fontana, 1985); N. F. R. Crafts, *British Economic Growth during the Industrial Revolution* (Oxford: Oxford University Press, 1985); Pat Hudson, *The Industrial Revolution* (London: Arnold, 1992); Patrick O'Brien and Roland Quinault (eds), *The Industrial Revolution and British Society* (Cambridge: Cambridge University Press, 1993); M. Daunton, *Progress and Poverty: An Economic and Social History of Britain, 1750–1850* (Oxford: Oxford University Press, 1995).

35 G. Kitson Clark, *The Making of Victorian England* (London: Methuen, 1962), pp. 6–7.

36 Price, 'Does the notion of Victorian England make sense?' p. 157. The revisionist work is diverse: see R. J. Morris, *Class, Sect and Party: The Making of the British Middle Class, Leeds 1820–1850* (Manchester: Manchester University Press, 1990); Patrick Joyce, *Democratic Subjects: The Self and the Social in Nineteenth-Century England* (Cambridge: Cambridge University Press, 1994); Dror Wahrman, *Imagining the Middle Class: The Political Representation of Class in Britain, c.1780–1840* (Cambridge: Cambridge University Press, 1995); Alan Kidd and David Nicholls (eds), *Gender, Civic Culture and Consumerism: Middle-Class Identity in Britain, 1800–1940* (Manchester: Manchester University Press, 1999).

37 Robin Gilmour, *The Victorian Period: The Intellectual Context of English Literature* (London: Longman, 1993), pp. 3, 14.

38 Bullen, 'Introduction' to *Writing and Victorianism*, p. 6.

39 See especially Leonore Davidoff and Catherine Hall, *Family Fortunes: Men and Women of the English Middle Class, 1780–1850* (London: Hutchinson, 1987).

40 Nancy Armstrong, *Desire and Domestic Fiction: A Political History of the Novel* (Oxford: Oxford University Press, 1997).

41 Amanda Vickery, *The Gentleman's Daughter: Women's Lives in Georgian England* (New Haven, CT: Yale University Press, 1998).

42 Price, 'Does the notion of Victorian England make sense?' p. 157.

43 Mark Bevir, 'The long nineteenth century in intellectual history', *Journal of Victorian Culture*, 6 (2001), pp. 313–35.

44 See: Kitson Clark, *The Making of Victorian England*, p. 276.

45 See: Martin Hewitt, unpublished paper delivered at the 'Boundaries' conference, department of English, University of Exeter, 2002. I am very grateful to the author for showing me a copy of the paper.

46 Rohan McWilliam, 'Melodrama and the historians', *Radical History*, 78 (2000), pp. 57–84.

47 Raymond Williams, *Marxism and Literature* (Oxford: Oxford University Press, 1977), pp. 121–7.

48 For literary studies that highlight the distinctiveness of the 1880s, see: Richard Altick, *Victorian People and Ideas* (London: J. M. Dent and Sons, 1974); and Peter Keating, *The Haunted Study: A Social History of the English Novel 1875–1914* (London: Fontana, 1991).

49 José Harris, *Private Lives, Public Spirit in Britain 1870–1914* (London: Penguin, 1994), pp. 32–3.

50 Edward Paxton Hood, *The Age and its Architects* (1852), p. 73, cited by Briggs, *Age of Improvement*, p. 446.

51 Harold Perkin, *The Origins of Modern English Society 1780–1880* (London: Routledge & Kegan Paul, 1969); Richard Altick, in *Victorian People and Ideas* (London, J. M. Dent & Sons, 1974), occasionally cited the queen's opinions in the course of discussing Victorian values, but did not consider her understanding of her reign. F. M. L. Thompson made no reference to Victoria, monarchy or empire in his compelling account, *The Rise of Respectable Society: A Social History of Victorian Britain, 1830–1900* (London, Fontana, 1988).

52 David Cannadine, 'The context, performance and meaning of ritual: the British monarchy and the "invention of tradition", *c.*1820–1977', in Eric Hobsbawm and Terence Ranger (eds), *The Invention of Tradition* (Cambridge: Cambridge University Press, 1983), pp. 101–64; and 'The last Hanoverian sovereign? The Victorian monarchy in historical perspective, 1688–1988', in A. L. Beier, David Cannadine and James M. Rosenheim (eds), *The First Modern Society: Essays in English History in Honour of Lawrence Stone* (Cambridge: Cambridge University Press, 1989), pp. 127–66; Dorothy Thompson, *Queen Victoria: Gender and Power* (London: Virago, 1990). For a review of some of recent work in this field, see Regenia Gagnier, 'Locating the Victorians', *Journal of Victorian Culture*, 6 (2001), pp. 113–24.

53 Joyce, *Democratic Subjects*; Regenia Gagnier, *Subjectivities: A History of Self-Representation in Britain, 1832–1920* (Oxford: Oxford University Press, 1991).

54 James Epstein, 'Victorian subjects', *Journal of British Studies*, 34 (1995), pp. 295–9.

55 Catherine Hall, Keith McClelland and Jane Rendall, *Defining the Victorian Nation: Class, Race, Gender and the Reform Act of 1867* (Cambridge: Cambridge University Press, 2000).

56 Richard Williams, *The Contentious Crown: Public Discussion of the British Monarchy in the Reign of Queen Victoria* (Aldershot: Ashgate, 1997), p. 265. See also: John Plunkett, *Queen Victoria: First Media Monarch* (Oxford: Oxford University Press, 2003).

57 The Baptist writer Marianne Farningham, for example, connected her autobiographical endeavour, begun in 1900, with the general experience of self-reflection prompted by the turn of the century and the death of the queen; see her *A Working Woman's Life: An Autobiography* (London: James Clarke & Co., 1907), p. 11. This retrospective mood may account for the significant rise in

autobiographical writing in the period 1900–14, detected by Robert Gray, who notes the preference for the term 'reminiscences' and 'recollections' rather than 'autobiography' and 'life' in such memoirs: R. Gray, 'Self-made men, self-narrated lives: male autobiographical writing and the Victorian middle class', *Journal of Victorian Culture*, 6 (2001), pp. 291–2.

58 Susan Pedersen and Peter Mandler (eds), *After the Victorians: Private Conscience and Public Duty in Modern Britain* (London: Routledge, 1994).

Timeline of Victorian studies,
1901–2002

1901–10

Victoria and her family

Death of Queen Victoria aged 81, 22 January 1901

Sidney Lee, *Queen Victoria: A Biography* (1902)

The Letters of Queen Victoria: A Selection from Her Majesty's Correspondence between the years 1837 and 1861, ed. A. C. Benson and Vct. Esher, 3 vols (1907)

Death of Edward VII aged 68, 6 May 1910

Prime ministers

Maurice Courcelle, *Disraeli* (Paris: Felix Alcan, 1902)

Wilfrid Meynell, *Benjamin Disraeli: An Unconventional Biography* (London: Hutchinson, 1903)

John Morley, *The Life of William Ewart Gladstone*, 3 vols (London: Macmillan, 1903)

Death of Lord Salisbury aged 73, 22 August 1903

Walter Sichel, *Disraeli: A Study in Personality and Ideas* (London: Methuen, 1904)

D. C. Lathbury, *Mr. Gladstone* (London: A. R. Mowbray, 1907)

W. F. Monypenny and G. E. Buckle, *The Life of Benjamin Disraeli, Earl of Beaconsfield*, 6 vols (London: John Murray, 1910–20)

Writers

L. Stephen, *George Eliot* (London: Macmillan, 1902)

New Letters and Memorials of Jane Welsh Carlyle, ed. Alexander Carlyle (London: John Lane, 1903)

G. K. Chesterton, *Robert Browning* (London: Macmillan, 1903)

The Works of John Ruskin, ed. E. T. Cook and Alexander Wedderburn (London: Longmans, 1903–12)

G. W. E. Russell, *Matthew Arnold* (London: Hodder & Stoughton, 1904)

A. C. Benson, *Walter Pater* (London: Macmillan, 1904)

A. C. Benson, *Alfred Tennyson* (London: Methuen, 1904)

G. K. Chesterton, *Dickens* (London: Methuen, 1906)

The Works of Mrs Gaskell, ed. A. W. Ward, 8 vols (London: John Murray, 1906)

Clement Shorter, *The Brontës: Life and Letters* (London: Hodder & Stoughton, 1908)

R. A. J. Walling, *George Borrow: The Man and His Work* (London: Cassell, 1908)
T. Wright, *The Life of Walter Pater* (London: Everett, 1907)
D. Duncan, *Life and Letters of Herbert Spencer* (London: Methuen, 1908)
The Works of W. M. Thackeray, ed. George Saintsbury, 20 vols (London: Oxford University Press, 1910)
The Collected Works of William Morris, ed. May Morris (London: Longmans, 1910–15)

Studies of the Victorian age

Louis Cazamian, *Le Roman social en angleterre* (Paris: Société nouvelle de librarie et d'édition, 1903)
J. W. C. Carr, *Some Eminent Victorians: Personal Recollections in the World of Wit and Letters* (London: Duckworth, 1908)

1911–20

Victoria and her family

Queen Victoria Memorial and Gardens opened on the Mall, outside Buckingham Palace, 1911

Prime ministers

Louis Napoleon Parker, *Disraeli: A Play* (New York: John Lane, 1911)
Benjamin Disraeli, *Whigs and Whiggism. Political Writings*, ed. William Hutcheon (London: John Murray 1913)
Early Correspondence of Lord John Russell, 1805–40, ed. R. Russell (London: T. Fisher Unwin, 1913)
Peel Papers to the British Musuem, 1917
H. H. Asquith, *Some Aspects of the Victorian Age*, Romanes Lecture (Oxford: Clarendon Press, 1918)
The Private Letters of Sir Robert Peel, ed. G. Peel (London: John Murray, 1920)

Writers

Herbert Jenkins, *The Life of George Borrow* (London: John Murray, 1912)
Frank Swinnerton, *George Gissing: A Critical Study* (London: Martin Secker, 1912)
Edward Thomas, *George Borrow: The Man and His Books* (London: Chapman & Hall, 1912)
May Sinclair, *The Three Brontës* (London: Hutchinson, 1913)
Edward Thomas, *Walter Pater: A Critical Study by Edward Thomas* (London: Secker, 1913)
D. A. Wilson, *The Truth about Carlyle: An Exposure of the Fundamental Fiction Still Current* (London: Alston Rivers, 1913)
Lord Alfred Douglas, *Oscar Wilde and Myself* (London: John Long, 1914)
George Bernard Shaw, 'On Dickens', *Dickensian*, 10 (June 1914)
Frank Harris, *Oscar Wilde: His Life and Confessions* (New York: privately printed, 1916)
Edmund Gosse, *The Life of Algernon Charles Swinburne* (London: Macmillan, 1917)
Poems of Gerard Manley Hopkins, ed. Robert Bridges (London: H. Milford, 1918)
W. W. Crotch, *The Secret of Dickens* (London: Chapman and Hall, 1919)

Studies of the Victorian age

The Oxford Book of Victorian Verse, chosen by Arthur Quiller-Couch (Oxford: Clarendon Press, 1912)

G. K. Chesterton, *The Victorian Age in Literature* (London: Williams & Norgate, 1913)

Holbrook Jackson, *The 1890s: A Review of Art and Ideas at the Close of the 19th Century* (London: Jonathan Cape, 1913)

T. H. S. Escott, *Great Victorians: Memories and Personalities* (London: Unwin, 1916)

Lytton Strachey, *Eminent Victorians* (London: Chatto & Windus, 1918)

Exhibitions

Robert Browning Centenary, Victoria and Albert Museum, 1912

Dickens Exhibition, Victoria and Albert Museum, 1912

1921–30

Victoria and her family

Lytton Strachey, *Queen Victoria* (London: Chatto and Windus, 1921)

David Carb, *Queen Victoria. A Play in Seven Episodes* (New York: E. P. Dutton, 1922)

Death of Princess Helena aged 77, 9 June 1923

The Letters of Queen Victoria, 2nd series: A Selection from Her Majesty's Correspondence and Journal between the Years 1862 and 1878, ed. G. E. Buckle, 3 vols (London: John Murray, 1926–28)

Frederick Ponsonby, *Sidelights on Queen Victoria* (London: Macmillan, 1930)

The Letters of Queen Victoria, 3rd series: A Selection from Her Majesty's Correspondence and Journal between the Years 1886 and 1901, ed. G. E. Buckle, 3 vols (London: John Murray, 1930–2)

Prime ministers

Lady Gwendolen Cecil, *Life of Robert, Marquis of Salisbury*, 4 vols (London: Hodder & Stoughton, 1921)

Frances Balfour, *The Life of George, 4th Earl of Aberdeen*, 2 vols (London: Hodder & Stoughton, 1922)

E. T. Raymond, *The Man of Promise, Lord Rosebery: A Critical Study* (London: T. F. Unwin, 1923)

D. C. Somervell, *Disraeli and Gladstone: A Duo-Biographical Sketch* (New York: George H. Doran, 1923)

Kingsley Martin, *The Triumph of Lord Palmerston* (London: Allen & Unwin, 1924)

The Later Correspondence of Lord John Russell, 1840–1878, ed. G. P. Gooch (London: Longmans, 1925)

E. T. Raymond, *Disraeli: The Alien Patriot* (London: Hodder & Stoughton, 1925)

Edward Clarke, *Benjamin Disraeli: The Romance of a Great Career 1804–1881* (London: John Murray, 1926)

Andre Maurois, *Disraeli: A Picture of the Victorian Age* (London: Bodley Head, 1927)

E. H. Thruston, *Earl of Rosebery, Statesman and Sportsman* (London: Tavistock Press, 1928)

A. A. W. Ramsay, *Sir Robert Peel* (London: Constable, 1928)

Death of Lord Rosebery aged 82, 21 May 1929

The Letters of Disraeli to Lady Bradford and Lady Chesterfield, ed. Marquis of Zetland, 2 vols (London: Ernest Benn, 1929)

Gladstone Papers presented to the British Museum, 1930

A. Wyatt Tilby, *Lord John Russell: A Study in Civil and Religious Liberty* (London: Cassell, 1930)

Bertram Newman, *Lord Melbourne* (London: Macmillan, 1930)

Writers

Harold Nicolson, *Tennyson: Aspects of His Life, Character and Poetry* (London: Constable, 1923)

D. A. Wilson, *Carlyle*, 6 vols (London: Kegan Paul, Trench, Trubner, 1923–34)

The Works of George Borrow, ed. C. Shorter, 16 vols (London: Constable, 1923–4)

C. E. M. Joad, *Samuel Butler (1835–1902)* (London: L. Parsons, 1924)

Arthur Quiller-Couch, *Charles Dickens and Other Victorians* (Cambridge: Cambridge University Press, 1925)

Complete Works of Algernon Swinburne, ed. E. Gosse and T. Wise, 18 vols (London: Heinemann, 1925–7)

The Bradenham Edition of the Novels and Tales of Benjamin Disraeli, 1st Earl of Beaconsfield, ed. P. Guedalla, 12 vols (London: P. Davies, 1926)

Mary Gretton, *The Writings and Life of George Meredith. A Centenary Study* (London: Oxford University Press, 1926)

Evelyn Waugh, *Rossetti: His Life and Works* (London: Duckworth, 1928)

H. Kingsmill, *Matthew Arnold* (London: Duckworth, 1928)

F. E. Hardy, *The Life of Thomas Hardy*, 2 vols (London: Macmillan, 1928–30)

Founding of the Trollope Society, Philadelphia, 1929

A. S. Whitfield, *Mrs. Gaskell: Her Life and Work* (London: G. Routledge, 1929)

George Eliot Fellowship established, 1930

Elizabeth Haldane, *Mrs. Gaskell and Her Friends* (London: Hodder & Stoughton, 1930)

Charles Simpson, *Emily Brontë* (London: Country Life, 1930)

Studies of the Victorian age

Michael Sadleir, *Excursions in Victorian Bibliography* (London: Chaundy & Cox, 1922)

Julia Cameron, *Victorian Photographs of Famous Men and Fair Women* (London: Hogarth Press, 1926)

J. H. Clapham, *The Economic History of Modern Britain*, 3 vols (Cambridge: Cambridge University Press, 1926–38)

A. Baumann, *The Last Victorians* (London: E. Benn, 1927)

E. H. Dance, *Victorian Illusion* (London: W. Heinemann, 1928)

Wanda F. Neff, *Victorian Working Women: An Historical and Literary Study of Women in British Industries and Professions, 1832–50* (George Allen & Unwin, 1929)

E. Wingfield-Stratford, *The Victorian Tragedy* (London: G. Routledge, 1930)

E. F. Benson, *As We Were: A Victorian Peep-Show* (London: Longmans, Green, 1930)

J. L. Hammond and Barbara Hammond, *The Age of the Chartists, 1832–1854: A Study of Discontent* (London: Longmans, Green, 1930)

Media
(All works listed under 'Media' were produced in the UK unless indicated otherwise)
Under the Greenwood Tree (Wardour, 1929)

Conservation and the built environment
Kenneth Clark, *The Gothic Revival: An Essay in the History of Taste* (London: Constable, 1928)

1931–40
Victoria and her family
Hector Bolitho, *Albert the Good* (London: Cobden-Sanderson, 1932)
P. Guedalla, *The Queen and Mr. Gladstone*, 2 vols (London: Hodder & Stoughton, 1933)
Mona Wilson, *Queen Victoria* (London: P. Davies, 1933)
The Prince Consort and His brother, the Duke Ernst II of Saxe-Coburg: Two Hundred New Letters, ed. Hector Bolitho (London: Cobden-Sanderson, 1933)
E. F. Benson, *Queen Victoria* (London: Longmans, 1935)
F. Hardie, *The Political Influence of Queen Victoria, 1861–1901* (Oxford: Oxford University Press, 1935)
E. Sitwell, *Victoria of England* (London: Faber & Faber, 1936)
Hector Bolitho, *Victoria and Albert* (London: Cobden-Sanderson, 1938)
Letters of the Prince Consort, 1831–1861, ed. K. Jagow (London: John Murray, 1938)
Death of Princess Louise aged 91, 3 December 1939

Prime ministers
F. W. Hirst, *Gladstone as Financier and Economist* (London: Ernest Benn, 1931)
Marquess of Crewe, *Lord Rosebery*, 2 vols (London: John Murray, 1931)
Lord Aberdeen Papers presented to the British Museum, 1932
Francis Birrell, *Gladstone* (London: Duckworth, 1933)
F. E. Hyde, *Mr. Gladstone at the Board of Trade* (London: Cobden-Sanderson, 1934)
Herbert C. F. Bell, *Lord Palmerston* (London: Longmans, Green, 1936)
Erich Eyck, *Gladstone* (London: George Allen & Unwin, 1938)
J. Hammond, *Gladstone and the Irish Nation* (London: Longmans, Green, 1938)
David Cecil, *The Young Melbourne, and the Story of His Marriage with Caroline Lamb* (London: Constable, 1939)

Writers
Rudolf Besier, *The Barretts of Wimpole Street* (London: Victor Gollancz, 1930)
E. F. Benson, *Charlotte Brontë* (London: Longmans, Green, 1932)
The Letters of Matthew Arnold to Arthur Hugh Clough, ed. H. F. Lowry (Oxford: Oxford University Press, 1932)
Georges Lafourcade, *Swinburne: A Literary Biography* (London: G. Bell, 1932)

C. G. Stillman, *Samuel Butler: A Mid-Victorian Modern* (London: Martin Secker, 1932)

A. Symons, *A Study of Walter Pater* (London: C. J. Sawyer, 1932)

Letters of Robert Browning, ed. T. L. Hood (London: John Murray, 1933)

Anna Theresa Kitchel, *George Lewes and George Eliot: A Review of Records* (New York: John Day, 1934)

Virginia Moore, *The Life and Eager Death of Emily Brontë. A Biography* (London: Rich and Cowan, 1936)

M. Muggeridge, *The Earnest Atheist: A Study of Samuel Butler* (London: Eyre & Spottiswoode, 1936)

A. Davidson, *Edward Lear: Landscape Painter and Nonsense Poet (1812–1888)* (London: John Murray, 1938)

The Complete Works of Lewis Carroll ed. Alexander Woolcott (London: Nonesuch Press, 1939)

George Orwell, 'Charles Dickens', in *Inside the Whale* (London: Gollancz, 1940)

Edmund Wilson, 'Dickens: the two Scrooges', *New Republic*, 102 (March 1940)

Studies of the Victorian age

Margaret Barton and Osbert Sitwell, *Victoriana: A Symposium of Victorian Wisdom* (London: Duckworth, 1931)

A. Bott, *Our Fathers, 1870–1900: Manners and Customs of the Ancient Victorians: A Survey in Pictures and Text of Their History, Morals, Wars, Sports, Writers and Politics* (London: Heinemann, 1931)

A. Bott, *Our Mothers: A Cavalcade in Pictures, Quotation and Description of Late Victorian Women Writers, 1870–1900* (London: Gollancz, 1932)

M. E. Perugrini, *Victorian Days and Ways* (London: Jarrolds, 1932)

Q. D. Leavis, *Fiction and the Reading Public* (London: Chatto and Windus, 1932)

Harold John Massingham and Hugh Massingham (eds), *The Great Victorians* (London: I. Nicholson & Watson, 1932)

Horace Wyndham, *Victorian Sensations* (London: Jarrolds, 1933)

David Cecil, *Early Victorian Novelists: Essays in Revaluation* (London: Constable, 1934)

G. M. Young (ed.), *Early Victorian England* (Oxford: Clarendon Press, 1934)

Hesketh Pearson, *Gilbert and Sullivan* (London: Hamish Hamilton, 1935)

Horace Wyndham, *Victorian Parade* (London: F. Muller, 1935)

R. C. K. Ensor, *England, 1870–1914* (Oxford: Clarendon Press, 1936)

G. M. Young, *Victorian England: Portrait of an Age* (London: Oxford University Press, 1936)

Peter Quennell, *Victorian Panorama: A Survey of Life and Fashion from Contemporary Photographs* (London: Batsford, 1937)

Edith Batho and Bonamy Dobrée, *The Victorians and After, 1830–1914* (London: Cresset Press, 1938)

Amy Cruse, *After the Victorians* (London: George Allen & Unwin, 1938)

E. L. Woodward, *The Age of Reform, 1815–1870* (Oxford: Clarendon Press, 1938)

R. Mowat, *The Victorian Age: The Age of Comfort and Culture* (London: G. G. Harrap, 1939)

Exhibitions

Victorian Pantomimes, Victoria and Albert Museum, 1933

William Morris Centenary, Victoria and Albert Museum, 1934

The Victorians and Their Books, National Book League, 1935
Pickwick Papers Centenary Display, Victoria and Albert Museum, 1936
Victorian Paintings, Birmingham Museum and Art Galley, 1937
Victorian and Edwardian Costume, Metropolitan Museum of Modern Art, New York, 1939
Victorian Photography, Victoria and Albert Museum, 1939

Media
The Hound of the Baskervilles (Ideal, 1931)
The Sign of Four (US, RKO, 1932)
Oliver Twist (US, Mono, 1933)
Jane Eyre (US, Mono, 1934)
The Old Curiosity Shop (BIP, 1934)
Becky Sharp (US, RKO, 1935)
David Copperfield (US, MGM 1935)
The Mystery of Edwin Drood (US, UN, 1935)
A Tale of Two Cities (US, MGM, 1935)
The Mill on the Floss (NPFD, 1937)
Victoria the Great (US, RKO, 1937)
A Christmas Carol (US, MGM, 1938)
The Adventures of Sherlock Holmes (US, Fox 1939)
The Hound of the Baskervilles (US, Fox 1939)
Wuthering Heights (US, United Artists, 1939)

Academic
Modern Philology publishes an annual bibliography of Victorian Studies (1932–57)

Conservation and the built environment
Harry Goodhart-Rendel gives Slade Lectures at Oxford on Victorian architecture, 1934
Crystal Palace burns to the ground, 30 November 1936
N. Pevsner, *Pioneers of the Modern Movement from William Morris to Walter Gropius* (London: Faber, 1936)
C. Hobhouse, *1851 and the Crystal Palace: Being an Account of the Great Exhibition and its Contents, of Sir Joseph Paxton, and His Masterpiece* (London: John Murray, 1937)

1941–50

Victoria and her family
Death of Prince Arthur aged 91, 16 January 1942
Death of Princess Beatrice aged 87, 26 October 1944

Prime ministers
T. J. P. Lever, *The Life and Times of Sir Robert Peel* (London: Allen & Unwin, 1942)
Russell's papers to the Public Record Office (1942)

Writers
Grant Richards, *A. E. Housman, 1897–1936* (London: Oxford University Press, 1941)

Hesketh Pearson, *Conan Doyle: His Life and Art* (London: Methuen, 1943)
The Letters and Private Papers of William Makepeace Thackeray, ed. Gordon N. Ray, 4 vols (Cambridge, MA: Harvard University Press, 1945–6)
F. B. Lennon, *Victoria Through the Looking-Glass: The Life of Lewis Carroll* (New York: Simon and Schuster, 1947)
Una Pope-Hennessy, *Canon Charles Kingsley: A Biography* (London: Chatto & Windus, 1948)
Lawrence and E. M. Hanson, *The Four Brontës: The Lives and Works of Charlotte, Branwell, Emily, and Anne Brontë* (London: Oxford University Press, 1949)
H. M. Hyde (ed.), *The Trials of Oscar Wilde* (London: William Hodge, 1948)
The Poems of Coventry Patmore, ed. Frederick Page (Oxford: Oxford University Press, 1949)

Studies of the Victorian age
H. House, *The Dickens World* (London: Oxford University Press, 1941)
Leslie Marchand, *The Athenaeum: A Mirror of Victorian Culture* (Chapel Hill: University of North Carolina Press, 1941)
F. R. Leavis, *The Great Tradition: George Eliot, Henry James, Joseph Conrad* (London: Chatto & Windus, 1948)
M. W. Disher, *Blood and Thunder: Mid-Victorian Melodrama and its Origins* (London: Muller, 1949)
Basil Willey, *Nineteenth Century Studies: Coleridge to Matthew Arnold* (London: Chatto & Windus, 1949)

Exhibitions
Victorian and Nineteenth-Century Pictures, Leicester Galleries, London, 1941
Aubrey Beardsley: Drawings and Books, Grolier Club, New York, 1945
Victorian Fiction, National Book League, 1947
The Personal History of David Copperfield, Victoria and Albert Museum, 1949

Media
Jane Eyre (US, Fox, 1943)
Great Expectations, dir. David Lean (Rank, 1946)
Nicholas Nickleby (Ealing, 1947)
Oliver Twist, dir. David Lean (Cineguild, 1948)
The Woman in White (US, Warner, 1948)
Ideas and Beliefs of the Victorians (BBC Third Programme, 1949)

Conservation and the built environment
H. M. Casson, *An Introduction to Victorian Architecture* (London: Art & Technics, 1948)

1951–60

Prime ministers
Hesketh Pearson, *Dizzy: The Life and Nature of Benjamin Disraeli, Earl of Beaconsfield* (London: Methuen, 1951)
David Cecil, *Lord M., or, The later life of Lord Melbourne* (London: Constable, 1954)

Philip Magnus, *Gladstone: A Biography* (London: John Murray, 1954)
W. B. Pemberton, *Lord Palmerston* (London: Batchworth Press, 1954)
Lord Melbourne's papers to the Royal Archives (1954)

Writers
Noel Annan, *Leslie Stephen: His Thought and Character in Relation to His Time* (London: MacGibbon and Kee, 1951)
The Letters of Anthony Trollope, ed. Bradford Allen Booth (London: Oxford University Press, 1951)
Lawrence and Elisabeth Hanson, *Marian Evans and George Eliot: A Biography* (London: Oxford University Press, 1952)
E. D. H. Johnson, *The Alien Vision of Victorian Poetry: Sources of the Poetic Imagination in Tennyson, Browning and Arnold* (Princeton, NJ: Princeton University Press, 1952)
Betty Miller, *Robert Browning: A Portrait* (London: John Murray, 1952)
The Diaries of Lewis Carroll, ed. R. L. Green, 2 vols (London: Cassell, 1953)
L. Stevenson, *The Ordeal of George Meredith: A Biography* (New York: Scribner, 1953)
Michael St John Packe, *The Life of John Stuart Mill* (London: Secker & Warburg, 1954)
Geoffrey Tillotson, *Thackeray the Novelist* (Cambridge: Cambridge University Press, 1954)
The George Eliot Letters, ed. Gordon Haight, 9 vols (London: Oxford University Press, 1954–78)
Founding of the William Morris Society, 1955
C. E. Carrington, *Rudyard Kipling: His Life and Work* (London: Macmillan, 1955)
E. P. Thompson, *William Morris: Romantic to Revolutionary* (London: Lawrence and Wishart, 1955)
G. N. Ray, *Thackeray*, 2 vols (London: Oxford University Press, 1955–58)
J. Lindsay, *George Meredith, His Life and Work* (London: Bodley Head, 1956)
The Diaries of John Ruskin, ed. Joan Evans and John Howard, 3 vols (Oxford: Clarendon Press, 1956–59)
John Butt and Kathleen Tillotson, *Dickens at Work* (London: Methuen, 1957)
The Correspondence of Arthur Hugh Clough, ed. F. L. Mulhauser (Oxford: Clarendon Press, 1957)
J. C. Reid, *The Mind and Art of Coventry Patmore* (London: Routledge and Kegan Paul, 1957)
Gardner B. Taplin, *The Life of Elizabeth Barrett Browning* (London: John Murray, 1957)
Boris Ford (ed.), *From Dickens to Hardy*, Pelican English Library (London: Penguin Books, 1958)
Winifred Gerin, *Anne Brontë* (London: Nelson, 1959)
Barbara Hardy, *The Novels of George Eliot: A Study in Form* (London: Athlone Press, 1959)
Ada Harrison and Derek Stanford, *Anne Brontë, Her Life and Work* (London: Methuen, 1959)
Journals and Papers of Gerald Manley Hopkins, ed. H. House and G. Storey (London: Oxford University Press, 1959)

Norman St John Stevas, *Walter Bagehot: A Study of his Life and Thought, Together with a Selection from His Political Writings* (London: Eyre & Spottiswoode, 1959)

The Swinburne Letters, ed. Cecil Y. Lang, 6 vols (New Haven, CT: Yale University Press, 1959–62)

R. K. Webb, *Harriet Martineau: A Radical Victorian* (London: Heinemann, 1960)

The Complete Prose Works of Matthew Arnold, ed. R. H. Super, 11 vols (Ann Arbor: University of Michigan Press, 1960–77)

Studies of the Victorian age

John Steegman, *Consort of Taste, 1830–70* (London: Sidgwick and Jackson, 1950)

Jerome Buckley, *Victorian Temper: A Study in Literary Culture* (New York: Vintage Books, 1951)

C. R. Fay, *Palace of Industry, 1851: A Study of the Great Exhibition and its Fruits* (Cambridge: Cambridge University Press, 1951)

F. A. Hayek, *John Stuart Mill and Harriet Taylor: Their Correspondence and Subsequent Marriage* (London: Routledge & Kegan Paul, 1951)

Margaret Hewitt, *Wives and Mothers in Victorian Industry* (London: Rockliff, 1951)

The Poems of Arthur Hugh Clough, ed. H. F. Lowry *et al.* (Oxford: Clarendon Press, 1951)

N. Pevsner, *High Victorian Design: A Study of the Exhibits of 1851* (London: Architectural Press, 1951)

Geoffrey Tillotson, *Criticism and the Nineteenth Century* (London: Athlone Press, 1951)

John Holloway, *The Victorian Sage: Studies in Argument* (London: Macmillan, 1953)

Asa Briggs, *Victorian People: Some Reassessments of People, Institutions, Ideas and Events* (London: Odhams Press, 1954)

George Rowell, *Victorian Theatre: A Survey* (London: Oxford University Press, 1956)

Kathleen Tillotson, *Novels of the Eighteen-Forties* (Oxford: Oxford University Press, 1956)

Basil Willey, *More Nineteenth Century Studies: A Group of Honest Doubters* (London: Chatto & Windus, 1956)

Richard Altick, *The English Common Reader: A Social History of the Mass Reading Public* (Chicago, IL: Chicago University Press, 1957)

Walter E. Houghton, *The Victorian Frame of Mind* (New Haven, CT: Yale University Press, 1957)

Roy Jenkins, *Sir Charles Dilke: Victorian Tragedy* (London: Collins, 1958)

Raymond Williams, *Culture and Society, 1780–1950* (London: Chatto & Windus, 1958)

T. S. R. Boase, *English Art, 1800–70* (Oxford: Clarendon Press, 1959)

H. J. Hanham, *Elections and Party Management: Politics in the Time of Disraeli and Gladstone* (London: Longmans, 1959)

Gertrude Himmelfarb, *Darwin and the Darwinian Revolution* (London: Chatto & Windus, 1959)

Exhibitions
Victorian Photography, Victoria and Albert Museum, 1951
1851 Pavilion at the Festival of Britain Exhibition, 1951
Victorian Decorative Arts, Victoria and Albert Museum, 1952
Era of Leopold and Victoria, Belgo-British Union, 1953
Victorian Paintings, Arts Council, 1955
Victorian America: Lithographs by Currier and Ives, Arts Council, 1955
Victorian Scene, Leicester, 1956
Victorian Era, Walker Gallery, Liverpool, 1957

Media
1851 Week (BBC Third Programme, 1951)
The Warden (BBC, 1951)
Pickwick Papers (BBC, 1952)
Pickwick Papers (Renown, 1952)
Wuthering Heights (BBC, 1953)
The Good Old Days (BBC, 1953–83)
Victorian Humanity (BBC Third Programme, 1955)
David Copperfield (BBC, 1956)
Jane Eyre (BBC, 1956)
Vanity Fair (BBC, 1956)
Nicholas Nickleby (BBC, 1957)
Our Mutual Friend (BBC, 1958)
A Tale of Two Cities (Rank, 1958)
The Last Chronicle of Barsetshire (BBC, 1959)
A Tale of Two Cities (BBC, 1959)
Barnaby Rudge (BBC, 1960)

Academic
Founding of journal *Victorian Studies*, 1957

Conservation and the built environment
Founding of the Victorian Society, 1958
H. Hitchcock, *Early Victorian Architecture in Britain*, 2 vols (London: Trewin Copplestone, 1954)

Other
Founding of the Elgar Society, 1951

1961–70

Victoria and her family
Dearest Child: Letters Between Queen Victoria and the Princess Royal, 1858–1861, ed. Roger Fulford (London: Evans Brothers, 1964; continued in 5 further volumes to 1990, the last volume edited by Agatha Ramm)
Elizabeth Longford, *Victoria, RI* (London, Weidenfeld & Nicolson, 1964)
Winslow Ames, *Prince Albert and Victorian Taste* (London: Evans Brothers, 1968)
Victoria in the Highlands: The Personal Journal of Her Majesty Queen Victoria, with Notes and Introductions, and a Description of the Acquisition and Rebuilding of Balmoral Castle, ed. David Duff (London: Frederick Muller, 1968)

Prime ministers

Norman Gash, *Mr Secretary Peel: The Life of Sir Robert Peel to 1830* (London: Longmans, 1961)

Robert Rhodes James, *Rosebery: A Biography of Archibald Philip, 5th Earl of Rosebery* (London: Weidenfeld & Nicolson, 1963)

Robert Blake, *Disraeli* (London: Eyre & Spottiswoode, 1966)

Rosebery's papers to National Library of Scotland (1966)

Gladstone's papers to Hawarden (1968)

The Gladstone Diaries, ed. M. R. D. Foot and H. C. G. Matthew, 14 vols (Oxford: Clarendon Press, 1968–94)

Jasper Ridley, *Lord Palmerston* (London: Constable, 1970)

Writers

Wayne Burns, *Charles Reade: A Study in Victorian Authorship* (New York: Bookman Associates, 1961)

The Letters and Diaries of John Henry Newman, ed. C. S. Dessain and T. Gornall, 31 vols (London: Nelson, 1961–77)

L. M. Packer *Christina Rossetti* (Berkeley: University of California Press, 1963)

The Collected Works of John Stuart Mill, ed. J. M. Robson (Toronto: University of Toronto Press, 1963–)

The Letters of Dante Rossetti, ed. O. Doughty and J. R. Wahl, 4 vols (Oxford: Oxford University Press, 1965–67)

The Collected Works of Walter Bagehot, ed. Norman St. John Stevas, 15 vols (London: Economist, 1965–78)

The Letters of Charles Dickens, ed. M. House and G. Storey, 12 vols (Oxford: Clarendon Press, 1965–2002)

The Letters of Mrs Gaskell, ed. J. A. V. Chapple and A. Pollard (Manchester: Manchester University Press, 1966)

Winifred Gerin, *Charlotte Brontë: The Evolution of Genius* (Oxford: Clarendon Press, 1967)

Gordon Haight, *George Eliot: A Biography* (Oxford: Oxford University Press, 1968)

Vivien Noakes, *Edward Lear: The Life of a Wanderer* (Boston: Houghton Mifflin, 1968)

Founding of the Browning Society, 1969

Founding of the Lewis Carroll Society, 1969

J. S. Mill, *Autobiography*, ed. Jack Stillinger (New York: Houghton Mifflin, 1969)

The Complete Works of Robert Browning, ed. Roma King, Jr. *et al.*, 13 vols (Athens, OH: Ohio University Press, 1969–95)

The Poems of Tennyson, ed. C. Ricks, 3 vols (London: Longman, 1969)

Founding of the Dickens Society, 1970

F. R. and Q. D. Leavis, *Dickens the Novelist* (London: Chatto and Windus, 1970)

The Letters of George Meredith, ed. C. L. Cline, 3 vols (Oxford: Clarendon Press, 1970)

Studies of the Victorian age

H. J. Dyos, *Victorian Suburb: A Study of the Growth of Camberwell* (Leicester: Leicester University Press, 1961)

J. E. Gloag, *Victorian Comfort: A Social History of Design, 1830–1900* (London: Adam & Charles Black, 1961)

David Newsome, *Godliness and Good Learning: Four Studies on a Victorian Ideal* (London: Cassell, 1961)

J. E. Gloag, *Victorian Taste: Some Aspects of Architecture and Industrial Design from 1820–1900* (London: Adam & Charles Black, 1962)

R. E. Robinson and J. T. Gallagher, *Africa and the Victorians: The Official Mind of Imperialism* (London: Macmillan, 1961)

G. Kitson Clark, *The Making of Victorian England* (London: Methuen, 1962)

Asa Briggs, *Victorian Cities* (London: Odhams Press, 1963)

K. Inglis, *Churches and the Working Classes in Victorian England* (London: Routledge & Kegan Paul, 1963)

Louis James, *Fiction for the Working Man, 1830–1850: A Study of the Literature Produced for the Working Classes in Early Victorian Urban England* (London: Oxford University Press, 1963)

F. M. L. Thompson, *English Landed Society of the 19th Century* (London: Routledge & Kegan Paul, 1963)

J. A. and O. Banks, *Feminism and Family Planning in Victorian England* (Liverpool: Liverpool University Press, 1964)

W. L. Burn, *The Age of Equipoise: A Study of the Mid-Victorian Generation* (London: Allen & Unwin, 1964)

Melvin Richter, *The Politics of Conscience: T. H. Green and His Age* (London: Weidenfeld & Nicolson, 1964)

Geoffrey and Kathleen Tillotson *Mid-Victorian Studies* (London: Athlone Press, 1965)

John Burrow, *Evolution and Society: A Study in Victorian Social Theory* (Cambridge: Cambridge University Press, 1966)

Steven Marcus, *The Other Victorians: A Study of Sexuality and Pornography in mid-Nineteenth Century England* (London: Weidenfeld and Nicolson, 1966)

John Vincent, *The Formation of the British Liberal Party, 1857–1868* (London: Constable, 1966)

Owen Chadwick, *The Victorian Church*, 2 vols (London: Adam & Charles Black, 1966–70)

Maurice Cowling, *1867: Gladstone, Disraeli and Revolution* (Cambridge: Cambridge University Press, 1967)

John Vincent, *Pollbooks: How Victorians Voted* (Cambridge: Cambridge University Press, 1967)

L. P. Curtis, *Anglo-Saxons and Celts: A Study of Anti-Irish Prejudice in Victorian England* (Bridgeport, CT: Conference on British Studies, 1968)

Gertrude Himmelfarb, *Victorian Minds* (London: Weidenfeld & Nicolson,1968)

George Levine, *The Boundaries of Fiction: Carlyle, Macaulay, Newman* (Princeton, NJ: Princeton University Press, 1968)

Sheldon Rothblatt, *The Revolution of the Dons: Cambridge and Society in Victorian England* (London: Faber, 1968)

Exhibitions

London, 1862: The International Exhibition, Victoria and Albert Museum, 1962

Sir Joseph Paxton, 1803–1865: A Centenary Exhibition, Victorian Society and the Arts Council, 1965

Aubrey Beardsley, Victoria and Albert Museum, 1966

Victorian Book Illustration, Victoria and Albert Museum, 1966
Millais, Walker Art Gallery, Liverpool and the Royal Academy of Arts, London, 1967
Victorian Christmas, Victoria and Albert Museum, 1967
Victorian and Edwardian Sculpture, Fine Art Society, London, 1968
Victorian Engravings, Victoria and Albert Museum, 1969
Victorian High Art, Leighton House, London, 1969
William Holman Hunt, Walker Art Gallery, Liverpool and Victoria and Albert Museum, 1969
Charles Dickens: An Exhibition to Commemorate the Centenary of His Death, Victoria and Albert Museum, 1970

Media
Oliver Twist (BBC, 1961)
The Old Curiosity Shop (BBC, 1963)
Silas Marner (BBC, 1964)
The Mill on the Floss (BBC, 1965)
The Woman in White (BBC, 1966)
Far from the Madding Crowd, dir. John Schlesinger (Warner, 1967)
The Forsyte Saga (BBC, 1967)
Wuthering Heights (BBC, 1967)
Nicholas Nickleby (BBC, 1968)
Oliver, dir. Carol Reed (Columbia, 1968)
The Tenant of Wildfell Hall (BBC, 1968)
Dombey and Son (BBC, 1969)
An Ideal Husband (BBC, 1969)
Daniel Deronda (BBC, 1970)
Villette (BBC, 1970)
The Woodlanders (BBC, 1970)

Academic
Victorian Poetry, Morgantown, WV, by University of West Virginia Press, 1963–
Victorian Studies Centre established at University of Leicester, 1966
Wellesley Index to Victorian Periodicals, ed. Walter Houghton *et al.* (Toronto: University of Toronto Press, 1966–88)
Tennyson Research Bulletin (Lincoln, UK: Tennyson Research Centre, 1967–)
Victorian Periodicals Newsletter (Toronto: University of Toronto, 1968–78; from 1978 published as *Victorian Periodicals Review*)

Conservation and the built environment
Victorian Society Exhibition, 1961
Euston Station Hotel (built 1881) demolished despite public campaign, 1963
Peter Ferriday (ed.), *Victorian Architecture* (London: Jonathan Cape, 1963)
R. F. Jordan, *Victorian Architecture* (Harmondsworth: Penguin, 1966)
New Scotland Yard (1890) saved from demolition and renamed the Norman Shaw Building, 1967
Albert Dock, Liverpool: Grade 1 status, 1968
John Summerson, *Victorian Architecture: Four Studies in Evaluation* (New York: Columbia University Press, 1970)

Other
Founding of the 1890s Society, 1963

1971–80

Victoria and her family
Cecil Woodham Smith, *Queen Victoria: Her Life and Times, 1819–61* (London: Hamish Hamilton, 1972)
Reginald Pound, *Albert. A Biography of the Prince Consort* (London: Michael Joseph, 1973)

Prime ministers
Norman Gash, *Sir Robert Peel: The Life of Sir Robert Peel after 1830* (London: Longman, 1972)
John Prest, *Lord John Russell* (London: Macmillan, 1972)
Robert Taylor, *Lord Salisbury* (London: Allen Lane, 1975)
R. W. Davis, *Disraeli* (London: Hutchinson, 1976)
Philip Ziegler, *Melbourne: A Biography of William Lamb, 2nd Viscount Melbourne* (London: Collins, 1976)
Disraeli Newsletter, published in Kingston, Ontario, Canada, 1976–81
Disraeli's papers transferred from Hughenden to the Bodleian, 1978
Lucille Iremonger, *Lord Aberdeen: A Biography of the 4th Earl Aberdeen* (London: Collins, 1978)

Writers
Founding of the A. E. Housman Society, 1973
Winifred Gerin, *Emily Brontë: A Biography* (Oxford: Clarendon Press, 1971)
Ian Jack, *Browning's Major Poetry* (Oxford: Clarendon Press, 1973)
The Letters of Thomas Babington Macaulay, ed. Thomas Pinney, 6 vols (Cambridge: Cambridge University Press, 1974–81)
Robert Gittings, *Young Thomas Hardy* (London: Heinemann, 1975)
Ruby Redinger, *George Eliot: The Emergent Self* (London: Bodley Head, 1975)
Winifred Gerin, *Elizabeth Gaskell: a biography* (Oxford: Clarendon Press, 1976)
Gissing Trust established 1978
Robert Gittings, *The Older Hardy* (London: Heinemann, 1978)
The Poems of George Meredith, ed. P. Bartlett, 2 vols (New Haven, CT: Yale University Press, 1978)
The Collected Letters of Thomas Hardy, ed. R. L. Purdy and M. Millgate, 7 vols (Oxford: Clarendon Press, 1978–88)
The Letters of Lewis Carroll, ed. M. N. Cohen and R. L. Green, 2 vols (London: Macmillan, 1979)
The Complete Poems of Christina Rossetti, ed. R. W. Crump, 3 vols (Baton Rouge: Louisiana State University Press, 1979–90)
Founding of the Wilkie Collins Society (1980)
R. B. Martin, *Tennyson: The Unquiet Heart* (Oxford: Clarendon Press, 1980)

Studies of the Victorian age
Geoffrey Best, *Mid-Victorian Britain, 1851–75* (London: Weidenfeld & Nicolson, 1971)

Brian Harrison, *Drink and the Victorians: The Temperance Question in England, 1815–72* (London: Faber, 1971)

J. F. C. Harrison, *Early Victorian Britain, 1832–51* (London: Weidenfeld & Nicolson, 1971)

Gareth Stedman Jones, *Outcast London: A Study of the Relationship between Classes in Victorian Society* (Oxford: Clarendon Press, 1971)

Isobel Armstrong, *Victorian Scrutinies: Reviews of Poetry, 1830–70* (London: Athlone Press, 1972)

H. J. Dyos and M. Wolff (eds), *The Victorian City: Images and Realities*, 2 vols (London: Routledge & Kegan Paul, 1973)

E. P. Hennock, *Fit and Proper Persons: Ideal and Reality in Nineteenth-Century Urban Government* (London: Arnold, 1973)

Martha Vicinus, *Suffer and Be Still: Women in the Victorian Age* (Bloomington: Indiana University Press, 1973)

P. Hollis (ed.), *Pressure from Without in Early Victorian England* (London: Arnold, 1974)

Edward Royle, *Victorian Infidels: The Origins of the British Secularist Movement, 1791–1866* (Manchester: Manchester University Press, 1974)

F. M. Turner, *Between Science and Religion: The Reaction to Scientific Naturalism in late Victorian England* (New Haven, CT: Yale University Press, 1974)

Martha Vicinus, *The Industrial Muse: A Study of Nineteenth Century British Working-Class Literature* (London: Croom Helm, 1974)

Derek Fraser, *Urban Politics in Victorian England: The Structure of Politics in Victorian Cities* (Leicester: Leicester University Press, 1976)

Robert Gray, *The Labour Aristocracy in Victorian Edinburgh* (Oxford: Clarendon Press, 1976)

D. C. Moore, *The Politics of Deference: A Study of the Mid-Nineteenth-Century English Political System* (Hassocks: Harvester, 1976)

John Sutherland, *Victorian Novelists and Publishers* (London: Athlone Press, 1976)

Anne Humphreys, *Travels into the Poor Man's Country: The Work of Henry Mayhew* (Athens: University of Georgia Press, 1977)

Oliver Macdonagh, *Early Victorian Government, 1830–70* (London: Weidenfeld & Nicolson, 1977)

Geoffrey Crossick, *An Artisan Elite in Victorian Society: Kentish London, 1840–1880* (London: Croom Helm, 1978)

Christopher Harvie, *Lights of Liberalism: University Liberals and the Challenge of Democracy, 1860–86* (London: Allen Lane, 1978)

Douglas Lorimer, *Colour, Class and the Victorians: English Attitudes towards the Negro in the Nineteenth Century* (Leicester: Leicester University Press, 1978)

Roy Strong, *And When Did You Last See Your Father? The Victorian Painter and British History* (London: Thames & Hudson, 1978)

Sandra Gilbert and Susan Gubar, *The Madwoman in the Attic: The Woman Writer in the Nineteenth Century Literary Imagination* (New Haven, CT: Yale University Press, 1979)

Rosemary Ashton, *The German Idea: Four English Writers and the Reception of German Thought, 1800–1860* (Cambridge: Cambridge University Press, 1980)

Winifred Hughes, *The Maniac in the Cellar: Sensation Novels of the 1860s* (Princeton, NJ: Princeton University Press, 1980)

Richard Jenkyns, *The Victorians and Ancient Greece* (Cambridge, MA: Harvard
   University Press, 1980)

Exhibitions

Dante Rossetti, Newcastle, 1971
Victorian Church Art, Victoria and Albert Museum, 1971
Victorian Glass, Victoria and Albert Museum, 1971
Victorian Publishers' Bindings, Victoria and Albert Museum, 1972
Marble Halls: Drawings and Models for Victorian Secular Buildings, Victoria and
   Albert Museum, 1973
Victorian Children's Books, Victoria and Albert Museum, 1973
Victorian Engravings, Victoria and Albert Museum, 1973
Ruskin Pottery, Victoria and Albert Museum, 1975
Printed Textiles of William Morris, Victoria and Albert Museum, 1978
Sir Gilbert Scott (1811–1878): Architect of the Gothic Revival, Victoria and Albert
   Museum, 1978
This Brilliant Year: 1887, Royal Academy of Arts, 1978
The Luxury of Good Taste: An Exhibition of Victorian Design, 1835–80, Victoria
   and Albert Museum, 1979
Victoria: The Life and Times of Queen Victoria, Tokyo, 1979

Media

Jude the Obscure (BBC, 1971)
The Moonstone (BBC, 1972)
Lord Arthur Savile's Crime (BBC, 1972)
Wessex Tales (BBC, 1973)
The Importance of Being Earnest (BBC, 1974)
The Picture of Dorian Gray (BBC, 1976)
Our Mutual Friend (Masterpiece Theatre, 1977)
Hard Times (Granada, 1977)
The Mayor of Casterbridge (BBC, 1978)
Wuthering Heights, sung by Kate Bush, tops the UK singles chart, 1978
Disraeli: Portrait of a Romantic (Anglia, 1979)
The Life and Adventures of Nicholas Nickleby (Royal Shakespeare Company, 1980)

Academic

Founding of *Browning Institute Studies: An Annual of Victorian Literature and
   Culture*, Princeton, NJ, 1973–90 (from 1990 published as *Victorian Literature
   and Culture*)
Waterloo Directory of Victorian Periodicals, ed. John North, Michael Wolff and
   Dorothy Deering (Waterloo: Wilfrid Laurier University Press, 1977–)
Pre-Raphaelite Review, Amherst, MA, 1977–80 (from 1980 to 1987 published as
   Journal of Pre-Raphaelite Studies, Peterborough, New Hampshire; 1987–89 as
   Journal of Pre-Raphaelite and Aesthetic Studies, University of British Columbia)
Carlyle Newsletter published by the University of Edinburgh, 1979–87 (1988–93
   as *Carlyle Annual*, Queen's College, New York; finally, 1994– as *Carlyle Studies
   Annual*, Illinois State University)

Conservation and the built environment

John Summerson, *The Architecture of Victorian London* (Charlottesville: University Press of Virginia, 1976)

Mentmore Towers (Joseph Paxton): auction of house contents and sale of property to Maharishi Mahesh Yogi, 1977

1981–90

Victoria and her family

Stephen Bayley, *The Albert Memorial: The Monument in its Social and Architectural Context* (Aldershot: Scolar Press, 1981)

John A. S. Phillips, *Prince Albert and the Victorian Age* (Cambridge: Cambridge University Press, 1981)

Elisabeth Darby and Nicola Smith, *The Cult of the Prince Consort* (New Haven, CT: Yale, 1983)

Hermione Hobhouse, *Prince Albert: His Life and Work* (London: Hamish Hamilton, 1983)

Robert Rhodes James, *Albert, Prince Consort: A Biography* (London: Hamish Hamilton, 1983)

Stanley Weintraub, *Victoria: Biography of a Queen* (London: Allen & Unwin, 1987)

Dorothy Thompson, *Queen Victoria: Gender and Power* (London: Virago, 1990)

Prime ministers

Kenneth Bourne, *Palmerston: The Early Years 1784–1841* (London: Allen Lane, 1982)

Sarah Bradford, *Disraeli* (London: Weidenfeld & Nicolson, 1982)

Richard Shannon, *Gladstone, 1809–65* (London: Hamish Hamilton, 1982)

Disraeli, *Letters*, ed. J. A. W. Gunn *et al.* (Toronto: University of Toronto Press, 1982–)

Broadlands Mss to University of Southampton, 1983

Muriel Chamberlain, *Lord Aberdeen: A Political Biography* (London: Longman, 1983)

Disraeli Lectures, Conservative Political Centre, 1985–

Colin Matthew, *Gladstone, 1809–74* (Oxford: Oxford University Press, 1986)

John Vincent, *Disraeli* (Oxford: Oxford University Press, 1990)

Writers

Park Honan, *Matthew Arnold: A Life* (London: Weidenfeld & Nicolson, 1981)

Letters of Tennyson, ed. Cecil Y. Lang and E. F. Shannon, 3 vols (Cambridge, MA: Harvard University Press, 1981–90)

Michael Millgate, *Thomas Hardy: A Biography* (Oxford: Oxford University Press, 1982)

The Complete Poetical Works of Thomas Hardy, ed. S. Hynes, 5 vols (Oxford: Clarendon Press, 1982–95)

F. Kaplan, *Thomas Carlyle: A Biography* (Cambridge: Cambridge University Press, 1983)

Browning Works, ed. Ian Jack *et al.* (Oxford: Clarendon Press, 1983–)

Letters of Trollope, ed. N. J. Hall (Stanford, CA: Stanford University Press, 1983)

The Brownings' Correspondence, ed. Philip Kelley and Ronald Hudson (Winfield, KA: Wedgestone, 1984–)

Founding of the Gaskell Society, 1985

Darwin Correspondence, ed. F. Burckhardt (Cambridge: Cambridge University Press, 1985–)

Tim Hilton, *Ruskin*, 2 vols (New Haven, CT: Yale University Press, 1985–2000)

Richard Ellman, *Oscar Wilde* (London: Hamish Hamilton, 1987)

Founding of the Gerald Manley Hopkins Society, 1987

Founding of the Trollope Society (London), 1987

Daniel Karlin, *The Courtship of Robert Browning and Elizabeth Barrett* (Oxford: Clarendon Press, 1987)

Ian Ker, *John Henry Newman* (Oxford: Clarendon Press, 1988)

H. F. Tucker, *Tennyson and the Doom of Romanticism* (Cambridge, MA: Harvard University Press, 1988)

Founding of the Arthur Conan Doyle Society, 1989

Peter Ackroyd, *Dickens* (London: Sinclair-Stevenson, 1990)

Elisabeth Jay, *Mrs Oliphant: 'A Fiction to Herself': A Literary Life* (Oxford: Clarendon Press, 1990)

The Poetical Works of Gerald Manley Hopkins, ed. N. H. Mackenzie (Oxford: Clarendon Press, 1990)

John Sutherland, *Mrs Humphry Ward: Eminent Victorian, Pre-eminent Edwardian* (Oxford: Clarendon Press, 1990)

Studies of the Victorian age

John Burrow, *A Liberal Descent: Victorian Historians and the English Past* (Cambridge: Cambridge University Press, 1981)

J. Mordaunt Crook, *William Burges and the High Victorian Dream* (London: John Murray, 1981)

Mark Girouard, *The Return to Camelot: Chivalry and the English Gentleman* (New Haven, CT: Yale University Press, 1981)

Martin Wiener, *English Culture and the Decline of the Industrial Spirit, 1850–1980* (Cambridge: Cambridge University Press, 1981)

David Vincent, *Bread, Knowledge and Freedom: A Study in Nineteenth Century Working Class Autobiography* (London: Europa, 1981)

C. Dellheim, *The Face of the Past: The Preservation of the Medieval Inheritance in Victorian England* (Cambridge: Cambridge University Press, 1982)

Joanne Shattock and Michael Wolff (eds), *The Victorian Periodical Press: Samplings and Soundings* (Leicester: Leicester University Press, 1982)

Gillian Beer, *Darwin's Plots: Evolutionary Narrative in Darwin, George Eliot and Nineteenth-Century Fiction* (London: Routledge and Kegan Paul, 1983)

Lucy Brown, *Victorian News and Newspapers* (Oxford: Oxford University Press, 1985)

Janet Oppenheim, *The Other World: Spiritualism and Psychical Research in England, 1850–1914* (Cambridge: Cambridge University Press, 1985)

R. M. Young, *Darwin's Metaphor: Nature's Place in Victorian Culture* (Cambridge: Cambridge University Press, 1985)

J. P. Parry, *Democracy and Religion: Gladstone and the Liberal Party, 1867–75* (Cambridge: Cambridge University Press, 1986)

Linda Peterson, *Victorian Autobiography: The Tradition of Self-Interpretation* (New Haven, CT: Yale University Press, 1986)

Elaine Showalter, *The Female Malady: Women, Madness and Victorian Culture, 1830–1980* (Princeton, NJ: Princeton University Press, 1986)

Leonore Davidoff and Catherine Hall, *Family Fortunes: Men and Women of the English Middle Class, 1780–1850* (London: Hutchinson, 1987)

The New Oxford Book of Victorian Verse, ed. Christopher Ricks (Oxford: Clarendon Press, 1987)

Edward Norman, *The Victorian Christian Socialists* (Cambridge: Cambridge University Press, 1987)

Ruth Richardson, *Death, Dissection and the Destitute* (London: Routledge & Kegan Paul, 1987)

George Stocking Jr., *Victorian Anthropology* (London: Collier Macmillan, 1987)

Boyd Hilton, *The Age of Atonement: The Influence of Evangelicalism on Social and Economic Thought, 1795–1865* (Oxford: Oxford University Press, 1988)

Sally Mitchell (ed.), *Victorian Britain: An Encyclopaedia* (New York: Garland, 1988)

Lynda Nead, *Myths of Sexuality: Representations of Women in Victorian Britain* (Oxford: Blackwell, 1988)

Mary Poovey, *Uneven Developments: The Ideological Work of Gender in Mid-Victorian England* (Chicago, IL: University of Chicago Press, 1988)

Adrian Desmond, *The Politics of Evolution: Morphology, Medicine, and Reform in Radical London* (Chicago, IL: University of Chicago Press, 1989)

Eric Griffiths, *The Printed Voice of Victorian Poetry* (Oxford: Clarendon Press, 1989)

Nicholas Temperley (ed.), *The Lost Chord: Essays on Victorian Music* (Bloomington: Indiana University Press, 1989)

J. F. C. Harrison, *Late Victorian Britain, 1875–1901* (London: Fontana, 1990)

G. Marsden (ed.), *Victorian Values: Personalities and Perspectives in Nineteenth Century Society* (London: Longman, 1990)

Thomas Richards, *The Commodity Culture of Victorian England: Advertising and Spectacle, 1851–1914* (Stanford, CA: Stanford University Press, 1990)

Exhibitions

D'Oyly Carte, Theatre Museum, 1981

Edward Lear, Royal Academy of Arts, 1985

A Vision Exchanged: Amateurs and Photography in Mid-Victorian England, Victoria and Albert Museum, 1985

Media

Tess, dir. Roman Polanski (France–UK, Columbia, 1981)

The Barchester Chronicles (BBC, 1982)

Wuthering Heights, dir. Luis Bunuel (Spain, Plexus, 1983)

Bleak House (BBC, 1985)

Silas Marner (BBC, 1985)

Litle Dorrit (Curzon, 1987)

Vanity Fair (BBC, 1987)

Victorian Values (Granada, 1987)

Eminent Victorians (Granada, 1989)

A Tale of Two Cities (Masterpiece Theatre, 1989)
Parnell and the Englishwoman (BBC, 1990)

Academic
Victorian Review: Journal of the Victorian Studies Association of Western Canada,
 Edmonton, 1990–

Conservation and the built environment
Colin Cunningham, *Victorian and Edwardian Town Halls* (London: Routledge &
 Kegan Paul, 1981)
Alfred Waterhouse, 1830–1905, Royal Institute of British Architects, 1983

1991–2000
Victoria and her family
Monica Charlot, *Victoria: The Young Queen* (Oxford: Blackwell, 1991)
Giles St Aubyn, *Queen Victoria: A Portrait* (London: Sinclair-Stevenson, 1991)
Frogmore House opens to public, 1992
The Duke of Edinburgh opens a Victorian time-capsule, 1993
Theo Aronson, *Prince Eddy and the Homosexual World* (London: John Murray,
 1994)
D. M. Potts and W. T. W. Potts, *Queen Victoria's Gene: Haemophilia and the Royal
 Family* (Stroud: Sutton, 1995)
Adrienne Munich, *Queen Victoria's Secrets* (New York: Columbia University Press,
 1996)
Margaret Homans and Adrienne Munich (eds), *Remaking Queen Victoria* (Cam-
 bridge: Cambridge University Press, 1997)
Stanley Weintraub, *Albert. Uncrowned King* (London: John Murray, 1997)
Chris Brooks (ed.), *The Albert Memorial: The Prince Consort National Monument,
 its History, Contexts and Conservation* (New Haven, CT: Yale, 2000)
Christopher Hibbert, *Queen Victoria: A Personal History* (London: HarperCollins,
 2000)
Jerrold M. Packard, *Farewell in Splendour: The Death of Queen Victoria and Her
 Age* (New York: Dutton, 2000)
Tony Rennell, *Last Days of Glory: The Death of Queen Victoria* (London: Viking,
 2000)

Prime ministers
Stanley Weintraub, *Disraeli: A Biography* (London: Hamish Hamilton, 1993)
Roy Jenkins, *Gladstone* (London: Macmillan, 1995)
Colin Matthew, *Gladstone, 1875–98* (Oxford: Oxford University Press, 1995)
Jane Ridley, *The Young Disraeli, 1804–46* (London: Sinclair-Stevenson, 1995)
Paul Smith, *Disraeli: A Brief Life* (Cambridge: Cambridge University Press, 1996)
L. G. Mitchell, *Lord Melbourne, 1779–1848* (Oxford: Oxford University Press, 1997)
Peter J. Jagger (ed.), *Gladstone* (London: Hambledon, 1998)
Andrew Roberts, *Salisbury: Victorian Titan* (London: Weidenfeld & Nicolson,
 1999)
Paul Scherer, *Lord John Russell: A Biography* (London: Associated University
 Presses, 1999)

Richard Shannon, *Gladstone: Heroic Minister, 1865–98* (London: Allen Lane, 1999)
E. D. Steele, *Lord Salisbury: A Political Biography* (London: UCL Press, 1999)

Writers
Rosemary Ashton, *G. H. Lewes: A Life* (Oxford: Oxford University Press, 1991)
Adrian Desmond and James Moore, *Darwin* (London: Michael Joseph, 1991)
Founding of the George Borrow Society, 1991
Victoria Glendinning, *Trollope* (London: Hutchinson, 1992)
Founding of the Martineau Society, 1993
Jenny Uglow, *Elizabeth Gaskell: A Habit of Stories* (London: Faber, 1993)
Juliet Barker, *The Brontës* (London: Weidenfeld & Nicolson, 1994)
Jan Marsh, *Christina Rossetti: A Literary Biography* (London: Jonathan Cape, 1994)
Fiona McCarthy, *William Morris: A Life For Our Time* (London: Faber, 1994)
Denis Donoghue, *Walter Pater: Lover of Strange Souls* (New York: Knopf, 1995)
The Letters of Charlotte Brontë: With a Selection of Letters by Family and Friends, ed. Margaret Smith 2 vols (Oxford: Clarendon Press, 1995–2000)
The Letters of Matthew Arnold, ed. Cecil Y. Lang (Charlottesville: University of Virginia Press, 1996–)
Founding of the Thomas Hardy Society of North America (1997)
The Letters of Christina Rossetti, ed. Anthony H. Harrison (Charlottesville: University of Virginia Press, 1997–)
D. J. Taylor, *Thackeray* (Chatto & Windus, 1999)
John Batchelor, *Ruskin: No Wealth but Life* (London: Chatto & Windus, 2000)
Further Letters of Mrs Gaskell, ed. J. Chapple and A. Shelston (Manchester: Manchester University Press, 2000)
Jerome McGann, *Dante Gabriel Rossetti and the Game that Must Be Lost* (New Haven, CT: Yale University Press, 2000)

Studies of the Victorian age
Michael Booth, *Theatre in the Victorian Age* (Cambridge: Cambridge University Press, 1991)
Stefan Collini, *Public Moralists: Political Thought and Intellectual Life in Britain, 1850–1930* (Oxford: Clarendon Press, 1991)
R. Gagnier, *Subjectivities: A History of Self-Representation in Britain, 1832–1920* (Oxford: Oxford University Press, 1991)
Patrick Joyce, *Visions of the People: Industrial England and the Question of Class, 1848–1914* (Cambridge: Cambridge University Press, 1991)
Judith Walkowitz, *City of Dreadful Delight: Narratives of Sexual Danger in Late-Victorian London* (London: Virago, 1992)
Isobel Armstrong, *Victorian Poetry: Poetry, Poetics and Politics* (London: Routledge, 1993)
Kate Flint, *The Woman Reader, 1837–1914* (Oxford: Clarendon Press, 1993)
David Morse, *High Victorian Culture* (London: Macmillan, 1993)
Peter Mandler and Susan Pedersen (eds), *After the Victorians: Private Conscience and Public Duty in Modern Britain. Essays in Memory of John Clive* (London: Routledge, 1994)

Michael Mason, *The Making of Victorian Sexuality* (Oxford: Oxford University Press, 1994)

Michael Wheeler, *Heaven, Hell and the Victorians* (Cambridge: Cambridge University Press, 1994)

Andrew Elfenbein, *Byron and the Victorians* (Cambridge: Cambridge University Press, 1995)

John Sutherland, *Victorian Fiction: Writers, Publishers, Readers* (Basingstoke: Macmillan, 1995)

Sally Shuttleworth, *Charlotte Brontë and Victorian Psychiatry* (Cambridge: Cambridge University Press, 1996)

First Biennial Nineteenth-Century Music Studies Conference, Hull, 1997

Sally Ledger, *The New Woman: Fiction and Feminism at the Fin de Siècle* (Manchester: Manchester University Press, 1997)

David Newsome, *The Victorian World Picture: Perceptions and Introspections in an Age of Change* (London: John Murray, 1997)

Peter Bailey, *Popular Culture and Performance in the Victorian City* (Cambridge: Cambridge University Press, 1998)

Gary Day (ed.), *Varieties of Victorianism: The Uses of a Past* (London: Macmillan, 1998)

K. T. Hoppen, *The Mid-Victorian Generation, 1846–86* (Oxford: Clarendon Press, 1998)

Alison Winter, *Mesmerized: Powers of Mind in Victorian Britain* (Chicago, IL: University of Chicago Press, 1998)

Richard Schoch *Shakespeare's Victorian Stage: Performing History in the Theatre of Charles Kean* (Cambridge: Cambridge University Press, 1998)

John Schad, *Victorians in Theory: From Derrida to Browning* (Manchester: Manchester University Press, 1999)

John Tosh, *A Man's Place: Masculinity and the Middle Class Home in Victorian England* (New Haven, CT: Yale University Press, 1999)

Herbert F. Tucker (ed.), *Companion to Victorian Literature and Culture* (Oxford: Blackwell, 1999)

Joseph Bristow (ed.), *The Cambridge Companion to Victorian Poetry* (Cambridge: Cambridge University Press, 2000)

Rupert Christiansen, *The Visitors: Culture Shock in Nineteenth-Century Britain* (London: Chatto & Windus, 2000)

J. Kucich and D. Sudoff (eds), *Victorian Afterlife: Postmodern Culture Rewrites the Nineteenth Century* (Minneapolis: University of Minnesota Press, 2000)

Exhibitions

William Morris, Victoria and Albert Museum, 1996

Victoria and Albert, Vicky and the Kaiser: ein Kapitel deutsch–englischer Familiengeschichte, Deutsches Historisches Museum, Berlin 1997

Media

Adam Bede (BBC, 1992)
Jane Eyre (Pathé, 1996)
Jude (Universal, 1996)
The Tenant of Wildfell Hall (BBC, 1996)
Mrs Brown (Buena Vista, 1997)

Victoria and the Jubilee (BBC, 1997)
Wilde (Polygram, 1997)
Our Mutual Friend (BBC, 1998)
Vanity Fair (BBC, 1998)
Wuthering Heights (Cinema Club, 1998)
David Copperfield (BBC, 1999)
1900 House (Channel 4, 1999)
Oliver Twist (ITV, 1999)

Academic
Journal of Victorian Culture established, 1996
Inaugural meeting of the British Association of Victorian Studies, 2000

Conservation and the built environment
Chris Brooks and Andrew Saint (eds), *The Victorian Church: Architecture and Society* (Manchester: Manchester University Press, 1995)
Completion of the restoration of the Albert Memorial, 1998

2001–2
Victoria and her family
Lynne Vallone, *Becoming Victoria* (New Haven, CT: Yale University Press, 2001)

Prime ministers
Michael Bentley, *Lord Salisbury's World: Conservative Environments in Late Victorian Britain* (Cambridge: Cambridge University Press, 2001)

Writers
L. Miller, *The Brontë Myth* (London: Jonathan Cape, 2001)
Rosemary Ashton, *Thomas and Jane Carlyle: Portrait of a Marriage* (London: Chatto & Windus, 2002)
Founding of the Oscar Wilde Society of America, 2002

Studies of the Victorian age
Deirdre David (ed.), *The Cambridge Companion to the Victorian Novel* (Cambridge: Cambridge University Press, 2001)
James Secord, *Victorian Sensation: The Extraordinary Publication, Reception and Secret Authorship of the Vestiges of the Natural History of Creation* (Chicago, IL: University of Chicago Press, 2001)
Matthew Sweet, *Inventing the Victorians* (London: Faber, 2001)
Philip Davis, *The Victorians*, Oxford English Literary History, vol. 8 (Oxford: Oxford University Press, 2002)
John Gardiner, *The Victorians: An Age in Retrospect* (London: Hambledon & London, 2002)
A. N. Wilson, *The Victorians* (London: Hutchinson, 2002)

Exhibitions
Exposed: The Victorian Nude, Tate Britain, 2001
Queen Victoria Before 1840, Buckingham Palace, 2001
The Victorian Vision, Victoria and Albert Museum, 2001

Media
Queen Victoria: The Early Years (BBC, 2001)
Victoria and Albert (ITV, 2001)
The Victorians Uncovered (Channel 4, 2001)
The Way We Live Now (BBC, 2001)
What the Victorians Did for Us (Channel 4, 2001)
The Importance of Being Earnest (Buena Vista, 2002)
Daniel Deronda (BBC, 2002)
Prince Albert ('Reputations', BBC, 2002)

Conservation and the built environment
National Trust purchase of Tytensfield, 2002

Index

Note: 'n' after a page reference indicates a note number on that page.